MASTERING TODAY'S SOFTWARE

THIRD EDITION

EDWARD G. MARTIN
City University of New York
CHARLES S. PARKER
The College of Santa Fe

The Dryden Press
Harcourt Brace College Publishers
Fort Worth Philadelphia San Diego New York Orlando Austin San Antonio
Toronto Montreal London Sydney Tokyo

Acquisitions Editor	Robb Linsky
Developmental Editor	Elizabeth Hayes
Project Editor	Michele Tomiack
Art Director	Melinda Welch
Production Manager	Ann Coburn
Product Manager	Scott Timian
Director of Editing, Design, and Production	Diane Southworth
Editor in Chief	Lyn Hastert Maize
Publisher	Diana Farrell
Project Management	Seaside Publishing Services
Composition	GTS Graphics
Text Type	11/12 Bodoni Book

Address for Editorial Correspondence
The Dryden Press, 301 Commerce Street, Suite 3700, Fort Worth, TX 76102

Address for Orders
The Dryden Press, 6277 Sea Harbor Drive, Orlando, FL 32887
1-800-782-4479, or 1-800-433-0001 (in Florida)

ISBN: 0-03-013914-7 Chapters 1–5
0-03-014067-6 Chapters 1–9

Printed in the United States of America

5 6 7 8 9 0 1 2 3 4 059 10 9 8 7 6 5 4 3 2 1

The Dryden Press
Harcourt Brace College Publishers

PREFACE

Computers have become an integral part of our lives. The writer may now use a keyboard instead of a pencil; the artist, a light pen instead of a brush. And yet, the magic of creativity remains in the *user* of technology, not in the technology itself. Computers are, after all, only tools, and like any tool, they exist to serve the people who use them.

The purpose of *Mastering Today's Software* is to teach both microcomputer concepts and hands-on skills in using microcomputers—skills designed to make a person more productive in virtually any field. With The Dryden Press's EXACT custom publishing concept, instructors can request their own custom-bound textbooks to enhance the mastery of these skills further.

We are in the midst of a computer applications revolution that shows no signs of letting up. If anything, it is accelerating. Today it is almost mandatory for anyone working in an office—or even out in the field—to know how to use a microcomputer. The computer revolution has left virtually no job untouched.

COVERAGE

As well as state-of-the-art coverage of microcomputer concepts, *Mastering Today's Software* includes a set of easy-to-use lab tutorials for learning today's most widely used software packages. The book is designed primarily for users of computer systems running under DOS or under Windows 3.1 or Windows 95. It is written with instructions that assist users of hard-disk, diskette, and network-based systems.

The EXACT custom publishing program lets instructors choose any combination of concepts modules and lab instructional manuals, as well as binding options. EXACT also provides a quick turnaround from the time an order is placed to its arrival on campus. The process is seamless, and the end result is a customized textbook tailored to your needs. The following concepts and lab modules are currently available for custom binding:

- *Concepts Modules.* Adopters have a choice of either five or nine full-color chapters on microcomputer concepts:
  - *Microcomputer Concepts:* This "short-concepts" version of the text contains five chapters covering the principles of microcomputing, hardware and software, telecommunications, and owning a microcomputer.
  - *Extended Microcomputer Concepts:* This "long-concepts" version of the text contains the five short-concepts chapters plus four additional chapters covering advanced software applications, applications development, systems development, and social issues created by technology.

  The concepts modules have been revised substantially since the last edition, with the following pronounced changes:
  - The topic of social issues in the technology field has been expanded to include all of Chapter 9. Other topics in that chapter from the previous edition have been transferred elsewhere—the sections on artificial intelligence and multimedia computing have been moved to Chapter 6, and the discussion on object-oriented programming is now in Chapter 7.
  - Chapters 3 and 4 have been expanded appreciably to cover the usage of graphical user interfaces (GUIs) and the Internet, respectively.
  - The hardware and software appendixes appearing at the end of Chapter 5 in the previous edition have been moved to Chapters 2 and 3. An illustrated glossary on the Internet has been added at the end of Chapter 4.

- A number of topics have grown in importance since this textbook was last published and have received greater attention in this edition. Among these are the Internet and the information superhighway, virtual reality, Windows 95, software suites, wireless networks and mobile computing, client-server computing, CD-ROM and multimedia applications, and graphical user interfaces.
- A user-oriented feature box has been added to each chapter. These boxes give students practical insights into a variety of end-user applications.

■ *Lab Manuals.* One or more lab (software) manuals can be bound with a concepts module or, if lab use only is required, bound into a book without concepts. Each of the available lab manuals—which usually contain three chapters and a reference appendix—is targeted to a particular release of one of the products in the following list. Check with your Dryden sales representative to learn about the latest releases and earlier releases in stock and also to learn of new software products being added to the series.
- Disk Operating System (DOS)
- Windows
- WordPerfect
- WordPerfect for Windows
- Word for Windows
- Lotus 1-2-3
- Lotus 1-2-3 for Windows
- Excel for Windows
- Quattro Pro
- Quattro Pro for Windows
- dBASE III PLUS
- dBASE IV
- dBASE V
- Paradox
- Paradox for Windows
- Access for Windows
- QBASIC

TEACHING AND LEARNING TOOLS

Each of the concepts modules and lab manuals contains a number of features that help students master the materials:

■ *Outline.* Beginning each chapter is a detailed outline that shows the major headings and subheadings within the chapter.

■ *Objectives.* Also at the beginning of each chapter is a list of learning objectives that serves as a yardstick, measuring what should be learned.

■ *Overview.* Each chapter starts with an overview that puts the subject matter into perspective and lets students know what they will be studying.

■ *Boldfaced Key Terms.* Important terms appear in boldfaced type as they are introduced in each chapter and are listed at the chapter's end.

■ *Illustrations and Photographs.* Illustrations and photographs are provided for further pedagogical support, showing such items as computer hardware, outputs that result when commands are executed, summaries of command and keystroke sequences, and informative tables that help with data entry.

■ *Summary and Quiz.* At the end of each chapter is a bulleted summary of the chapter's contents and a 30-question quiz. The quiz features true/false, multiple-choice, and matching questions.

■ *Exercises.* Every chapter ends with a set of written and hands-on computer exercises designed to reinforce mastery of concepts and software use.

The following additional features can be found in each of the lab manuals:

■ *Graduated Chapter Organization.* Chapters in each manual are arranged with respect to beginning, intermediate, and advanced materials, making it easy for students and instructors to progress to a given level of expertise.

■ *Step-by-Step Command Layout.* Commands in each software package are laid out in an easy-to-execute, step-by-step fashion. As students progress, the "press-this-key" approach slowly gives way to a less detailed list of instructions. In this manner, students do not mindlessly follow keystrokes but learn to master specific tasks.

- *Marginal Icons.* Shortcut icons or toolbar buttons are displayed in the margins for easy reference.
- *Independent Instruction Sequences.* At times, the steps to be followed depend on whether a student is working from a hard disk, floppy disks, or a network; or whether a student is using a mouse, a keyboard, or a combination of both. To provide flexibility in using the software, separate instruction sequences are displayed for users of each option.
- *Applications.* Problem exercises within each chapter allow students to test their skills while building applications.
- *Checkpoints.* Checkpoints throughout each chapter enable students to review information and, before going further, to try out their new skills.
- *Tips.* Each chapter contains short, boldfaced tips at strategic points to provide hints about improving software skills, warnings of pitfalls, or suggestions for new commands to try.
- *Reference Appendix.* After the chapters in each manual is a comprehensive reference appendix. For the package under study, each appendix summarizes important keystrokes and provides alphabetical listings of critical operations.
- *Glossary and Index.* At the end of each manual are a glossary and an index. The glossary defines all key terms from the manual and shows the pages on which terms are first discussed. The index provides an alphabetical listing of important topics.

INSTRUCTOR AND STUDENT SUPPLEMENTS

An *Instructor's Manual and Test Bank* is available to adopters of *Mastering Today's Software.* For the student, a data disk accompanies many of the software manuals. Also included in the instructional package are a wide variety of electronic supplements. Classroom presentation software, videos, still images selected from both conepts modules and lab manuals on CD-ROM, and tutorial software for students are all available on adoption of either version of the concepts modules. See your Dryden sales representative about the most current offerings available in these areas.

Instructor's Manual and Test Bank. The *Instructor's Manual and Test Bank,* given free to each adopter of the textbook, helps teachers organize materials in *Mastering Today's Software* for classroom use. Included in the instructor's manual portion for each chapter is an outline, a list of commands and tips, answers to exercises, and supplementary problems.

The test bank portion of the manual contains hundreds of test items in various formats, including true/false, multiple-choice, fill-in, and matching questions. Answers are provided for all of the questions. The test bank is available in both hard-copy and computerized forms. The electronic versions—available for use with IBM, IBM-compatible, and Macintosh microcomputers—allow instructors to preview, edit, or delete questions, as well as to add their own questions, print scrambled forms of tests, and print answer keys.

Data Disk. The final chapter in each lab manual offers advanced topics. A *data disk* is available with text and graphics files that students can use to reduce the amount of keystroking required to complete the chapter.

ACKNOWLEDGMENTS

A project of this magnitude could never have been completed had it not been for the efforts of a large number of people, working in a variety of capacities.

First, we wish to thank the following reviewers, whose thoughtful comments on preliminary drafts of *Mastering Today's Software* improved both the technical accuracy of the text and the selected materials: Sarah Alexander, *Palm Beach Community College;* Paul F. Anderson, *Florence-Darlington Technical College;* Jan Bamford, *Northern Alberta Institute of Technology;* Michael P. Barnes, *Hardin-Simmons University;* Nick Bearce, *Bluefield State College;* Harry Benham, *Montana State University;* David Boyd, *Valdosta State College;* Elizabeth C. Boyd, independent consultant; Catherine J. Brotherton, *Riverside Community College;* Jan Carroll, *Sam Houston State University;* Frank Cress, *Butte College;* Eli Cohen, *Eastern New Mexico University;* Robert C. Coleman, *Pima Community College;* Terry Cooper, *Medicine Hat College;* Jack Cundiff, *Horry-Georgetown Technical College;* Donald L. Dershem, *Mountain View College;* Eugene T. Dolan, *The University of the District of Columbia;* Mary Eisele, independent consultant; Benedict Eng, independent consultant; Pat Rajski Flanagan, *El Paso Community College;* Jody Frankel, *City University of New York;* Leonard S. Gorney, *King's College;* Rosemary Gross, *Creighton University;* Evonne Hanson, *Gannon University;* Donald L. Harris, *Lincoln Land Community College;* Sherry Hemphill, *Wenatchee Valley College;* Keith Hendrick, *Wallace State College;* Barbara Corbett Howard, *Northern Virginia Community College;* Lorraine Hoyt, independent consultant; Fatima T. Husain, *North Dakota State University;* Julius Inman, *Coastal Carolina College;* Elwood Jones, *Broward Community College/Data Processing;* Shashidhar Kaparthi, *University of Northern Iowa;* Rose M. Laird, *Northern Virginia Community College;* Charles Donald Lake, *Faulkner State College;* Robert Landrum, *Jones Junior College;* Kenneth R. Lee, *Delaware Valley College;* Barbara J. Maccarone, *North Shore Community College;* Robert MacDonald, *East Stroudsburg University;* Ana R. Malitske-Goes, *Northern Virginia Community College—Alexandria Campus;* William H. McDaniel, Jr., *Northern Virginia Community College—Alexandria Campus;* Kathleen J. Noce, *Gannon University;* Cathleen Paprocki, *William Rainey Harper College;* Gene Phillips, *Bakersfield College;* Herbert F. Rebhun, *University of Houston—Downtown;* Mark Sabet, *California State University, Los Angeles;* Arline Sachs, *Northern Virginia Community College;* Ali Salehnia, *South Dakota State University;* Judith Scheeren, *Westmoreland County Community College;* Stephen J. Sheel, *Coastal Carolina University;* Jean Smelewicz, *Quinsigamond Community College;* T. Michael Smith, *Austin Community College;* John F. Walker, *Dona Ana Community College;* Karen Watterson, independent consultant; Mark W. Weiss, *University of Nebraska—Omaha;* Paula J. Worthington, *Northern Virginia Community College—Annandale Campus;* M. I. Zahid, *The Citadel.*

We would also like to thank the following individuals for their contributions in the writing of several manuals: Charles Kee, *City University of New York, Kingsborough Community College;* Terry Duke and Craig Collins, *University of Texas at El Paso;* and Marilyn Wertheimer Meyer, *Fresno City College.*

At The Dryden Press, special thanks goes to our publisher, Diana Farrell; our editor-in-chief, Lyn Maize; our acquisitions editor, Robb Linsky; and our developmental editor, Elizabeth Hayes, for the suggestions and accommodations they made to produce a better manuscript. We would also like to thank Scott Timian, product manager; Michele Tomiak, project editor; Ann Coburn, production manager; Melinda Welch, designer; and the many others who worked hard on behalf of this project.

Edward G. Martin / Charles S. Parker

CONTENTS

MC 1 Introduction to Computing

OUTLINE

LEARNING OBJECTIVES

After completing this chapter, you will be able to:

1. Describe the role of the input, processing, output, and storage functions of the computer system.
2. Explain the functions performed by data, programs, memory (RAM), secondary storage, hardware, and software.
3. Appreciate how data are stored in a computer system.
4. Describe how data are organized and accessed in a computer system.
5. Name several types of hardware and software and explain the roles served by each.
6. Describe the various elements of a microcomputer system and how they work together to process applications.

OVERVIEW

This is a book about microcomputers and their uses. Through a variety of learning materials, it focuses on making you—the reader—more savvy about using computer technology to become more productive in your chosen field. Whether you become an accountant, engineer, stockbroker, real-estate agent, lawyer, architect, doctor, or teacher, you will be able to work both faster and smarter if you know how to use a microcomputer.

Computers did not always play so prominent a role in helping people with their work. Prior to 1980, before microcomputers were introduced, computers were prohibitively expensive and few people other than computer professionals had access to them. Also, using computers generally required a lot of technical knowledge.

Just as the telephone, automobile, and airplane each changed the nature of business in earlier years, microcomputers have dramatically changed the face of computing. Because microcomputers are inexpensive, there are thousands of times more computers in use today than before microcomputers were invented. And because microcomputers are readily available, powerful, and small enough to put almost anywhere, there are thousands of times more people involved with computers today than just a decade or so ago.

Along with the surge in computer use, there has been explosive growth in high-quality computer products: products that help you type and write books; products that let you analyze numbers up, down, and sideways; products that provide you access to virtually any sort of fact that is stored electronically; products that not only keep track of your stocks, but also pick winners and dump losers; products that help you file taxes; and products that give you electronic access to thousands of newspapers and journals from your home. We are today in the midst of a computer applications revolution that is showing no signs of slowing down (see Figure MC 1-1).

At the heart of the applications revolution lies a class of products that is the major focus of this textbook. *Productivity software* refers to computer programs that turn microcomputers into useful work tools, thereby making people more productive at their jobs. Among the most widely used and familiar types of productivity software are word processing packages, spreadsheets, and database management systems.

A major goal of this chapter is to introduce several fundamental computer concepts and to familiarize you with the terminology of computing. We will first look at what a computer is and how it works. Then we will cover in depth some important elements found in every computer system and, after that, several critical computer concepts. Finally, we will look at an in-depth example of a microcomputer user in action.

COMPUTERS AND COMPUTER SYSTEMS

A **computer** is a device that can rapidly perform arithmetic, make comparisons, and store and retrieve facts. When a computer is put together with other elements so that it can perform useful work, the result is a **computer system.** The small computer systems that can fit on a desktop or on a lap are often called **microcomputer systems.**

To understand fully the distinction between a computer and a computer system, refer to Figure MC 1-2. Depicted in the figure are several pieces of equipment most commonly found in a microcomputer system: a system unit, a monitor (display device), a printer, disk drives, a keyboard, and a mouse. Inside the system unit is a circuit board, with a special, fingernail-sized chip plugged into it that performs the main computing for the entire system. It is

FIGURE MC 1-1 **Computers shaping the workplace.** (a) Personal desktop workstations are rapidly becoming a necessity for office work. (b) Portable computers enable data to be electronically accessed and gathered out in the field. (c) and (d) People are increasingly buying computers for personal use, making it easier than ever before to run home-based businesses and to cater to high-tech hobbies.

(a) (b) (c) (d)

this chip that is commonly called "the computer," or **central processing unit (CPU).** Small as it is, such a computer is capable of performing millions of arithmetic operations per second. It enables a single human to perform in an afternoon work that would take years for a roomful of clerks to do manually.

Thus, the computer is only one of the pieces of equipment that make up the computer system. Also, a computer system consists of far more than just equipment. Other elements include the instructions and data the computer processes, as well as operating manuals, procedures, and the people who use the system. In other words, all the components that contribute to making the computer a useful tool can be said to be parts of a computer system.

INPUT, PROCESSING, OUTPUT, AND STORAGE

Four words sum up the operation of every computer system: input, processing, output, and storage. To see what these words mean, let's look at something you probably have in your own home—a stereo system.

FIGURE MC 1-2 **A microcomputer system.** Featured in the photo, clockwise from the left, are a printer, monitor (often called a display device), system unit (under the monitor), keyboard, and mouse. The system unit contains the computer itself and the disk drives.

A simple stereo system usually consists of a tape recorder and compact disk (CD) player, an amplifier, and a pair of speakers. To use the system you might place a CD in the CD player and turn the system on. The player converts the patterns in the tracks into sounds and transmits them to the amplifier as electronic signals. The amplifier takes the signals, strengthens them, and transmits them to the speakers. The result is music. In computer terms, the CD player sends signals as *input* to the amplifier. The amplifier *processes* the signals and sends them to the speakers, which produce a musical *output.* The CD player is an input device, the amplifier is a processing unit, and the speakers are output devices. The amplifier is the heart of the system, whereas the CD player, tape recorder, and speakers are examples of support—or *peripheral*—equipment.

Most stereo systems have a variety of other support equipment. An antenna, for example, is a kind of input device. Headphones are an output device. A tape recorder is both an input and output device: you can use it to send signals to the amplifier or to receive signals from it. The CDs and tapes in your collection are, in computer terms, *input/output (I/O) media.* They store music in a machine-readable form—a format that the associated input device (CD player and tape recorder) can recognize (that is, "read") and convert into signals for the amplifier to process.

All the elements in a stereo system have their counterparts in a computer system. At the heart of the computer system, performing the processing function, is the CPU. Input to the computer system is through either a keyboard or a mouse. Output is through the display device and printer. Storage is made available through disk drives. The disks that are mounted on their respective drives are examples of I/O media. The same board that contains the microprocessor chip within the system unit also contains memory chips—another form of storage.

DATA AND PROGRAMS

The material that a computer receives as input is classified as either data or programs. **Data** are essentially raw unorganized facts. **Programs** are instructions that tell the computer how to process those facts to produce the results that you want.

Data

Almost any kind of fact or set of facts can become computer data—a letter to a friend, a 300-page book, a budget, a colorful graph, or a set of employee records.

Data can exist in many forms. The four types of data that are commonly handled by computer systems are text, graphics, audio, and video (See Figure MC 1-3).

Text data have been around the longest. These data usually consist of standard alphabetic, numeric, and special characters—that is, the type of data one normally sees in a simple word-processed letter, a budget, or a printed report.

Graphics data consist of *still* pictures such as drawings, graphs, photographs, and illustrations. Graphics data often require more sophisticated equipment than that used by text because they are naturally more complicated and are often in color.

Audio data are the type of data exchanged during an ordinary telephone call. Any type of sound—including music and voice—is considered audio

FIGURE MC 1-3 **Data.** The four types of data that are most commonly handled by computer systems are text, graphics, audio, and video.

data. Today's modern computers can store sounds in machine-readable form just as they store any other type of data.

Video data consist of *motion* pictures, such as a movie or a live conference. Today, many microcomputer systems come with powerful CPUs and are capable of handling video data.

Programs

Like many other machines, the amplifier in your home stereo system is a special-purpose device. It is designed to support only a few specific tasks—playing a CD, making a recording on tape, playing music into speakers or headphones, and so forth. Most of these functions are built into its circuitry; it is "hardwired" to perform a very limited number of specific tasks. Even a programming capability, when present, will be extremely limited.

Most computer systems, in contrast, are general purpose. They must do an enormous variety of tasks, any one of which may involve extremely complex processing. For example, you may need a computer system to scan a list of customer accounts and print a report of all customers with overdue balances. Minutes later, you may want to create a series of color charts to present at a meeting. And tomorrow, you may need the computer to help prepare a sales brochure for clients.

Because most computers must be flexible, they cannot be hardwired to do all or even most of the tasks they need to do. Instead, they rely predominantly on programs for guidance. As mentioned before, a program is a list of instructions. Often a program is read into the computer system, accompanied by the data it is to process. The program and its inputs then direct the circuits in the computer to open and close in the manner needed to do whatever task needs doing.

The types of products you will likely be working with in your school computer lab—word-processing packages, spreadsheet packages, and database management systems—are all examples of programs. In fact, each of these products consists of a *system* of interrelated programs. A word-processing package, for example, consists of the main word-processing program itself, a program that enables you to install the word processor on your specific type of computer system, a program to check for spelling errors, and many other programs.

Programs cannot be written in ordinary English. They must be written in a *programming language*—a dialect the computer system can read and translate into the electronic pulses that make it work. Virtually all of the programs—or *software*—you buy today in a computer store or through the mail are in "package" form (see Figure MC 1-4). Typically, such a *software package* consists of program disks, operating instructions, training tutorials, a warranty, and reference manuals inside a shrink-wrapped box. All of the program disks have been written in some programming language, such as C or assembly language. As a general rule, you will not have to learn the language the package is written in—or, for that matter, be required to learn any language at all—to be able to use the package.

FIGURE MC 1-4
Software packages.
Software packages normally consist of program disks, operating instructions, training tutorials, a warranty, and printed or electronic reference manuals inside a shrink-wrapped box.

A CLOSER LOOK AT COMPUTER STORAGE

So far we have seen that if you want to get something done on a computer system, you must supply it with both facts (data) and instructions (a program) specifying how to process those facts. For example, if you want to use Paradox to prepare payroll reports, you must supply such data as employees' names, social security numbers, and salaries. You must also have the Paradox program available on your computer system. The directions you give to Paradox must "tell" the computer system how to compute taxes, how to take deductions, and so forth. The computer system relies on a memory (storage) to remember all these details as it is doing the work. Actually, as hinted earlier, computer systems contain two types of storage—RAM and secondary storage.

RAM **Memory**—or **RAM** (for **random access memory**)—is generally contained in the system unit, the device that houses the computer. It holds the data and programs the computer is currently processing. Thus RAM functions like a scratch pad; the data are stored only temporarily, as they are needed for processing. When data are temporarily captured in the computer's RAM, they can be rearranged or recombined by the instructions in the program.

Secondary Storage Data and programs the computer does not immediately need for the job at hand are stored in **secondary storage.** On microcomputer systems, the most common forms of secondary storage are *diskette, hard-disk,* and *CD-ROM* units that are fitted into the system unit. These pieces of equipment are called *secondary storage devices.* They enable us to save large quantities of data and programs conveniently in machine-readable form, on a relatively long-term basis, so that we need not rekey them into the system every time we use them. Secondary storage devices on microcomputer systems are usually capable of storing thousands of programs and millions of pieces of data.

When the CPU needs a certain program and set of data, it requests them from the secondary storage device—much as you might request a particular song from a jukebox—and reads them into RAM for processing. Unlike the jukebox, however, which puts the original copy in play, the CPU puts a duplicate copy of the original program or data into RAM for use.

The difference between RAM and secondary storage is similar to the difference between your own memory and this textbook. You read this textbook by bringing a few facts at a time into your memory and processing them through your brain. As you read, there become two copies of many of the facts—the copy in the textbook and the copy in your memory. The facts in the textbook, like data in secondary storage, are long-term; they will not disappear if you take the weekend off to go camping. Many of the facts saved in your own memory, however, will disappear as soon as your mind moves on to something else—just like data in RAM.

DATA AND PROGRAM REPRESENTATION

The electronic components of digital computer systems work in just two states: a circuit is either open or closed, a magnetic spot is either present or absent, and so on. It is convenient to think of these **binary** states as the 0-state and the 1-state. Computer people refer to such 0s and 1s as **bits** (a contraction of the term *bi*nary digi*ts*). Being primarily electronic, computers do all their processing and communicating by representing programs and data in bit form. Binary, then, is the symbol set that forms the computer's "native tongue."

People, of course, do not speak binary. You are not likely to go up to a friend and say,

`0100100001001001`

which in one binary-based coding system translates as "Hi." People communicate with one another in natural languages, such as English, Chinese, and

Spanish. In our part of the world, we speak English. Also, we write with a 26-character alphabet, and we use a number system with 10 rather than just 2 digits. Computers, however, understand only 0 and 1. So in order for us to interact with a computer, our messages to it must be translated into binary form and its messages to us must be translated from binary into a natural language.

The programming languages most people use to interact with computer systems consist of a wide variety of natural-language symbols. When we type a message at a keyboard, the computer system must translate all the natural-language symbols in the message into 0s and 1s. After processing is finished, the computer system must translate the 0s and 1s it has used to represent the program's results into natural language.

ASCII

Computer systems use a variety of binary-based codes to represent programs and data. For example, when data and programs are being sent to or from the CPU, a fixed-length, binary-based code called **ASCII** (American Standard Code for Information Interchange) is often used to represent each character transmitted. ASCII, developed largely through the efforts of the American National Standards Institute, is used on virtually all microcomputers. It is also widely adopted as the standard for data communications systems.

ASCII represents each printable character as a unique combination of a fixed number of bits (see Figure MC 1-5). ASCII originally was designed as a 7-bit code that could represent 128 (2^7) characters. Several 8-bit versions of ASCII have been developed because computers are designed to handle data in chunks of 8 bits. A group of 8 bits has 256 (2^8) different combinations;

FIGURE MC 1-5 **ASCII.** This common fixed-length code represents characters in byte form.

Character	Standard ASCII 8-Bit Representation	Character	Standard ASCII 8-Bit Representation
0	00110000	I	01001001
1	00110001	J	01001010
2	00110010	K	01001011
3	00110011	L	01001100
4	00110100	M	01001101
5	00110101	N	01001110
6	00110110	O	01001111
7	00110111	P	01010000
8	00111000	Q	01010001
9	00111001	R	01010010
A	01000001	S	01010011
B	01000010	T	01010100
C	01000011	U	01010101
D	01000100	V	01010110
E	01000101	W	01010111
F	01000110	X	01011000
G	01000111	Y	01011001
H	01001000	Z	01011010

therefore, ASCII can represent up to 256 characters. This is more than enough to account for the 26 uppercase and 26 lowercase characters, the 10 decimal digits, and several special characters.

The Byte Concept

The eight bits used to represent a character are collectively referred to as a **byte.** In many computer systems, one byte represents a single addressable storage location. For this reason, computer manufacturers use the byte measure to define their machines' storage capacity.

As you may have noticed, computer advertisements are filled with references to kilobytes, megabytes, and gigabytes. One **kilobyte (KB)** is equal to a little more than 1,000 bytes (1,024, to be precise), one **megabyte (meg** or **MB)** equals about one million bytes, and one **gigabyte (GB)** equals about one billion bytes. So, for example, when you read about a 200 KB file on a 300 MB hard disk, it means that the file takes up 200,000 characters of space, and the disk unit has space for a total of 300 million characters.

The conversion from natural-language words and numbers to their ASCII equivalents and back again usually takes place on an I/O device. For example, when a user types in a message at a keyboard, a specialized processor inside the keyboard usually translates the message into ASCII and sends it as a series of bytes to the CPU. The output the CPU sends back to the display or some other output device is also in ASCII, which the output device—usually with the aid of another embedded specialized processor—translates into understandable words and numbers.

Machine Language

Before your computer can execute any program instruction, the instruction must be converted into a binary-based code known as **machine language.** An example of a typical 32-bit machine-language instruction follows:

```
01011000011100000000000100000010
```

A machine-language instruction may look like a meaningless string of 0s and 1s, but it actually consists of groups of bits that represent specific storage locations and operations. The instruction shown here, for instance, transfers data between two specific memory locations.

In the earliest computers, including the first microcomputers, all programs were written in machine language. Today, although it is still possible to write in machine language, hardly anybody does. Instead, most people rely on *language translators,* special programs that convert instructions automatically into machine language. For instance, when you type instructions into your spreadsheet package, the package has a built-in language translator that automatically converts your instructions into machine language. This translation is so smooth that most users are not even aware that it is taking place.

Each computer has its own machine language. A code that is used on an IBM Aptiva computer (which uses an Intel CPU chip) will be totally foreign to an Apple Power Macintosh (which uses a PowerPC CPU chip). Thus, when you buy a program package such as a word processor or spreadsheet, you must get the version intended for your specific type of computer system. You certainly do not want the program package translating all of your commands to, say, the PowerPC's machine language if you have an IBM Aptiva computer that understands another brand of machine language. Most microcomputer systems sold today are said to be either "IBM-compatible"—meaning they primarily use Intel CPU chips—or "Macintosh-compatible"—meaning they use PowerPC CPU chips.

ORGANIZING DATA

Data, as mentioned earlier, are essentially raw facts. But you cannot just randomly input a collection of facts into a computer system and expect to get results. Data to be processed in a computer system must be organized in a systematic way. A common procedure is to organize data into fields, records, files, and databases. Each of these words has a precise meaning in a computing environment, and you should use them with care.

A **field** is a collection of characters (such as a single digit, letter of the alphabet, or special symbol like a decimal point) that represents a single type of data. A **record** is a collection of related fields. A **file** is a collection of related records. A **database** is a collection of related files.

Databases, files, records, and fields normally are stored on an input/output medium such as a disk or tape. Your school, for example, probably has a file, perhaps stored on disk, of all students currently enrolled (See Figure MC 1-6). The file likely contains a record for each student. Each record has several fields containing various types of data about each student: ID number, name, street, city, state, major subject area, and the like. Your school's student database may contain the contents of a student address file such as the one in Figure MC 1-6, a student grade file (courses completed and grades earned by each student), and perhaps other student data. Each file and database is given a name so that it can be easily accessed.

Programs, too, are usually organized into files. For instance, if you displayed the full contents of your word-processing or spreadsheet program on the screen, you would see a list of file names. Each name corresponds to a specific program file, and collectively these related program files make up the "package" you are using.

FIGURE MC 1-6 **Differences among a file, record, and field.** The file shown contains name and address data on students enrolled at a college. If there are 2,000 active students at the college, this file would contain 2,000 records. Each record in the file has six data fields—the student's number, name, street, city, state, and major.

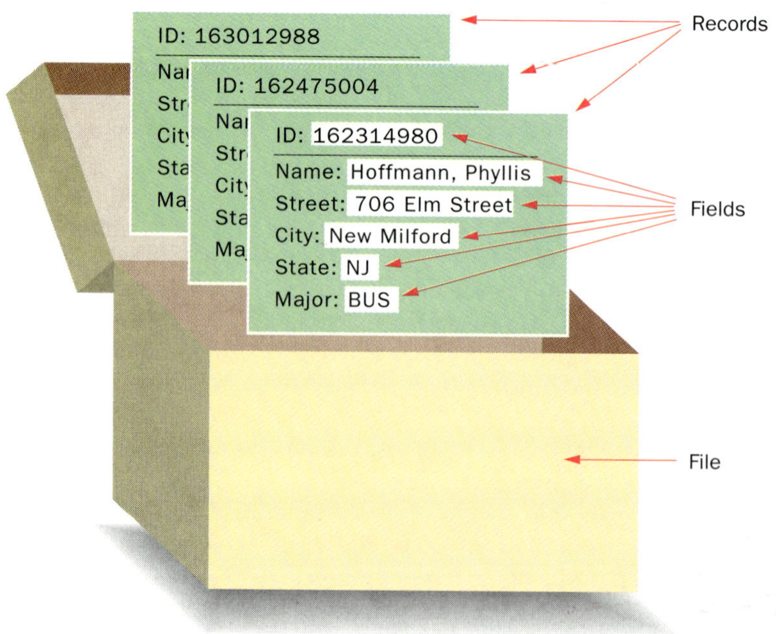

HARDWARE AND SOFTWARE

In the world of computers, it is common to distinguish between hardware and software. **Hardware** refers to the actual machinery that makes up a computer system—for example, the CPU, I/O devices, and storage devices. **Software** refers to computer programs.

Hardware

Hardware falls into one or more of five categories: input devices, processing devices, storage devices, output devices, and communications devices.

Input devices, such as the keyboard and mouse, enable data and programs to be read into the computer system. *Processing devices,* such as the computer and related equipment, allow computations and comparisons to be made on the input. *Storage devices*—such as RAM and the disk units—hold input, processed results, and output for further use. *Output devices,* such as the monitor and printer, place computer output into a form that humans can understand. *Communications devices* assist in the transmission of data and programs over long distances, from one hardware device to another.

It is not unusual for a particular hardware device to fall into more than one of these five categories. For instance, storage devices are capable of both input and output. In the next chapter we will look in detail at the first four types of these hardware devices. In Chapter 4, we will address communications.

Any hardware device that is ready for or in communication with the computer at a given time is said to be *online* at that time. If a device isn't online, it's *offline.*

Software

There are two principal classes of software: applications software and systems software.

Applications Software People use **applications software** to perform tasks such as computing the interest or balance in bank accounts, preparing bills, creating documents, preparing budgets, managing files and databases, playing games, scheduling airline flights, diagnosing hospital patients' illnesses, and analyzing data for trends or unusual happenings (see chapter User Tip). In other words, applications software makes possible the types of "computer work" people have in mind when they acquire a computer system. You can buy prewritten applications software or write it yourself. If you write it yourself, you must be familiar with a specific programming language.

Productivity software packages are the class of applications software designed to make workers more productive at their jobs. Some important types of productivity software available for microcomputers are listed and described in Figure MC 1-7. Of the packages listed in the figure, word processors, spreadsheets, presentation graphics, database management systems, and communications software are often referred to as the "Big Five." These packages far outsell other types of productivity software packages.

Systems Software **Systems software** consists of "background" programs that enable applications software to run on a given set of hardware. One of the most important pieces of systems software is the *operating system,* the main set of control programs that coordinates the computer system's work. Several operating systems are available for microcomputers. Among the best known of these are MS-DOS and Microsoft Windows.

Operating systems are developed to conform to the physical limitations of specific CPU chips. Often they are written in the special programming

USER TIP

Using Computers to Win a Pulitzer Prize

Did you ever think you could use a computer to win a Pulitzer Prize? Computer analyses won one for the *Miami Herald.* Just days before the start of 1993, the Florida paper printed a report that shocked state residents. Using computers and mapping software to analyze some 60,000 damage reports filed in the wake of Hurricane Andrew as well as some seven million home-inspection records, the paper had made some chilling discoveries.

When a map of wind speeds was superimposed on a map showing damage, it was found that many of the worst-hit areas were not where the worst winds occurred. And when a home's age, value, size, construction material, and other factors were correlated with damage, one strong relationship stood out—the newer the house, the worse it tended to fare. These discoveries led to a trail of unenforced building codes, shoddy construction practices, and fraudulent inspections.

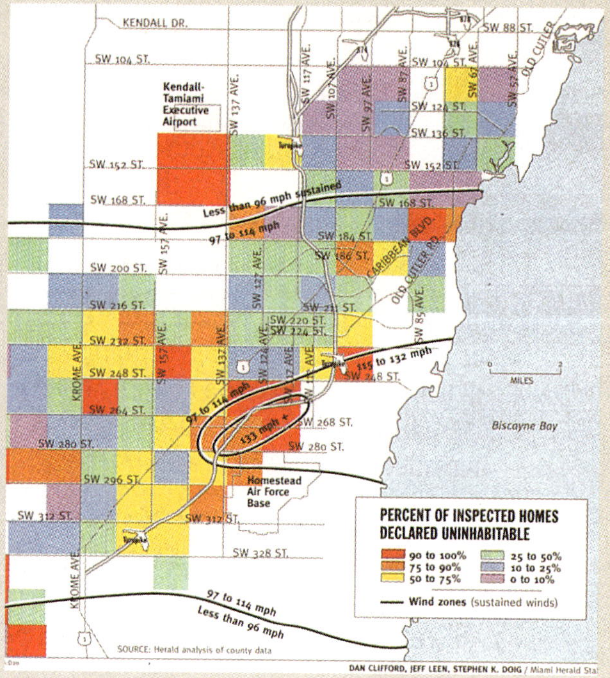

Miami vice. Computer analyses uncovered a subtle trail of corruption.

language available with the chip. These programming languages, which address specific memory hardware and storage areas, are not interchangeable. Since application programs are written to interface with particular operating systems, an applications program that works with one operating system usually does not work with another, unless modified. Thus, choosing the right operating system is critical. When buying productivity software packages, make sure you get the specific version of the software intended for *both* your computer system and your operating system.

USING MICROCOMPUTERS: A COMPREHENSIVE EXAMPLE

Now that we have briefly seen how a computer system works, we will "walk through" a hypothetical applications environment within a typical organization to put many of the concepts you have just read about into sharper focus. We will also introduce a few new concepts along the way—ones that you should know before using a microcomputer system or any type of productivity software package.

Lydia Maxwell is the catering manager at a large resort. She finds the desktop microcomputer system shown in Figure MC 1-8 a useful tool in her work.

Hardware

The principal hardware in Lydia's microcomputer system consists of six separate pieces of equipment: a keyboard, a mouse, a monitor or display device, a printer, speakers, and a system unit. Within the *system unit* are the

FIGURE MC 1-7 **Types of productivity software.** Productivity software packages are designed to make both ordinary users and computer professionals more productive at their jobs.

Package Type	Description
Word processing	Turns the computer system into a powerful typewriting tool
Spreadsheet	Turns the computer system into a sophisticated electronic calculator and analysis tool
Presentation graphics	Turns the computer into a tool that can be used to prepare overheads, slides, and presentation materials for meetings
Database management system	Turns the computer system into an electronic research assistant, capable of searching through mounds of data
Communications software	Enables users to call up remote computers for such things as financial information, mail, and news
Desktop publishing	Turns the computer system into a tool that can be used to produce documents that look like they were produced at a professional print shop
Desk accessory	Provides the electronic equivalent of tools commonly found on an office desktop—calendars and address files, for instance
CASE (computer-aided software engineering)	Automates and integrates many of the tasks performed by computer professionals.
Expert system	Enables workers to tap into expert knowledge to support them in their work
CAD (computer-aided design)	Gives people such as architects and product designers the ability to bring products to market faster

CPU chip, RAM, and secondary storage devices—two diskette drives, a hard-disk drive, and a CD-ROM drive—as well as circuitry we will cover later.

The *keyboard*, which resembles that of an ordinary typewriter, enables Lydia to direct the microcomputer system to do what she wants. Everything

FIGURE MC 1-8 **Lydia Maxwell's microcomputer system.** Represented in Lydia's system is the equipment commonly found in a microcomputer system—a system unit with built-in disk drives, speakers, a display device, a printer, a keyboard and mouse, and a communications feature.

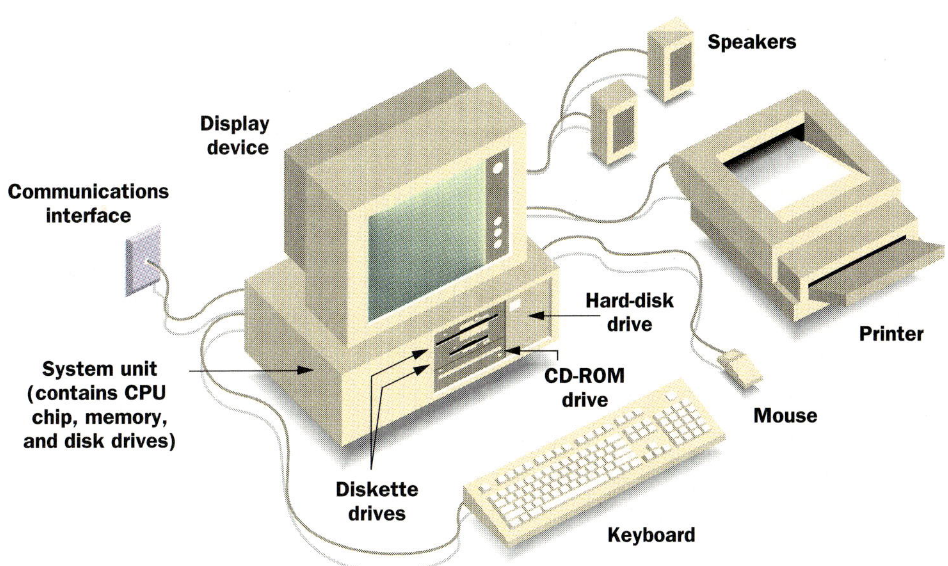

she inputs at the keyboard, as well as the computer system's responses to these inputs, is shown on the *monitor,* which resembles a television screen. When she wants something printed out, she directs the computer system to send the output to her *printer*. The *mouse* can be used to perform some types of keyboard operations faster.

The *diskette unit* on Lydia's microcomputer system consists of two drives. On the drives, Lydia can mount diskettes, or floppy disks—small platters capable of storing, say, 100 or more pages of data or programs in electronic form. The diskettes must be properly inserted into the computer system's disk drives if the system is to access the programs and data on them. The *hard-disk unit* on Lydia's system has several hundred times the capacity of a single diskette and permits much quicker accessing of both programs and data.

The *CD-ROM* (for compact-disk, read-only memory) drive and *speakers* on Lydia's system are part of a multimedia kit. CD-ROM disks enable her to watch video presentations on her display and to install new software packages, while the speakers provide accompanying audio output, such as voice and music. The term *multimedia* refers to the fact that such technologies as CD-ROM bring to the desktop multiple data types—audio and video along with the more traditional text and graphics. Lydia also has a multimedia computer system at home that her children use to play games.

Getting Started

The software and data that people need to access to make them more productive can be on hard disk, diskette, or CD-ROM. Most people who have hard-disk computer systems—including Lydia—will store copies of the programs and data they most frequently use on their hard disks. Duplicate (backup) copies of these programs and data, as well as less frequently used materials, are typically maintained offline, on diskette.

To make her computer system ready to use, Lydia first turns on the power. As soon as the computer is turned on, it automatically loads portions of the operating system into RAM. The operating system either returns a message called a *prompt* to the display or returns a graphical screen, indicating that it is ready to receive instructions from the user. This process of readying the computer system for applications processing is called *booting*.

Next, after the system is booted up, Lydia must type in a specific command at the keyboard (or make a selection with a mouse) that tells the computer which program she wishes to work on—say, her word-processing package or her spreadsheet. Once she invokes this command, certain portions of the selected applications program are loaded from hard disk or CD-ROM into RAM. At this point the applications program takes over control of the computer system from the operating system. Typically, the computer system will then display an introductory screen or two on the monitor, indicating that the applications program is being successfully loaded. Finally, the user will be given a screen that asks for some type of opening response. At this time, the user can fetch an existing data file from hard disk, load in data from a diskette, begin typing in new data, or issue other sorts of preparatory instructions.

Once a program and its data are activated, the computer is transformed into a powerful calculating tool.

Applications Processing

One application for which Lydia finds her computer system useful is *word processing*. For instance, when a letter must be quickly prepared and sent to a client to confirm a booking date or to thank the client for his or her patronage, Lydia uses a word-processing software package and a "canned" form letter stored on her hard disk. To word process, she either types a command at the operating-system prompt or selects a screen icon with her mouse so that the proper operating-system routine (in RAM) retrieves her word-processing program. She can then use the program to make changes in the letter. When the letter is finished, she will select a command to have the letter printed out on her printer.

Lydia also frequently uses her microcomputer system to prepare budgets, a task that requires her to use a *spreadsheet* software package. To work with the package, Lydia invokes a special command to exit her word-processing program. This automatically brings her back to the operating system. Then, she invokes a command from the operating system to summon the spreadsheet program. At this point, she is ready to prepare budgets. She can send completed budgets to her printer when she requires them in printed form.

To plan meals, Lydia uses a *database management system.* To get this application up and running, she leaves the spreadsheet program and invokes a command from the operating system to recognize the database management package. The database program is especially useful in assisting Lydia with searching through descriptions of food dishes to find ones that will fit a particular client's needs. On her hard disk is stored a file of hundreds of filled-in "forms," or records, one for each food dish she can offer to guests (see Figure MC 1-9). Each form contains three separate fields of data—the name of the dish, its ingredients, and a few remarks.

If Lydia is helping a client plan a Saturday night banquet over the phone, she can summon the database program to search for all forms on her entrees disk file in which "ingredients" contains "beef" and "mushrooms" and "remarks" contains "dinner." Then she can have the names of these dishes directed to her display screen.

Lydia could rely on her memory, but having the computer system make the search for her often turns up good alternatives that did not cross her mind. Also, she can save a lot of phone time by having her computer system do the searching in the background while she attends to other matters with the client.

FIGURE MC 1-9 Meal planning data stored on disk. Lydia's meal-planning data file consists of several filled-in electronic forms. Several thousand such forms can be stored on a hard disk.

Lydia's database manager lets her add new forms to the file when she wants them, delete forms, and modify forms. She does this with a *screen menu* of processing alternatives (not to be confused with a food menu) that the database manager sends to her display screen, asking her what she wants to do (see Figure MC 1-10).

Lydia also has a *communications interface,* which enables her computer to get data from other computers located miles away. For instance, Lydia uses her computer to place food and beverage orders automatically with a distributor located across town. The communications interface is made up of hardware and software elements that enable Lydia's computer to call up the distributor's computer and transfer a food and beverage order, electronically, over regular telephone lines. The distributor's computer will even relay back a confirmation of the order, and will also allow Lydia to inspect the stock levels of goods and the latest prices.

Lydia's communications interface also connects her to the *Internet,* a web of computer networks that links tens of millions of people and organizations worldwide (see Figure MC 1-11). She finds the Internet especially useful for mingling with colleagues in the restaurant and travel industries and for posting *electronic bulletin board* messages to potential clients about the hotel's facilities. The Internet is a public network that contains thousands of bulletin boards on subjects ranging from astrology to dog care to Zen.

One reason for Lydia's success at her job is her skill at quickly pulling together key information when dealing with clients, managers, and suppliers.

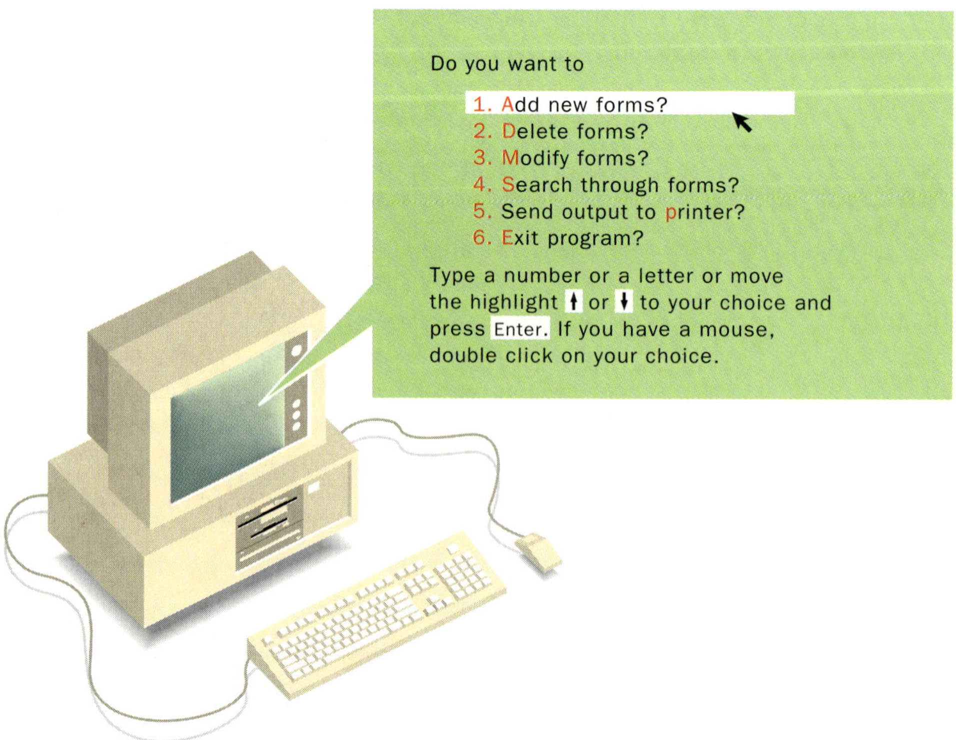

FIGURE MC 1-10 **A screen menu.** Screen menus beckon a user to choose a specific course of action. Using them effectively requires neither typing skills nor an extensive knowledge of computers.

FIGURE MC 1-11 **The Internet.** The Internet is a massive, worldwide web of computer networks through which tens of millions of computer users exchange ideas.

The database management system and word processor allow Lydia to give clients first-class service. Hotel management appreciates the value of this; a $50,000 booking can easily be won or lost on the quality of service. The spreadsheet allows Lydia quickly to prepare important financial information for management and to analyze that information in ways that would not be feasible if she had to do it by hand. Also, the communications interface enables Lydia to place orders more efficiently, saving time and lowering costs, and to explore new channels for marketing the hotel's services. These are but a few of the benefits that computers and their productivity software provide.

Summary

- The small computer systems that can fit on a desktop or on a lap are called microcomputer systems.
- Four words sum up the operation of every computer system, including microcomputer systems—input, processing, output, and storage.
- The material that a computer receives as input is of two kinds: data and programs. Data are essentially raw, unorganized facts. Programs are instructions that tell the computer system how to process those facts.
- Computer systems contain two types of storage. Memory (or RAM, for random access memory) provides temporary storage for the data and programs

the computer is currently processing. Programs and data are kept on a more long-term basis in secondary storage.

- As data and programs are sent to and from the computer, they are coded in ASCII by input and output devices. Language translators within the computer system further convert any programs being input into a common machine language so the computer can process the programs.
- Data to be processed by a computer system are often organized into fields, records, files, and databases.
- Hardware refers to the equipment in a computer system. Hardware is often classified as falling into one or more of five categories: input devices, processing devices, output devices, storage devices, and communications devices.
- Software refers to computer programs. The two principal classes of software are systems software (which includes the operating system) and applications software (which includes productivity software such as word processors and spreadsheets).
- Chapter 1 concludes with a comprehensive example that ties together many of the materials presented in the chapter.

Key Terms

Shown in parentheses are the page numbers on which key terms are boldfaced.

Applications software (MC 11)
ASCII (MC 8)
Binary (MC 7)
Bit (MC 7)
Byte (MC 9)
Central processing unit (CPU) (MC 3)
Computer (MC 2)
Computer system (MC 2)
Data (MC 5)
Database (MC 10)
Field (MC 10)
File (MC 10)
Gigabyte (GB) (MC 9)
Hardware (MC 11)
Kilobyte (KB) (MC 9)
Machine language (MC 9)
Megabyte (MB) (MC 9)
Memory (MC 7)
Microcomputer system (MC 2)
Productivity software (MC 11)
Program (MC 5)
Random access memory (RAM) (MC 7)
Record (MC 10)
Secondary storage (MC 7)
Software (MC 11)
Systems software (MC 11)

Quiz

True/False

___ 1. The CPU is the computer that runs your microcomputer system.

___ 2. Data and programs are essentially the same thing.

___ 3. Word processors are types of computer operating systems.

___ 4. RAM means random access memory.

___ 5. Diskettes are a type of memory.

____ 6. Data sent to and from the computer are commonly coded in ASCII.

____ 7. A megabyte is larger than a gigabyte.

____ 8. A field is a collection of related files.

____ 9. The operating system is an example of productivity software.

____ 10. Software refers to computer programs.

Multiple Choice

____ 11. The main role of the CPU is
a. processing.
b. storage.
c. input.
d. output.
e. long-distance communication.

____ 12. The main role of the display device is
a. processing.
b. storage.
c. input.
d. output.
e. long-distance communication.

____ 13. Which of the following is not a type of data?
a. Text
b. Software
c. Graphics
d. Video
e. Audio

____ 14. Memory
a. holds data and programs temporarily.
b. is also called RAM.
c. is not the same as secondary storage.
d. often is found in the system unit.
e. All of the above

____ 15. ASCII often represents characters as eight
a. bytes.
b. megabytes.
c. bits.
d. kilobytes.
e. gigabytes.

____ 16. A kilobyte is roughly ______________ bytes.
a. 8
b. 64
c. 640
d. 1,000
e. 1,000,000

____ 17. Which of the following is not an example of binary coding?
a. Machine language
b. Byte
c. Natural language
d. ASCII
e. Bit

___ 18. Which of the following represents the smallest unit of measure?
a. File
b. Field
c. Database
d. Record
e. Answer cannot be determined from the information given.

___ 19. Which of the following represents the largest unit of measure?
a. File
b. Field
c. Database
d. Record
e. Answer cannot be determined from the information given.

___ 20. Any hardware device that is ready for or in communication with the computer at any given time is said to be
a. binary.
b. electronic.
c. offline.
d. auxiliary.
e. online.

Matching

Select the term that best matches each phrase:

a. Software
b. Hardware
c. Machine language
d. Computer
e. Data
f. Field
g. RAM
h. Diskette
i. ASCII
j. Kilobyte
k. Megabyte
l. File

___ 21. Equipment in a computer system

___ 22. Another name for memory

___ 23. Approximately a million bytes

___ 24. A collection of related records

___ 25. A code consisting of seven or eight bits

___ 26. Another name for the CPU

___ 27. A collection of unorganized facts

___ 28. A type of secondary storage

___ 29. Another name for programs

___ 30. A form into which every program is translated

Answers

True/False: 1. T; 2. F; 3. F; 4. T; 5. F; 6. T; 7. F; 8. F; 9. F; 10. T

Multiple Choice: 11. a; 12. d; 13. b; 14. e; 15. c; 16. d; 17. c; 18. b; 19. c; 20. e

Matching: 21. b; 22. g; 23. k; 24. l; 25. i; 26. d; 27. e; 28. h; 29. a; 30. c

Exercises

1. Create on paper a small file of data—say, employee data or data about your favorite movies. Identify the number of records and the contents of each of the fields.

2. Go to your school library or a local bookstore and find six to eight journals that focus on microcomputers. For each journal, list the following information:
   a. The name of the journal
   b. The frequency with which the journal is published (for example, weekly, monthly, bimonthly)
   c. The audience to which the journal is principally targeted (for example, users of IBM and IBM-compatible microcomputers, users of Apple computers, network users, users of Microsoft software, desktop publishers)

3. In each of the following productivity software areas—word processing, spreadsheets, and database management systems—identify at least two packages that are used on IBM microcomputers and IBM-compatible machines. Also, identify at least two packages in each area that can be used on the Apple Macintosh and Macintosh-compatible computers.

4. Look in a computer magazine for an advertisement of a microcomputer system for sale. What are the principal hardware components and the function of each? What software is being offered in the deal and what does each of these software packages do? Is the system complete for your needs or do additional items have to be purchased separately?

MC 2 HARDWARE

OUTLINE

Overview
Input Hardware
  Keyboards
  Digitizers
  Other Input Devices
Processing Hardware
  Types of Microcomputers
  Looking inside the System Unit
Secondary Storage Hardware
  Properties of Secondary Storage Systems
  Diskettes
  Hard Disks
  Optical Disks
  Cartridge Disks
  Cartridge Tapes
Output Hardware
  Monitors
  Printers
  Special-Purpose Output Devices
Appendix: Tips for Buying Microcomputer Hardware

LEARNING OBJECTIVES

After completing this chapter, you will be able to:

1. Describe several types of input, output, and storage devices and the purpose served by each.
2. Distinguish among the various types of microcomputer systems.
3. Identify the components of the system unit and explain the roles they perform.
4. Name several properties of disks and appreciate situations in which each type is appropriate.
5. Describe several of the key features of keyboards, monitors, printers, and other input and output devices, as well as some of the differences among them.

OVERVIEW

When people think of computers or computer systems, hardware seems to come to mind most readily. Hardware refers to the exciting pieces of equipment that make your computer system look like a computer system. As you will learn in this chapter, a rich variety of microcomputer hardware is available in today's marketplace.

The hardware discussed in this chapter is divided into four areas. First you will learn about input hardware, the devices used to enter data and programs into the computer system. Then the chapter addresses the processing function of the computer system. Here you will learn about the types of microcomputer systems in the marketplace as well as the devices within a typical desktop system unit. Next we cover secondary storage, with an emphasis on disk systems—the secondary storage alternatives with which you are most likely to interact. The chapter closes with a discussion of output equipment, by far the most diverse class of hardware in terms of the functions it performs. An appendix providing tips for buying microcomputer hardware is located at the end of the chapter.

INPUT HARDWARE

Input hardware devices enable users to enter data into the computer system. A wide variety of hardware is available for input, including keyboards, several types of digitizers, and numerous other devices.

Keyboards

For most people, a microcomputer system would be useless without a **keyboard,** which often is the main vehicle for input. Keyboards vary tremendously with respect to such factors as number of keys, key arrangement, types of special keys, and touch. Figure MC 2-1 shows a typical microcomputer keyboard.

The keyboards on most microcomputer systems have several special keys that involve specific software routines. The *Delete* key and the *Backspace* key, for example, erase characters from the screen and from memory, and the *Insert* key enables characters to inserted. In many software packages, the *Enter* key is used to enter into the computer a character or a command that you have just selected.

On virtually all keyboards there are *Ctrl, Alt,* and *Shift* keys. These keys work by being held down while another key is pressed. If you hold down the Shift key and strike a letter key, for instance, the corresponding letter will be capitalized on the screen—just as it would be capitalized in print if you were using a conventional typewriter. Holding down the Shift key and striking *PrtSc,* on the other hand, will usually output the current screen image to the printer.

Usually several **function keys** (see top part of Figure MC 2-1) are available to users. These keys, typically labeled F1, F2, F3, and so on, are located in a cluster at the top or on the left-hand side of the keyboard. When pressed by the operator, these keys initiate a command or even an entire computer program. Generally speaking, each software package you work with will define the function keys differently. For example, pressing the F2 key may enable you to search for text strings with your word processor but to edit cells with your spreadsheet package.

Most keyboards also have a *numeric keypad* (see right part of Figure MC 2-1), which is activated by the *Num Lock* key and makes it easy to enter numbers quickly.

FIGURE MC 2-1 **Enhanced keyboard.** This 102-key keyboard, which resembles many keyboards sold today, has keys that are conveniently located for the popular software packages.

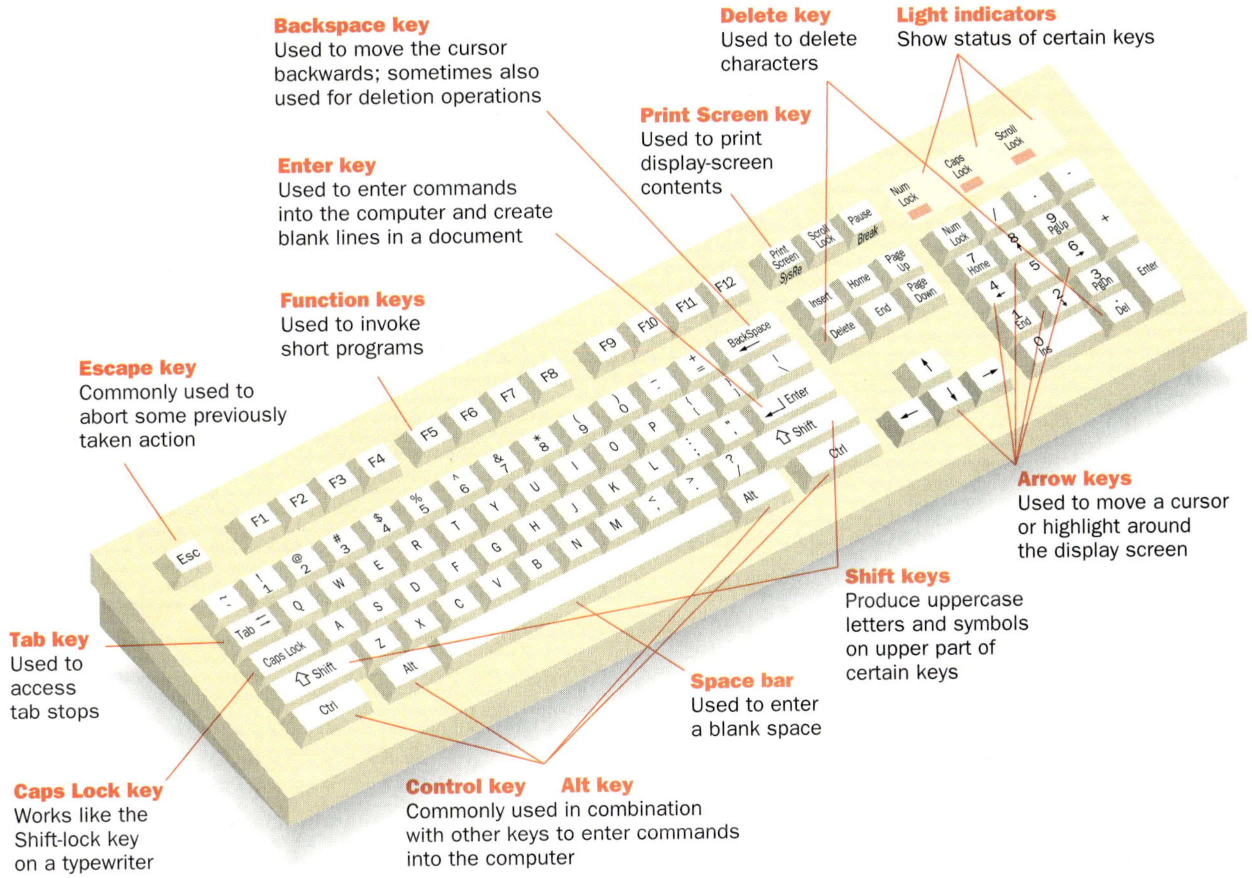

Digitizers

A *digitizer* is a screen-pointing device that converts a measurement into a digital value. Digitizers determine a position, distance, or speed, and move the cursor on the display screen accordingly. Six common types of digitizers are the mouse, light pen, joystick, trackball, crosshair cursor, and digitizing tablet.

Mouse Many people supplement keyboard operations with a **mouse,** which is the most widely used type of digitizing device (see Figure MC 2-2). When the mouse is moved along a flat surface, the cursor on the display screen moves correspondingly. Mice are useful for moving the cursor rapidly from one location to another on a display screen. Using a mouse in this way often is much faster than pressing combinations of cursor-movement (arrow) keys on the keyboard. Mice are especially handy to use when pointing to **icons** on the screen—small graphics symbols that represent commands or program options. When you use the mouse to move an icon on the display screen, you make that icon active by *clicking* a button on the mouse. By instead clicking the mouse button twice in rapid succession—an action called *double clicking*—you generally invoke, or execute, the choice rather than merely highlight it.

Light Pen A *light pen* contains a light-sensitive cell at its tip. When the tip of the pen is placed close to the screen, the display device can identify its

FIGURE MC 2-2 Mouse input. When the mouse is moved along a flat surface, the cursor on the display screen moves correspondingly.

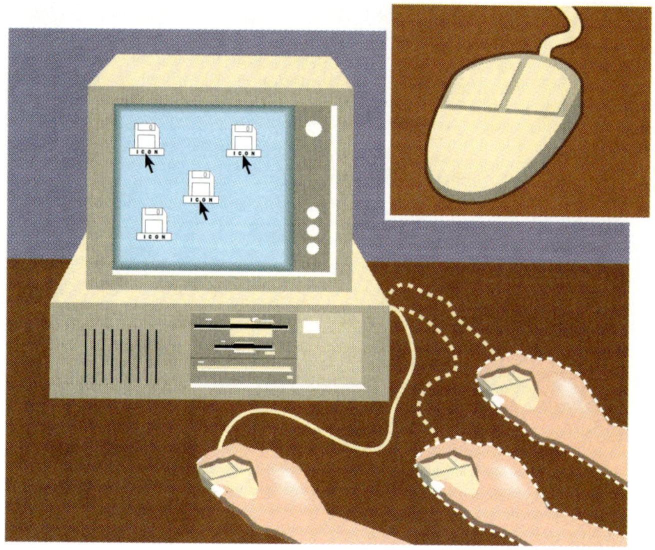

position and the pen can be used to select items. One of the most common applications of light pens is in *pen-based computers,* which are notebook-sized devices targeted to workers who need to use a computer while on the move. Figure MC 2-3a shows a pen-based computer in use.

Joystick A *joystick* (see Figure MC 2-3b), which looks like a car's stick shift, is often used for computer games and for computer-aided design (CAD) work. With many joysticks, the speed at which they move and the distance they travel determine the speed and distance traveled by the screen cursor. Today, some electronic games employ gloves with built-in sensors in place of joysticks, to enable the computer to detect hand movements directly.

Trackball A *trackball* consists of a sphere resting on rollers, with only the top of the sphere exposed outside its case (see Figure MC 2-3c). The screen cursor travels in whatever direction the operator spins the sphere. A mouse is merely a trackball turned upside down. Many people prefer a trackball to a mouse because it requires less desk space to be used.

Digitizing Tablet A *digitizing tablet* employs either a *crosshair cursor* or a *pen.* The operator uses one or the other of these devices to trace over an image on the flat tablet (see Figure MC 2-3d). The image is digitized into the computer system's memory as the cursor passes over it. Think of the tablet as a matrix of thousands of tiny dots. Each dot has a machine address. When you trace a line on the tablet, the stylus or cursor passes over some of the dots, causing their status in computer memory to change from a 0-state to a 1-state. When the drawing is complete, it is stored in electronic form as a large matrix of 0s and 1s and may be recalled at any time.

Other Input Devices

Whereas keyboards and digitizers are the most common types of input devices, many other devices are available for specialized applications.

FIGURE MC 2-3 **Digitizers.** The wide variety of digitizing devices on the market today powerfully illustrates the many ways for ordinary users to input data at their desktops. (a) Light pen being used on a pen-based computer. (b) Joystick. (c) Trackball. (d) Digitizing tablet with pens and a crosshair cursor on top of it.

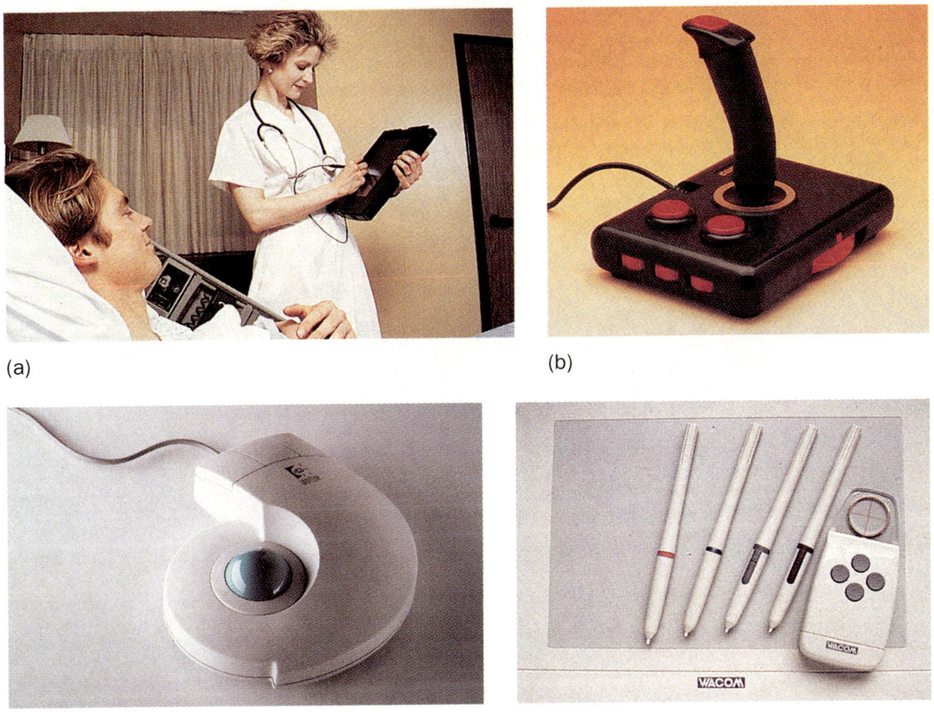

(a) (b) (c) (d)

For instance, *image scanners,* such as the ones in Figure MC 2-4, are used to convert images such as photographs, drawings, and documents into a collection of tiny dots and store them in computer memory. Many image scanners sold with microcomputers scan at a resolution of 300 or 600 dots per inch (dpi). As you might expect, the more dots the computer uses to store the image, the better the resolution will be when the image is finally output. (Typeset-quality imaging, available through professional print shops, generally starts at a resolution of about 1,000 dpi.) Many image scanners are "dumb," meaning that they cannot recognize any of the text they read. "Intelligent" image scanners, on the other hand, are accompanied by software that enables them to recognize as well as read characters. When text is recognized, it can be manipulated with a word processor or spreadsheet.

Voice-input devices—machines that can convert spoken words into digital form for computer storage and processing—are another type of specialized input device. If you stop to think about how complicated the interpretation of spoken words can be for humans, you can realize how tricky it is to design a voice-input device to do essentially the same thing. Two people, for instance, may pronounce the same word differently because of accents, personal styles of speech, and the unique quality of each person's voice. Unfortunately, most voice-input devices can recognize only a limited number of isolated words and whole sentences composed of continuous speech. Thus, the complexity of the messages to which they can respond is quite limited. Today, voice-input devices are commonly used to enter numbers into the computer system. Even-

FIGURE MC 2-4 **Image scanners.** Image scanners are used to digitize images of photographs, drawings, and filled-in form documents into computer storage. (a) A page scanner with faxing capabilities. (b) A portable, motorized scanner.

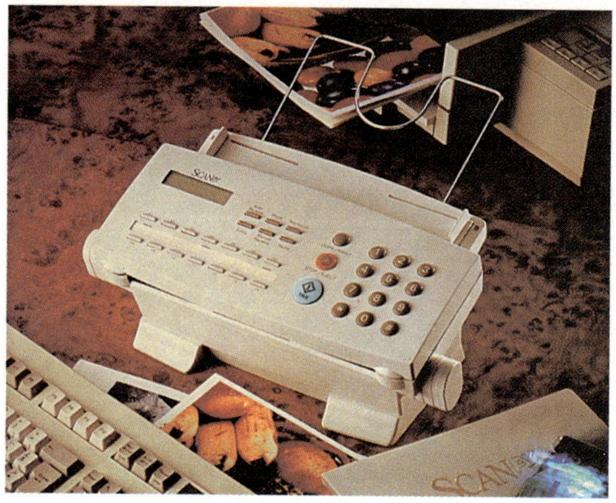

(a)

(b)

tually, they will probably play a major role for text input in word-processing applications.

PROCESSING HARDWARE

The processing device in a microcomputer system is called the **system unit.** This device contains the microprocessor chip (CPU) and RAM. It also usually houses the secondary storage devices and a number of other hardware units.

Types of Microcomputers

As illustrated in Figure MC 2-5, the system units accompanying most microcomputer systems can be classified as being either desktop, portable (including laptop), or handheld.

Desktop Units **Desktop computers** are those found most often in schools, homes, and businesses. These are the computer systems that have become household names—the IBM PC and PS/2 lines; Apple Macintosh and PowerMac lines; Compaq Deskpro and ProLinea series; and so forth. Desktop units fall into one of two categories: single-user systems and multiuser systems. Single-user systems, as their name implies, can be operated by only one user at a time, whereas multiuser systems can accommodate several users concurrently.

Portable and Laptop Units *Portable computers* are designed for users who would like to use the same microcomputer at several sites. These computers are lightweight (1 to 18 pounds) and compact (able to fit into a briefcase). The most lightweight portable computers—which can be used on one's lap, if desired—are called **laptop computers,** or sometimes *notebook computers.* Although many portables are just as powerful as their larger desktop cousins, they tend to be more expensive, have smaller screens, and have a denser arrangement of keys. These disadvantages notwithstanding, portability

FIGURE MC 2-5 **Four microcomputer systems.** (a) IBM ValuePoint P60/D Pentium desktop computer. (b) Apple Power Macintosh 8100/80 desktop computer. (c) IBM ThinkPad 755C laptop computer. (d) Sharp Travel Organizer handheld computer.

(a)

(b)

(c)

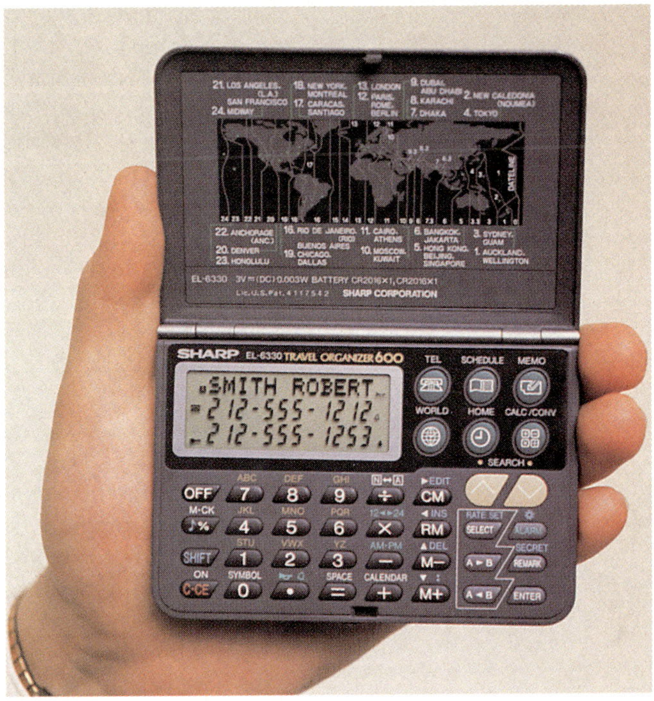

(d)

is "in" these days, and laptop computers currently are one of the fastest-growing segments of the microcomputer industry.

Handheld Units *Handheld computers*—or *palmtop computers*—look and behave a lot like standard pocket calculators. You can generally hold the entire computer system in your hand while operating it. Today, most handheld computers are relegated to specialized tasks—keeping track of golf or bowling scores, helping translate words into foreign languages, maintaining address books and phone directories, and providing synonyms and antonyms for words.

Looking inside the System Unit

Here we "flip the lid" off a typical system unit to see how the parts inside fit together. The system unit usually consists of at least a CPU chip, memory (RAM and ROM) chips, boards on which these and other chips are mounted, ports that provide connections for external devices, a power supply, and internal circuitry to hook everything together (see Figure MC 2-6). In addition, system units often have built-in diskette and hard-disk units, and possibly even built-in CD-ROM or tape units (or both). Disks and tapes will be covered later in the chapter.

Microprocessor Chips Every microcomputer system unit contains a specific microprocessor chip as its CPU. This chip is put into a carrier package, as shown in Figure MC 2-7, and the carrier package is mounted onto a special board—called the **system board**—that fits inside the system unit. This board is located on the floor of the system unit shown in Figure MC 2-6.

Most microcomputer systems made today use CPU chips that are manufactured by either Intel or Motorola. The Intel line of chips—such as the 8086, 8088, 80286, 80386, 80486, and Pentium chip—is used on the microcomputer systems made by IBM as well as by Compaq, Dell, AST, and scores of other companies that make IBM-compatible microcomputer systems. Many Intel chips are commonly referred to by their last three digits—for example, a 486 refers to an 80486 chip. Sometimes the chip numbers come with special suffixes—for instance, DX (or no suffix) is the standard chip, whereas DX2 and DX4 are faster versions of the chip, SX is an economy version, and SL is a low-power-consumptive version.

The Motorola line of chips—including the 68000, 68020, 68030, and 68040—is found primarily on Apple Macintosh computers made before 1994. Recently, Apple, Motorola, and IBM have teamed up on the PowerPC chip, which has become the standard CPU on Macintoshes and on some microcomputers made by IBM and others. The new chip is smaller and generally less expensive than the Intel Pentium. Some CPU chips in the PowerPC line are the 601, 603, 604, and 620.

The type of CPU chip in a computer's system unit greatly affects what you can do with the computer system. Software is written to work on a specific chip, and a program that works on one chip may not function on another unless modified. For instance, software is not very portable between Intel and Motorola chips, because these chips employ a somewhat dissimilar design philosophy. Also, a program designed for an Intel 80486 chip may not work on the earlier 80286 chip, which is less capable. And, even though a program designed for an 80286 chip may work on an 80486 chip, some of the 80486's power will be wasted.

Working alongside the CPU chip in many system units are specialized processor chips, such as numeric coprocessors and graphic coprocessors. The role of these "slave chips" is to perform specialized tasks for the CPU, thereby enhancing overall system performance. For instance, a *numeric (math) coprocessor* chip helps the CPU perform arithmetic; a *graphic coprocessor* chip helps the CPU with the computationally intensive chore of creating complex screen displays. It is not unusual to boost the speed of a computer system several times over by using such specialized chips.

FIGURE MC 2-6 The inside of a system unit. With the cover of the system unit removed, you can see the parts inside. Generally, the system board is located on the floor of the system unit. Most system units also contain a fan to keep the parts from overheating.

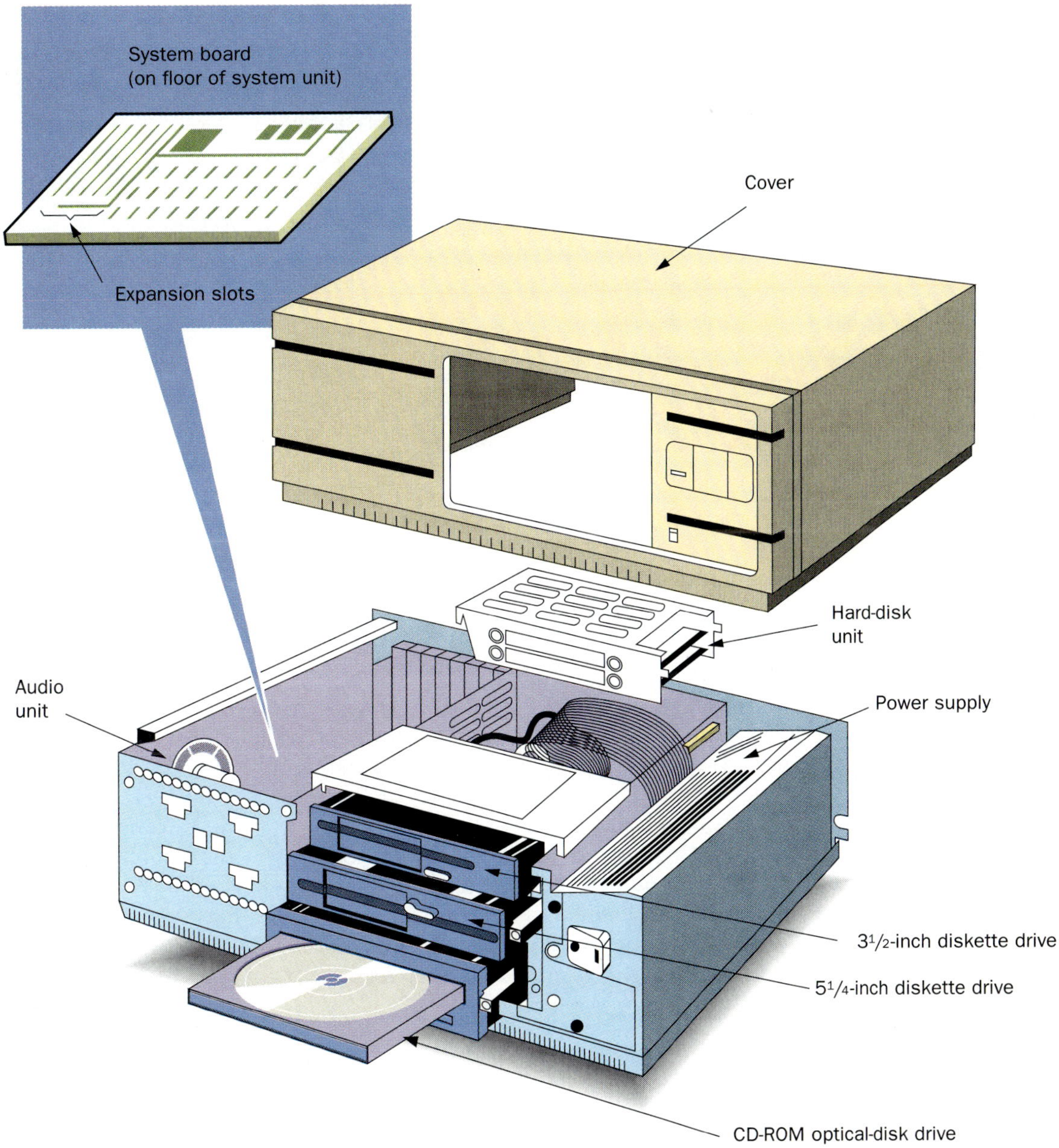

RAM **RAM** (for **random access memory**) is used to store the programs and data on which the computer is currently working. Like the microprocessor, the RAM of a microcomputer system consists of circuits etched onto silicon chips. These chips are mounted onto carrier packages, like the CPU is, and the packages are plugged into the system board. Most desktop microcomputer systems in use today have enough RAM to store several million bytes of data. Many computer systems allow memory expansion (within limits) directly on the system board or through add-in boards (discussed shortly) when RAM is insufficient.

FIGURE MC 2-7 **CPU chips.** Both the Pentium and PowerPC chips run more than 300 times faster than the original Intel 8088 chip that ran the IBM PC in the early 1980s. (a) Two Intel Pentium chips, mounted in carrier packages, with their covers nearby. (b) A PowerPC chip.

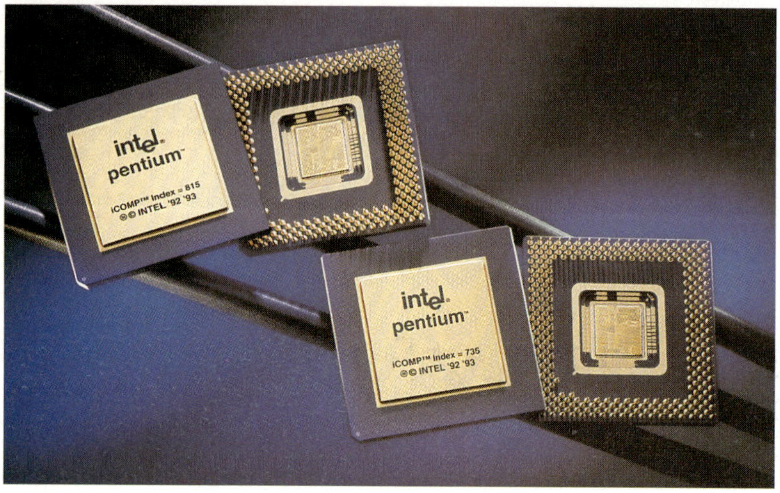

(a)

(b)

Most RAM is *volatile,* meaning that the contents of memory are lost when the computer is shut off. This is in contrast to secondary storage, which is *nonvolatile.*

ROM **ROM,** which stands for **read-only memory,** consists of nonerasable hardware modules that contain programs. Like RAM, these modules are mounted onto carrier packages that, in turn, are plugged into one or more boards inside the system unit. You can neither write over these ROM programs (that is why they are called *read-only*) nor destroy their contents when you shut off the computer's power (that is, they are nonvolatile). A program stored in ROM can be fetched more quickly by the CPU than it could if it were stored on disk, where it would have to be loaded into RAM before the computer could work on it. Often key pieces of systems software are stored in ROM.

Add-in Boards Many microcomputer-system vendors enable you to customize your system by choosing your own **add-in boards.** These boards are cardlike pieces of hardware that contain the circuitry for performing one or more specific functions. They plug into expansion slots within the computer's system unit and thereby enable you either to interface with specific types of peripheral devices or to add new capabilities. For example, if you want a certain model of display unit attached to your computer, you may need a special *display adapter board* that contains the proper interfacing routine for establishing the connection. Similarly, you can get your computer system to communicate with facsimile (fax) machines and with the Internet by getting a *fax/modem board.*

Many types of add-in boards currently are available in the marketplace. Most of these boards provide either a basic function that is unavailable with the system unit or a "value-added" capability that enhances an existing function. With new machines and new capabilities being announced regularly, the number and types of add-in boards are changing rapidly.

Ports Most system units contain built-in sockets that enable you to plug in other hardware devices. These sockets, which often are found on the exterior of the system unit, are known as **ports** (see Figure MC 2-8). Printers, for instance, generally hook up to desktop microcomputers through either *parallel* ports or *serial* ports (see Figure MC 2-8a). IBM microcomputers and similar devices typically interface printers with parallel ports; many Apple computers interface printers with serial ports. Most computers also use serial ports to permit connection to remote devices over phone lines.

When an input/output (I/O) device needs to be "plugged into" a desktop system unit and there is not a built-in port for it, you normally must buy a special add-in board that has a port on it. When you install the board, the port will extend through a hole in the back of the system unit so that you can plug the I/O device into it.

For laptop and handheld computers, *PCMCIA* (Personal Computer Memory Card International Association) *ports* have recently become quite popular. These ports enable storage and communications devices to be made available through a credit-card-sized interface card (see Figure MC 2-8b). The card is plugged into the computer's PCMCIA port and then connected by a wire jack—like those used to plug touch-tone phones into walls—to the peripheral device.

Buses The CPU connects to RAM, ROM, boards, and ports through circuitry called an I/O **bus,** as shown in Figure MC 2-9. The I/O bus links the CPU to every hardware device in the system, enabling data to be exchanged and processed.

Today, a number of I/O bus standards are in existence. The three most state-of-the-art standards are IBM's *Micro Channel Architecture* (used on the high end of some IBM microcomputers), Apple's *NuBus* (used on the most recent Macintoshes), and *EISA,* or *Enhanced Industry Standard Architecture* (used on many IBM and IBM-compatible microcomputers). Each of these bus architectures is based on a 32-bit *word size*—meaning data travel along the bus in 32-bit "chunks" (words). An older and less powerful standard, *ISA* (for *Industry Standard Architecture*), which is based on a 16-bit word size, is also very widely seen in practice. The choice of an I/O bus is critical because boards are generally not interchangeable between different types of buses.

To provide even faster display response time as we march further along into the age of desktop video, many hardware manufacturers have recently split bus functionality into two separate hardware units: the I/O bus (or *main bus*) and the local bus. The *local bus* serves peripheral devices that need extremely fast response time—such as the display, the disk drives, and memory. All other

FIGURE MC 2-8 **Ports.** Ports enable external peripheral devices to be connected to the computer system. (a) Desktop port. (b) Laptop PCMCIA port.

(a) (b)

FIGURE MC 2-9 How devices are linked. A set of wires or circuits called a *bus* allows the CPU to communicate with RAM, ROM, and peripheral devices connected through either boards or ports.

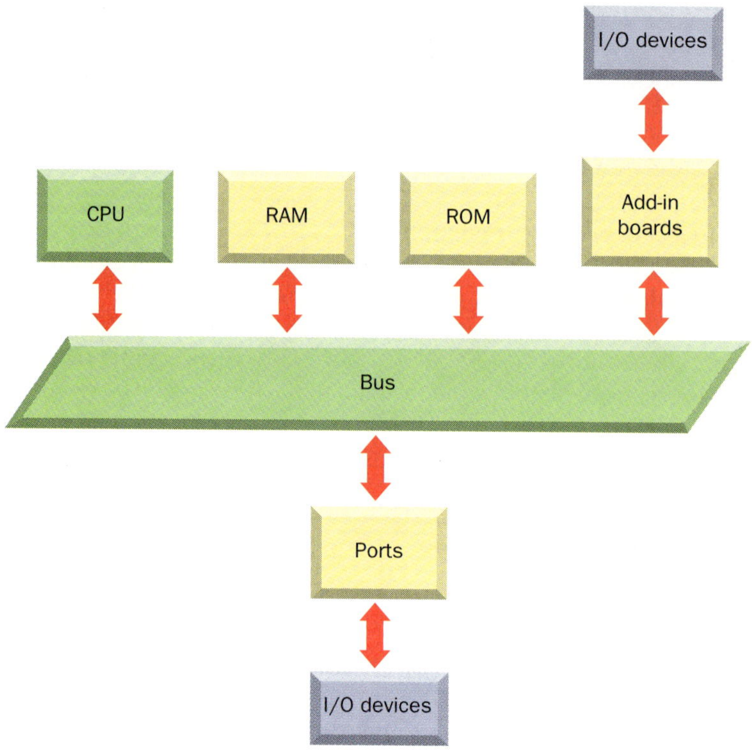

(slower) devices—such as the mouse, communications devices, and sound boards—work off the I/O bus.

In the IBM-compatible microcomputer world, two local bus standards have become dominant during the last few years. The first, *VESA* (Video Electronic Standards Association), is sometimes referred to as the *VL* bus. The second standard is *PCI* (Peripheral Component Interconnect). The difference between the two is largely technical. Some video-intensive computer programs (such as computer games) may require that you have a specific type of local bus in your system.

SECONDARY STORAGE HARDWARE

The most popular secondary storage alternative on microcomputer systems is the disk—floppy disk, hard disk, and CD-ROM optical disk. Less widely used alternatives are other types of optical disk, disk cartridges, and magnetic-tape cartridges. But before we look in depth at any of these secondary storage alternatives, we will turn first to the properties that define and differentiate them.

Properties of Secondary Storage Systems

Secondary storage systems are often discussed in terms of their physical parts, media removability, and access capabilities.

Physical Parts Any secondary storage system involves two physical parts: a *peripheral device* and an *I/O medium.* A disk unit and a tape unit are examples of peripheral devices; magnetic disk platters and magnetic tape cartridges are types of media. Data and programs are written onto and read from some type of medium. The medium must be situated on a peripheral device for the CPU to process its contents.

The peripheral storage device can be internal or external. *Internal devices*—such as diskette, hard-disk, and CD-ROM drives—typically come configured in the system unit when you buy a computer system, whereas *external devices* are stand-alone hardware devices that connect via cable to a port on the back of the system unit. External devices may also require a special add-in board to be inserted into the system unit.

In most secondary storage systems, media must pass by a *read/write head* in the peripheral device to be read from or written to.

Removable versus Nonremovable Media In many secondary storage systems, although the peripheral device is online to the computer, the associated medium must be loaded into the device before the computer can read from it or write to it. These are called *removable-media* secondary storage systems. Diskettes, some types of hard disks, magnetic tape cartridges, and optical disks are examples of removable media used on such systems. Most hard disks, by contrast, are *fixed-media* secondary storage systems, in which the disk is encased in a sealed unit within the system unit and cannot be conveniently removed.

Removability of media provides virtually unlimited storage capacity, because the medium can be replaced when it is full. Removability also facilitates backup (covered extensively later in the chapter). *Backup* occurs when a duplicate set of data or programs are written onto a disk or tape and are stored offline, for use if the originals are lost or destroyed. *Security* is also enhanced by removability, because programs or data do not have to stay on the disk unit. Finally, removability makes it possible to assign a specific application to a specific medium—say, assigning all customer accounts to one disk and all vendor accounts to another. Fixed media, in contrast, generally offer the advantages of higher speed, greater online storage capacity, and better reliability.

Sequential versus Direct Access When the computer system is instructed to use data or programs residing in secondary storage, it first must be able to find the materials. The process of retrieving data and programs in storage is called *access.*

Two basic access methods are available: sequential and direct. With **sequential access,** the records in a file can be retrieved only in the same order in which they are physically stored. With **direct access,** also called *random access,* records can be retrieved in any order.

The distinction between sequential and direct access can be seen on a typical home stereo system. Suppose you have both a cassette tape and a CD of the same music. You want to hear the fifth song on the CD, and this song is also the fifth selection on the tape. With the tape, you must pass sequentially through the first four songs to hear the fifth one. With the CD, however, you can go directly to the fifth song and listen to it immediately.

Music CDs are also effective for sequential access. You can start at the beginning and play tunes in sequence. Thus, the CD is really both a sequential- and direct-access medium because you can play a series of songs sequentially or pick individual ones in random order.

Diskettes

Diskettes, or **floppy disks,** are small, round platters encased in plastic jackets. The platters are made of a tough Mylar plastic and coated with a magnetizable substance. Each side of the diskette contains concentric **tracks,** which are encoded with 0- and 1-bits when you write data and programs to them (see Figure MC 2-10). The jacket is lined with a soft material that cleans the disk as it spins.

Sizes of Diskettes Several types of diskettes are commercially available. If one were to cite a single property that most distinguishes one diskette from another, that property would likely be size.

Diskettes targeted to today's microcomputer systems users are widely available in two principal sizes (diameters): 3½ inches and 5¼ inches (see Figure MC 2-11). The 5¼-inch diskettes came along first; then came the 3½-inch diskettes. The 5¼-inch diskettes are contained in flexible, plastic-coated, cardboard jackets, whereas the 3½-inch diskettes are contained in rugged plastic cases that can fit into a shirt pocket. Strange as it may seem, 3½-inch diskettes can store more data than can 5¼-inch ones.

Despite their small size, diskettes can store a respectable amount of data. Common capacities are 360 kilobytes and 1.2 megabytes for 5¼-inch diskettes, and 720 kilobytes, 1.44 megabytes, and 2.88 megabytes for 3½-inch diskettes. A 360-kilobyte diskette can store more than 100 typewritten pages of information; thus, 1.44-megabyte diskettes can store up to 400 pages and 2.88-megabyte diskettes can store up to 800 pages. The 1.2- and 1.44-megabyte diskettes are often called *high-density* diskettes; the 360- and 720-kilobyte diskettes are called *double-density* or *low-density* diskettes. The 2.88-megabyte diskettes, which began being installed on some microcomputer systems in 1992, are sometimes referred to as *extra-density* diskettes. (Density refers to how tightly bits of data are packed on the diskette.)

FIGURE MC 2-10 **Surface of a disk.** Unlike a phonograph record, which bears a single spiral groove, a disk is composed of concentric tracks. The diskette shown here has 80 tracks. Hard disks commonly have hundreds of tracks.

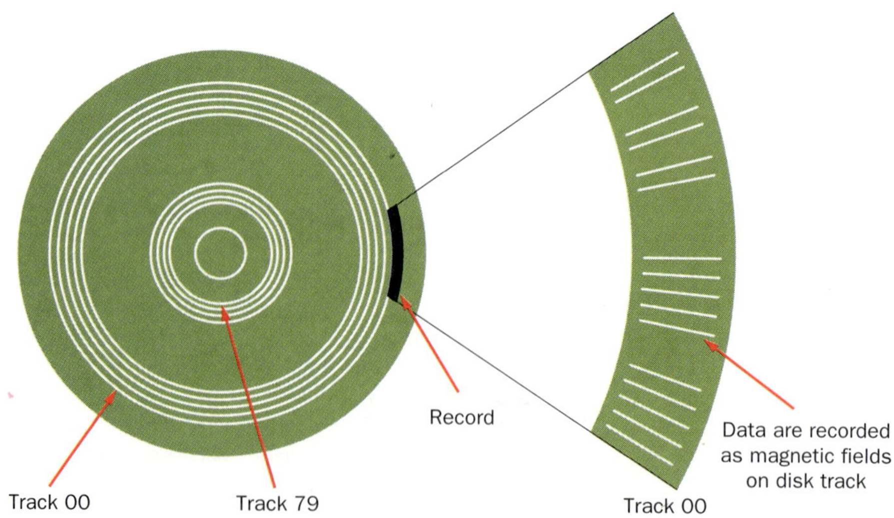

FIGURE MC 2-11 **5¼-inch and 3½-inch diskettes compared.** (a) In a 5¼-inch diskette, the recording window is always open, meaning the disk surface is constantly exposed. (b) In a 3½-inch diskette, the recording window exposes the disk surface only when the shutter mechanism is slid to the left, which happens during reading and writing operations. In addition to offering this improved design feature, having a more rugged cover, and being a more compact size, 3½-inch diskettes can store more data than can 5¼-inch diskettes.

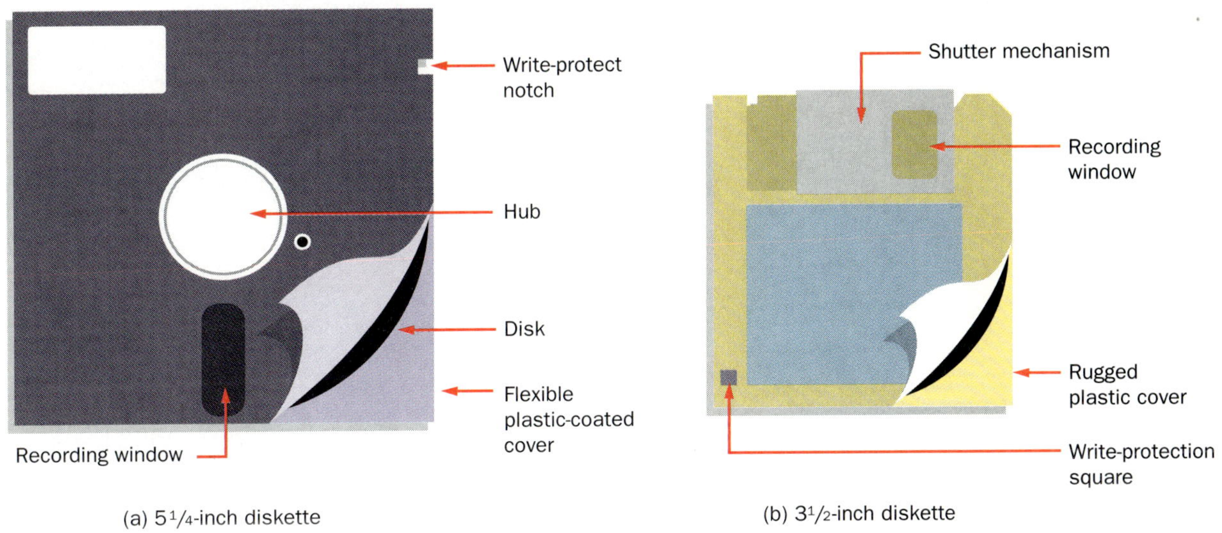

To protect data, diskettes also contain a *write-protect notch* or *square* (refer again to Figure MC 2-11). This prevents the user from accidentally writing on the disk. Covering the notch on 5¼-inch diskettes makes it impossible to write on the surface. The convention on 3½-inch diskettes is the opposite: exposing the notch or square makes writing impossible.

Sectoring on Diskettes Computer systems differ in the number of **sectors** into which they divide, or format, a disk. Sectors divide a diskette into addressable, pie-shaped pieces. For example, diskettes on IBM and similar computer systems commonly are formatted into 8, 9, 15, or 18 sectors depending on the type of diskette and operating system used. Often there are 512 bytes per sector (see Figure MC 2-12). **Formatting** the diskette shown in Figure MC 2-12 causes it to be divided into 9 pie-shaped sectors, 0 through 8. Because the diskette has 40 tracks, this results in $9 \times 40 = 360$ addressable storage locations per side. On most microcomputer systems, a *Format* command is used to format the diskette, and a diskette is not usable for storage unless it has been formatted.

A **file directory** on the diskette, which the computer system automatically maintains, keeps track of the contents of each location. This directory shows the name of each file, its size, and the location at which it begins.

Using Diskettes To use a diskette, the operator inserts it into a device called a *diskette unit,* or *diskette drive* (see Figures MC 2-13 and MC 2-14). There are two basic designs for disk doors. Doors with *latches* require you to latch the door after placing a disk in the drive—thereby making the disk available for processing—and unlatch the door to remove the disk. Doors with *eject buttons* automatically accept a disk that has been inserted properly—you will

FIGURE MC 2-12 **Formatting (sectoring) a diskette.** IBM microcomputers and similar machines use the same number of sectors on every track with both 3½- and 5¼-inch diskettes. Shown here is the organization of a 9-sector, 360-kilobyte, 5¼-inch diskette.

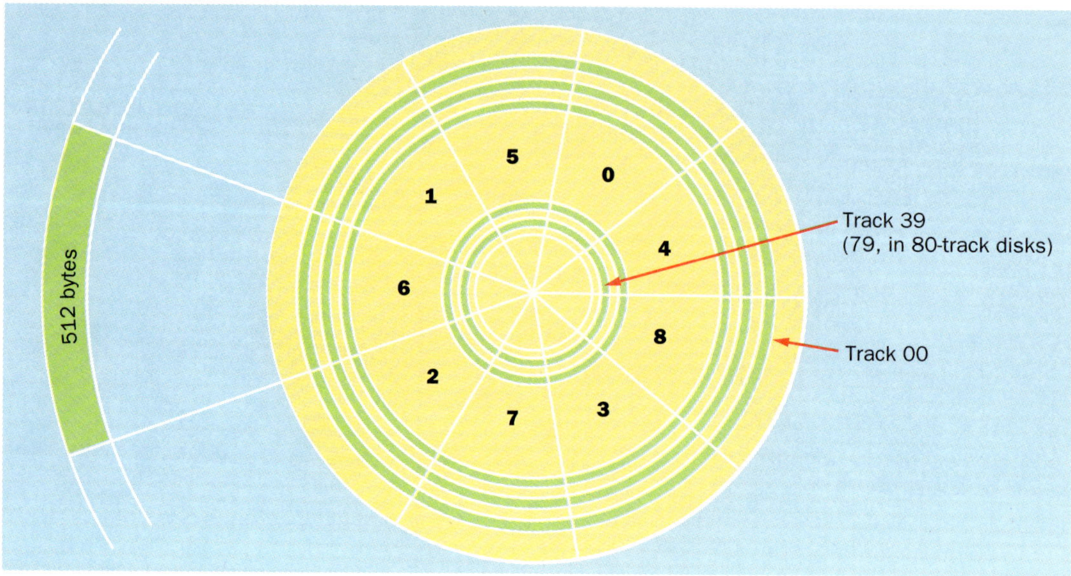

FIGURE MC 2-13 **Inserting a diskette into a drive.** Diskettes correctly fit into the drive only one way—usually with the label up and the recording window toward the drive door, as shown.

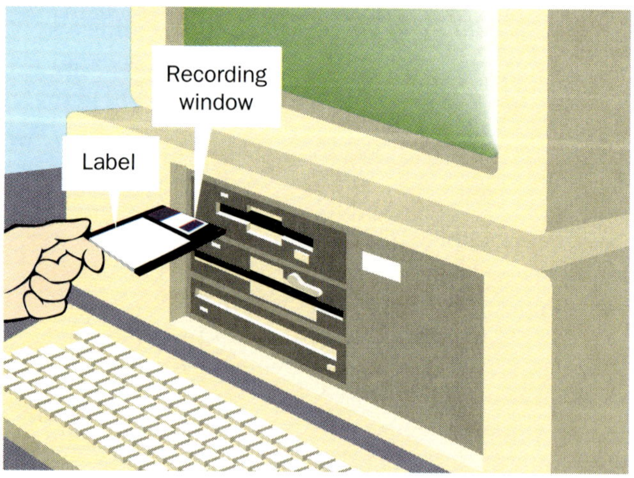

hear a click when this happens—and require you to press the eject button to remove the disk. The trend in drive doors is toward eject buttons. There is only one correct way to insert the diskette into the drive—with the disk label facing up and the recording-window end going in first.

While the diskette is rotating, *read/write heads* access tracks through the *recording window.* While the *indicator light* for a drive is on, meaning that the

FIGURE MC 2-14 **Disk-drive doors.** (a) Doors with latches require you to latch the door after placing a disk in the drive—thereby making the disk available for processing—and unlatch the door to remove the disk. (b) Doors with eject buttons automatically accept for processing a disk that has been inserted properly—you will hear a click when this happens—and require you to press the eject button to remove the disk.

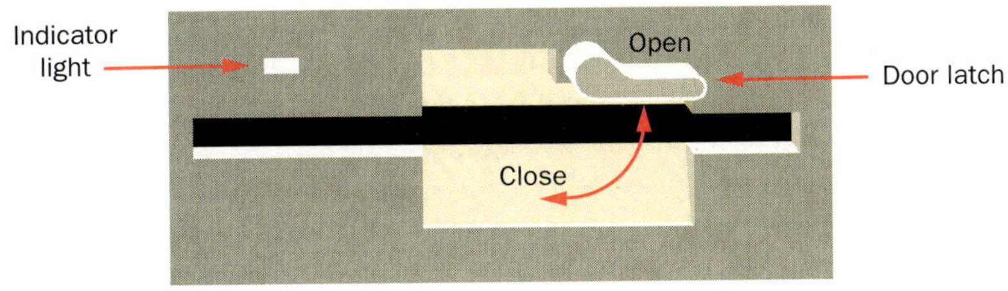

(a) Door with latch

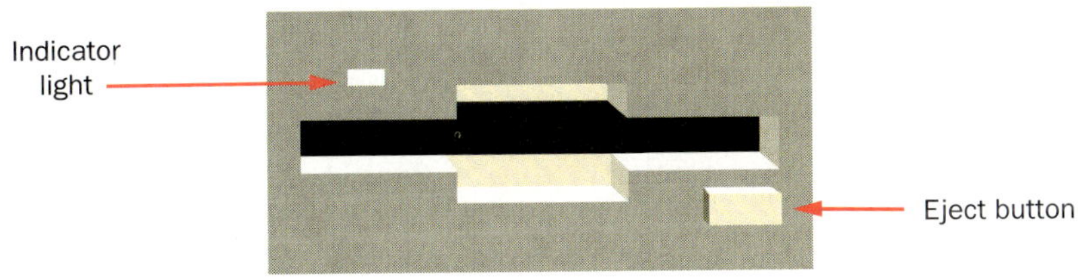

(b) Door with eject button

read/write heads are reading from or writing to the diskette in the drive, you must not try to remove the diskette.

Caring for Diskettes Diskettes may look like inert sheets of plastic, but they are extremely sensitive items and must be cared for accordingly. For instance, never touch an exposed diskette surface or bend the diskette in any way. Also, keep the diskette away from magnetic objects, motors, stereo speakers, and extreme temperatures. Furthermore, never subject the diskette to pressure, say, by using a ballpoint pen to write something on an attached label.

Hard Disks

Although many microcomputer systems still depend on diskettes alone, systems that use a magnetic hard disk are the norm. **Hard disks,** which consist of rigid rather than flexible platters, are especially appropriate when an organization needs greater amounts of online storage and faster access to programs and data than diskettes can provide.

Characteristics Hard disks for microcomputer systems usually employ a *Winchester* technology. In a Winchester disk system, the disks and their read/write heads are hermetically sealed into a single nonremovable module called a *hard-disk unit.* Because the disks are completely sealed and free from air contamination, the disk unit results in fewer operating problems if cared for properly. Unlike floppy disks, which spin only when accessed, hard disks are spinning constantly when the computer system is on.

Hard-disk units for microcomputers are most commonly available today in capacities of several hundred megabytes or more. For desktop microcomputers, hard disks are most widely available in 3½-inch diameters.

As hinted earlier, hard-disk units on microcomputer systems can be internal or external. An *internal* hard-disk system—by far the most common type—is fitted into a bay in your computer's system unit (see Figure MC 2-15). An *external* system is a detached hardware unit that has its own power supply.

In a hard-disk system, a read/write head never touches the surface of a disk at any time, even during reading and writing. Head and disk are very close, however; the head often glides millionths of an inch above the recording surfaces. A human hair or even a smoke particle present on a surface will damage the disks and heads; the result will be like placing a pebble on your favorite phonograph album while playing it. Such an event, called a *head crash,* results whenever the disk head makes contact with the disk or a foreign object, causing damage to the disk or head. Diskettes do not crash as do hard disks because they rotate at a much slower speed, their read/write heads are much larger, and their flexible surface gives way if extra pressure is exerted.

Backup A critical operation on disk-based systems—especially on hard disk, where more data are stored—is backup. **Backup** refers to making a duplicate copy of any file you cannot afford to lose. Most operating systems contain commands that will allow you to make extra copies of individual files, a set of related files, or the contents of an entire disk.

Whenever you back up a disk, make sure the backup files are not stored on the same disk as the originals. In theory, they should not even be in the same room or building. That way, if a serious accident such as a fire or flood occurs at one location, the files at the other location will usually be safe. A variety of mishaps that can destroy programs and data—mishaps that all offer good reasons to back up disks—are listed in Figure MC 2-16.

Backup is commonly performed on floppies, writeable optical disks, cartridge magnetic disks, or cartridge tapes. A discussion of the latter three types of products follows.

FIGURE MC 2-15 **An internal hard-disk unit.** Hard-disk systems for microcomputers are most commonly found in capacities of several hundred megabytes or more.

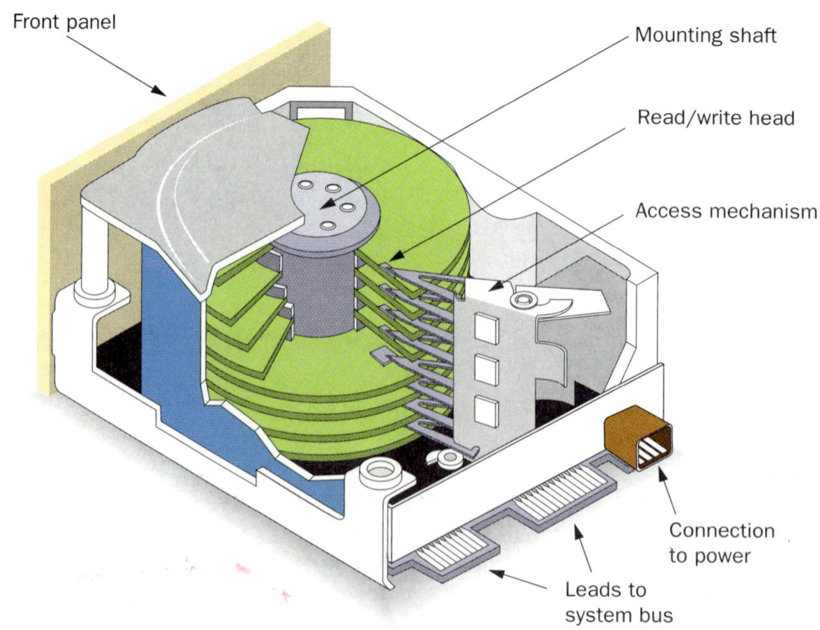

FIGURE MC 2-16 Good reasons for backing up a disk. Taking a few extra minutes to make duplicate copies of important files can avert a potential disaster.

Why Back Up?

A disk sector goes bad, destroying part of a file.

A file you thought you no longer had need for, and erased, turns out to be important.

You modify a file in an undesirable way, and the damage done is irreversible.

You accidentally reformat a disk.

The disk suffers a head crash.

A power brownout or failure, at the time of saving a file, causes "garbage" to be saved.

You save a file to the wrong subdirectory, overwriting a different file that has the same name.

While rushing your work, you make a mistake that causes the wrong files to be erased.

You unwittingly destroy a file while working on it—say, by deleting parts of it erroneously and then saving the file.

Malfunctioning hardware or software causes files to be erased.

A computer virus enters your system and destroys files.

Your disk is physically destroyed—for instance, a diskette is left in the sun or the hard disk is given a jolt. Alternatively, a fire or flood may destroy the disk.

Someone steals your diskette or hard disk.

Optical Disks

For applications that involve large secondary storage requirements, **optical disk** systems are coming into increasing use on microcomputer systems (see Figure MC 2-17). Data are placed onto optical disks with high-intensity laser beams that burn tiny holes into the surface. Then a lower-intensity laser beam reads the data inscribed. Most optical disk units are of the *CD-ROM* (Compact Disk/Read-Only Memory) type; that is, you buy a prerecorded disk and "play" (read) it on the optical disk unit on your computer. You cannot write new data to the disk in any way. Systems also are available that will let you write once to the disk. Once written, the data cannot be erased. These are called *WORM* (Write Once, Read Many) disk systems. In addition, fully erasable optical disk systems, which allow you to erase unwanted data an unlimited number of times, have recently become available. These systems use a combination of magnetic and optical technology to read and write data; consequently, fully erasable optical disks are sometimes referred to as *magneto-optical (MO) disks.*

Today many optical disks can store about one gigabyte of data. They are commonly used in entertainment products and in applications where encyclopedia or reference material is kept online to users (see Figure MC 2-18).

Cartridge Disks

Cartridge disk devices, which are popular for backup and for transporting data between computer systems, are commonly found on microcomputers. These devices are external hardware units that accept removable high-capacity magnetic disk cartridges (see Figure MC 2-19). The disk is packaged into a hard case (that is, the cartridge) to protect the disk's contents. The operator inserts a cartridge into a cartridge drive in a manner similar to inserting a diskette into a diskette drive. Cartridge disks commonly have capacities of 100

FIGURE MC 2-17 Optical disk units and their optical disks. (a) A CD-ROM optical disk in a protective plastic case. CD-ROMs must be removed from their cases before being used. (b) A CD-ROM optical disk unit, with an optical disk loaded on a drive tray, on an IBM Aptiva computer. (c) A magneto-optical (MO) disk in a protective cover. The MO's cover—like that of a floppy—is not removed when the disk is inserted into the disk unit. (d) An optical jukebox with a magazine containing several optical disks. The entire magazine is loaded into the jukebox at one time.

(a)

(b)

(c)

(d)

megabytes or more. Their biggest pluses are large storage capacity and, because of their removability, backup and security. The biggest drawback is cost—the disk unit can cost several hundred dollars and the cartridges retail for about $100 apiece. The drive shown in Figure MC 2-19 can accept 150 MB cartridges as well as lower-capacity cartridges. Two widely used cartridge-disk products are the Bernoulli Box and the SyQuest drive.

Cartridge Tapes

Like cartridge disks, **cartridge tape** is useful for transporting data between systems and for backing up the contents of a hard disk (see Figure MC 2-20). The tape, which is enclosed in a plastic cartridge, is made of a thin plastic that is coated with a magnetizable substance. To be read from or written to, the tape must be mounted on a device called a *tape unit*. Like disk units, tape

FIGURE MC 2-18 **Optical disk applications.** (a) A game product. (b) An encyclopedia that is part of an online bookshelf of several reference works. (c) A corporate training application.

(a)

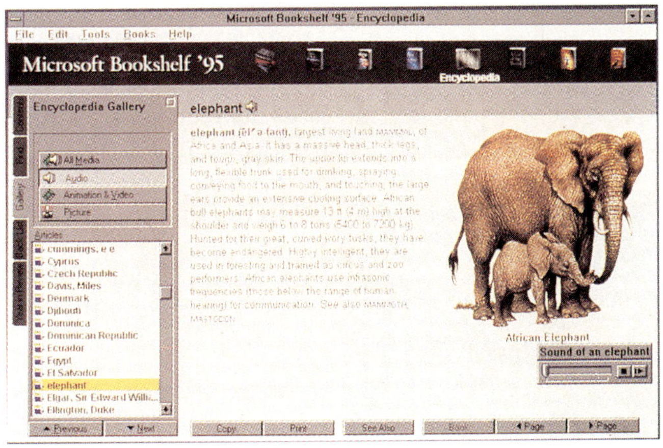

(b)

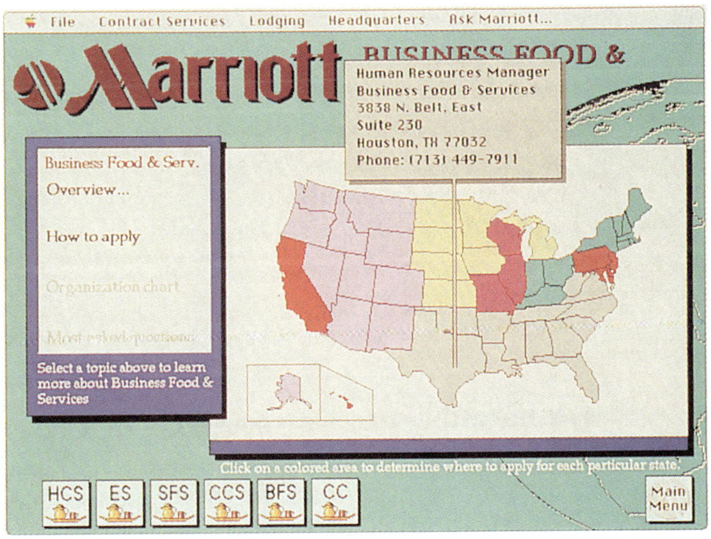

(c)

units can be internal or external. A ¼-inch tape up to 1,000 feet long can hold hundreds of megabytes of data and copy the contents of a disk in a matter of minutes.

OUTPUT HARDWARE

Output devices are perhaps the most diverse type of hardware. Most of them convert strings of bits the computer uses back into natural-language form or picture form to make them understandable to humans.

Most output devices produce output for screen display, or output onto paper or film. **Soft copy** generally refers to display output—that is, output that is temporary and of limited portability. **Hard copy,** on the other hand,

FIGURE MC 2-19
A microcomputer cartridge disk.
A cartridge disk provides a storage alternative that approaches the capacity and performance of a conventional hard disk and has the removability advantage of a diskette.

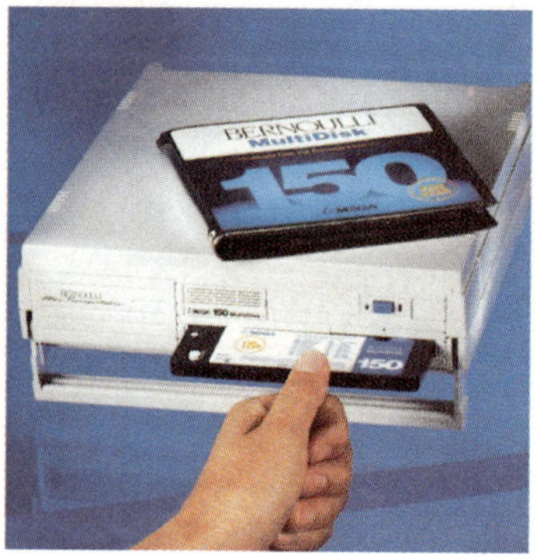

refers to output that has been recorded onto a medium such as paper or microfilm—in other words, output that is in a permanent and highly portable form.

Monitors

Monitors are hardware devices that contain a televisionlike viewing screen. One commonly finds them plugged into and sitting on top of the system units of microcomputers. As each key on the keyboard is pressed, the corresponding character representation of the key appears on the monitor screen at the cursor position. The **cursor** is a highlighted position on the screen indicating where the next character to be typed in will be placed. Alternatively, the cursor may point to the option the operator can select next.

Many features differentiate the hundreds of monitors currently on the market (see Figure MC 2-21). A discussion of some of the more noteworthy features follows.

Data Displayed Most of the monitors sold today are capable of providing text, graphics, and video output. *Text* output consists of only letters, digits, and special characters. Two examples are accounting worksheets and letters to friends. *Graphics* output includes complex picture images, such as charts, maps, and drawings. *Video* output, which is often accompanied by speaker audio output, is essentially graphics in motion.

Resolution A key characteristic of any monitor is resolution, or sharpness of the screen image. On most displays, images are formed by lighting up tiny dots on the screen. On such devices, resolution is measured by the density of these dots, or **pixels** (contraction of the phrase *picture elements*). The more pixels per square inch of screen, the higher the resolution (that is, the clearer the picture). A display resolution of, say, 640 by 480 means that the screen

FIGURE MC 2-20 **Microcomputer cartridge tape.** Cartridge tapes are commonly used to back up the contents of a hard disk. Featured here are two *internal* tape units (left), which fit into the computer's system unit, and an *external* tape unit (right).

FIGURE MC 2-21 **Monitors.** A wide variety of monitors is available in today's equipment marketplace. Two common types of monitors are (a) the CRT (cathode-ray tube), which resembles a standard television screen, and (b) the flat-panel display. Whereas most monitors today are of the CRT type, flat-panel displays are rapidly improving and gaining acceptance—especially on laptop computers.

(a)

(b)

consists of 640 columns by 480 rows of dots—that is, 640 × 480 = 307,200 pixels.

Text characters are formed on the screen in a dot-matrix configuration, as shown in Figure MC 2-22. Generally, several specific matrix sizes—say, 5 by 7 (= 35 pixels) or 8 by 14 (= 112 pixels)—are available for users to display text. For instance, a user may be able to display 25 rows of 80-character lines for one application and 50 rows of 132-character lines for another. The more pixels used to form each character, the higher the text resolution.

Graphics Standards A number of standards for display devices are currently in effect. In the IBM microcomputing world, standards such as Hercules monochrome, Monochrome Display Adapter (MDA), Color Graphics Adapter (CGA), Multi-Color Graphics Array (MCGA), and Enhanced Graphics Adapter (EGA) are widely found on display devices made before 1987. Video Graphics Array (VGA), the current standard, has been dominant over the last several years. VGA is available in three principal variants—the original VGA standard (VGA), Super VGA (SVGA), and Extended VGA (XGA). The Apple Macintosh line has a similar set of graphics standards.

Graphics standards specify "modes" in which the display device can run. For example, VGA can run in 17 different modes. One mode, for instance, divides the screen into a matrix of 320 by 200 pixels and allows 256 colors to be displayed simultaneously; another divides the screen into a matrix of 720 by 400 pixels and permits monochrome display only. SVGA and XGA allow even larger pixel matrices than these. An SVGA display, for instance, shows about 2½ times the amount of information as a VGA display of the same size (see Figure MC 2-23). A major drawback to SVGA when compared with VGA

FIGURE MC 2-22
The C character as formed by a 5-by-7 dot matrix of pixels. The more dots available in the matrix to form characters, the better the character resolution.

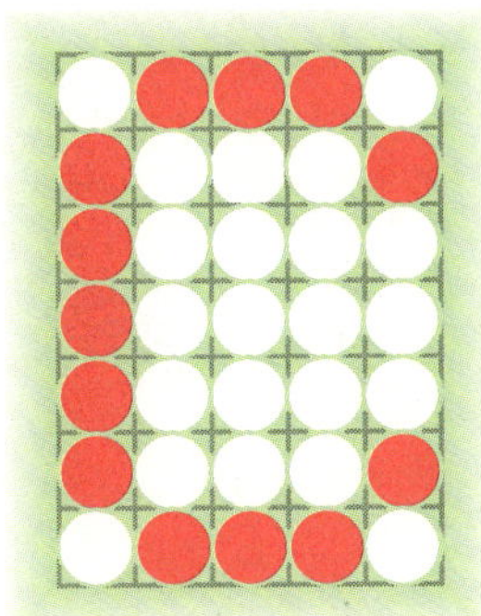

FIGURE MC 2-23 **VGA versus SVGA.** (a) VGA screen. (b) SVGA screen. Because an SVGA screen has more than twice as many pixels as a VGA screen of the same size, the SVGA screen can contain more than twice the amount of information. SVGA is ideal for applications in which users wish to squeeze more information onto a single screen.

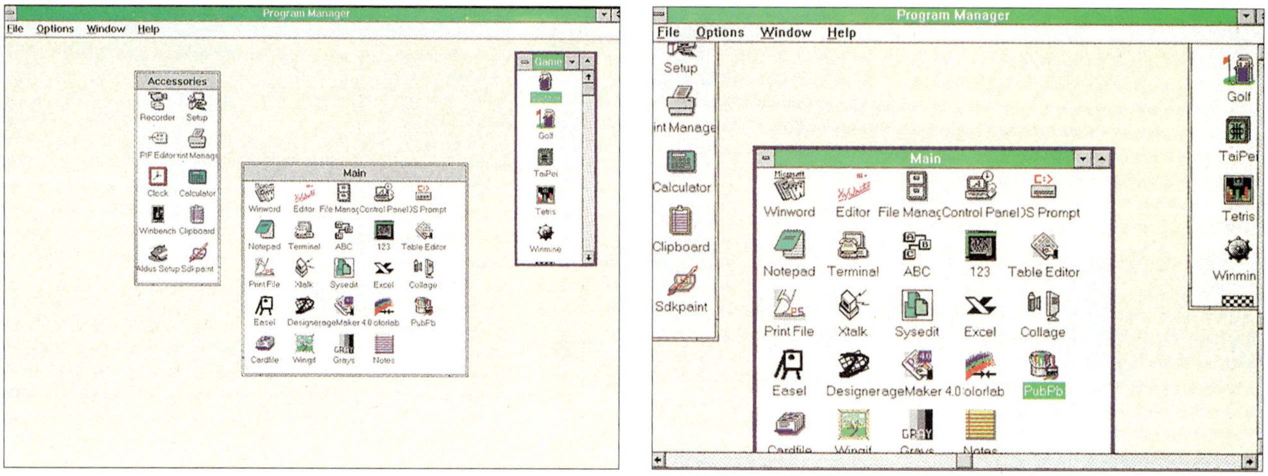

(a) (b)

is that its characters are minimally readable on a 14- or 15-inch display—and generally unreadable on a laptop screen. Another drawback is speed; because there is more information showing on an SVGA screen, the screen takes longer to rewrite every time it is changed.

One of the largest markets for graphics display devices today is in the engineering, science, and art fields. Powerful devices called *technical workstations* are used for mapping, circuit design, architectural and engineering design (see Figure MC 2-24a), drafting, art, advertising, and other graphics-intensive tasks. Such applications collectively fall under the heading of *computer-aided design (CAD).*

Another large market for computer graphics is in the business sector. Managers can easily become overwhelmed as they try to make decisions from piles of raw data. A possible solution lies in the old adage "A picture is worth a thousand words." Using a graphics image, a decision maker can more easily spot problems, opportunities, and trends. Many business applications of computer graphics fall into the general category of *presentation graphics.* With presentation graphics, computer images are used to increase the effectiveness of presenting data to others (see Figure MC 2-24b).

Recently, computer graphics techniques have brought many businesses squarely into the age of *electronic document imaging,* in which digital images of paper documents are electronically maintained by organizations and processed by workers at their computer workstations (see Figure MC 2-24c). The paper documents and any associated pictures may be initially read into the computer system with a scanner. Once in electronic form, the images are stored on a high-capacity optical disk system. Workers having access to the system can summon documents to their workstations, where they can cull, sort, summarize, or repackage the information to their heart's content. Workers may also be authorized to annotate certain documents with comments or approvals and send them to other workers who are hooked into the system.

FIGURE MC 2-24 Common graphics applications. (a) Architectural and engineering design. (b) Business presentation graphics. (c) Electronic document imaging.

(a)

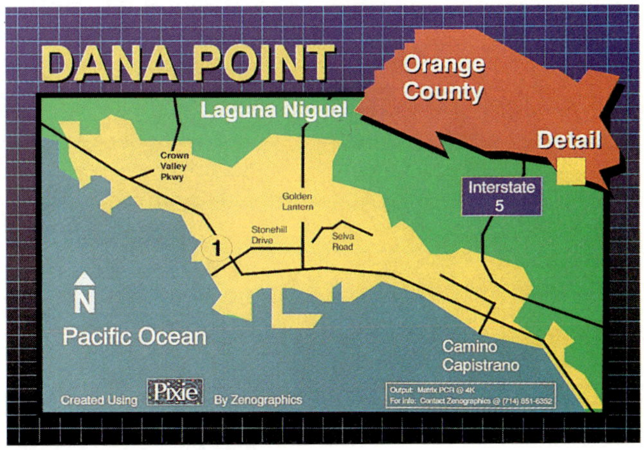

(b)

(c)

Color versus Monochrome Most monitors in use today are classifiable as either color or monochrome.

Most *color* displays (see Figure MC 2-21) are of the red-green-blue (RGB) type. That is, colors are formed by intermixing light beams of these three colors. Depending on such factors as the sophistication of the display unit itself and the amount of RAM available with the computer, users may be able to display only a few colors to millions. Today, color is the standard for virtually all desktop computing systems and is rapidly becoming the preferred choice for laptop computer systems, too.

Monochrome monitors output images using a single foreground color. Many of the earliest monochrome devices were of the black-and-white variety, providing white text on a black background. Over the years, a number of studies have shown that people became less fatigued when working with amber or green on a black background, so many of the monochrome monitors now available in the marketplace are of the amber or green type. Monochrome, being cheaper than color, is typically found in environments where color is not needed and where buyers are extremely price sensitive.

CRT and Flat-Panel Display Devices Traditionally, most monitors have used a large picture-tube element similar to the one inside a standard television set. This type of monitor, shown in Figure MC 2-21a, is commonly called a **CRT (cathode-ray tube).** CRT technology is relatively mature. Over the years, CRTs have become inexpensive and capable of providing excellent color output. These features notwithstanding, CRTs are bulky, fragile, and consume a great deal of power.

Over the last decade, monitors that use charged chemicals or gases sandwiched between panes of glass have become popular alternatives to CRTs. These slim-profile devices are called **flat-panel displays** (see Figure MC 2-21b). Although they can be relatively expensive, can produce glare, and have only recently become commercially viable for color output, flat-panel displays are compact, are lightweight, and require little power. Because of these features, they are commonly found on laptop computers.

Printers

Monitors have two major limitations as output devices: (1) only a small amount of data can be shown on the screen at one time, and (2) output, being in soft-copy form, is not portable. You must be physically present at a monitor to get any results. **Printers** overcome these limitations by producing hard copy—a permanent record of output.

Printers targeted to microcomputers come in a variety of types, the most common of which are solid-font, impact dot-matrix, ink-jet, thermal-transfer, and laser. Of these types, by far the most common are the impact dot-matrix, ink-jet, and laser printers.

Solid-Font Printers A *solid-font printer* has a printing element with fully formed characters similar to those found on the spokes of conventional typewriters. Two popular solid-font elements used on microcomputer systems are the daisywheel and print thimble. Solid-font printers are targeted to text rather than graphics applications. Whereas they operate at very slow speeds—often in the neighborhood of 30 to 80 characters per second—their output quality is very high. A few years ago, before low-cost laser printers dominated sales in the high-output-quality category, solid-font printers were far more popular than they are today.

Impact Dot-Matrix Printers Most microcomputer-based printers in use today print dot-matrix rather than fully formed characters, and many of them use a print head that is an impact dot-matrix mechanism. Typically, an impact dot-matrix mechanism constructs printed characters by repeatedly activating one or more vertical rows of pins, which strike a paper or ribbon as illustrated in Figure MC 2-25. **Impact dot-matrix printers** are usually much faster than solid-font printers; a speed of 100 to 200 characters per second is common. By overstriking characters and by making tiny shifts of the paper in the print carriage, moderately priced impact dot-matrix printers can produce an output quality that rivals that of solid-font printers.

Ink-Jet Printers **Ink-jet printers** (see Figure MC 2-26) spray small dots of electrically charged ink onto a page to form images. Many models hold several color cartridges simultaneously, so they are excellent for producing color output (see the User Tip box). Ink-jet printers are flexible enough to be used as plotters (output devices discussed later in the chapter) and as transparency-making machines. Recently, ink-jet technology has become very popular, and ink-jet printers are challenging dot-matrix printers at the low end of the desktop market. Canon calls its popular line of personal ink-jet devices—which

FIGURE MC 2-25 **Impact dot-matrix printing.** This character-formation technique is similar to the one used to light up electronic scoreboards at sports stadiums. The printing mechanism contains a vertical line of pins that form the characters on the paper. Depending on the character to be represented, different pins in the mechanism are activated. The characters shown here are formed from a 5-by-7 dot matrix. The more dots in the matrix, the higher the quality of the printed character.

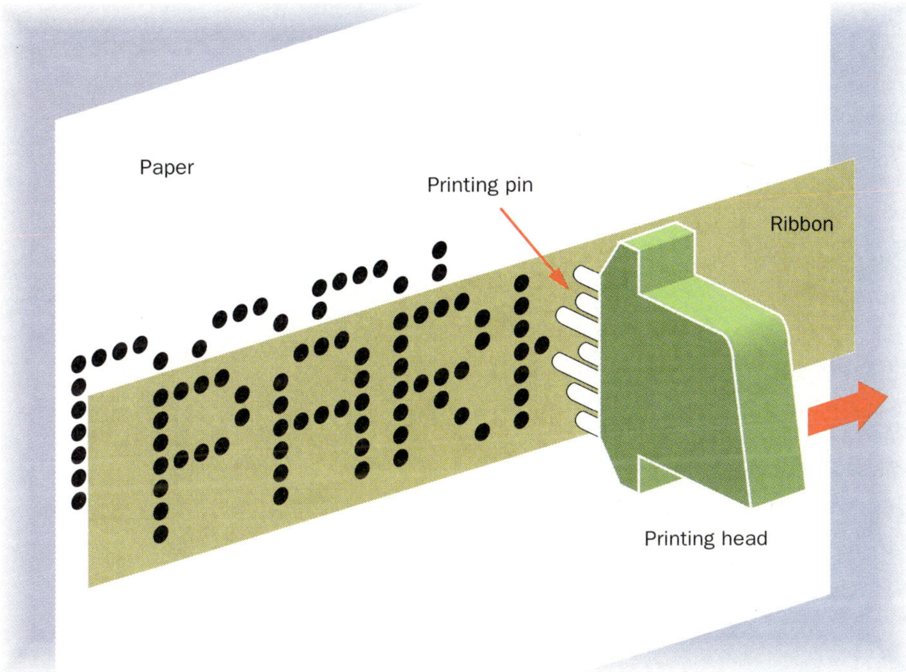

FIGURE MC 2-26 **Ink-jet printer.** Ink-jet printers are used for both color output and black-and-white text. The cost of ink-jet devices has dropped dramatically in recent years, and they are encroaching on the low end of the printing market once dominated by impact dot-matrix printers.

USER TIP

Color Printers

During the last couple of years, prices on desktop color printers have been rapidly dropping, with both performance and quality increasing. Many types of color printers are available, but for most needs, ink-jet devices are by far the most popular. You can now buy one that produces color output for less than $300—dirt cheap, when you consider that most other types of color printers cost well over $1,000. Ink-jet printers are best at producing simple color outputs, like the one shown in the accompanying figure; a more complicated color page may take 15 minutes or longer to print and may appear grainy.

Before you buy, consider the cost of consumable items—cartridges, special (nonsmearable and nonfadable) paper, and so on. Over a short period of time, these items can cost just as much as the printer itself. And, of course, look at the quality of the text the printer produces if you will also be using it to output standard text documents.

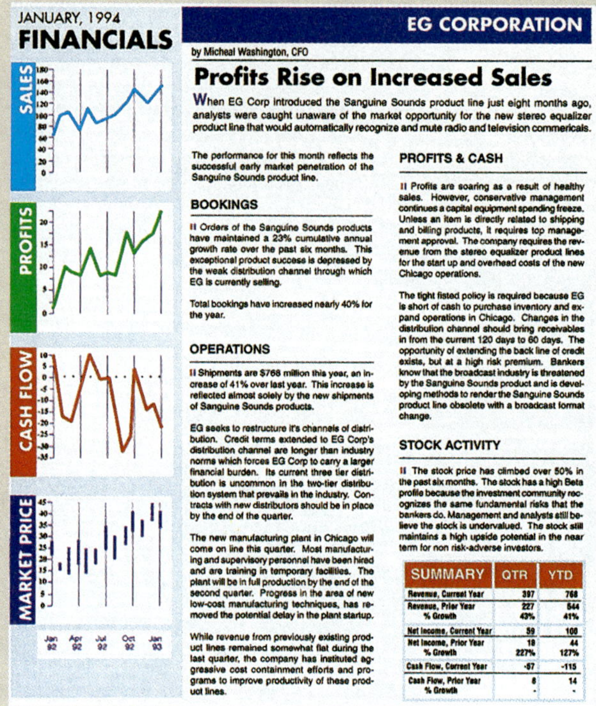

JANUARY, 1994
FINANCIALS

SALES
PROFITS
CASH FLOW
MARKET PRICE

Jan 92 Apr 92 Jul 92 Oct 92 Jan 93

EG CORPORATION

by Micheal Washington, CFO

Profits Rise on Increased Sales

When EG Corp introduced the Sanguine Sounds product line just eight months ago, analysts were caught unaware of the market opportunity for the new stereo equalizer product line that would automatically recognize and mute radio and television commericals.

The performance for this month reflects the successful early market penetration of the Sanguine Sounds product line.

BOOKINGS

Orders of the Sanguine Sounds products have maintained a 23% cumulative annual growth rate over the past six months. This exceptional product success is depressed by the weak distribution channel through which EG is currently selling.

Total bookings have increased nearly 40% for the year.

OPERATIONS

Shipments are $768 million this year, an increase of 41% over last year. This increase is reflected almost solely by the new shipments of Sanguine Sounds products.

EG seeks to restructure it's channels of distribution. Credit terms extended to EG Corp's distribution channel are longer than industry norms which forces EG Corp to carry a larger financial burden. Its current three tier distribution is uncommon in the two-tier distribution system that prevails in the industry. Contracts with new distributors should be in place by the end of the quarter.

The new manufacturing plant in Chicago will come on line this quarter. Most manufacturing and supervisory personnel have been hired and are training in temporary facilities. The plant will be in full production by the end of the second quarter. Progress in the area of new low-cost manufacturing techniques, has removed the potential delay in the plant startup.

While revenue from previously existing product lines remained somewhat flat during the last quarter, the company has instituted aggressive cost containment efforts and programs to improve productivity of these product lines.

PROFITS & CASH

Profits are soaring as a result of healthy sales. However, conservative management continues a capital equipment spending freeze. Unless an item is directly related to shipping and billing products, it requires top management approval. The company requires the revenue from the stereo equalizer product lines for the start up and overhead costs of the new Chicago operations.

The tight fisted policy is required because EG is short of cash to purchase inventory and expand operations in Chicago. Changes in the distribution channel should bring receivables in from the current 120 days to 60 days. The opportunity of extending the back line of credit exists, but at a high risk premium. Bankers know that the broadcast industry is threatened by the Sanguine Sounds product and is developing methods to render the Sanguine Sounds product line obsolete with a broadcast format change.

STOCK ACTIVITY

The stock price has climbed over 50% in the past six months. The stock has a high Beta profile because the investment community recognizes the same fundamental risks that the bankers do. Management and analysts still believe the stock is undervalued. The stock still maintains a high upside potential in the near term for non risk-adverse investors.

SUMMARY	QTR	YTD
Revenue, Current Year	397	768
Revenue, Prior Year	227	544
% Growth	43%	41%
Net Income, Current Year	59	100
Net Income, Prior Year	18	44
% Growth	227%	127%
Cash Flow, Current Year	-57	-115
Cash Flow, Prior Year	8	14
% Growth	-	-

Color printing. Ink-jet printers are ideal for outputs that require only a splash of color.

discharge ink bubbles out of nozzles that are finer than a human hair—*bubble-jet printers.*

Laser Printers **Laser printers** (see Figure MC 2-27) form images by charging thousands of dots on a platen with a high-intensity laser beam. Then, as with photocopiers, toner is affixed to the charged positions and, when paper is pressed against the platen, an image is formed. Laser printers are fast at producing high-resolution text and graphics, but they are usually relatively expensive—about $600 or more. Laser printers, however, have dropped enough in price over the last decade to be affordable by most businesses and by many individuals. Laser printers, consequently, have forged into the lead as the preferred type of printer for business applications.

Thermal-Transfer Printers *Thermal-transfer printers,* which represent a relatively new technology, thermally transfer ink from a wax-based ribbon or thermally transfer dye onto plain paper. The dye printers can produce photographic-quality output (see Figure MC 2-28). Thermal-transfer printers can also produce overheads for use at meetings.

Special-Purpose Output Devices

A very large number of output devices are available for specialized uses. Four such devices are speakers, plotters, voice-output devices, and film recorders.

Speakers Most computer systems targeted for home use today come with a set of *speakers.* Speakers provide audio output for such consumer-oriented, multimedia applications as playing computer games, listening to background music on compact disk, and watching television in a screen window. Common

FIGURE MC 2-27 **Laser printer.** Laser printers are most useful for producing high-resolution, black-and-white text and graphics—at a reasonable speed and for a reasonable price. They work on a principle similar to that of copying machines.

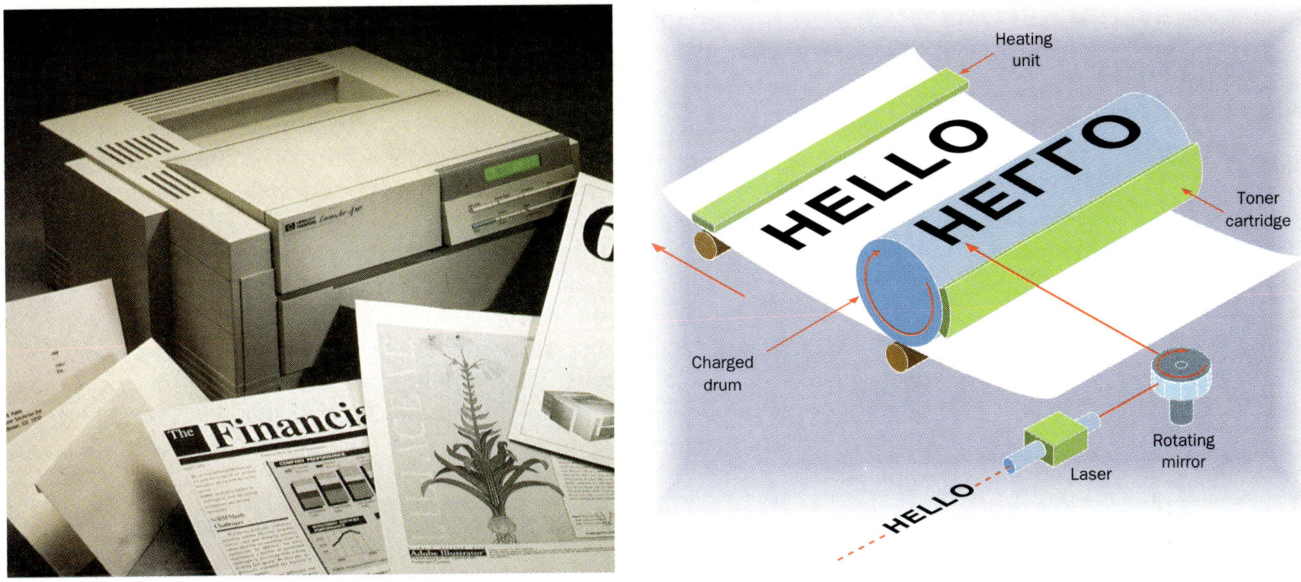

FIGURE MC 2-28 **Thermal-transfer printer output.** Thermal-transfer printers that use dyes can produce photographic-quality output, like that which you see on many magazine covers.

business applications include video demonstrations and presentations as well as computer videoconferencing. Computer systems that are packaged with speakers and CD-ROM devices are often called *multimedia PCs.* Figure MC 2-29 shows both a desktop multimedia PC and a laptop version, the latter sporting built-in speakers.

Plotters A **plotter** is an output device that is used primarily to produce charts, drawings, maps, three-dimensional illustrations, and other forms of graphics-oriented hard copy (see Figure MC 2-30). While many printers double as plotters, users with specialized graphics needs—such as an engineer who produces oversized drawings—will want to consider a device that is principally targeted to plotting rather than text applications. The two most common types of plotters are ink-jet and electrostatic plotters. An *ink-jet plotter* is an output device that uses ink-jet technology to create images, whereas an *electrostatic plotter* works through principles similar to those of a copying machine. Electrostatic plotters are much faster than ink-jet plotters but tend to be more expensive. Whether they employ ink-jet or electrostatic printing, plotters are of either the flatbed or drum type. *Flatbed plotters* resemble drafting boards, whereas *drum plotters*—like those in Figure MC 2-30—draw on paper that is rolled onto a drumlike mechanism.

Voice-Output Devices How often have you dialed a phone number only to hear "We're sorry, the number you are trying to reach is no longer in service"? *Voice-output devices,* which are responsible for such messages, convert electronic data into spoken messages. These messages may be constructed as needed from a file of prerecorded words, or they may be synthesized using other techniques. Computerized voice output is used extensively at airline terminals to broadcast information about flight departures and arrivals, in the securities business to quote the prices of stocks and bonds, and in the super-

FIGURE MC 2-29 **Speakers and multimedia PCs.** Multimedia PCs are microcomputer systems that are configured with a high-end CPU and graphics display, speakers, a CD-ROM disk unit, and video and sound boards. (a) Desktop system with detached speakers. (b) Laptop system with built-in speakers.

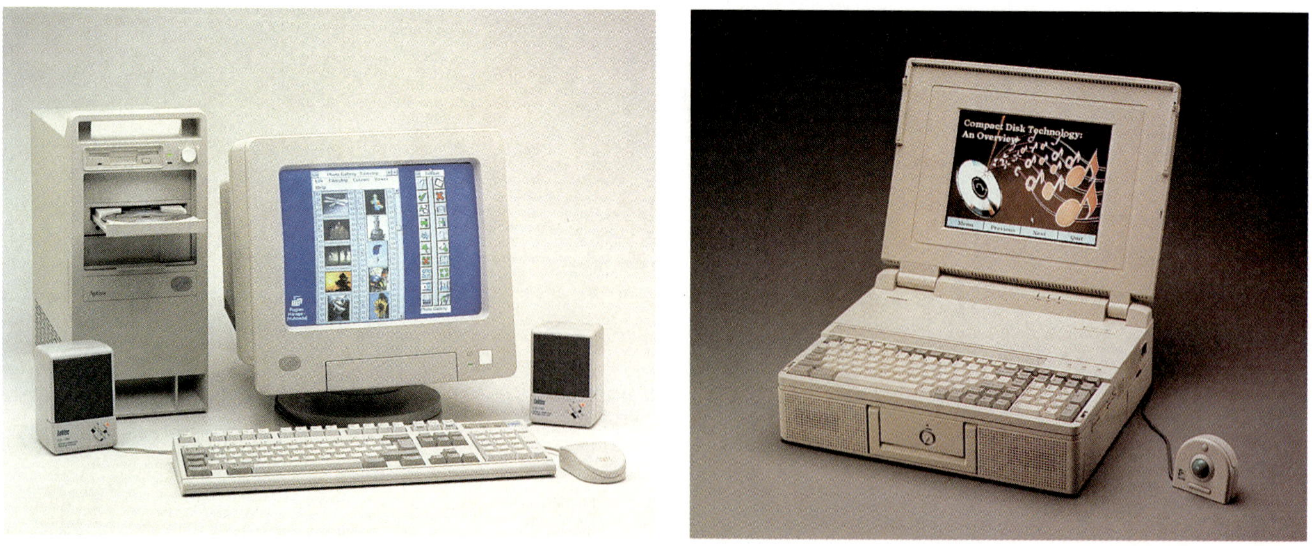

(a) (b)

FIGURE MC 2-30 **Plotters.** Plotters are used to produce charts, drawings, maps, and other forms of graphical hard copy. (a) Ink-jet plotters. (b) An electrostatic plotter.

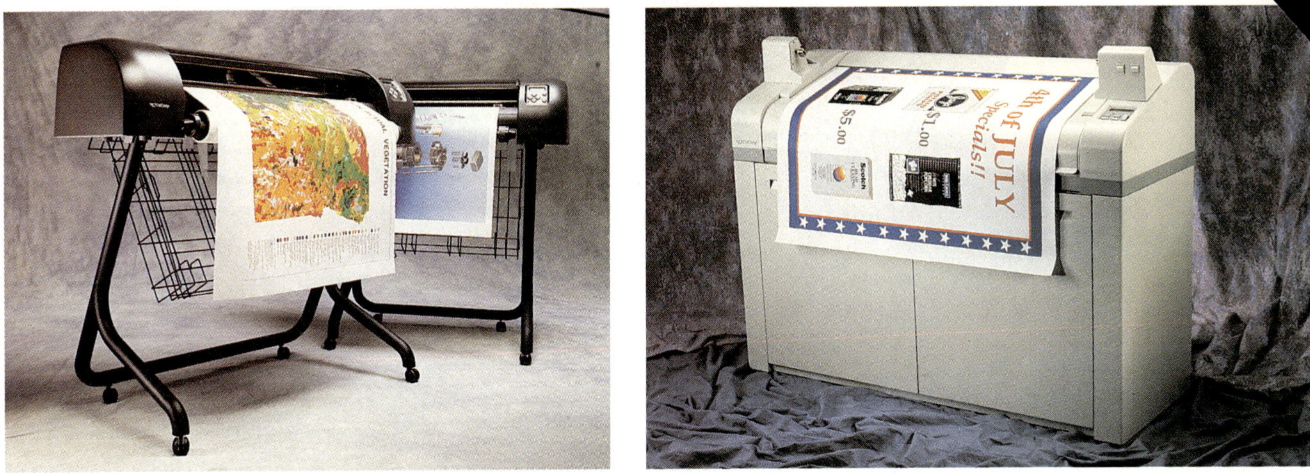

(a) (b)

market industry to announce descriptions and prices of items as they are scanned. Most voice-output devices have a vocabulary of a several hundred words and a limited ability to combine words dynamically to form intelligible sentences.

Film Recorders *Film recorders* are cameralike devices that capture high-resolution computer-generated images directly onto 35-millimeter slides, transparencies, and other film media. A few years ago, film recorders served only large computers, with which they were used for applications such as art, medical imaging, and scientific design work. Today they are increasingly being used with microcomputers for applications such as spicing up corporate business meetings or client presentations with slide shows. Virtually any image that can be captured on a monitor can be preserved for later use with a film recorder.

Summary

- Five important classes of hardware are input devices, processing devices, storage devices, output devices, and communications devices. The first four types are discussed in this chapter, the fifth in chapter 4.
- Input hardware includes such equipment as keyboards, digitizers (such as the mouse, light pen, joystick, trackball, crosshair cursor, and digitizing tablet), image scanners, and voice-input devices. The keyboard and mouse are by far the most widely used of these.
- The principal processing device is the system unit, which contains the CPU (processor) chip. In the microcomputing world, system units are classified as desktop computers, portable or laptop computers, or handheld devices. The system unit of a typical microcomputer system includes microprocessor chips, RAM, ROM, add-in boards, ports, and a bus. Also, most of them have bays to insert secondary storage units.
- Most microcomputer systems use magnetic disk devices—diskette and hard disk (or both)—for secondary storage. Other secondary storage devices that

are commonly employed include those that use optical disk, magnetic-disk cartridges, and magnetic-tape cartridges.

- Output devices are perhaps the most diverse types of hardware. Most people using a microcomputer system will have a monitor and a printer for output. Other output devices used frequently are speakers, plotters, voice-output devices, and film recorders.

Key Terms

Shown in parentheses are the page numbers on which key terms are boldfaced.

Add-in board (MC 32)
Backup (MC 40)
Bus (MC 33)
Cartridge disk (MC 41)
Cartridge tape (MC 42)
CRT (cathode-ray tube) (MC 48)
Cursor (MC 44)
Desktop computer (MC 28)
Direct access (MC 35)
Diskette (MC 36)
File directory (MC 37)
Flat-panel display (MC 48)
Floppy disk (MC 36)
Formatting (MC 37)
Function key (MC 24)
Hard copy (MC 43)
Hard disk (MC 39)
Icon (MC 25)
Impact dot-matrix printer (MC 48)
Ink-jet printer (MC 48)
Keyboard (MC 24)
Laptop computer (MC 28)
Laser printer (MC 50)
Monitor (MC 44)
Mouse (MC 25)
Optical disk (MC 41)
Pixel (MC 44)
Plotter (MC 52)
Port (MC 33)
Printer (MC 48)
Random access memory (RAM) (MC 31)
Read-only memory (ROM) (MC 32)
Sector (MC 37)
Sequential access (MC 35)
Soft copy (MC 43)
System board (MC 30)
System unit (MC 28)
Track (MC 36)

Quiz

True/False

____ 1. The mouse was designed as a replacement for the keyboard.

____ 2. A trackball is a mouse turned upside down.

____ 3. Function keys are located on the keyboard's numeric keypad.

____ 4. "Laptop" refers to a type of handheld computer.

____ 5. The system board is generally located on the floor of the system unit.

____ 6. ROM is used for secondary storage, as an alternative to the hard disk.

____ 7. The recording window is used to access the data on a disk.

____ 8. A hard disk contains RAM.

____ 9. Most CRTs are of the flat-panel type.

____ 10. A laser printer is an example of a daisywheel printer.

Multiple Choice

___ 11. Small programs are generally executed by pressing which of the following keys?
  a. Numeric-keypad keys
  b. Function keys
  c. Ctrl key
  d. Alt key
  e. Shift key

___ 12. Which of the following is not a digitizer?
  a. Mouse
  b. Plotter
  c. Trackball
  d. Crosshair cursor
  e. Joystick

___ 13. Which of the following technologies is still mostly in the pioneering stage?
  a. Keyboarding
  b. Mouse technology
  c. Voice input
  d. Display
  e. Printing

___ 14. Which of the following types of computer is most likely to be used for such tasks as keeping track of an individual's golf score and personal itinerary?
  a. Mainframe
  b. Minicomputer
  c. Handheld computer
  d. Desktop computer
  e. Laptop computer

___ 15. Nonerasable hardware modules that contain programs are referred to as
  a. ROM.
  b. RAM.
  c. Winchesters.
  d. EISA.
  e. ports.

___ 16. The words parallel and serial best describe
  a. laptop computers.
  b. boards.
  c. microprocessor chips.
  d. ROM.
  e. ports.

___ 17. Disks are commonly formatted into pie-shaped areas called
  a. sectors.
  b. ports.
  c. quads.
  d. slicerettes.
  e. directories.

___ 18. The term *head crash* is used to describe something bad happening to a
a. computer.
b. display device.
c. disk.
d. plotter.
e. mouse.

___ 19. All of the following are output devices except the
a. plotter.
b. trackball.
c. display device.
d. film recorder.
e. laser printer.

___ 20. The acronym WORM is often applied to certain types of
a. diskettes.
b. desktop computers.
c. optical disks.
d. magnetic tape.
e. film recorders.

Matching

Select the term that best matches each phrase:

a. CD-ROM
b. Mouse
c. Image scanner
d. Keyboard
e. Winchester
f. Port
g. Numeric coprocessor
h. Local bus
i. High-density
j. Film recorder
k. Plotter
l. Pixel

___ 21. PCI and VESA are examples

___ 22. A term that describes a type of optical disk

___ 23. A term that describes a type of diskette

___ 24. The most widely used type of input device

___ 25. A device that can be used to bring a drawing of something into computer storage

___ 26. Users of this device might double-click it

___ 27. A device that can speed up processing in a computer system

___ 28. A term commonly used to describe the resolution of a monitor

___ 29. A device that is very similar to a camera

___ 30. Two types are ink-jet and electrostatic

Answers

True/False: 1. F; 2. T; 3. F; 4. F; 5. T; 6. F; 7. T; 8. F; 9. F; 10. F

Multiple Choice: 11. b; 12. b; 13. c; 14. c; 15. a; 16. e; 17. a; 18. c; 19. b; 20. c

Matching: 21. h; 22. a; 23. i; 24. d; 25. c; 26. b; 27. g; 28. l; 29. j; 30. k

Exercises

1. By looking at pictures in computer journals or by inspecting computers at a local store, state whether each of the computer lines listed below is exclusively laptop, exclusively desktop, both laptop and desktop, or neither desktop nor laptop.
   a. IBM Aptiva series
   b. IBM Thinkpad series
   c. Apple Power Macintosh series
   d. Apple Powerbook series
   e. IBM 3090 series
   f. Compaq Contura series

   Microcomputer journals containing the information needed for this exercise may be available in your college or town library. Such journals are also carried by many bookstores and computer stores.

2. Compare at least two IBM Aptiva models or at least two Apple Power Macintosh models with respect to the following:
   a. Resident CPU chip (and speed)
   b. Maximum RAM available
   c. CD-ROM availability
   d. Hard-disk capacity
   e. Number of parallel and serial ports
   f. Number of expansion slots

   Note that Aptiva and Power Macintosh computers come in different configurations, so be sure to identify the specific configuration on which your response is based. Microcomputer journals containing the information needed for this exercise may be available in your college or town library. Such journals are also carried by many bookstores and computer stores.

3. For any one of the following types of storage devices—MO optical disk unit, cartridge disk unit, cartridge tape unit—find, by looking through microcomputer journals or by consulting another information source, the following information:
   a. The name of one of the leading models
   b. An approximate price for the model
   c. The approximate unit price and the capacity of the removable medium involved.

   Microcomputer journals containing the information needed for this exercise may be available in your college or town library. Such journals are also carried by many bookstores and computer stores.

4. For three of the following printers—Brother HL-630, HP LaserJet 4 Plus, HP LaserJet 4M Plus, Canon BJ-200e Bubble Jet, HP DeskJet 540, HP Deskjet 1200C/PS, and Fujitsu DL 6400—determine the following:
   a. The printing technology in use (for example, ink-jet, laser)
   b. The approximate cost
   c. The approximate speed
   d. Whether or not color output is possible

Facts about specific printer models are available in microcomputer journals such as *PC Magazine* (see especially the annual printer issue). Microcomputer journals containing the information needed for this exercise may be available in your college or town library. Such journals are also carried by many bookstores and computer stores.

APPENDIX Tips for Buying Microcomputer Hardware

When buying a system unit, storage, a monitor, a keyboard, or a printer, be sure to get answers to the following questions.

System Unit

Laptop or desktop? If you need portability, you need a laptop computer. Laptop buyers should expect to pay about $500 more than they would for a comparable desktop model. A critical decision in the laptop area is battery life; most have to be recharged every two to eight hours. Desktop computer systems are generally easier to upgrade than laptops, and their bigger screens and keyboards make them better choices for most uses.

Which platform? The two main choices are going with an IBM or IBM-compatible computer—most of which run under some version of Microsoft Windows—or, alternatively, going with a computer in the Apple Macintosh line. Over 80 percent of PCs sold today are Windows-based, but the Macintosh is extremely popular in the desktop publishing and graphic arts fields. Because there is less competition in the Macintosh arena, expect to pay slightly higher prices if you decide to become a Mac owner.

Does the system unit have enough power to meet current and future applications needs? Most computers sold today are 32-bit machines and run at speeds of from 75 to 150 megahertz (MHz) or more. You should buy a system that will last for several years.

RAM

How much memory is necessary? The computer you buy should have enough RAM to run your most memory-intensive program and then some—say, enough to be able to accommodate an upgrade to the next version of the program. (A good rule of thumb is to expect memory requirements to double.) Expect to pay about $40 to $50 per megabyte of RAM.

Can memory be expanded later if you need more? Determine in what increments and to what maximum it can be extended. As an example, many machines allow memory expansion in 1-MB or 2-MB increments.

Secondary Storage

Will you need one or two diskette drives? What disk diameter and capacity will you need? Recall that drives accommodate either 3½-inch or 5¼-inch disks and that disk capacities usually run from 360 KB to 2.88 MB. Many people today use systems that have one 1.44 MB 3½-inch drive and one 1.2 MB 5¼-inch drive.

Will you need a hard disk? Most business software requires a hard disk to run. Hard disks today range from several hundred megabytes to a few gigabytes in capacity, and most use either an IDE, an ESDI, or a SCSI format. Computer professionals often advise that you figure out the minimum amount of storage you will need and at least double or triple that figure to meet future needs.

What about a CD-ROM unit? CD-ROMs are increasing in popularity and are now a standard item for home-based microcomputers. When buying a CD-ROM unit, you should also equip your computer system with speakers, a sound and video card, and a good graphics board.

Monitor

Do you need a color or a monochrome monitor? Most business software made today is optimized for use on desktop, CRT-type color monitors. Monochrome displays are still in wide use on laptop computers, but both quality and price on color displays have improved substantially in recent years, and color is now the norm rather than the exception in the laptop area.

How readable is the screen? Always inspect the output of the monitor you are considering before making a purchase. Monitors often work in several different display modes, some suitable for text and others for graphics. You only have one pair of eyes, so if you are going to be spending many hours at a monitor screen each day, a monitor choice can be extremely important.

Which graphics standards (for example, VGA and SVGA) does the monitor support? If you are working in a graphical environment, consider an SVGA display or, alternatively, a larger-than-normal screen size. If the work you do requires especially fine resolutions, make sure that you evaluate how well the monitor produces such outputs.

Does the monitor have adjustable features? Especially important are an adjustable base, which helps ward off glare, and brightness and contrast controls.

Keyboard

Does the keyboard feel comfortable as you type on it? If possible, type on the keyboard before buying; notice especially the key spacing and how the keys feel to your touch.

Does the keyboard have an assortment of special keys and features? Many people like light indicators showing whether certain keys are active.

Are the keys placed in an arrangement that you prefer? Although most people use the QWERTY key arrangement, several other keyboard layouts are available. Also, make sure that the special keys are conveniently located.

Does the keyboard have adjustable features? It is especially important that the keyboard is detachable, enabling you to move it to suit your comfort, and that it has an adjustable slope.

Printer

What type of printer is best for your needs? For most people, the choice will be between an impact dot-matrix, ink-jet, and laser printer. Laser printers deliver the best print quality and speed but are the most expensive. If you are running a business on your computer, a laser printer should be your first choice. Many ink-jet printers can produce highly affordable color output. Impact dot-matrix printers are yielding to ink-jet printers in popularity at the low end of the market.

How fast is the printer? Impact dot-matrix printers typically are rated at several hundred characters per second (cps), whereas most microcomputer-oriented laser printers print anywhere from 2 to 16 pages per minute. Ink-jet printers normally output at speeds somewhere between laser and impact dot-matrix printers.

What types of outputs can the printer produce? Be sure to examine closely both the range and the quality of outputs. Some laser printers, for instance, will print large-point-size text with jagged contours and will not reproduce photographs well. You should never buy a printer unless you first see its outputs—and as wide a range of outputs as possible.

Other Hardware

If you are buying other hardware, make sure that your system has enough ports and expansion slots to accommodate it.

If you are buying a modem, decide whether you want it to be internal or external, how fast it must be, and whether it meets the communications standards prescribed by the application for which you intend it. Unless you need the modem on more than one computer, buy the internal type. Most modems sold today come with fax capabilities. (Chapter 4 discusses modems in detail.)

If you are thinking about buying a mouse, consider also the possibility of getting a trackball or trackpad. Many people dislike using a mouse because it must be moved around a desktop; trackballs and trackpads, in contrast, are stationary.

MC 3 Software

OUTLINE

Overview

The User Interface
- Command Syntax
- Shortcut Keystrokes
- Graphical User Interfaces

Elements of a Graphical User Interface
- Menus
- Windows
- Dialog Boxes
- Online Help

Systems Software
- Operating Systems
- Language Translators
- Utility Programs

Productivity Software
- Word Processors
- Spreadsheets
- Database Management Systems
- Other Productivity Software Packages

Appendix: Tips for Buying Microcomputer Software

LEARNING OBJECTIVES

After completing this chapter, you will be able to:

1. Explain the differences among user interfaces.
2. Identify the elements commonly found in a graphical user interface, and explain their functions.
3. Describe the roles played by such systems software as operating systems, language translators, and utility programs.
4. Identify several microcomputer-based operating systems and explain the major differences that exist among them.
5. Describe what word processors, spreadsheets, database management systems, and a number of other types of productivity software packages are designed to do.

OVERVIEW

In the previous chapter, you read about the hardware parts of a computer system. But hardware by itself cannot process data any more than the instruments in an orchestra can play a symphony without musicians, a conductor, and a musical score. Without software a computer system would be interesting to look at, perhaps, but essentially it would represent useless hunks of metal.

As mentioned earlier, *software* refers to computer programs. Two important types of software that we will cover in this chapter are systems software and applications software. These are the types with which most microcomputer users must become familiar.

We begin the chapter with software user interfaces. Not long ago, most professionals who used computers had to learn how to write in a programming language. Over the last few years, the situation has radically changed. With sophisticated computer graphics now widely available on the desktop level, graphical user interfaces have evolved and have made using a computer much easier. Important components of graphical user interfaces will be covered here.

Next we turn to systems software. Systems software refers to the background programs that make it possible for other programs to run. Such software allows you to start up your computer system, format disks, copy files from one medium to another, recover lost files, and do many other useful applications-support tasks. Everybody who uses a computer system must in some way interact with systems software.

Finally, we cover productivity software. Productivity software refers to the class of applications software designed to make end users better at performing tasks that would otherwise have to be done the old-fashioned way—manually. By far the most common types of productivity software are word processors, spreadsheets, and database management systems. The chapter covers these as well as a number of other types of productivity software packages. An appendix providing tips for buying microcomputer software is located at the end of the chapter.

THE USER INTERFACE

Users interact with software in a variety of ways. Those working with Microsoft's MS-DOS operating system, for instance, often type in DOS-language commands at a prompting character in order to perform their work. A user of Microsoft's Windows package, on the other hand, makes selections from menus—with a mouse—to perform similar types of operations. The manner in which a program package makes its resources available to users is known as its **user interface.** In this section, we will look at elements commonly found in user interfaces.

The backbone of most software packages is their command set. It is by issuing commands that you get the package to perform any desired action. Commands are most commonly invoked by typing statements that conform to a command syntax, by using shortcut keystrokes, or by making selections from a graphical user interface with a mouse or a keyboard.

Command Syntax

Command syntax was the first type of user interface and, until the last decade or two, the only type available. At some type of system **prompt,** the user must type in a command that conforms to a strict command syntax. **Syntax** refers to the grammatical rules that govern the structure and content of statements in a particular language.

For instance, when you are using the MS-DOS operating system, you will generally type commands at the operating-system prompt. If, say, you are pointed to the DOS directory on the C drive and want to erase a file named "FRED" from the A drive, then at the

```
C:\DOS>
```

operating-system prompt, you must type

```
ERASE A:FRED
```

If you instead type

```
ERADICATE A:FRED
```

or

```
ERASE FRED FROM A
```

an error message will display on the screen, indicating the command does not conform to the "official" syntax of the MS-DOS language.

Unfortunately, using a command syntax effectively is often beyond the patience and capabilities of most potential users. Syntax can be mathematically exacting, and the average person tends to be casual and prone to make mistakes. For instance, imagine having regularly to create DOS statements such as

```
DEVICE=C:\DOS\DRIVER.SYS /D:0 /F:1
```

Not only do you have to be very careful in making sure each of the characters in the statement is correct—including blank spaces appearing where they should be—but, if you cannot remember the syntax, you have to look it up.

To make software available to as wide an audience as possible, many software vendors have added features such as shortcut keystrokes and graphical user interfaces to simplify the issuing of commands. Keep in mind, however, that such new developments have not completely eliminated the use of command syntax. Although shortcut keystrokes and graphical user interfaces have certainly made it easier to use computers, many applications—such as creating computer programs and customizing software packages to work in nonstandard ways—require learning a programming language.

Shortcut Keystrokes

Shortcut keystrokes enable you to invoke commands with a minimal number of keystrokes. For instance, when you want to indent text with WordPerfect, you strike the

F4

function key. Next, you type the text you want indented. To turn off the indent, you press the Enter key. To perform the same type of task with a command syntax—something people had to do during the early days of word processing—would take much greater effort (see Figure MC 3-1).

In version 6 of WordPerfect, to change from single to double spacing in a document is just as easy. You hold down the Shift key while tapping the F8

FIGURE MC 3-1 Shortcut keystrokes. Shortcut keystrokes make it possible for you to issue commands with minimal keystroking. (a) In using a command syntax, you must type complete commands to indent a text paragraph, and, later, to turn off the indent. (b) With shortcut keystrokes, you can perform the same task with far fewer keystrokes and with less memorizing.

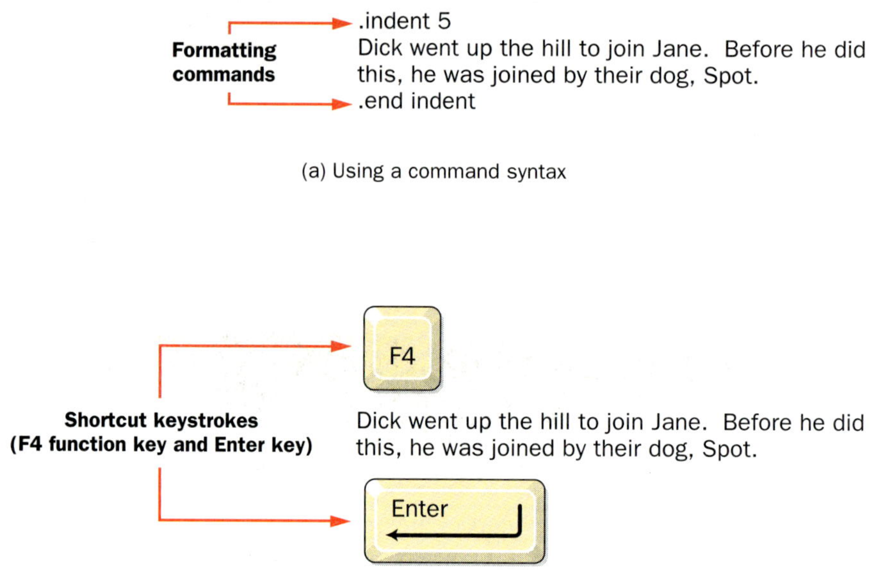

(a) Using a command syntax

(b) Using shortcut keystrokes

function key, followed by striking the 1 key, the 3 key, and the 2 key in succession. The way that this might be represented is as follows:

⇧ Shift + F8, 1, 3, 2

Shortcut keystrokes are a major time-saver when compared to conventional command syntax. However, they also suffer from the problem of taxing the user's memory. If you have to issue a seldom-used command, and you cannot remember the shortcut keystrokes for it, you have to look them up.

Graphical User Interfaces

Graphical user interfaces (GUIs) have become popular in recent years with the availability of high-resolution, graphics-display screens and powerful CPUs. Before these types of hardware came into the market, GUIs were not practical. Graphics monitors often displayed output that looked crude, and even if the screens were attractive, the graphics took too long to generate on the computer.

GUIs employ such devices as pull-down menus, windows, and icons to make it easier for users to navigate successfully through their favorite software packages (see Figure MC 3-2). Instead of having to remember a complicated command syntax or shortcut-keystroke sequence, you simply look for the command on a menu, point to it with a mouse or keyboard, and select it. If you cannot recall instantly the specific command to perform a specific operation, a variety of online tools are available to assist you.

GUIs also provide a means of customizing screens to suit your own personal work style. Menus can be personalized with your favorite commands and moved anywhere on the screen. Also, the screen can be laid out in a variety of different ways to suit your specific tastes.

FIGURE MC 3-2 Graphical user interfaces (GUIs). By representing command choices as menu items or as colorful icons, GUIs make it easy for users to point and click with a mouse when making selections.

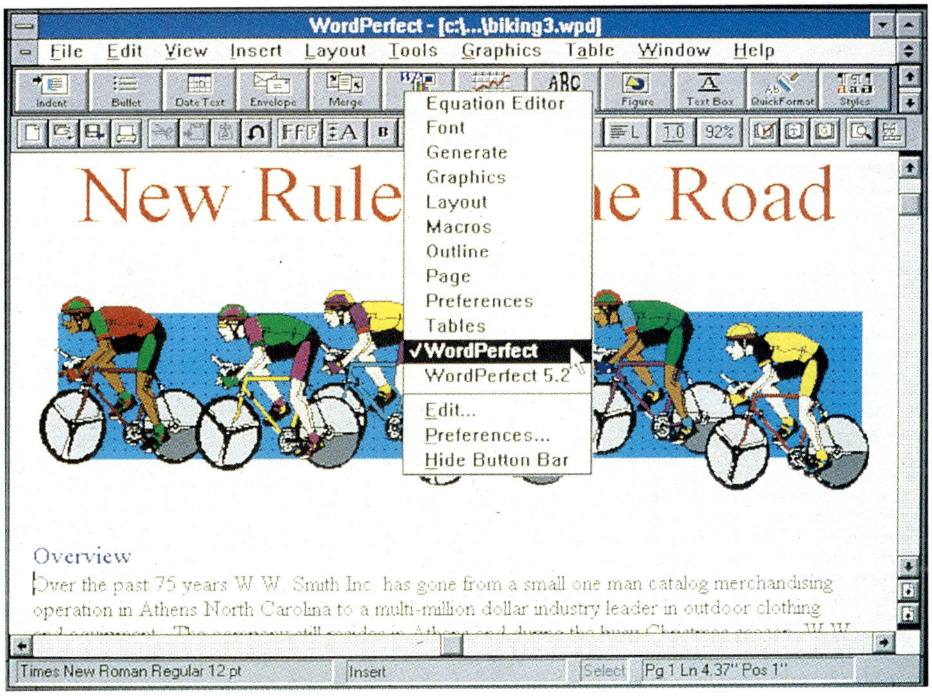

Despite the usefulness of GUIs, many users will not want to resort to them exclusively. For example, longtime users of WordPerfect may find it faster to work with familiar shortcut keystrokes than to select comparable commands off a menu. Also, longtime users of DOS often prefer to format and copy disks using DOS's command syntax rather than perform the same operations by making selections from Windows menus. And many users have complained that mouse pointing makes their arms tired after several hours. GUIs are particularly helpful, however, for seldom-used commands, when you are at your computer screen and need a memory jogger. Today, most software packages offer a combination of command syntax, shortcut keystrokes, and GUIs and let users switch between these alternatives at will.

ELEMENTS OF A GRAPHICAL USER INTERFACE

Most users of computer systems today work with software that sports a GUI of some type. Consequently, anyone learning about computers should know how GUIs work.

Menus

A **menu** is a set of options from which you can choose a desired action. Several types of menus are available.

Menu Bars At the top of many GUI screens is a **menu bar** showing the main command set governing the screen (see Figure MC 3-3). Generally, commands can be selected with a mouse or by some simple shortcut-keystroke

FIGURE MC 3-3 **Menu bar and pull-down menu.** Top-of-screen menu bars show the command set governing a screen. When a command is chosen from a menu bar, a pull-down menu of subcommands typically appears underneath the selected command, as illustrated here for the File command.

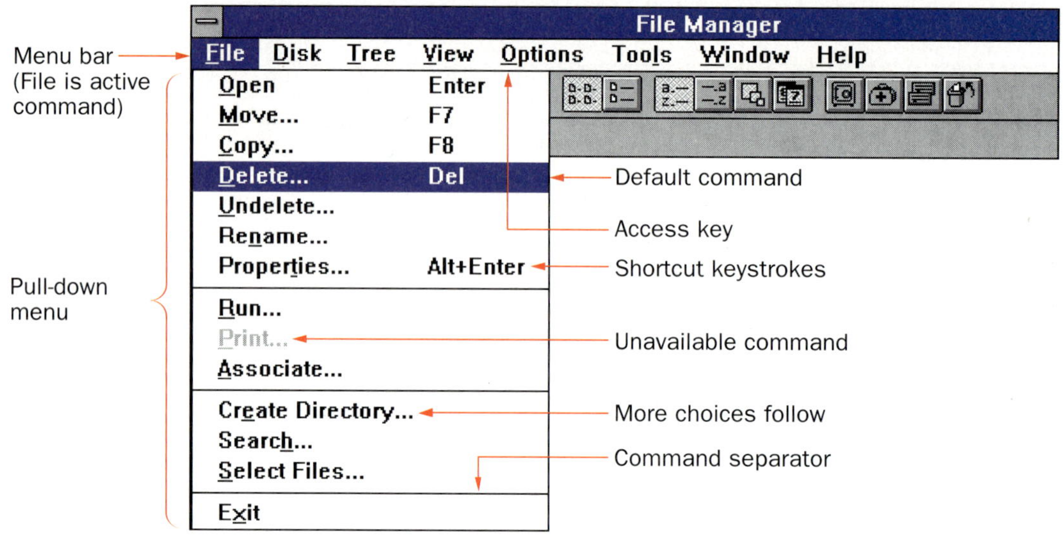

procedure. For instance, to select the File command on the menu bar in Figure MC 3-3, you can either click on it with a mouse or—with the keyboard—hold down the Alt key while tapping the F key. Generally, the key that is to be struck in combination with the Alt key (or other similar control key) is either highlighted or underlined on the menu. Such highlighted or underlined keys are commonly called *access keys.*

Once a selection is made from a menu bar, a pull-down menu usually appears under the chosen option, as shown in the figure.

Pull-Down Menus **Pull-down menus** (or *drop-down menus*) are displayed onscreen when you make a choice on a menu bar or on another pull-down menu. The options on the pull-down menus correspond to subcommands that prompt you for finer levels of detail.

Pull-down menus will typically conform to certain conventions. One is the *command separator,* a horizontal line used to group related commands. Several others are discussed in the following five subsections.

- **Active and Default Choices** Active and default commands are always highlighted on both the menu bar and any pull-down menu. The *active* command (File, in Figure MC 3-3) is the command that you have already selected, whereas the *default* command (Delete, in Figure MC 3-3) can be selected merely by striking the Enter key. You can often escape out of an active command through the Escape key. To select a choice other than a default, you can click on it with a mouse or—with a keyboard—either invoke its access key or, alternatively, move to it with the appropriate arrow key and then press Enter.

- **Shortcut Keystrokes** Many GUIs show shortcut keystrokes next to options on pull-down menus, such as Del for the Delete choice and Alt + Enter for the Properties choice in Figure MC 3-3. You have the choice of executing the command with either the appropriate access key (the T key, for Properties) or the corresponding shortcut-keystroke sequence (pressing the Alt key while also pressing the Enter key).

- **FADED TYPE** On the File pull-down menu in Figure MC 3-3, the Print subcommand is shown in *ghosted* or *faded type.* This means that this particular choice is unavailable in the context of what you are currently doing. For example, if you have not yet opened a document, you will not be able to print it.
- **ELLIPSES** Command options shown with an *ellipsis (. . .),* such as Move and Copy in the figure, mean that by selecting them you will be confronted with yet another set of choices. The choices are generally in the form of a dialog box (discussed shortly). If, instead of an ellipsis, a right-pointing triangle (▶) appears, a new list of choices in the form of another pull-down menu will unfurl alongside if the command option is selected.
- **CHECK MARKS** An item with a *check mark* to the left of it means that the associated option is "active" or "selected" (see Figure MC 3-4). For instance, the check by Toolbar in the figure means that the toolbar at the top of the screen is currently activated. Software packages also have a way of letting you deselect options—that is, making check marks disappear. One widely used procedure is to highlight the checked option and then strike the Enter key. Alternatively, you could deselect by clicking the mouse on the option. So, for instance, if you deselect Toolbar, the toolbar would disappear from the screen.

Icon Menus Often, menus are in the form of a set of **icons.** The toolbar just discussed is one example. An icon can represent a computer program or group of computer programs, a command or group of commands, a document (such as a letter, piece of art, or faxed transmission) or group of documents, and the like. As you can see, virtually anything that can go into a computer file or a collection of files can be represented onscreen as an icon. When you select an icon from the displayed arrangement, the corresponding action is taken by the software package. Figure MC 3-5 shows several icon menus.

Icon menus go by a variety of names, depending on the software package you are using. Such terms as *toolbars, toolboxes, button bars, smarticons,* and *palettes* all refer to icon menus of one sort or another. Icon menus can often be customized, meaning users can design their own icons, sequence icons in different ways, or move menus around the screen.

FIGURE MC 3-4 **Check marks.** Check marks to the left of choices indicate that the choices are active, or currently selected. Software packages also provide procedures that enable you to deselect active items.

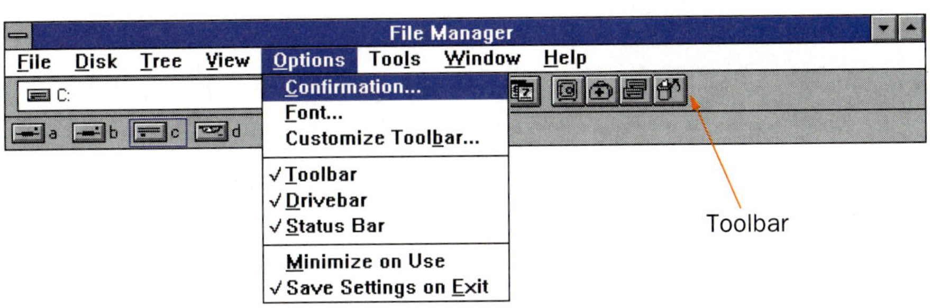

FIGURE MC 3-5 **Icon menus.** (a) The Lotus Notes icon menu illustrated here lets you launch into any of 30 applications. (b) Microsoft Word's *standard toolbar* provides access to the most widely used word-processing commands, and its *formatting toolbar* lets you choose typefaces and their sizes, boldface or italicize text, and select among a number of indenting styles. The *hyperlinks* at the top right of the screen let you launch into other software packages in the Microsoft Office suite of applications. (c) Both the Apple Macintosh (featured here) and Microsoft Windows GUIs represent files and the directories into which they are organized as icons.

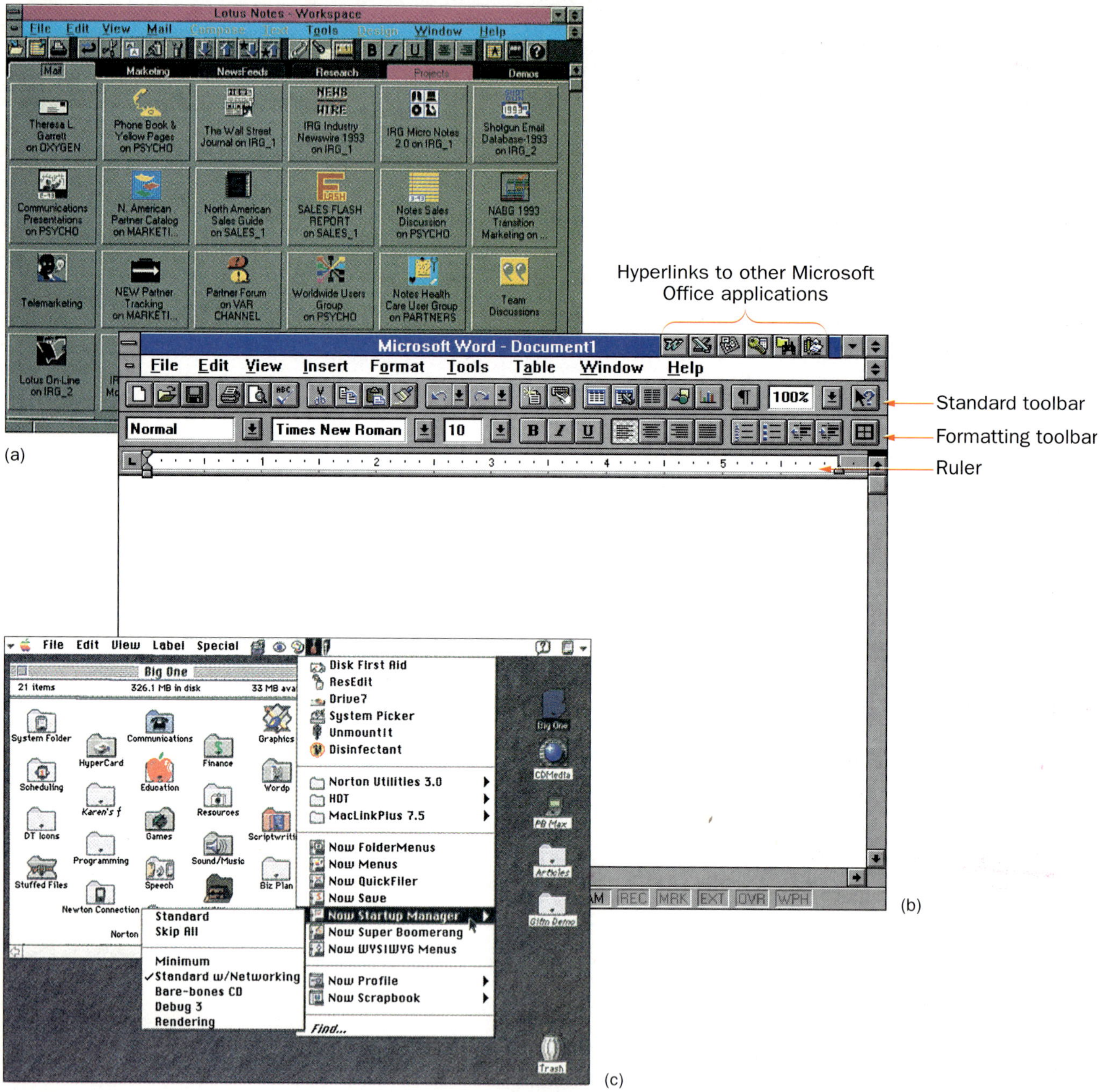

Dialog Boxes Menu items also often appear in *dialog boxes* that pop up onto the screen. These items—which include radio buttons, check boxes, and list boxes—will be discussed shortly.

Pop-Up Menus Users of Windows 95 and the Apple Macintosh often deal with *pop-up menus.* These menus look like pull-down menus (see Figure MC 3-5c) but instead appear on the screen when icons are clicked with the secondary mouse button.

Windows

The staple of the GUI is the **window**—a box of information that is overlaid on the display screen. A window can contain facts about software use, menu items, instructions, and a variety of other types of data.

Customizing Windows Often, windows can be tailored to meet your applications needs. Several of the ways this can be done are described in the following four subsections.

- **Tiling or Cascading Windows** As shown in Figure MC 3-6, users can arrange windows onscreen in either of two ways—by *tiling* them side by side (Figure MC 3-6a) or by *cascading* them one on top of another (Figure MC 3-6b). Tiling enables you to see information in several windows at the same time, whereas cascading lets you see as much information as possible in the foreground window but only the titles of the windows underneath. Whatever method you use to arrange windows, only one window can be active at a time. The active, or foreground, window often has a darkened title bar or darkened border (or both). The *title bar* contains the name of the window, and the *border* encloses the window's viewing area.
- **Resizing Windows** Windows can often be made larger or smaller. It might be possible to resize the active window by selecting a window border with a mouse, and—with the mouse button depressed—moving the *mouse pointer* (the onscreen arrow associated with the mouse) outward or inward on the screen. Alternatively, by clicking on a *corner* formed by two adjacent borders, it may be possible to resize along both borders. In Windows 95, *sizing handles* are used instead of borders and corners to resize windows.
- **Moving Windows** A window can generally be moved from one part of the screen to another. Typically, this is done by selecting the window with a mouse, and—with the mouse button pressed—*dragging and dropping* the window to the desired location. Often, when a window is in the process of being moved or resized, its border will dim or change to a dotted line.
- **Minimizing or Maximizing Windows** Windows can be *minimized* to icon size or *maximized* to fill the entire screen. For instance, by clicking on the left sizing button shown in Figure MC 3-6, the window is minimized; by instead clicking on the right button, the window is maximized. A program that has been minimized is still actively running in the background, so you can still issue commands from it. To leave the program entirely, you must click on the *control-menu icon* at the top left of the title bar. In Windows 95, the two sizing buttons and the control-menu icon all appear at the far right of the title bar and are represented by different symbols than those shown in Figure MC 3-6 (see Figure MC 3-19, which appears later).

As you perform work within screen windows, the mouse pointer often visibly changes in a **context-sensitive** way. In other words, the shape of the pointer is automatically altered with respect to the operation you are performing. Figure MC 3-7 shows a sampling of some of the shapes that you may see on the screen. For instance, when you are cropping an image, the pointer may resemble a pair of scissors. When you move the pointer over a boldfaced topic that can be selected on a list, the pointer may change to a hand with a pointed finger.

FIGURE MC 3-6 Tiled and cascaded windows. Tiling enables multiple windows on a screen to be placed side by side, whereas cascading overlaps them.

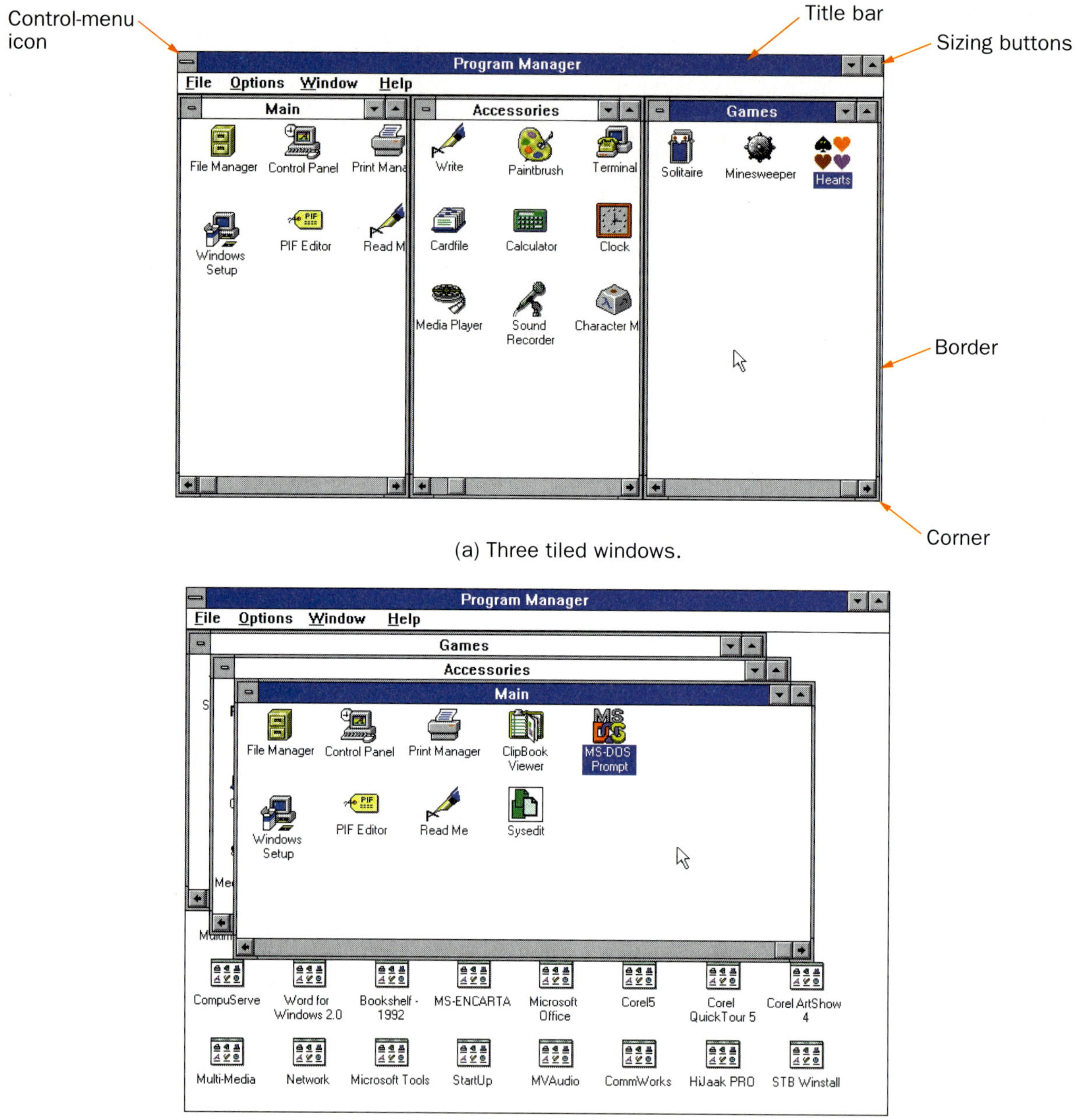

(a) Three tiled windows.

(b) Three cascaded windows.

Scroll Bars Often, a screen window is not big enough to display all the information it needs to at any one time. When this happens, **scroll bars** appear at the bottom or to the right of the window (or both) (see Figure MC 3-8), and you can use them to display the rest of the information.

Scrolling lets you move contiguous lines of text up and down—and even sideways—on the window or screen, similar to the way the roll on a player piano unwinds. When scrolling down, for example, as lines successively disappear from the top of the window or screen, new ones appear at the bottom.

FIGURE MC 3-7 **Context-sensitive pointer shapes.** Many software packages make the mouse pointer context-sensitive, changing its shape with respect to the operation you are performing.

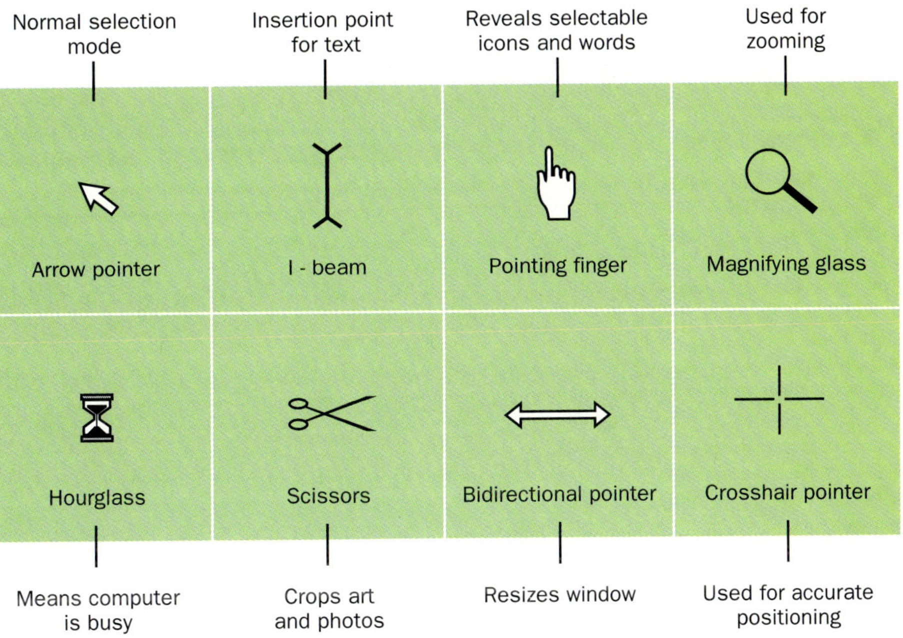

FIGURE MC 3-8 **Scroll bars.** Scroll bars enable you to see offscreen information. Clicking on a scroll *arrow* scrolls text a line at a time, whereas clicking before or after a scroll *box* scrolls a page at a time. For faster scrolling, drag the scroll box.

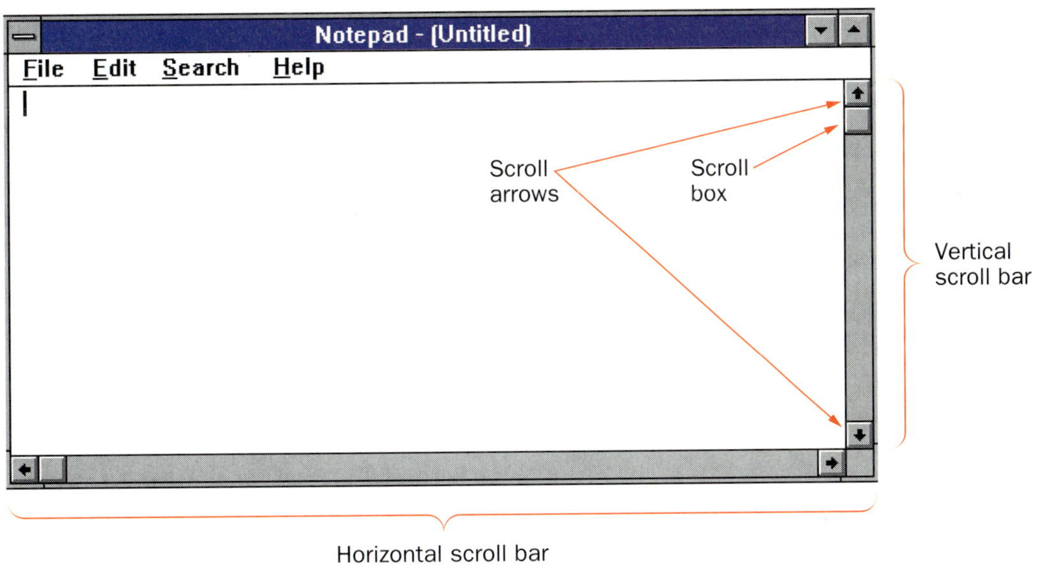

By activating a *scroll arrow* on any one of the scroll bars, you scroll the window a small amount at a time in the direction of the arrow to see offscreen information. The principle is similar to slowly moving a magnifying glass (the window) over a map (the information).

Between its two scroll arrows, each scroll bar contains a *scroll box.* By dragging this box up or down (or to the left or right) in the direction of the desired information, the scrolling can be done at a much higher speed. For instance, if the scroll box is at the top of the scroll bar and you drag it to the middle, it will take you to the halfway point of the information list. Clicking before or after the scroll box scrolls text a page at a time.

In Windows 3.1, scroll boxes are square; in Windows 95, they are sized in proportion to the percentage of information currently displayed. Instead of the scroll bar, you can usually use the keyboard's cursor-movement keys to scroll up or down or to the left or right.

Dialog Boxes

Dialog boxes are special windows that prompt the GUI user to supply further information. Information can be supplied in a number of ways.

Radio Buttons In the left part of the dialog box in Figure MC 3-9 are *radio buttons,* or *option buttons.* These rounded buttons work like the push buttons on many old radios in that only one choice in the panel can be active at any one time. Buttons can be activated or deactivated by clicking on them.

FIGURE MC 3-9 **Radio buttons.** Radio buttons—sometimes called option buttons—work like the push buttons on old radios in that only one button in a particular button panel can be active at one time.

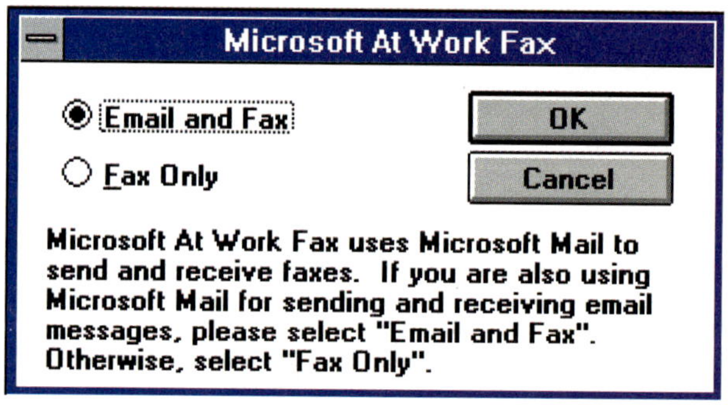

FIGURE MC 3-10 **Check boxes.** When an "X" is placed in a check box, the check box is selected. Check boxes are different from radio buttons in that several, none, or all of the boxes in a particular check-box panel can be active at one time.

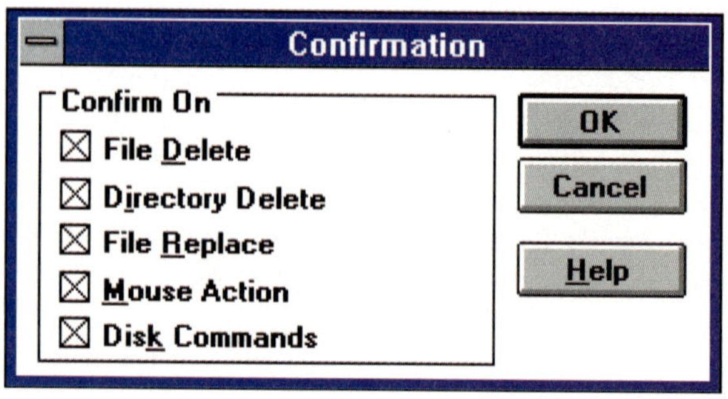

FIGURE MC 3-11 **Text box.** Text boxes enable you to type information (such as a file name or a percentage) into the computer.

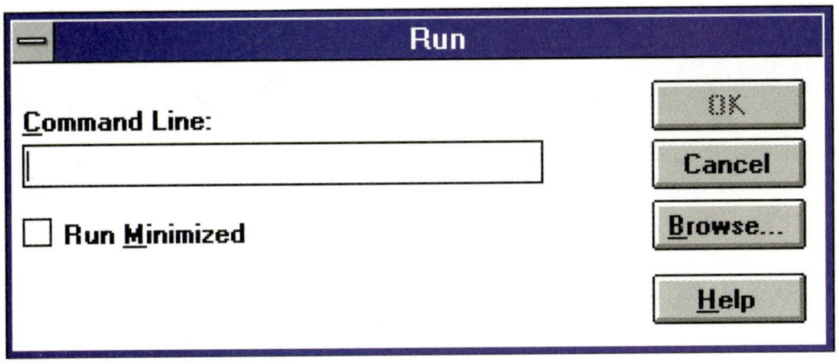

Check Boxes In the left part of the dialog box in Figure MC 3-10 is a set of *check boxes.* To make any of the choices in a check box active, you place an "X" in them by clicking on the box with a mouse. Check boxes differ from radio buttons in that more than one option in the panel can be active at one time, or even none of the options. Check boxes can be deactivated by clicking on them with a mouse.

Text Boxes Figure MC 3-11 shows a *text box.* Text boxes allow you to type information into the computer, such as a percentage, an absolute amount, or the name of a file or directory. After you finish typing the information, pressing the Tab key will generally allow you to move to the next item in the box.

List Boxes A *list box* is similar to a pull-down menu in that it contains a list of options, any one of which can be selected. Often, the list is too big to fit in its window at one time, in which case a vertical scroll bar or similar mechanism is used to enable you to see parts of the list that are not onscreen (see Figure MC 3-12). To save even more space, a *drop-down list box* is sometimes used. This displays only the first selection and reveals others when the user selects the *drop-down arrow* (↓) to the right of it.

Message Boxes A *message box* pops up on the screen when status information needs to be given or when a potential problem is unfolding. One common type of message box contains a *warning,* and it appears when you are attempting to execute an improper command or when you are performing an operation that may have grave consequences if you have not properly thought it through (see Figure MC 3-13). In any type of message box, the user must acknowledge the message by choosing one of the supplied command buttons before proceeding.

FIGURE MC 3-12
List box. In a list box, you select a choice by clicking on it with a mouse or by reaching it through the up or down arrow key and pressing Enter. Many list boxes have a vertical scroll bar or similar mechanism that lets you access choices not currently onscreen.

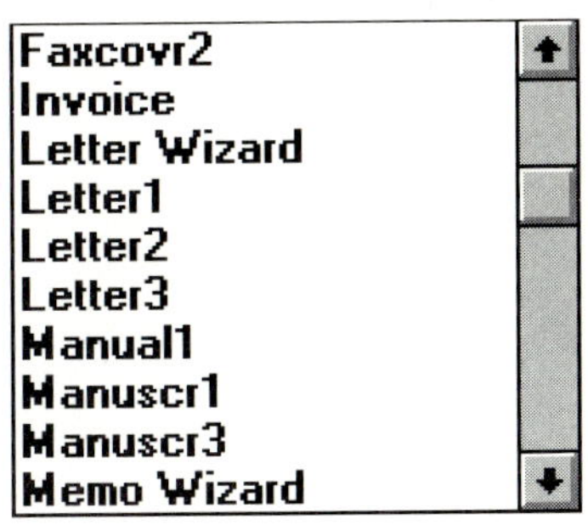

Online Help

Most people will eventually run into problems or think of questions when they are working with a software package. To make it as easy as possible to get help when you are at your computer, many GUIs have an *online help feature.* Often, the assistance provided will be context-sensitive—that is, the help routine tries to recognize the type of operation you are performing and then automatically attempts to provide the appropriate aid.

An online help feature can be an extremely vital component of a package. According to a recent study at Carnegie-Mellon University, a user interface that could slice one-eighth of a second off a critical, repetitive task such as order entry could save a company more than a million dollars.

FIGURE MC 3-13 **Message box.** A message box often appears on the screen when a potential problem is unfolding, such as when you are trying to execute an improper command or are facing a potentially dangerous situation.

Software packages employ a variety of tools in providing online assistance to users. Some of these tools are discussed in the following subsections.

Indexing Many help routines sport an *indexing feature* that lets you choose from a lengthy list of help topics. The topics are displayed in a list box, and you can scroll to the topic you need. There is a way, however, that lets you search even faster. As illustrated in Figure MC 3-14, you can position the screen cursor in a typing area, and then begin to type the word you want to look up in the index. As you key in each letter, the list-box display changes accordingly. As soon as the topic you want to look up appears in the display window, you can point to it and select it.

Online Tutorials With online secondary storage capacity for the average PC user approaching the gigabyte range, many vendors are providing online, graphical tutorials with their software packages. These tutorials enable you to do such things as learn how to use the package and observe examples and demonstrations.

Task Simplification A recent trend in software help is the development of tools to help users more quickly perform repetitive tasks. Depending on the vendor of the software package you are using, these tools may be called *wizards, coaches, tutors, experts, advisors,* or something else. Such tools guide the user in a step-by-step fashion through such tasks as preparing letters, invoices, or reports, and the like—either by providing directed tutorials or performing difficult parts of the task automatically.

SYSTEMS SOFTWARE

Systems software consists of support programs that coordinate the various parts of the computer system to make it run rapidly and efficiently. They perform such tasks as formatting disks so that they are suitable for storing budgets or word-processed documents, copying program files or data files from one disk to another, and enabling whatever brand of applications software you use to work on your printer or display device. There are three basic types of systems software: operating systems, language translators, and utility programs.

Operating Systems

The **operating system** serves as the gateway to applications programs, their data, and other system resources. It enables applications programs to be accessed and support activities to be carried out on program or data files.

FIGURE MC 3-14 **Indexing.** Most help routines have an indexing feature so that you can select a help topic from a large list. You can either scroll to a topic or—for faster access—partially type it, as shown here.

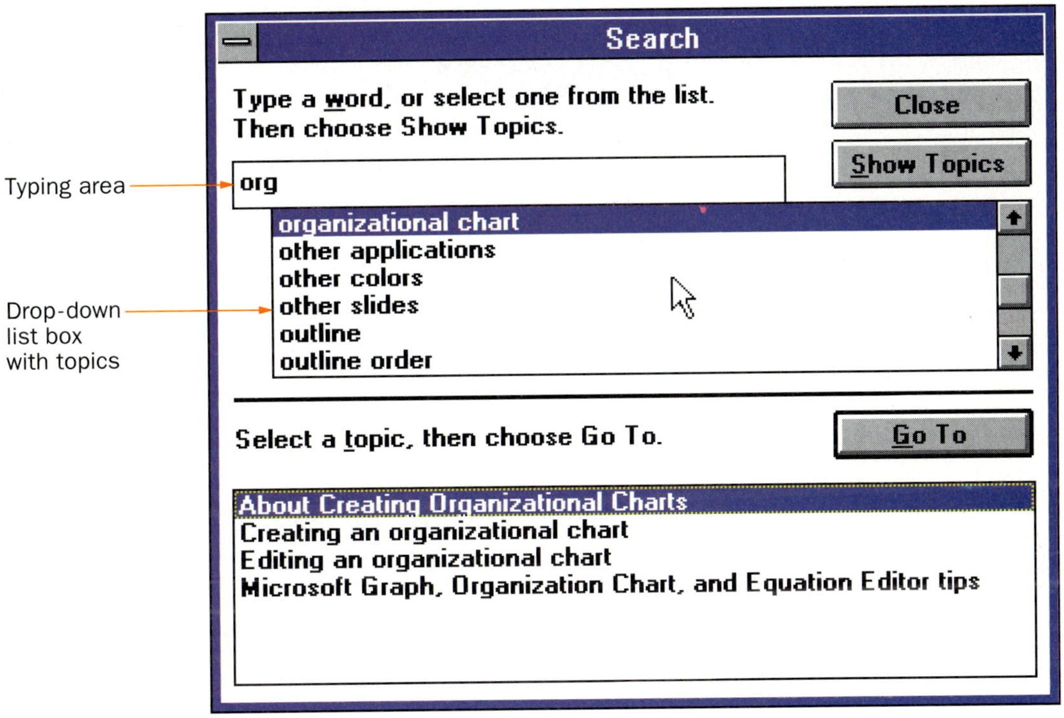

Because of the central role of the operating system in coordinating the computer system's activities, many consider it the most critical piece of software in the computer system. Without an operating system, none of the other programs can run.

Figure MC 3-15 shows the principle by which most operating systems work. Generally, when you turn on your computer system, you are immediately confronted with the operating system. If, say, you wish to create a document with your word processor, you would invoke your word-processing program by invoking a specific command from the operating system. If, later, you want to write a BASIC program, you must first exit your word-processing program; this action places you back into the operating system. Then, from the operating system, you would invoke BASIC (that is, the BASIC language translator). The marketplace offers a wide selection of operating systems for microcomputer users (see Figure MC 3-16).

Now, we briefly cover several of the most widely used operating systems to give you a feel for their principal characteristics and to help you understand how they differ from one another. The operating systems we discuss in this section include MS-DOS and PC-DOS, Windows 95, Windows NT, Macintosh System Software, UNIX, OS/2, and NetWare. Also covered is the Microsoft Windows 3.x *operating environment*—the GUI shell program that is widely used with MS-DOS and PC-DOS.

MS-DOS and PC-DOS Since the 1980s, DOS* (for Disk Operating System) has been the predominant microcomputer-based operating system for most

*For simplicity, when used in this text, DOS refers strictly to MS-DOS and PC-DOS. DOS, however, is not a proprietary name, and there are a few other, lesser-known operating systems that use the name DOS—Tandy TRSDOS and Apple ProDOS, for instance.

FIGURE MC 3-15 The gateway role of the operating system. The operating system makes available computer system resources to the user. Everyone using a computer system must interact with the operating system in some way.

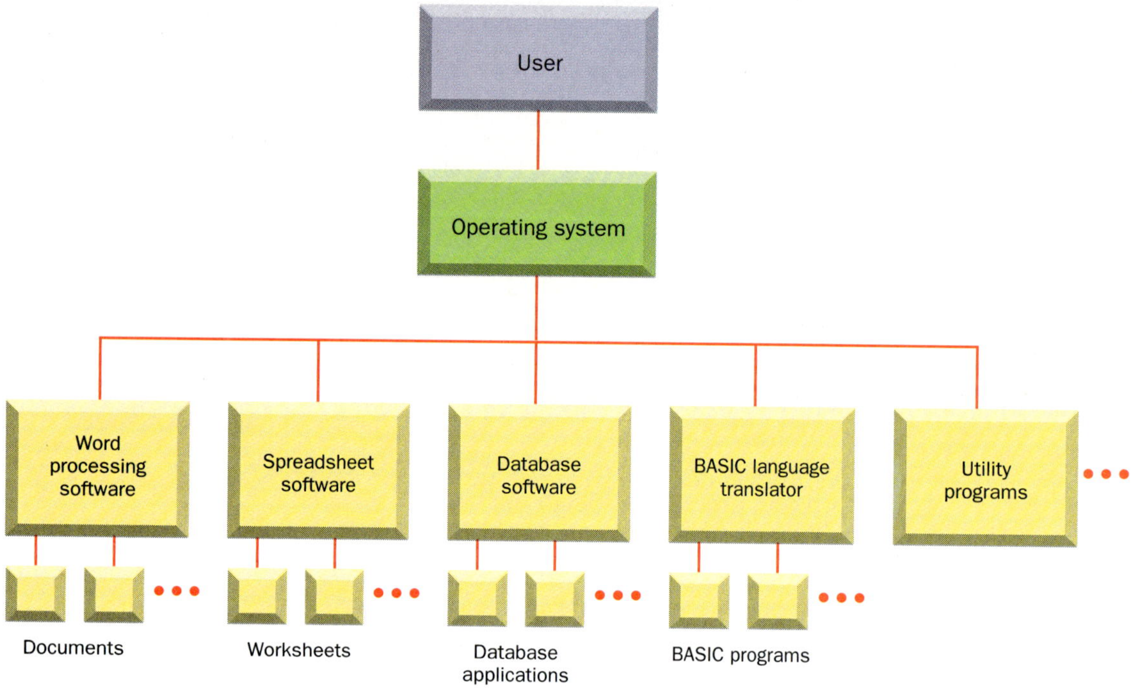

FIGURE MC 3-16 Popular microcomputer operating systems. DOS and Windows are the most widely used, with millions of copies sold.

Operating System	Description
Macintosh System Software	The operating system used on the Apple Macintosh line of microcomputers
MS-DOS	The most widely used operating system on IBM-compatible microcomputers
NetWare	The most widely used operating system on local area networks (LANs)
OS/2	The operating system designed for the high end of IBM's PS/2 line of microcomputers
PC-DOS	The operating system most widely used on IBM microcomputers
Windows 3.x*	Refers to the Windows 3.0 and Windows 3.1 operating environments (and variants such as Windows for Workgroups 3.11). Windows 3.x is a graphically oriented shell program for Microsoft's MS-DOS operating system
Windows 95	The operating system that is the heir apparent to both MS-DOS and Windows 3.x, combining the functionality of both programs into a single package
Windows NT	Microsoft's high-end, graphically oriented operating system, targeted primarily to corporate networking applications
UNIX	An operating system used on high-end microcomputers and on bigger computers

*Not a full operating system

businesses. Millions of copies of it have been sold to date, making it the most widely used software package ever developed. It has been estimated that more than 70 percent of today's microcomputer systems use DOS.

The two principal forms of DOS are MS-DOS and PC-DOS. Both were originally developed by Microsoft Corporation, of Redmond, Washington. But for a few minor differences, these operating systems are virtually identical. **PC-DOS** was created originally for the IBM PC, whereas **MS-DOS** was devised to operate on computer systems that look and work a lot like the IBM PC.

Both MS-DOS and PC-DOS have been revised many times since they were first developed. Each major revision is referred to as a *version.* All versions starting with the number 1 (such as 1.0 and 1.1) were designed for the earliest microcomputer systems, such as the original IBM PC, which used only floppy disks and cassette tapes for secondary storage. DOS was later extended to work with hard disks and networks and is today up to Versions 6 and 7. Later versions of DOS also support a limited amount of **multitasking,** a feature that enables the computer system to perform work on two or more programs or program tasks concurrently. Yet because it was originally designed around 16-bit CPU chips—which supported limited amounts of RAM—16-bit DOS cannot take full advantage of the power of new chips.

Today, it is not clear whether the successor to 16-bit DOS will be Windows 95, Windows NT, OS/2, UNIX, or some other advanced operating system. Although DOS has become technologically obsolescent, it is likely that DOS and DOS-based applications will be prevalent for the remainder of this decade. So many DOS-based computers are around today that vendors of new software are still supplying—in force—DOS-based applications to the marketplace. Furthermore, products such as Microsoft Windows 3.x have extended the popularity of DOS.

DOS with Windows 3.x Microsoft **Windows 3.x**—often referred to loosely as *Microsoft Windows* or just *Windows*—is an interconnected series of programs that supplies a graphical operating environment for computer systems (see Figure MC 3-17). Both the latest versions of this product (Windows 3.1 and Windows for Workgroups 3.11) and earlier versions are not full-fledged operating systems; they are merely GUI shell programs for the DOS (MS-DOS or PC-DOS) operating system. They turn your display into an electronic desktop. Just as an ordinary desktop may be arranged with a calendar, clock, calculator, and notepads on top of it—along with papers stacked one on top of another or placed so that each is in full view—so, too, can the Microsoft Windows 3.x desktop be arranged. As with the conventional desktop, the electronic desktop gives you the freedom to rearrange items at will or to make them disappear from view.

Windows provides several advantages over "plain" DOS, including the following:

- It replaces the DOS command line with a system of menus, information boxes called *windows*, and icons, thereby eliminating the need to remember a command syntax.
- It lets users easily work on more than one program at a time; for example, you can temporarily abandon your word processor to work with a spreadsheet program and then return to the word processor at the same place you left off.
- It lets users perform more than one task at a time; for example, you can be typing in one document while printing out another.
- It has built-in utilities that make it easy for users to share data among applications; this feature allows you to, say, prepare a graph with your spreadsheet program and store it in a word-processed document (see Figure MC 3-18).
- It encourages a consistent user interface; once you learn how to use one Windows program it becomes easier to learn others.
- It provides a variety of desk accessory programs—such as a card file, calendar, and calculator—that support doing work in a business environment.

FIGURE MC 3-17 **Microsoft Windows 3.1.** Microsoft Windows 3.1 provides computers running the MS-DOS and PC-DOS operating systems with a GUI. Annotated in the figure are some of the principal elements of the Windows electronic desktop.

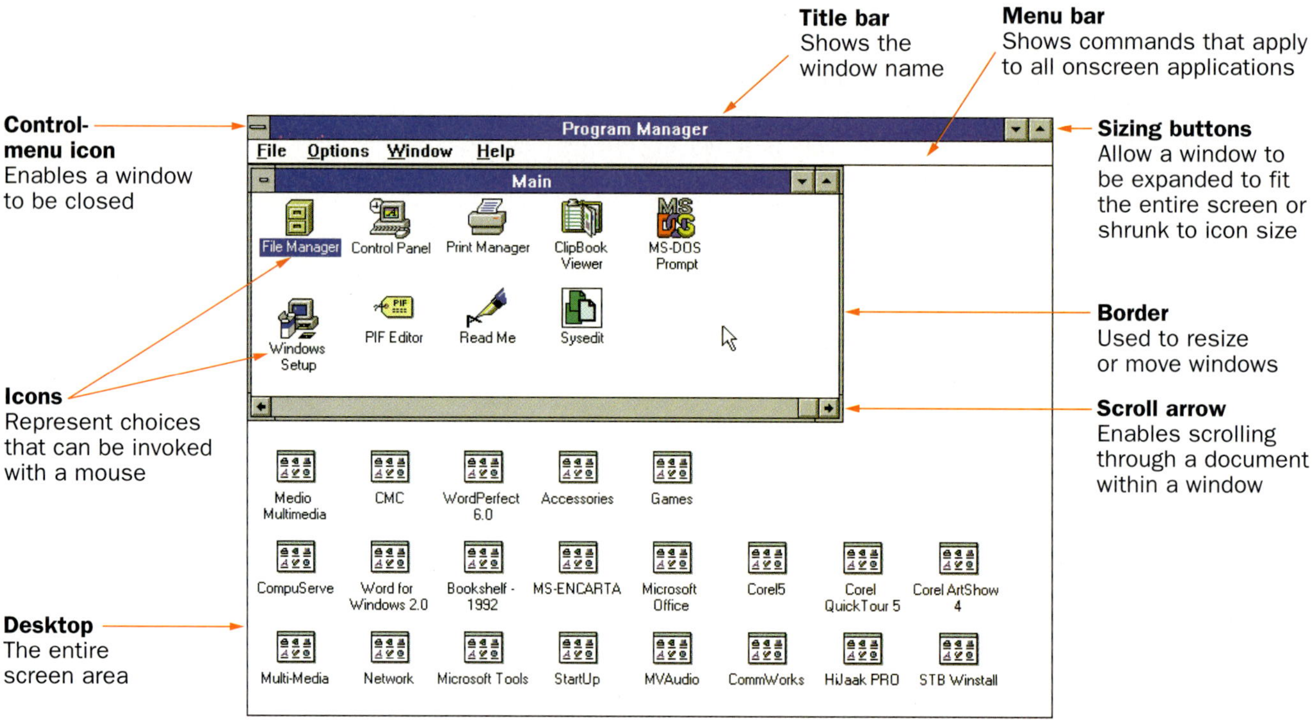

- It furnishes a cohesive system under which all the applications can be easily managed.

Windows 95 Although Windows 3.x has been immensely successful, it is only a graphical shell—not an entire operating system. This shell strategy has posed some problems for Microsoft. One is that you have to buy two separate programs—DOS and Windows—that have to work together seamlessly. Another, far more serious problem, is that DOS was designed when microcomputer chips were not very powerful. Thus, DOS is not capable of performing certain types of operations that the newer chips have made possible.

Microsoft's path out of the shell strategy has been twofold. First, it had to move to develop Windows as a full-fledged operating system—a product with both the familiarity and functionality of DOS and Windows 3.x. This would provide a smooth upgrade path to the 100 million or so DOS-with-Windows 3.x users. Second, it had to build new features into Windows that went well beyond the limited capabilities of DOS.

In 1994, the software giant announced that all versions of Windows after Windows 3.1 would bundle language commands (including those in DOS) and a GUI into a single product. It also announced a new numbering system. Instead of calling the next upgrade Windows 4.0, as many had anticipated, it would instead number new versions of Windows with respect to the year of release. So, for instance, **Windows 95** refers to the 1995 version of Windows.

Windows 95 employs a similar but easier to learn and use GUI than its predecessor, Windows 3.x (see Figure MC 3-19). It also provides *preemptive multitasking* (or "true" multitasking), meaning there are no delays, say, when

FIGURE MC 3-18 **Sharing data among applications.** Programs such as Microsoft Windows enable users to work on two or more programs or tasks concurrently. Here, a mouse is being used to drag and drop a chart from a spreadsheet application into a word-processed document.

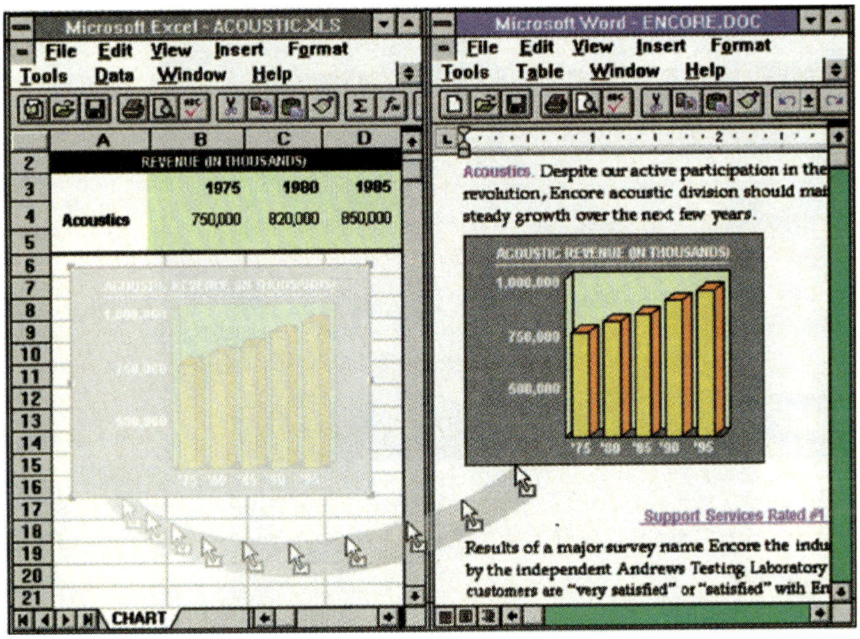

you are trying to type in one document while another is printing out. Windows 3.x, by contrast, provides only *cooperative multitasking,* in which one task (such as typing) may have to yield to another task (such as printing) when two tasks are currently active. Additionally, Windows 95 permits longer filenames than DOS and makes it far easier to configure peripheral hardware (this latter feature is called *plug-and-play* support).

Windows NT **Windows NT** (for New Technology), or NT for short, is a multitasking operating system developed by Microsoft Corporation for high-end, 32-bit computer systems. It is primarily targeted to corporate networking applications. Unlike Microsoft Windows 3.x, NT is a full operating system rather than a mere graphical shell.

One of NT's principal features is its ability to be run on a variety of computer systems, not just those using conventional Intel chips. Thus, applications written for Windows NT can be developed on a Pentium-based desktop PC and run on an engineering workstation that uses another, radically different type of computing chip.

NT is available in two versions. A *client* edition is available for desktop workstations, whereas a *server* version is targeted to computers that control communications networks.

Macintosh System Software **Macintosh System Software** is the proprietary, graphically oriented operating system that comes with the Apple Macintosh line of computers. The Apple Macintosh, introduced in 1984, has set the standard for GUIs. Today, many operating systems are trying to copy what the Mac originally started.

FIGURE MC 3-19 **Windows 95.** Windows 95 combines MS-DOS and Windows 3.x functionality into a single program and adds several new features as well, including an improved user interface, faster and more responsive applications processing, and plug-and-play support.

Macintosh System Software has grown with the times, keeping pace with the increases in power made available with each new Motorola and PowerPC CPU chip and each new Macintosh computer system. The latest version of Macintosh System Software, Version 7, can be used on virtually all recent Macintoshes that have at least two megabytes of RAM.

Macintosh System Software is found, almost exclusively, on computers in the Apple Macintosh line. An example of the GUI provided with the Macintosh is shown in Figure MC 3-20. Macintosh owners also frequently use UNIX, a flexible operating system that is not tied to any particular brand of computer.

UNIX UNIX was originally developed more than two decades ago at Bell Laboratories as a highly portable operating system for small computers. Many properties make UNIX a compelling choice for the new breed of 32-bit microcomputers arriving in the marketplace.

First, UNIX already has a long, successful track record as a multiuser, multitasking operating system. During the 20 years it has been available, it has attracted a large, loyal following.

Second, UNIX is flexibly built, so it can be used on a wide variety of computers. Unlike other operating systems—such as DOS and OS/2, which are based on Intel chips, or Macintosh System Software, which is based on PowerPC chips—UNIX is not built around a single family of processors. Computers from micros to mainframes can run UNIX, and a variety of devices from

FIGURE MC 3-20 **Macintosh system software.** Macintosh System Software sported the first commercially successful graphical interface for operating systems, and it is still one of the most popular. Annotated in the figure are some of the principal elements of the Macintosh electronic desktop. Although the names and appearance of many of the features differ from those in the Windows desktop, the types of tasks that you can perform are virtually identical to those in Windows.

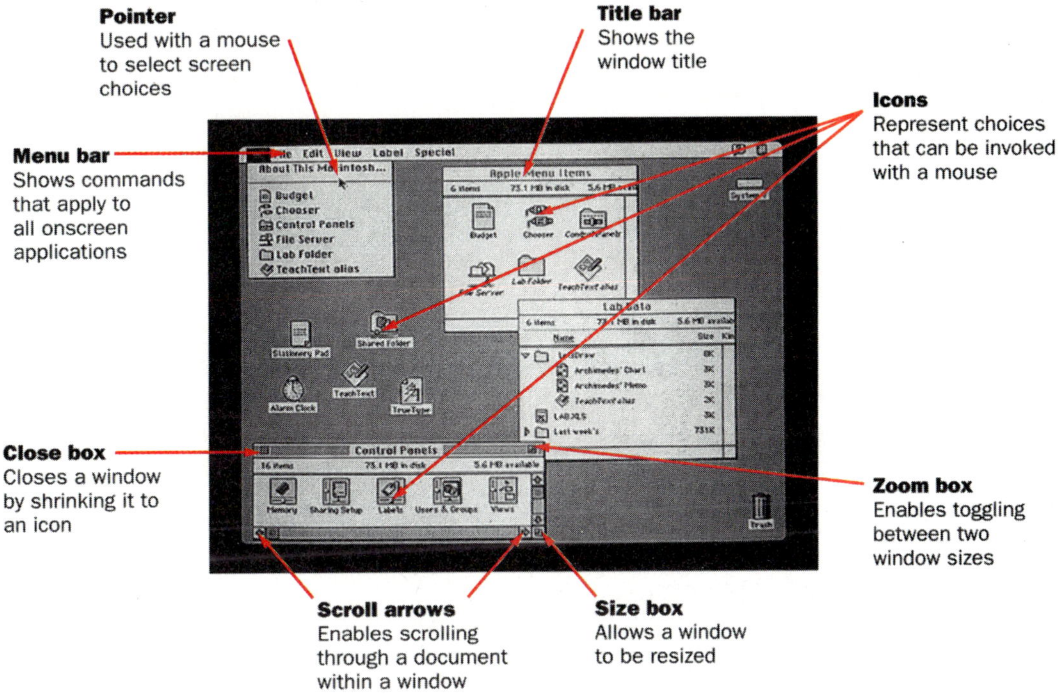

different manufacturers can easily run under UNIX while hooked into the same network.

But UNIX also has certain disadvantages. Many people complain that it is not very easy to use. Also, its flexibility makes UNIX slower than operating systems tailored around a particular microprocessor when UNIX is used in a network dominated by that particular microprocessor. Still another disadvantage of UNIX is that there are several "brands" of it now available, and many of them are incompatible with each other.

OS/2 OS/2 is a multiuser, multitasking operating system originally developed by IBM for the high end of the PS/2 line of computers and similar devices. It provides a graphical, display-screen interface (called Presentation Manager) similar to the one that accompanies Microsoft Windows. In fact, OS/2 can even run Microsoft Windows.

The OS/2 operating system makes possible the addressing of 16 megabytes (MB) of RAM. It can be operated in one of two modes. In the *real (compatibility) mode,* OS/2 is capable of running programs that were created to run under 16-bit DOS. Because DOS can address only 640 kilobytes of RAM, so, too, can the real mode address only this amount of space. In the *protected mode,* by contrast, OS/2 is designed to run applications that are created specifically for OS/2 and to take advantage of its capability to address 16 megabytes of RAM and to preemptively multitask. When OS/2 runs in the protected mode, a memory protection feature ensures that multiple tasks will not collide with each other in RAM—say, one program writing over the data created by another. OS/2 cannot run DOS programs in the protected mode.

NetWare **NetWare**—developed by Novell, Inc., during the mid-1980s—is today the most widely used operating system on microcomputer-based networks. Most users of NetWare will interact with it when they are logging in to the network, or when they are dealing with a printer or hard disk that is not part of their immediate workstation environment. NetWare provides a shell over the user's chosen operating system, thereby enabling the retrieving or saving of files on a shared hard disk and the printing of files on a shared printer.

Here is how a typical NetWare session works on a network of IBM microcomputers or similar machines. When you turn on a workstation that is hooked into the network, the network will send a prompt to your display. Often, the prompt is

```
F>
```

At this point, you can decide to work on or off the network.

If you wish to work on the network, a login message must next be typed. For instance, if the network recognizes you as KJOHNSON, you might have to type at the system prompt

```
LOGIN KJOHNSON
```

At this point, you have *access rights* to the network, and you are free to do any network operation within the access rights that have been assigned to you. Access rights cover such matters as which files you are allowed to retrieve or modify. When you are working at the F prompt, which typically corresponds to the shared hard disk on the network, you treat this disk as if it were just a local disk drive—but one, of course, with the full facilities of the network available to it.

Language Translators

As mentioned in Chapter 1, computers can execute programs only after the programs have been translated into machine language. There are two reasons why people do not generally write programs in this language. First, machine-language instructions consist of complex-looking strings of 0s and 1s, for example,

```
01011000011100000000000100000010
```

Few people enjoy or are successful at writing long programs consisting of statements like this. Second, machine-language instructions must be written at the most detailed level of exposition. This involves a technical computer knowledge that is well beyond the grasp of most users.

A **language translator** is a systems program that converts an applications program written in a programming language into machine language. The two most common types of language translators are compilers and interpreters.

Compilers A **compiler** translates a program entirely into machine language before the program is executed. Every compiler-oriented language requires its own special compiler. Thus, a COBOL program needs a COBOL compiler; it cannot run on a BASIC compiler.

The program that you write in a programming language and enter into the computer is called a *source module.* The machine-language program that the compiler then produces is called an *object module.* Object modules can be saved, so the program does not have to be recompiled each time it is run.

Interpreters An **interpreter,** unlike a compiler, does not create an object module. Interpreters read, translate, and execute source programs one line at a time. The translation into machine language is performed while the program is running.

Interpreters have advantages and disadvantages relative to compilers. Two major advantages are that interpreters are easier to use and they enable errors to be more quickly discovered in programs. The major disadvantage of interpreters is that they are less efficient than compilers and, consequently, programs run more slowly on them. Because interpreters translate each program statement into machine language just prior to executing it, they can take up a lot of time—especially when the same statements are executed thousands of times during the course of program execution and must be reinterpreted every time they are encountered.

Utility Programs

Some tasks are performed so often in the course of processing that it would be extremely inefficient if every user had to code them into programs over and over again. Sorting records, formatting disks and tapes, and copying programs from one medium to another are examples of such tasks. To save users and programmers from wasting time writing such routines, computer systems normally have available a library of **utility programs** to perform these types of operations. Typically, utility programs reside in secondary storage and are summoned from the operating system when needed.

Utility programs are packaged in a variety of ways. Sometimes they are bundled into an operating system. For instance, utility programs for formatting disks, copying the contents of disks, and checking the allocation of disk space are part of MS-DOS. In other cases, utility routines are built into applications programs. For instance, many productivity software packages that run under DOS have their own built-in sort routines. In still other cases, utilities are independent programs that can be acquired from third-party vendors and made to run with a given operating system or productivity software package. For instance, "disk utilities" are available that go well beyond the disk-handling capabilities of DOS, doing such things as reorganizing data on disk.

Figure MC 3-21 lists several important types of utility programs and the purposes they serve.

PRODUCTIVITY SOFTWARE

Productivity software refers to the class of applications software designed to make end users better at performing their jobs. In this section, we look at several different types of productivity software, to give you a feel for the variety of products currently in the market. Of the types of software that are discussed, word processors, spreadsheets, and database management systems are the most widely used.

Word Processors

One of the most widespread applications of computers today is word processing. **Word processing** refers to the use of computer technology to create, manipulate, and print text materials such as letters, legal contracts, or manuscripts—that is, the sort of material that traditionally has been prepared with typewriters. Fortunately, word processing is among the easiest to learn of all

FIGURE MC 3-21 Types of utility programs. Utility programs, which provide a variety of system support functions, supplement the activities of the operating system.

Utility	Description
Backup utilities	Give users the ability to back up the contents of a hard disk quickly
Device drivers	Used to install software that allows specific brands or types of hardware to be accessed by the computer system
Disk utilities	Used to perform tasks such as recovering damaged or erased files, compressing data, and allocating disk space to optimize disk performance
Display utilities	Used to improve the display environment, such as turning the display screen off after so many minutes or outputting characters in a compressed mode
Performance monitors	Enable users to discover how efficiently the computer system is working
Print utilities	Used to provide existing software with enhanced printing capabilities, such as printing sideways on paper, printing with better resolution, or adding new typefaces
Sort utilities	Used to arrange records
Vaccine programs	Used to protect the system from computer virus attacks

computer applications. It is such a time-saver that most people who learn to do it let their typewriters gather dust.

For example, a major problem with conventional typewriting is that you type directly onto paper. Mistakes are hard to correct, you can produce only one "original" copy of each document, and you must retype any previously typewritten materials that have to be inserted into documents. With a word processor, on the other hand, keystrokes are saved electronically—making it easy to correct mistakes, create new documents by "cutting and pasting" them together from previously stored documents, and print multiple "original" copies of documents. In addition, many other types of text editing and print formatting activities are possible with a word processor—you can search for and replace text strings, check spelling and locate synonyms with automatic assistance, merge address files with form letters so that a stack of letters can be printed automatically, and so on (see Figure MC 3-22).

Among today's best-selling general-purpose word-processing packages are WordPerfect, Microsoft Word, and Ami Pro. Word and WordPerfect are the undisputed leaders in the word-processing marketplace today, with close to a combined 75 percent market share. You might pay as little as $100 for a software package or as much as several hundred dollars, depending on the size of the computer you are using and the level of sophistication you require from the software.

Spreadsheets

An electronic **spreadsheet package** is a software product that produces computerized counterparts to the ruled, ledger-style worksheets with which accountants frequently work (see Figure MC 3-23). Electronic spreadsheets first came to public notice in the late 1970s when a Harvard Business School student named Dan Bricklin and a programmer friend produced a microcomputer package called VisiCalc ("the VISIble CALCulator"). Bricklin conceived of the idea watching his accounting professor erase large chunks of blackboard every time a single number changed in an interdependent series of calculations. Awed by the amount of repetitive labor involved, Bricklin quickly saw the potential of computerized worksheets.

FIGURE MC 3-22 **Text editing and print formatting.** Text-editing operations allow you to "cut and paste" text materials in electronic memory. Print-formatting operations let you output those materials in a visually appealing way.

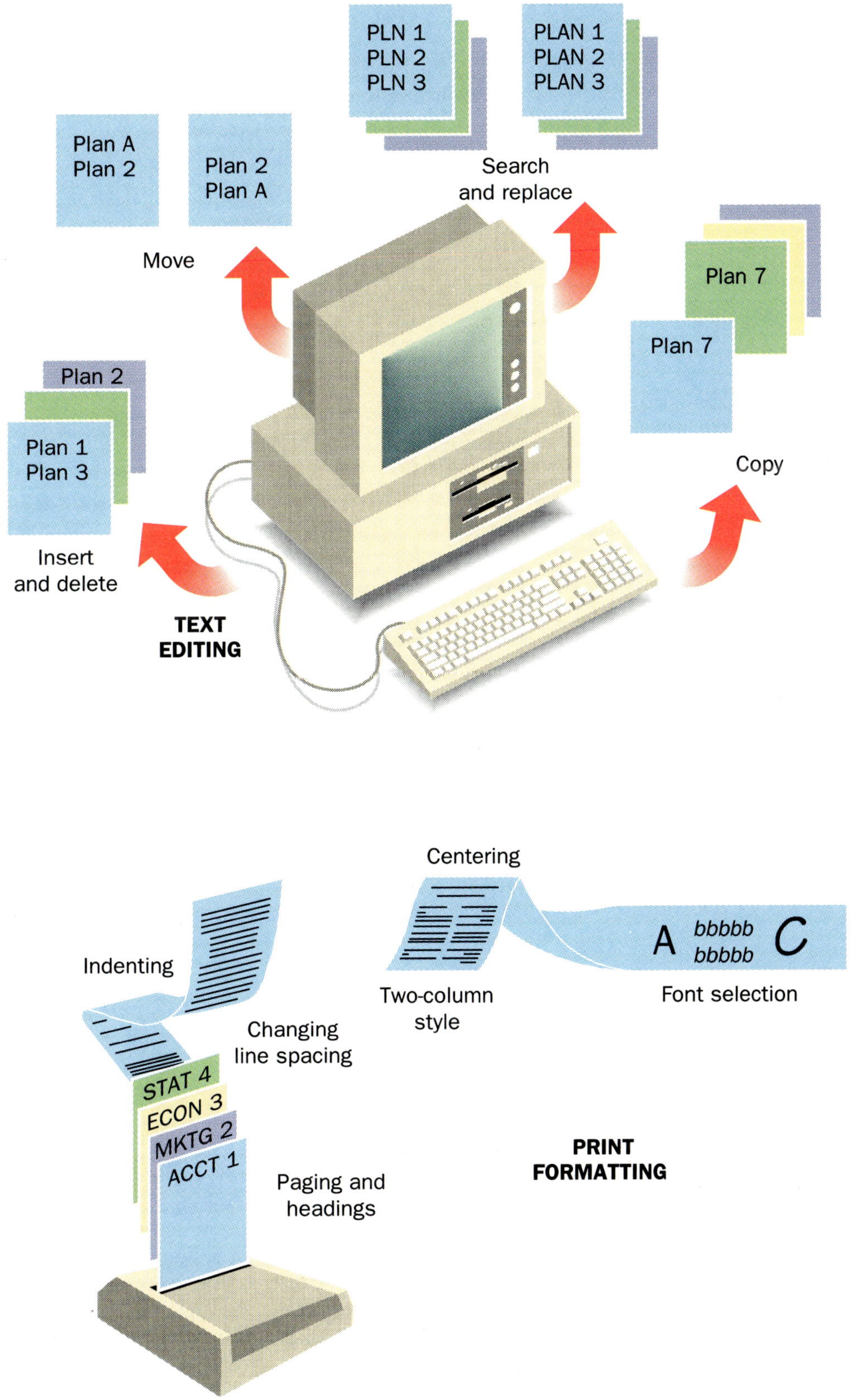

FIGURE MC 3-23 Manually prepared and electronic worksheets. An electronic spreadsheet package produces computerized counterparts to the ruled, ledger-style worksheets with which accountants frequently work.

(a) Manually prepared worksheet

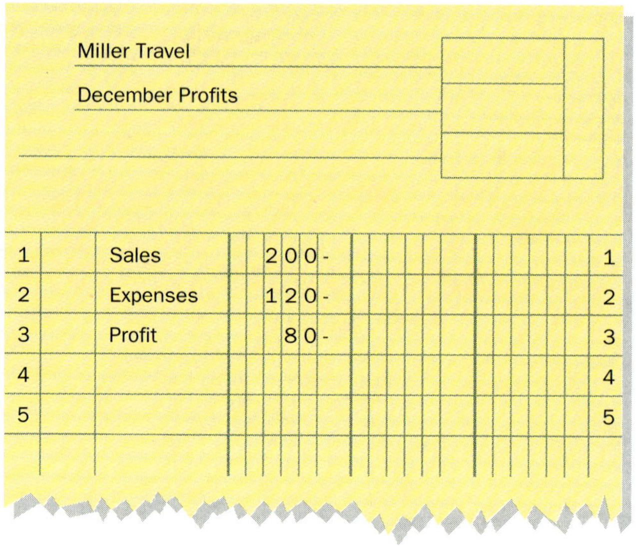

(b) Worksheet prepared by electronic spreadsheet package

	A	B	C	D	E
1	Sales	200			
2	Expenses	120			
3	Profit	80			
4					
5					
6					

Today, although VisiCalc is gone from the scene, spreadsheet software for all sizes of computers abounds in the marketplace. Among the leading spreadsheet packages currently available for microcomputers are 1-2-3, Excel, Quattro, and SuperCalc, with 1-2-3 and Excel leading in sales. Technically speaking, most of these products are *integrated software packages* in that they supplement spreadsheeting capabilities with one or more other functions, including database processing, presentation graphics, and, most recently, mapping (see the chapter User Tip box). The topic of integrated software packages will be more fully addressed later in the chapter.

Just as word processors were a leap forward over conventional typewriters, spreadsheets were a major advancement over pocket calculators. Whereas pocket calculators allow the user to make a single calculation at a time, the result of which is displayed in a tiny screen area, spreadsheets allow the user to make a large set of interrelated calculations at a time, with several results

USER TIP

Mapping Software

For hundreds of years, when new information had to be recorded on a map, it was drawn on the map's surface. Transparency overlays, introduced later, allowed different types of data to be added to a map. Several overlays were often used jointly, but use of too many could make the maps confusing.

Then, in the late 1980s, computerized *mapping software* products—sometimes called *geographic information systems*—were created. Stored in the mapping software's database are the maps and the data to be graphed on them. Virtually any data that you can graph—animal and foliage populations, land-use statistics, traffic patterns, mineral use, and pollution—can be stored in the database and reflected in the graph. Arby's is one of dozens of companies using mapping software to evaluate franchises and to select new sites. Today, mapping systems are merging with spreadsheets, either as a built-in part of a package or as an optional, add-on routine.

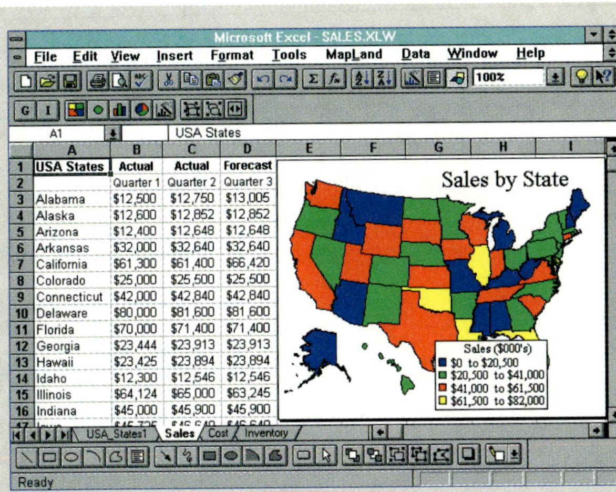

Mapping software. With spreadsheet software, you, too, may be able to create maps.

showing simultaneously on a large screen area. In addition, spreadsheets are almost as easy to use as pocket calculators.

Database Management Systems

A **database management system (DBMS)** is a software system that integrates data in storage and provides easy access to them. The data themselves are placed on disk in a database, which is simply an integrated collection of related files.

Microcomputer DBMSs are predominantly *relational.* Relational DMBSs are relatively simple to learn and use as compared with DBMSs on large computer systems. Many relational databases come with only a single proprietary language that has commands to set up, use, and modify database data, as well as to develop database applications.

Data in relational databases are organized into *tables,* such as those in Figure MC 3-24. Each table has a name, such as EMPLOYEE and OFFICE in the example. These tables are similar in concept to *files.* Moreover, the rows of the tables are like *records* and the columns are like *fields.* Many of the tables have one or more columns in common with other tables. It is through these columns that the data in the tables are *related.* In our example, the EMPLOYEE and OFFICE tables are related through the "city" column in each (called OFFICE-LOCATION in one and LOCATION in the other).

If, say, we wanted to retrieve the names of all employees in the San Diego office, we could use a command such as

```
SELECT NAME
      FROM EMPLOYEE
WHERE OFFICE-LOCATION = 'SAN DIEGO'
```

The system would access the EMPLOYEE table to select the names of all employees who worked in San Diego. This command request, as you can see, involves only one table.

FIGURE MC 3-24 **A relational database with two tables.** In relational database management systems, data exist in tables. Two or more tables can be combined, or *related*, through their common fields. Through the use of simple database commands, the user can extract and output information from single or combined tables.

EMPLOYEE		
NAME	OFFICE - LOCATION	DEPARTMENT
Doney	Phoenix	Acctg.
Black	Denver	Sales
James	Cleveland	Sales
Giles	San Diego	Acctg.
Smith	Miami	Acctg.
Fink	San Diego	Sales
. . .	. . .	. . .

OFFICE	
LOCATION	MANAGER
San Diego	Hurt
Cleveland	Holmes
Miami	Jonas
Phoenix	Alexis
. . .	. . .

The power of relational database systems, however, rests in their ability to link the data in more than one table. Suppose, for example, we wanted to know which employees worked under the office manager named Jonas. We would enter another command to do this. The database system would find the name Jonas in the OFFICE table, determine that Jonas managed the office in Miami, and then use the EMPLOYEE table to find all employees who worked in Miami. In other words, the system would "cut and paste" these tables together to retrieve the needed information.

This principle, applied on a large scale to databases with many tables and many interrelations, provides users with considerable freedom in the retrieval of information. Commands similar to the ones described here make it possible to modify, insert, or delete entries or tables in the database, as well as to retrieve information. In addition, when several such commands are put together and saved, they form a program. Other commands packaged into microcomputer-based DBMSs allow users to loop, compare, and perform arithmetic on data fields.

Some of the more widely used microcomputer-based database management packages are dBASE, Paradox, Foxbase and Foxpro, Oracle, Access, Superbase, and Approach. DBMS-like programs that let you collect information from individual files but do not automatically integrate files for you are called *file managers.* File managers, although not as powerful as DBMSs, are generally less expensive and easier to learn.

Other Productivity Software Packages

Whereas word processors, spreadsheets, and DBMSs are the most common types of productivity software packages used on microcomputer systems, a wide variety of other types of packages exist.

Desktop Publishing Packages **Desktop publishing** refers to microcomputer-based publishing systems that fit on a desktop. These systems let you combine on a page such elements as text (in a variety of typefaces), art, and photos, thus creating attractive documents that look like they came off a printer's press. As you can see from studying the image in Figure MC 3-25, the basic difference between word processing and desktop publishing is principally one of document "look." Whereas word processing deals mainly with straight, nontypeset text—and maybe a few simple typefaces for emphasis—desktop publishing involves much more sophisticated types of typesetting and imagesetting. Today's trend in desktop publishing packages is to supply users with a complete suite of publishing tools, including page-makeup, illustration, and photo-manipulation capabilities.

Presentation Graphics Packages A **presentation graphics package** is a software product that is capable of creating, arranging, or displaying

FIGURE MC 3-25 **Desktop publishing.** Desktop publishing lets you combine on a page such elements as text, art, and photos in highly sophisticated ways, thus creating documents that look professionally prepared.

FIGURE MC 3-26 **Presentation graphics.** Presentation graphics software makes it easy for users to prepare graphs from business data.

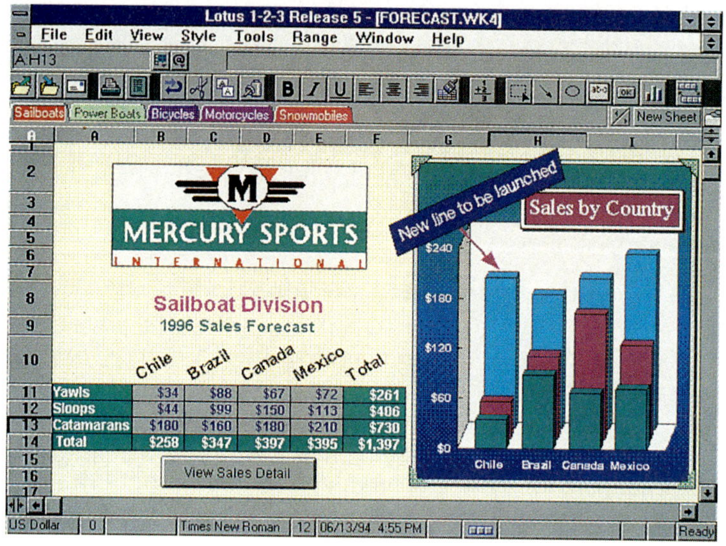

outputs such as business graphs and charts. A software package that is targeted to the creation of images such as the one shown in Figure MC 3-26 is, in whole or in part, a presentation graphics package. So, too, are the software products used to help people arrange such outputs in proper sequence, so they may later be displayed in a slide show on a monitor or room screen. A wide variety of presentation graphics packages exist in the marketplace. Most of them are either sold as independent products or—like the one in the figure—bundled (integrated) with spreadsheet software.

Suite and Integrated Software For users who wish to tie together several applications, either a software suite or an integrated software package may be the solution (see Figure MC 3-27).

- **SOFTWARE SUITES** *Software suites*—such as Microsoft Office, Lotus SmartSuite, and Borland Office—provide a set of compatible, full-featured software products at a reduced price. For instance, Lotus SmartSuite assembles the full-featured versions of Ami Pro, 1-2-3, Freelance Graphics, Organizer, and cc:Mail at a price lower than it would cost to buy all of the packages individually. Thus, you have all the desktop tools you need to do word processing, spreadsheeting, data management, graphics, communications, and organizing at your complete disposal.

  Software suites have become the hottest new way to package software. Microsoft—the leader in suite sales—claims it sells more copies of its popular word processor, Word, in suite form than it does as individual units.

  A trend in suites is the development of applications interfaces, so users need know only a single set of commands to operate any package in the suite. Figure MC 3-18, covered earlier in the chapter, illustrates how easy it is to select any object (like a graph or chart) from one application in the suite and bring it into another.

- **INTEGRATED SOFTWARE PACKAGES** *Integrated software packages* compress the functions you would get in a software suite into a single package.

FIGURE MC 3-27 **Software suites and integrated software.** Software suites and integrated software packages give you a lot of functionality at a reduced price. (a) Lotus SmartSuite software suite. (b) Microsoft Works integrated software package.

(a)

(b)

So, for instance, instead of getting a full-featured word processor or spreadsheet, you are getting slightly "watered down" versions with fewer features available. Not that this is a huge limitation. Integrated packages are far cheaper than suites, and most people who buy full-featured software wind up using only a tiny percentage of the features, anyway. Today, one of the most popular integrated software packages is Microsoft Works, which bundles word processing, spreadsheeting, data management, graphics, and communications.

Accounting Packages Virtually every business must support a number of routine operations, most of which involve some form of tedious recordkeeping. Because these operations—such as paying employees, recording customer purchases and payments, and recording vendor receipts and payments—involve the processing of business transactions, they are called *transaction processing* systems. **Accounting packages** are specialized integrated software products that pull together a number of related transaction processing functions. In many cases, the packages also enable management to get up-to-the-minute reporting on transaction volume during a period as well as key decision-making information about inventories, open orders, and overdue payments or overdue rental merchandise.

Desk Accessories **Desk accessories,** or *desktop organizers,* are software packages that provide the electronic equivalent of items commonly found on an office desktop. Desk accessory software varies among vendors, but many offer features such as an appointment calendar, clock, alarm, notepad, calculator, Rolodex-type file, and phone directory (see Figure MC 3-28). Typically,

FIGURE MC 3-28 **Desk accessory.** Many desk accessory packages incorporate a calendar, a to-do list, a planner, an address book, an electronic mail capability, and a variety of other useful features.

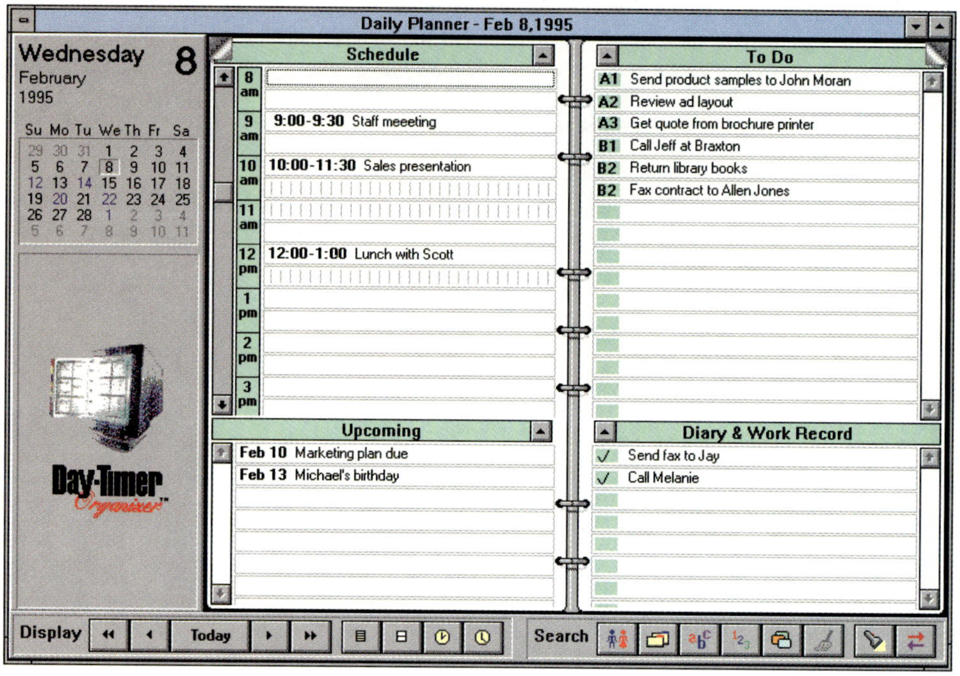

each feature is activated through a screen window that appears when a specific icon is selected. Increasingly, desk accessory features are being built into operating-system software.

Project Managers A **project manager** (see Figure MC 3-29) is a software product that helps people plan and schedule projects—say, bringing a new product to the marketplace or installing a new computer system and getting it to work. Because computers can "crunch" numbers much more quickly and accurately than can people working by hand, the projects solved by computer can be large and complex. Many microcomputer-based project managers can coordinate more than 50,000 interdependent project activities. With a project manager, the user can quickly try out several dozen project alternatives in a relatively short period of time, to see which one works best.

CAD Software Using **computer-aided design (CAD) software,** people can dramatically reduce the time it takes to design products, as well as improve the way products are presented to consumers. Using the computer, designers can electronically modify design alternatives onscreen until they achieve the desired results. CAD is especially helpful in designing products such as automobiles, aircraft, ships, structures (see Figure MC 3-30), electrical circuits and computer chips, and even shoes and clothes. Although not long ago CAD was confined to large computer systems, it now represents a major applications area within the microcomputing world.

Vertical-Market Software Applications software products such as word processors, spreadsheets, and DBMSs are broadly targeted to a general class

FIGURE MC 3-29 **Project management.** Large projects are often managed with the assistance of a software product called a *project manager.* Many project managers, like the one featured here, provide a project timetable and graphs showing how pieces of the project fit together.

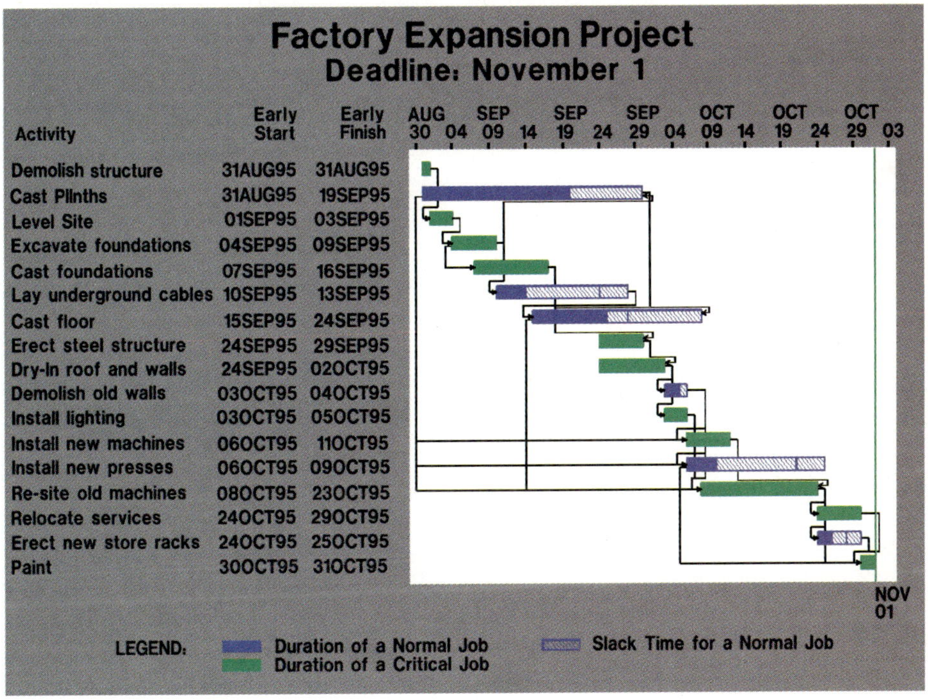

FIGURE MC 3-30 **Computer-aided design.** Architects modeling with computers often employ light sources and reflective algorithms to produce renderings of near-photographic quality. Use of such tools often makes it easier to sell design concepts to clients.

of users. Spreadsheets, for instance, are used by accountants, financial analysts, salespeople, teachers, and people in many other professions. Furthermore, the users of spreadsheets are drawn from a number of industries—banking, the automotive industry, chemicals and pharmaceuticals, academia, and so on. **Vertical-market software,** on the other hand, refers to software targeted to a narrow group of users—that is, a "niche market." An example is medical office software. Such packages consist of customized accounting systems that are targeted to the particular type of record management faced by doctors and dentists.

Statistical Packages Statistics involves the interpretation of data. It is a science that deals with such concepts as averages, trends, predictions, and differences between groups. For instance, through the use of statistics, a researcher can make statements about whether a shift in consumer-preference data is significant enough to warrant management attention; how likely it is that sales next year will be between 100,000 and 120,000 units based on production, price, and spending estimates; or how much consumers are expected to spend next year on automobiles or computers. **Statistical packages** are programs that allow researchers in industry, government, academic institutions, and special groups to study such phenomena and make descriptive or predictive statements.

Artificial Intelligence and Expert Systems The ability of computer systems to perform in ways that would be considered intelligent if observed in humans is commonly referred to as *artificial intelligence (AI).* The field of AI evolved from attempts to write programs that would enable computers to rival skilled humans at games such as chess and checkers, to prove difficult mathematical theorems, and so forth.

Expert systems—programs that incorporate the knowledge base and reasoning patterns of human experts—are an outgrowth of the chess-playing programs of the 1950s and 1960s. Today expert systems are successfully used in many fields. In medicine, for instance, an expert system might be used to incorporate the thinking patterns of some of the world's leading physicians. For example, a system might be given a configuration of symptoms exhibited by a patient. If these symptoms might lead to the diagnosis of a disease the program knows something about, the program might ask the attending physician for information about specific details. Ultimately, through questioning and checking the patient's condition against a large database of successfully diagnosed cases, the program might quickly draw conclusions that the attending physician might have reached much more slowly, if at all. Expert systems also have enormous potential in business.

Summary

- The manner in which a program package makes its resources available to users is known as its user interface. Three common types of user interfaces are command syntax, shortcut keystrokes, and graphical user interfaces (GUIs).
- GUIs employ a number of easy-to-use tools, including an electronic desktop arranged with icons and windows, a system of menus and submenus, scroll bars, dialog boxes, and a context-sensitive online help feature.
- Systems software consists of support programs that coordinate the various parts of the computer system to make it run rapidly and efficiently.
- There are three principal types of systems software: operating systems, language translators, and utility programs. The operating system serves as the

gateway to programs, their data, and other system resources. Language translators translate programs into machine language. Utility programs perform system support tasks for the operating system.

- Some of today's most widely used operating systems include MS-DOS and PC-DOS, Windows 95, Windows NT, Macintosh System Software, UNIX, OS/2, and NetWare. Microsoft Windows 3.1, a graphically oriented operating environment for DOS users, is another widely used product.
- Productivity software refers to the class of applications software designed to make end users better at performing their jobs.
- Three of the most important types of productivity software are word processors, spreadsheets, and database management systems (DBMSs). Other types of productivity software that are also popular include desktop publishing packages, presentation graphics software, integrated software packages, software suites, accounting packages, desk accessories, project managers, computer-aided design (CAD) software, vertical-market software, statistical packages, and expert systems.

Key Terms

Shown in parentheses are the page numbers on which key terms are boldfaced.

Accounting package (MC 91)
Compiler (MC 82)
Computer-aided design (CAD) software (MC 92)
Context sensitive (MC 69)
Database management system (DBMS) (MC 87)
Desk accessory (MC 91)
Desktop publishing (MC 89)
Dialog box (MC 72)
Expert system (MC 94)
Graphical user interface (GUI) (MC 64)
Icon (MC 67)
Interpreter (MC 83)
Language translator (MC 72)
Macintosh system software (MC 79)
Menu (MC 65)
Menu bar (MC 65)
MS-DOS (MC 77)
Multitasking (MC 77)
NetWare (MC 82)
Operating system (MC 74)
OS/2 (MC 81)
PC-DOS (MC 77)
Presentation graphics package (MC 89)
Productivity software (MC 83)
Project manager (MC 92)
Prompt (MC 62)
Pull-down menu (MC 66)
Scroll bar (MC 70)
Shortcut keystroke (MC 63)
Spreadsheet package (MC 84)
Statistical package (MC 94)
Syntax (MC 62)
Systems software (MC 74)
UNIX (MC 80)
User interface (MC 62)
Utility program (MC 83)
Vertical-market software (MC 94)
Window (MC 69)
Windows 3.x (MC 77)
Windows 95 (MC 78)
Windows NT (MC 79)
Word processing (MC 83)

Quiz

True/False

___ 1. Shortcut keystrokes are used to issue commands.

___ 2. The scroll bar's scroll box enables scrolling to take place more rapidly.

___ 3. Multitasking is a feature that enables an operating system temporarily to become a language translator.

___ 4. The latest release of UNIX is called OS/2

___ 5. Windows 95 and Windows NT are two different names for the same software product.

___ 6. Macintosh System Software is an operating system that works primarily through users remembering a command syntax.

___ 7. Windows 3.1 is a shell program that fits over the MS-DOS operating system, thereby enhancing it with a graphical user interface.

___ 8. Lotus Development's 1-2-3 is one of today's leading word processors.

___ 9. CAD is an acronym for computer-age deskwork.

___ 10. Expert systems, although useful in the medical field, are not expected to play a major role in business.

Multiple Choice

___ 11. Radio buttons
   a. allow only one choice in a panel to be active at a time.
   b. allow several choices in a panel to be active at a time.
   c. allow no choices in a panel to be active at a time.
   d. are used to activate a sound card and speakers on the computer system.
   e. are also known as check boxes.

___ 12. Windows that are overlapped are
   a. cascaded.
   b. tiled.
   c. maximized.
   d. minimized.
   e. smarticons.

___ 13. All of the following are operating systems except
   a. UNIX.
   b. OS/2.
   c. WordPerfect.
   d. Windows 95.
   e. MS-DOS.

___ 14. Both PC-DOS and MS-DOS were originally developed by
   a. IBM Corporation.
   b. Lotus Development Corporation.
   c. Abbott Laboratories.
   d. Microsoft Corporation.
   e. Robotic Engineering, Inc.

____ 15. An example of a software product that is a graphical shell operating environment as opposed to a full operating system is
a. MS-DOS.
b. Windows NT.
c. Windows 3.1.
d. UNIX.
e. OS/2.

____ 16. All of the following are productivity software packages except
a. WordPerfect.
b. Lotus 1-2-3.
c. dBASE.
d. UNIX.
e. Excel.

____ 17. Such software as vaccine programs, device drivers, and programs that recover lost disk files are examples of
a. operating systems.
b. language translators.
c. utility programs.
d. productivity software.
e. operating environments.

____ 18. VisiCalc is an example of an early
a. word processor.
b. DBMS.
c. desktop publishing system.
d. CAD system.
e. electronic spreadsheet package.

____ 19. A medical office system is an example of a
a. word processor.
b. project manager.
c. vertical-market software package.
d. CAD system.
e. spreadsheet package.

____ 20. The ability of computer systems to perform in ways that would be considered intelligent if observed in humans is commonly referred to as
a. artificial intelligence.
b. robotics.
c. martinizing.
d. windowing.
e. virtual reality.

Matching

Select the term that best matches each phrase:

a. OS/2	g. 1-2-3
b. Paradox	h. NetWare
c. DOS	i. Windows NT
d. PageMaker	j. VisiCalc
e. WordPerfect	k. Works
f. GUI	l. UNIX

____ 21. The first spreadsheet package

____ 22. The multiuser, multitasking operating system developed at Bell Laboratories

____ 23. Refers to a graphical interface presented to the software user

____ 24. A word-processing package

____ 25. The most widely used operating system of all time

____ 26. A contemporary spreadsheet package

____ 27. A DBMS

____ 28. An integrated software package

____ 29. An operating system targeted specifically to microcomputer-based networks

____ 30. An IBM operating system with real and protected modes

Answers

True/False: 1. T; 2. T; 3. F; 4. F; 5. F; 6. F; 7. T; 8. F; 9. F; 10. F

Multiple Choice: 11. a; 12. a; 13. c; 14. d; 15. c; 16. d; 17. c; 18. e; 19. c; 20. a

Matching: 21. j; 22. l; 23. f; 24. e; 25. c; 26. g; 27. b; 28. k; 29. h; 30. a

Exercises

1. For the latest releases of three of the following software packages—WordPerfect (for Windows), Lotus 1-2-3 (for Windows), Excel (for the Apple Macintosh line), and Paradox (for Windows)—determine the minimum number of bytes of RAM and hard disk required. (Be sure to identify the release number of the product as part of the exercise.)
2. What are the recommended minimum RAM and hard-disk requirements for running Windows 95 and the latest comparable version of OS/2?
3. By looking through computer journals or through reports at your local computer store or computer center, identify a software package in one of the following areas: presentation graphics, accounting software, desktop publishing software, CAD software. Report to the class about the package, telling its suggested list price, explaining its principal features, and describing the hardware on which it is designed to work. (Microcomputer journals containing information needed for this exercise may be available in your college or town library. Such journals are carried as well by many bookstores and computer stores. You can also get useful information for this exercise by calling or writing directly to vendors; their 800-area-code numbers and addresses often appear in journal advertisements.)
4. By looking through computer journals or through reports at your local computer store or computer center, identify a software package in a specific vertical market. Report to the class about the package, telling its suggested list price, explaining its principal features, and describing the hardware on which it is designed to work. (Microcomputer journals containing the infor-

mation needed for this exercise may be available in your college or town library. Such journals are carried as well by many bookstores and computer stores. You can also get useful information for this exercise by calling or writing directly to vendors; their 800-area-code numbers and addresses often appear in journal advertisements.)

5. Refer to the two tables in the following tiny relational database and answer these questions:
   a. What is the average salary of an employee in the Sales Department?
   b. Which employees does Jonas control?
   c. What is the average salary of employees under Hurt's supervision?
   d. In which of the previous questions was it necessary to relate data in both tables to get an answer? How were the tables related?

Employee Table

Name	Location	Department	Salary
Doney	Phoenix	Accounting	$58,000
Black	Denver	Sales	$71,000
James	Cleveland	Sales	$44,000
Giles	San Diego	Accounting	$62,000
Smith	Miami	Accounting	$73,000
Fink	San Diego	Sales	$54,000
. . .	. . .	. . .	. . .

Office Table

Location	Manager
San Diego	Hurt
Cleveland	Holmes
Miami	Jonas
Phoenix	Alexis
. . .	. . .

APPENDIX Tips for Buying Microcomputer Software

When buying applications software such as word processors, spreadsheets, and database management systems, be sure to get answers to the following questions.

Word Processing

Does the package contain all the features that you want? Make a list of features and check a reference manual, trade book, or product review to see what the package has or lacks. Most of the leading word processors contain the same basic set of features.

Will the package fit on your system? Look closely at the RAM and the hard-disk requirements of the package to see if it fits. Most packages will run comfortably on 8 megabytes of RAM and a hundred megabytes of hard disk.

Will the package run smoothly on your hardware configuration? Keep in mind that printing attractive fonts, proportionally spaced text, and graphics usually requires a laser or ink-jet printer. If the package lets you preview graphics output before printing them, which most packages do, you must have a graphics-oriented monitor. Many word processors produced today require the power of at least an 80486 computer.

Does the package implement word processing features in a way you find compatible with your work style? The best way to answer this question is to try out the system at a store, in school, or at a friend's house. Of course, be sure to check that the package exists in a version that will work on your computer system.

Spreadsheets

Does the package contain all the features that you want, and does it implement them in a way that is comfortable with your work style? Most major spreadsheet packages are remarkably alike. They contain virtually the same types of commands and many of them closely follow the user interface of Lotus Development Corporation's 1-2-3, Microsoft's Excel, and Novell's Quattro Pro. The most important differences among these spreadsheets are support and the "bells-and-whistles" items.

Will the package fit on your system? Consider the RAM and hard-disk requirements of the package. Most spreadsheets will run comfortably on 8 megabytes of RAM and a hundred megabytes of hard disk.

Will the package work on your hardware configuration? Check the graphics requirements of the package. If you are going to be doing a great deal of presentation graphics, you will probably want at least an 80486-based CPU and a laser or an ink-jet printer.

Database Management Systems

Do you have enough capacity? Compared with other types of productivity software, database management systems are very data-intensive. If you need to relate files so that the contents of several files are available simultaneously, you will almost certainly need lots of RAM and a large hard disk. An 80486 computer with 8–16 megabytes of RAM and several hundred megabytes of hard disk is recommended.

Does the package contain all of the features that you want and implement them in a way that you find comfortable with your work style? Both a DBMS package's features and its look and feel can vary tremendously from vendor to vendor. Before buying a package, make a checklist of the features that you need and see how they are implemented in the packages under consideration.

Will the package work on your hardware configuration? Check that the package exists in a version that will work on your system.

How easy is the package to learn and use? Database management is generally harder to master than word processing or spreadsheets. Some packages, in fact, are targeted more toward programmers than toward ordinary users. Make sure that the package you want to buy comes with documentation, demo disks, or learning manuals that you are able to read and understand. If the vendor learning and documentation tools are mediocre, check for the availability of good trade books to help you get started.

How fast is the package? Because database management packages are data intensive, the speed with which they can retrieve information is extremely critical. It will probably be difficult for you to design a benchmark test to test speed before you buy, so to judge the package under consideration, read closely the results of the comparative product tests that are published regularly in computer journals.

What type of file-backup procedures do you plan to use? One of the worst of all computer nightmares is having a large database destroyed when a hard disk malfunctions and there is no backup. When buying a DBMS, you should consider what backup options are available. A backup tape unit or an MO optical disk unit are most convenient for large databases but will add to the cost of having database management in your applications portfolio.

Other Considerations

For users who wish to link several applications, choosing either a software suite or an integrated software package may be the solution. *Software suites*—such as Microsoft Office—provide many more useful features than *integrated software packages*—such as Microsoft Works—but cost more and require more storage. Both types of software products have the advantages of requiring the user to know only a single GUI and seamlessly allowing the user to cut and paste items from one application into another.

MC 4 TELECOMMUNICATIONS CONCEPTS

OUTLINE

LEARNING OBJECTIVES

After completing this chapter, you will be able to:

1. Describe several uses of telecommunications technology.
2. Describe how the Internet works and identify some of the important applications along the information superhighway.
3. Name various types of telecommunications media and explain how messages can be sent over them.
4. Name some of the types of communications services and network facilities that organizations may acquire.
5. Explain the conventions used by devices to communicate with each other.
6. Identify some of the strategies used to manage networks.

OVERVIEW

Telecommunications refers to communications over a distance—over phone lines, via privately owned cable, or by satellite, for example. Today, telecommunications technologies are integrated in a variety of ways into many organizations' routine operations. Through telecommunications, for example, a marketing manager at a personal computing workstation can instantly receive information on inventories from a warehouse at another location and then transmit that information to a division office across the country or even across the globe. Later, the manager can use that same workstation to dial up a computer owned by a supplier 1,000 miles away to get a list of prices. The manager may even be able to work at home some days by using another personal computer workstation to do the same types of tasks performed in the office.

Telecommunications has become increasingly critical to many organizations in recent years because of the increased pace at which business is done, the globalization of economies, the distribution of data in electronic form to ever more points, and the new, flexible lifestyles made possible by computers and related technologies. The popularity of the Internet and the realization of an information superhighway has pushed interest in telecommunications into the public mainstream.

In this chapter, we will look first at several business applications of telecommunications. Then we will turn to how data are sent over distances. We will begin by describing the media that carry data, such as phone lines and microwaves, as well as the types of signals that encode the data. Next, we will discuss the various ways in which people and organizations can get the resources they need to transmit data. Finally, we will examine several issues concerning the management of telecommunications systems traffic.

TELECOMMUNICATIONS APPLICATIONS

Today a wide variety of important business applications involve telecommunications. Here we will briefly discuss several of them.

Distributed Transaction Processing

At one time, transaction processing operations such as accounts receivable and order entry were totally centralized. As communications systems made it possible to *distribute* workloads to multiple sites, many organizations modified their systems accordingly. The airlines' passenger reservation system is one noteworthy example; thousands of agents located across the globe use display terminals or microcomputer workstations to tap into computerized databases located elsewhere that contain flight, hotel, and rental-car information. While a computer in, say, Chicago is processing a Cerritos, California, agent's request for flight information, that same agent may be processing a ticket for another client back in California.

Virtually every large organization today has several types of distributed transaction processing systems in place. For instance, retail stores often collect and process data locally, then transmit these data to a headquarters site for timely analysis. Mail-order firms frequently process orders at one site and then transmit transaction data to a warehouse site to initiate packing and delivery. The applications are virtually endless.

Recently, many companies have gone a step further with their distributed transaction processing systems by creating *interorganizational systems (IOSs),* in which their computers are linked directly to the computers of key customers or suppliers. One type of interorganizational information system used by many companies is *electronic data interchange (EDI)*. EDI enables standard business documents such as purchase orders and invoices to be exchanged directly from one company's computer system to the computer system of another company. By some counts, companies by the tens of thousands are now involved in one way or another with EDI. Many companies also let their key suppliers monitor their inventory data and automatically replenish any goods that need reordering.

Electronic Messaging

A variety of technological means are available for accommodating electronic messages—from short reminders to two-way discussions on issues to complete documents.

Electronic Mailboxes and Voice Mail **Electronic mailboxes** are the computer-age equivalents of traditional mailboxes. They consist of files on hard disk, belonging to specific individuals or accounts, authorized to receive electronic messages. In one common application, a person types a memo and electronically routes it to the electronic mailbox of a friend or business associate (see Figure MC 4-1).

Voice mail, which involves voice data, is a telecommunications technology that takes electronic mailboxes one step further. In a voice-mail system, the sender's spoken messages are digitized and stored in bit form on an answering device at the receiver's location. When the receiver presses a "listen" key, the digitized message is reconverted to voice data.

Bulletin Boards Whereas electronic mailboxes usually consist of several individual files, each accessible by one specific person, an **electronic bulletin board** is a file that is shared by many people. Each person with access

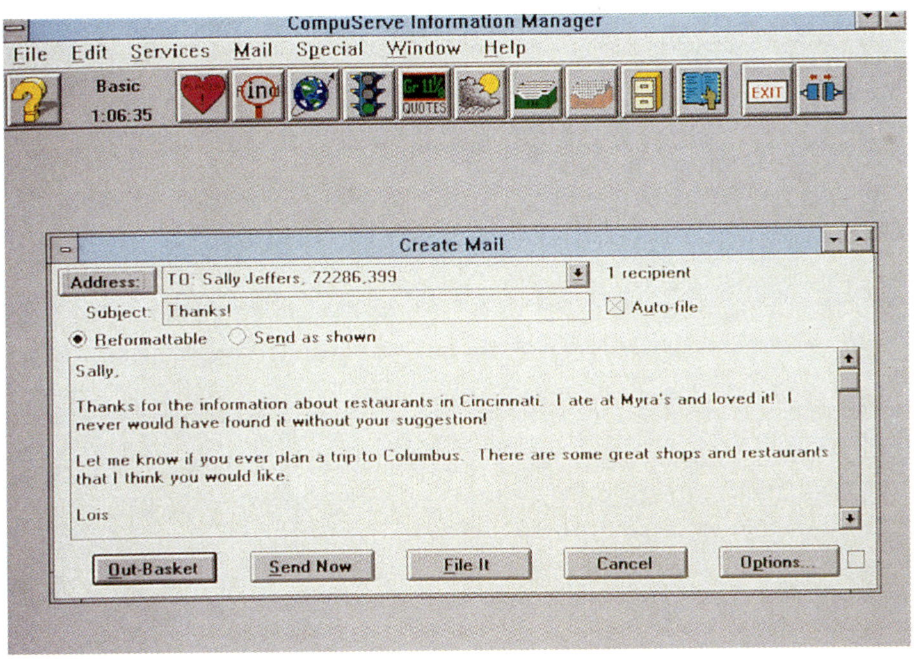

FIGURE MC 4-1 **Electronic mailboxes.** With an electronic mail package, users can create or summon electronic memos and documents and route them to the electronic mailboxes of selected individuals.

to the bulletin board can see the information "posted" on it, add information, and delete information.

Many organizations use in-house bulletin boards to carry out a high-tech phenomenon known as *computer conferencing*. Computer conferencing allows a meeting to take place by computer—even when all the participants are not using their computer workstations at the same time. For instance, Figure MC 4-2 shows conferencing software tracking memos sent as part of a discussion on medical products. Computer conferencing might also be available to a group of executives who are investigating the feasibility of a big merger during a hectic two-week period. At any time, participants can broadcast messages to all other participants and can retrieve all or any part of the proceedings of the "conference."

Both electronic mailboxes and bulletin boards are increasingly being used to perform workgroup computing. In **workgroup computing,** office workers perform their jobs by sharing work over the computer system. Workgroup computing, say many industry watchers, may completely revolutionize the way work is done in organizations.

Facsimile **Facsimile (fax) machines** enable hard-copy images of documents to be sent from one location to another over ordinary phone lines. For example, a secretary in Kansas City may place a short document containing both text and pictures into a fax machine, such as the one shown in Figure MC 4-3a. The fax machine will digitize the page images and transmit them over ordinary phone lines to New York. In New York another fax machine will receive the electronic page images and reproduce them in hard-copy form. All of this may take place in less than a minute.

Facsimile machines have been in use for many years. If you are an old-movie buff, you may remember the 1948 flick *Call Northside 777,* in which a

FIGURE MC 4-2 **Computer conferencing.** Computer conferencing enables meetings to take place even when participants are scattered all over the world and are not using their computers at the same time. Conferencing software, shown here, can organize the contents of an ongoing discussion.

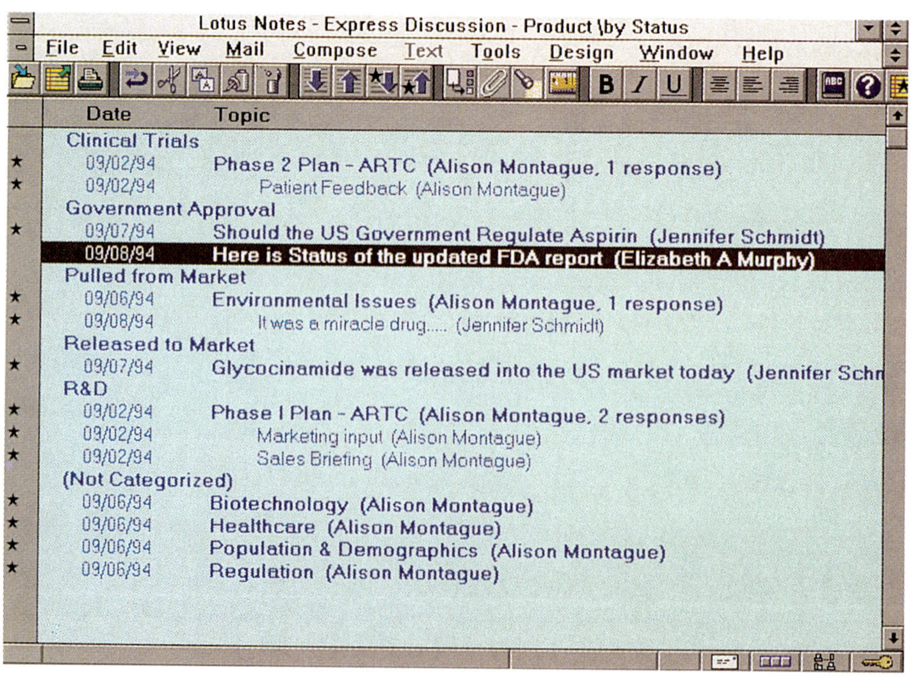

FIGURE MC 4-3 **Faxing.** Fascimile (fax) technology enables document images to be sent from one location to another, over ordinary phone lines. (a) Fax machines send and receive hard-copy documents. (b) Fax software lets users send and receive faxed documents with ordinary computer systems in soft-copy form.

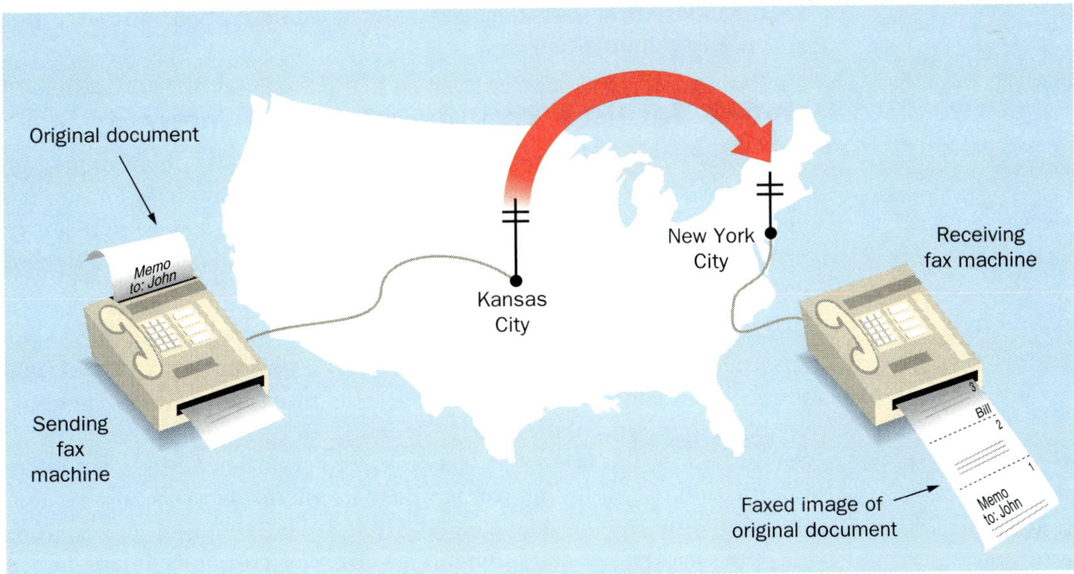

(a)

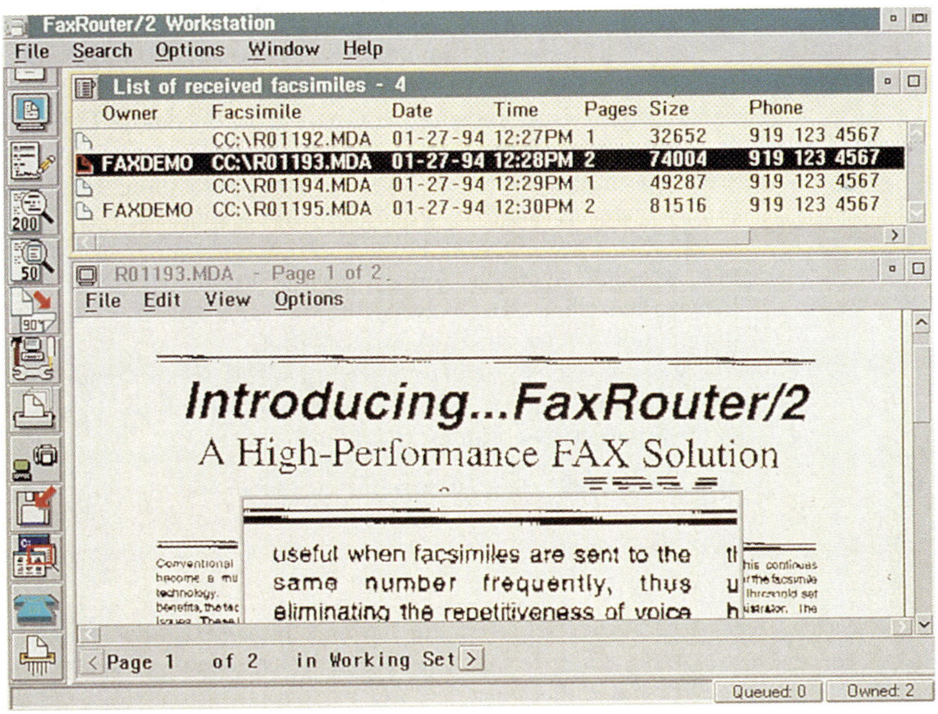

(b)

young Jimmy Stewart proves a key trial witness has lied by summoning from across the country a timely fax image contradicting her testimony. It has only been since the recent development of both the microprocessor and improved manufacturing techniques, however, that inexpensive faxing—and the ensuing boom in personal fax machines—has occurred.

Microcomputer systems can also be equipped with *fax boards* and fax software (see Figure MC 4-3b) that enable them to communicate with both fax machines and other computers with a faxing capability. The advantages to computer-to-computer faxing are that paper is saved, there is no waiting in line for the office fax machine, and faxed documents can be electronically saved and easily routed elsewhere.

Online Services Providers and the Internet

The assortment of information you can get over the phone lines today is, in a word, amazing. Thousands of private and public databases are currently available for online information retrieval. Among these are services for recreational users, shoppers, businesses, researchers, travelers, and other microcomputer users with specialized information needs.

Subscription Services Many people get their online information through a particular services provider, which works similarly to a cable television company. When you subscribe to the services provider, you gain access to the variety of participating databases to which it, in turn, subscribes. Prodigy, CompuServe, GEnie, the Microsoft Network, and America Online, for instance, target information useful to the average person, including news and weather, personal investing and money management, travel, and shopping (see Figure MC 4-4).

Businesspeople can summon a variety of corporate financial reports, such as those available from Moody's, Standard & Poor's, and Dun & Bradstreet. Also available is a never-ending stream of information from news wires such as those of Dow Jones and Reuters.

For researchers and others who read a lot, virtually every major general-interest or trade magazine, newspaper, and journal published worldwide is now online. Also, many regional newspapers in dozens of U.S. cities are available in electronic versions that can be "delivered" to your monitor screen. There are even clipping services that will scan publications for you and save articles in an electronic mailbox on subjects you designate.

Professionals such as lawyers and doctors also have databases targeted to their specialized needs. Mead Corporation, one of the largest electronic publishers, has been extremely successful with Lexis, a legal database. And for the medical professional, there is Medis.

Many services providers have a monthly fee and an hourly hookup charge. They may also impose special charges for some types of services—say, access to the Internet (see Figure MC 4-5).

The Internet The **Internet** is a global web of tens of thousands of networks connecting, collectively, millions of users, businesses, schools, government agencies, and other groups. Uses of the Internet vary widely; following is a small sample:

- A publisher relies on the Internet to coordinate work on a 20-volume book series, which is being prepared by thousands of contributors scattered all over the globe.
- A politician uses the Internet to communicate with voters in his area, and, also, to access satellite weather information so that he can plan outdoor campaign activities.
- One company sends design drawings and spreadsheets to other companies over the Internet, while another uses it to provide software and support to customers.
- The newsletter of a government organization has increased circulation tremendously since the publication became available in electronic form over the Internet.

FIGURE MC 4-4 **Online services providers.** Services providers—such as America Online, featured here—offer subscribers a wide variety of online information and services, including news, sports, weather, personal finance, shopping, computer games, electronic mail, bulletin boards, and Internet connectivity. Shown here is (a) an opening menu and (b)–(d) several submenus providing access to specific types of information.

FIGURE MC 4-5 **The Internet.** Most online services providers—such as Prodigy, featured here—offer access to the Internet. The type of provider chosen can be critical, because not all of them deliver the same Internet features at the same price and some have better tools for navigating the Internet than others.

- A dentist consults with specialists at an insurance company by sending to them over the Internet X-rays of patients' teeth and other data.
- One user has joined a *UseNet* bulletin board on the Internet that allows him to exchange thoughts about comic books with other users throughout the world having this interest. (UseNet, a screen from which is shown in Figure MC 4-6, contains thousands of bulletin boards organized by topic.)

The Internet dates back to the late 1960s—the radical era that also gave birth to Woodstock and massive protests against the war in Vietnam. Back then, and throughout most of its history, Internet was called *ARPANET.* It was named for the group that sponsored its development, the Advanced Research Project Agency of the Department of Defense (DOD).

During its first few years, ARPANET enabled scientists at a few dozen universities to communicate with each other and with government agencies on projects. Within a decade or so, however, hundreds of universities were in on the act.

The DOD got much more than it bargained for in connecting the university scientists. With the Vietnam war in full swing during the early years of the network, the electronic mail facility accommodated not only legitimate research but also heated debates about U.S. involvement in Southeast Asia. Also, as students began to access the network, computer games such as Space

FIGURE MC 4-6 UseNet. UseNet is a network of newsgroups—Internet bulletin boards—that collectively cover thousands of topics (see main part of screen for a small sample). Participation in most newsgroups is completely free; that is, you can post or read messages without paying a membership or usage fee.

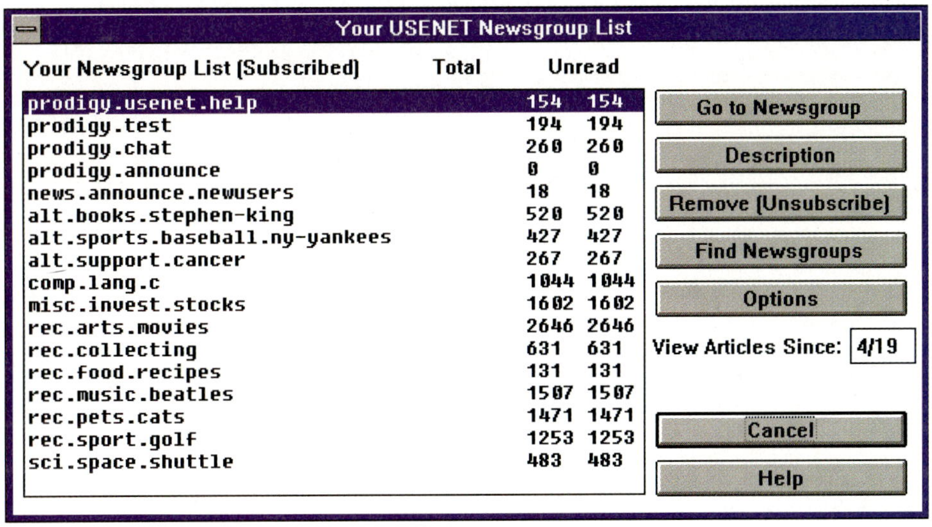

War found their way into the roster of applications, as well as bulletin boards to discuss game strategies. Over the years, the Internet evolved into a general-purpose vehicle for technically oriented people to communicate electronically about anything from politics to science to sports.

Despite its success in academia, however, the Internet went virtually unnoticed by the general public for over two decades. Then, in the early 1990s, government and business started talking seriously about building a national *information superhighway* (called "Iway" for short) to link homes, businesses, schools, libraries, hospitals—you name it—with high-speed data paths. Such paths might enable students to read electronic books in libraries all over the country and consumers to watch at the click of a few keystrokes any movie or television show ever made (see Figure MC 4-7).

When government and business began considering a software vehicle to deliver all of the new electronic "products" that an Iway would conceivably make possible, two possibilities loomed large—either building a delivery vehicle from scratch or taking an already existing vehicle and improving it. Because the Internet already reached large numbers of people over a wide number of computer platforms, it quickly became the front-running choice. As interest soared, scores of companies began looking for ways to make the Internet more accessible to people and to make more services available.

Currently, you can hook up to the Internet in one of three principal ways: (1) through a general-purpose online services provider such as Prodigy, CompuServe, or America Online, (2) through an Internet-dedicated services provider such as Delphi, The Pipeline, or NetScape, and (3) by connecting directly on your own (which requires greater technical knowledge). The dedicated services providers can provide you with faster access, a wider range of Internet services, and full peer status on the Internet. However, if you need more than the Internet's resources, you will need to use a general-purpose online services company.

Whether the Internet will become the Iway's main delivery vehicle remains to be seen. Several obstacles must first be overcome. The first obstacle is that

FIGURE MC 4-7 What's aboard the information superhighway? Funds are still pouring into building pieces of it, so nobody can say for sure. However, all of the services listed here are currently available.

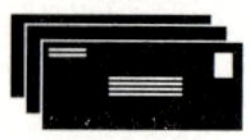

Electronic mail. Internet mail service now links people in more than 150 countries. Futurists predict that, eventually, there will be a universal electronic mail network similar to the phone system.

Bulk file transfer. Products such as electronic newspapers and magazines—as well as software and music—are now beginning to be distributed to consumers over networks, saving the cost of print media, disks, and mailing.

Discussion groups and forums. You can now take part in worldwide discussions and forums on matters of personal interest; you browse the network to find topics in which you wish to participate.

On-demand movies and television shows. In the future, it will be possible to order virtually any movie and television show by computer, your own choosing viewing times. Before this takes place, video mass-delivery systems will need to improve by several orders of magnitude.

Computer games. Games are now available over networks; as video and communications capabilities improve, expect the games to be more spectacular—for instance, computer network versions of television game shows.

Shopping and procurement. It is now becoming possible to search through hundreds of electronic malls for products and to use "intelligent agents" that help you find exactly what you want.

Customer support. Many companies—including Compaq and Dell—are already offering customer support over the Internet. The Internet is also widely used to distribute advertising literature about products and to update software.

News and weather. News and weather from all over the globe are updated regularly. You can even access satellite data and make your own weather predictions.

Access to electronic libraries. Eventually, you will be able to access millions of books online instead of having to go to your local library to find them.

Access to remote computing. If your own computer is not powerful enough to perform certain types of computing, you can access larger computers located elsewhere—and their software, too.

Conferencing. Futurists predict that the so-called picture phone—a phoning device that enables people to see each other as they speak—will someday be a standard feature on the information superhighway.

FIGURE MC 4-8 Shopping the Iway with Mosaic. As interest soars in the Internet, friendly point-and-click interfaces like Mosaic are becoming available to let nontechnical users browse.

the Internet was built for use by scientists. Accessing information often requires the use of complicated search procedures. Recently, however, a number of tools have been developed to help ordinary users navigate. Three such tools are Gopher, intelligent agents, and the World Wide Web.

- **Gopher** *Gopher* is a browsing tool developed at the University of Minnesota. It generates hierarchical menus that allow you to access the Internet's resources by making selections with an onscreen pointer. If you can't find what you want in a particular file, at a particular Internet site, or in a particular multisite database, you have the option of moving elsewhere to see what's available there.

- **World Wide Web (WWW)** The *World Wide Web (WWW)* is a browsing program that works through hyperlinks to data. A *hyperlink* is an icon or a highlighted word or phrase that, when selected, provides access to the information implied by the icon, word, or phrase. For instance, in Figure MC 4-5, the underlined blue words and phrases—such as "Prodigy Help Index"—are hyperlinks to other screens of data. Hyperlinks make it easy for users to access data without learning cryptic programming sequences or Internet addresses. Graphical user interfaces (GUIs)—sporting names like Mosaic and Cello—have been developed to make it easier for ordinary people to navigate the WWW (see Figure MC 4-8 for a Mosaic screen).

- **Intelligent Agents** Intelligent agents are software routines that enable users to more easily frame queries to do searches. For instance, when shopping for a new computer over the Internet, you might ask an agent to check every electronic shopping mall and flag all 90-MHz-or-better Pentium-based desktop computers that cost less than $2,000, have a built-in CD-ROM, and have more than 600 MB of disk storage and more than 16 MB of RAM.

USER TIP

Netiquette

Just as people with bad manners drive on the nation's roads, so, too, do folks with atrocious manners appear on the information superhighway. In order to avoid being impolite, watch your *netiquette*—that is, your etiquette when dealing with others on networks. Here are some tips to follow:

- As a newcomer to a particular newsgroup or discussion forum, check the frequently-asked-question (FAQ) file for answers to queries you may have instead of bothering someone first.
- As a newcomer to a particular newsgroup or discussion forum, observe what others are saying before jumping in with a topic that may be disruptive or out of context.
- Keep in mind that when you send a message in capital letters over the Internet, experienced users regard it as "shouting"; use capital letters only for emphasis.
- Remember that the people you communicate with over the Internet come from a variety of backgrounds, cultures, and political persuasions, so be tactful in controversial matters.
- Do not burden an entire group with your comments if they can be directed to a single person.

Manners count. Never forget that you are communicating with people, not computers.

A second obstacle to widespread use is security. In 1988, a prankster planted a computer virus in the Internet, causing havoc on thousands of computers worldwide. This and other breaches of security have made many businesses think twice about the Internet—especially for applications where the damage potential is great. Discussions concerning a private-access version of the Internet are currently under way.

A third obstacle is the size of the Iway itself. Can the Internet continue to handle the combined needs of users, businesses, educational institutions, consumers, and other groups? Will complex services like full-motion video work over a single system like the Internet? No one really knows.

A Glossary of common Internet terms appears in the appendix at chapter's end. The chapter User Tip covers *netiquette*—etiquette as it is practiced over computer networks.

COMMUNICATIONS MEDIA

Figure MC 4-9 shows a simple telecommunications system. Two hardware units that are distant from each other transfer messages over some type of **communications medium.** The hardware units may be a display terminal and a computer, two computers, two fax machines, or some other combination of two devices. The medium may be private or public phone lines, microwaves, or some other alternative. When a message is transmitted, one of the hardware units is designated as the *sender* and the other as the *receiver*. There are several ways to send the message over the medium, as this section will demonstrate.

FIGURE MC 4-9 A simple telecommunications system. As complicated as telecommunications systems may seem to the casual observer, they basically involve one device being able to communicate effectively with another.

Types of Media

Communications media fall into one of two classes: *wire* and *wireless.*

Wire Three types of wiring are widely used in telecommunications systems today: twisted-pair wires, coaxial cable, and fiber optic cable.

- **TWISTED-PAIR WIRES** **Twisted-pair wires,** in which strands of wire are twisted in twos, is the communications technology that has been in use the longest. The telephone system, which carries most of the data transmitted in this country and abroad, still consists primarily of twisted-pair wires. In some cases, several thousand pairs may be placed into single cables, which might connect switching stations within a city. In contrast, only a few pairs are needed to connect a home phone to the closest telephone pole. Twisted-pair wires can be manufactured and installed at a very low cost, but they are appropriate only for relatively unsophisticated applications such as low-speed text and voice transmission.

- **COAXIAL CABLE** **Coaxial cable,** the medium pioneered by the cable television industry, was developed primarily to provide high-speed, interference-free video transmission. Coaxial cable is now also widely used in other types of communication systems and is employed extensively by the phone companies, typically as a replacement for twisted-pair wires in large "trunk" lines.

- **FIBER OPTIC CABLE** One of the most successful developments in cable technology in recent years has been fiber optics. An innovation whose potential is just beginning to be realized, **fiber optic cable** consists of hundreds of clear glass fiber strands, each approximately the thickness of a human hair. Transmission is made possible by the transformation of data into light beams, which are sent through the cable by a laser device at speeds on the order of billions of bits per second.

  Each hairlike fiber strand has the capacity to carry a few television stations or several thousand two-way voice conversations. By contrast, a wire strand can carry at most only a couple of dozen phone calls—and may weigh 20 times as much. The principal advantages of fiber optics over wire media include speed, size, weight, resistance to tapping, and longevity. The speed differences between wire and fiber optic cable can be enormous; in the six seconds it takes to transmit a page of Webster's *Unabridged Dictionary* over wire, the entire 2,000-plus pages of the work can be transmitted over a single fiber strand. Fiber optic cable is especially suitable in situations involving heavy point-to-point transmission between two stations.

Wireless Wireless technology has become especially popular in recent years. It allows communications in situations in which wiring is impractical, and the lack of wiring facilitates device portability. Three widely used technologies that cater to wireless communications are microwave transmission, cellular transmission, and infrared transmission.

■ **Microwaves** **Microwaves** are high-frequency radio signals. Text, graphics, audio, and video data can all be converted to microwave impulses. Microwave transmission works by what is called the *line-of-sight principle.* The transmission stations need not actually be within sight of each other; however, they should have a relatively unobstructed path along which to communicate. When one microwave station receives a message from another, it amplifies the message and passes it on to others. Because of mountains and the curvature of the earth, microwave stations often are placed on tall buildings and mountaintops to ensure an obstacle-free transmission path.

Microwave signals can be sent in two ways: via terrestrial stations or by way of satellite. Both can transmit data in large quantities and at much higher speeds than can twisted-pair wires.

Terrestrial microwave stations must be no more than 25 to 30 miles apart to communicate with each other directly. This limitation arises because the moisture at the earth's surface causes interference, which impedes communication between stations. As you can imagine, it is quite impractical to build all the repeater stations needed to connect distant locations.

Communications satellites were developed to reduce the cost of long-distance transmission via terrestrial repeater stations and to provide a cheaper and better overseas communications medium than underseas cable. Communications satellites are placed into an orbit thousands of miles above the earth. Because they travel at the same speed as the earth's rotation, they appear to remain stationary over a given spot.

Both communications satellites and terrestrial microwave stations are most appropriate for transmitting large amounts of data one way at a time. Thus, they are ideal for applications such as television and radio broadcasting.

■ **Cellular Transmission** Recently, cellular networks—and especially cellular phones—have become quite popular. **Cellular phones** are mobile phones that do not need to be hooked up to a standard phone outlet in order to work. They can put two people into communication with each other anywhere, even if the individuals are in motion.

Cellular phones operate by keeping in contact with transmitter stations called *cell stations,* or *cells.* These stations, which resemble tall metal telephone poles, are strategically placed throughout a calling area. Cells perform two essential functions: (1) They provide an interface with the regular public phone network, and (2) they enable a moving vehicle with a phone to receive uninterrupted transmitting power by passing signals off to contiguous cells located in the zone into which the vehicle is moving.

Currently those who most benefit from the cellular phone boom are people who need to be in constant contact with the office or clients but must be on the move as well—such as a busy executive, salesperson, field worker, or real estate agent. Such a user might, for instance, take a cellular phone out of a briefcase and use it while waiting for a train (see Figure MC 4-10), sitting at a traffic light, or taxiing down a runway. People who work outdoors, such as farmers and refinery workers, who may need to be in contact with others but cannot afford the time it takes to get to a regular phone, are also reaping the benefits of cellular phone technology.

Cellular phones are also becoming a big hit internationally, especially in less developed countries such as Poland and China. In places such as these, communication systems are crude by North American standards; it is much easier to build new, cellular networks than to upgrade current facilities or to put in wired systems.

FIGURE MC 4-10 Cellular phones. Cellular phones are useful for people who are on the go, need to keep in contact with the office, or do not have convenient access to a conventional phone.

■ **INFRARED TECHNOLOGY** *Infrared technology* has become popular in recent years for setting up wireless links between office microcomputers. As opposed to microwave and cellular tchnologies, which use radio waves, infrared technology relies on sending data as *light*, and the distances involved are usually short. One interoffice system uses a device on each computer that sends and receives messages via a ceiling transmitter that has an unobstructed line-of-sight path to and from the computers.

Media Mode

Communications media also can be classified in terms of whether they can send messages in two directions. In the terminology of communications, transmission mode is said to be simplex, half-duplex, or full-duplex.

In **simplex transmission,** data can be transmitted only in a single, prespecified direction. Two examples from everyday life are television and AM/FM radio. Although simplex lines are cheap, they are relatively uncommon for many types of computer-based telecommunications applications, which generally involve two-way communication. Even devices that are designed primarily to receive information, such as printers, must communicate an acknowledgment back to the sender device.

In **half-duplex transmission,** messages can be carried in either direction, but only one way at a time. The press-to-talk radio phones used in police

FIGURE MC 4-11 **Analog and digital transmission.** Most business computing equipment today uses digital transmission, whereas the phone system is still primarily analog.

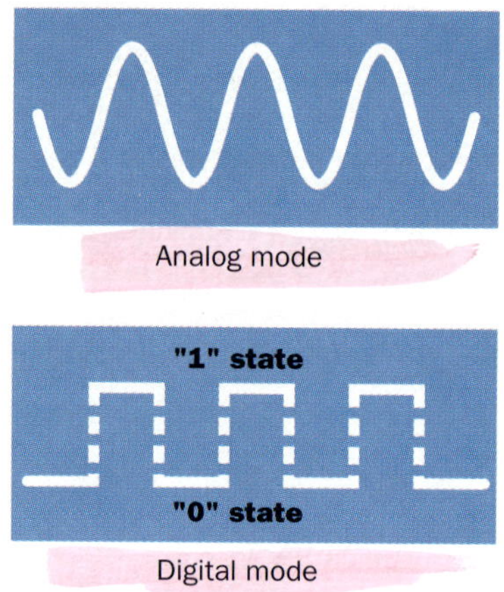

cars employ this mode of transmission; only one person can talk at a time. Often the line between a workstation and its host CPU is half-duplex. If the computer is transmitting to the workstation, the operator cannot send new messages until the computer is finished.

Full-duplex transmission is like traffic on a busy two-way street: the flow moves in two directions at the same time. Full duplexing is ideal for hardware units that need to pass large amounts of data between each other, as in computer-to-computer communication. Full-duplex channels generally are not needed for workstation-to-host links, because the workstation operator's response usually depends on the results sent back from the computer.

Media Signal

Signals sent along a medium can be analog or digital. The phone system, established many years ago to handle voice traffic, carries signals in an **analog** fashion—that is, by a *continuous* sine wave over a certain frequency range. The continuous wave reflects the myriad variations in the pitch of the human voice. Unfortunately, most business computing equipment is **digital;** it is built to handle data coded in two *discrete* states—that is, 0- and 1-bits. This difference between analog and digital states is illustrated in Figure MC 4-11.

Modems Because digital impulses cannot be sent over analog phone lines, some means of translating each kind of signal into the other had to be developed. Conversion of signals from digital to continuous-wave form is called *modulation,* and translation from continuous waves back to digital impulses is termed *demodulation.* A single device called a **modem** (coined from the words *MOdulation* and *DEModulation*) takes care of both operations. As Figure MC 4-12 shows, when one device sends another a message that must be carried over an analog line, a modem is needed at both the sending end (to convert from digital to analog) and the receiving end (to convert from analog to digital).

Modems are often classified as either external or internal (see Figure MC 4-13). *External modems* are hardware devices that are separate from the system units or terminals they serve. *Board (internal) modems,* which have become possible with advances in microcircuitry, are built onto add-in boards that are inserted into an expansion slot inside the computer's system unit. A standard jack is used to connect the port on the board to a wall outlet. Board

FIGURE MC 4-12 **How modems work.** An operator at a microcomputer workstation types in data that are encoded digitally and sent to modem A. Modem A converts the data to analog form and sends them over the phone lines to modem B. Modem B reconverts the data back to digital form and delivers them to another CPU. When this second CPU transmits data back to the originating workstation, these steps are reversed.

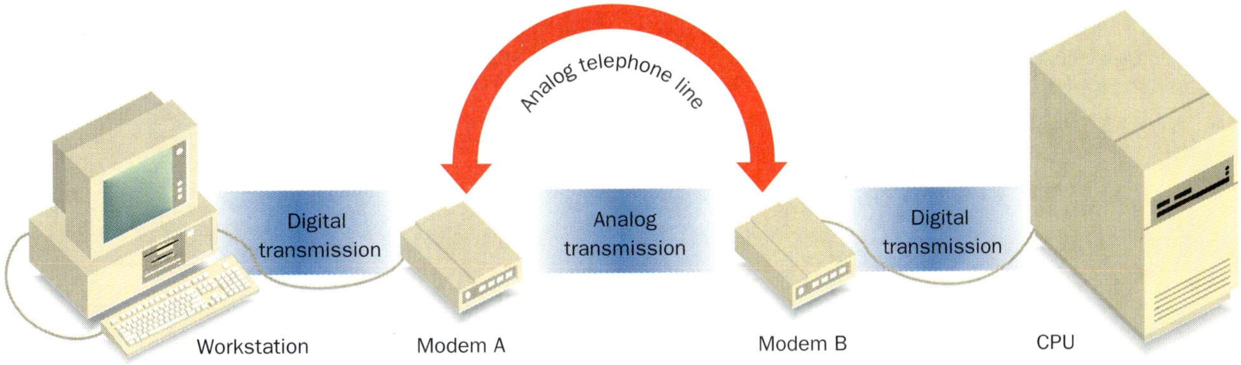

modems have the advantage of requiring no desk space but the disadvantage of using up one of the limited number of expansion slots.

Recently, wireless external modems have become available for users of laptop computers (see Figure MC 4-14).

Modems and bps Rates Common transmission rates on modems targeted to microcomputer users are 1,200, 2,400, 4,800, 9,600, 14,400, and 28,800 **bits per second (bps).** Often modems capable of higher speeds have independent circuitry that enables them to function at the lower rates as well.

FIGURE MC 4-13 **External and internal modems.** Modems are either external or internal. (a) An external modem is detached from the system unit and can be hooked up two or more computers simultaneously. (b) A board (internal) modem fits in an expansion slot within the system unit and is the kind recommended for most personal uses.

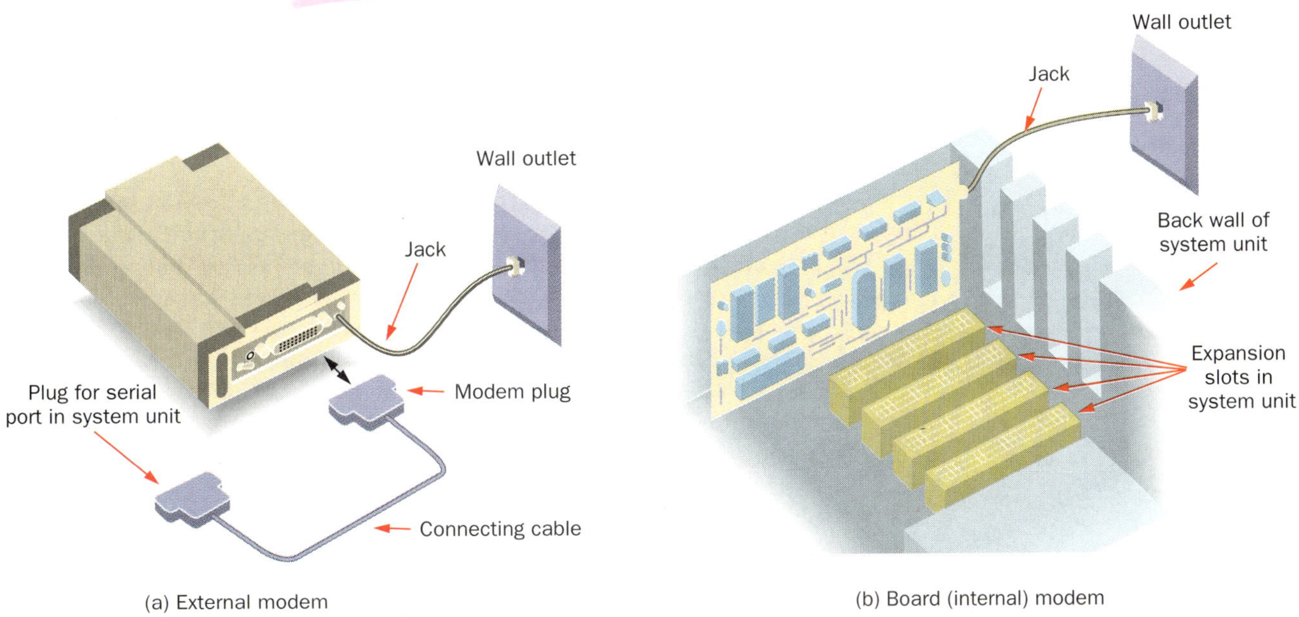

FIGURE MC 4-14 **Wireless modem.** The Sierra Wireless PocketPlus modem, featured here, works by cellular transmission and lets laptop users send and receive data directly, without having to plug into a cellular phone.

Digital Lines Although wire traditionally has been analog, *digital lines* are also available. These lines—which are most commonly fiber optic and of the ISDN (for integrated services digital network) type—can transmit data significantly faster and more accurately than their analog counterparts. With digital lines, several types of data (say, text, audio, and video) can feasibly be sent along the same circuit. And, of course, no modem is necessary. The public phone network is still far from being all digital, but urban areas are rapidly moving in that direction. Also, digital satellites—which provide television viewers much clearer reception than the traditional analog satellite—have recently been launched. (Digital satellites are the ones that broadcast to 18-inch-diameter rooftop dishes.)

Parallel versus Serial Transmission

The bits used to represent characters transmitted between devices may be sent by parallel or serial means. If, for example, all the 8-bits needed to convey the letter *A* are sent out at once along eight separate paths, **parallel transmission** is being used. On the other hand, if the bits representing *A* are sent out one at a time over a single channel, **serial transmission** is occurring. Figure MC 4-15 illustrates the difference between the two. Shortly, we will discuss the role of the *parity bit* that accompanies the transmission.

As Figure MC 4-15 suggests, parallel transmission is much faster than serial transmission. However, because parallel cable requires many more paths, it is also more expensive. Thus, parallel transmission usually is limited to short distances.

Microcomputer modems almost always communicate by serial means. A standard serial interface known as *RS-232C* is commonly used for such transmission on IBM microcomputers. An enhanced form of this interface, the *RS-422*, is widely used on Apple's Macintosh line.

FIGURE MC 4-15 **Serial and parallel transmission.** (a) In serial transmission, all of the bits of a byte follow one another over a single path. (b) In parallel transmission, the bits of a byte are split into nine channels (for each of the eight bits and a parity bit) and transmitted. Parallel transmission is faster but more expensive per foot of cable used. Shown in the figure is transmission of the ASCII representation of the letter *A*.

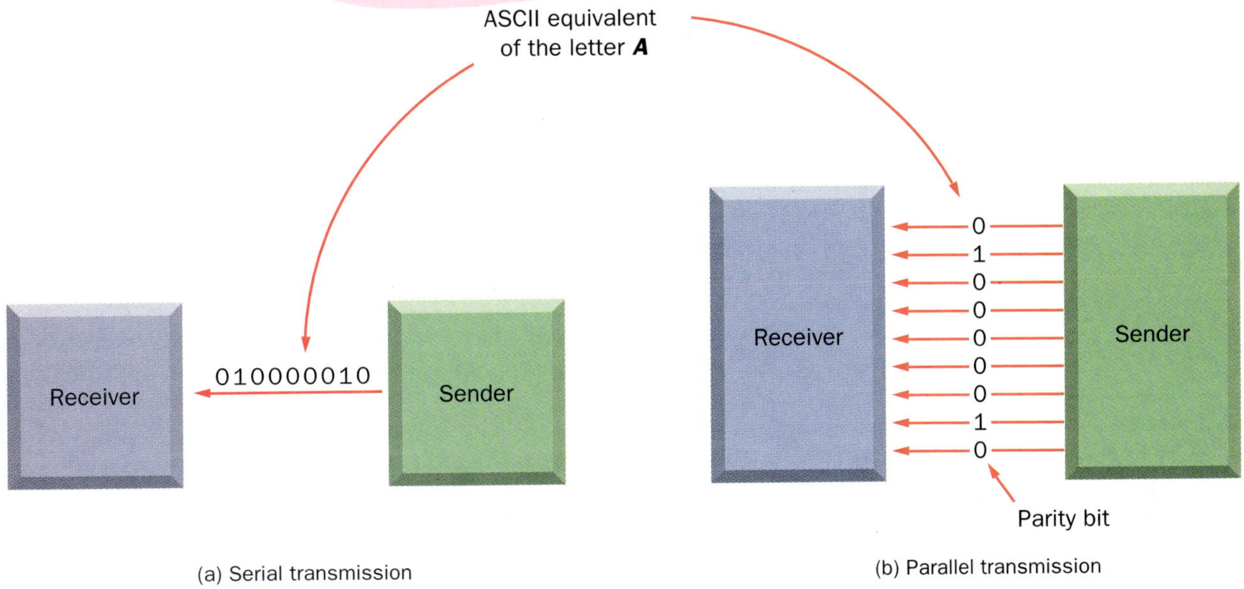

The microcomputer's system unit must communicate with nearby peripherals, such as the keyboard, disk drives, and printer, at high speeds. Since the distance involved is short—say, a few feet—parallel transmission is usually feasible for this purpose. In many IBM microcomputers, nearby printers are connected in parallel to the computer's system unit with a popular standard known as the *Centronics* interface.

The Parity Bit The *parity bit* is used to check for transmission errors. For example, suppose you are at a keyboard and press the B key. If the keyboard processor supports ASCII coding, it will transmit the byte "01000010" up the line to the CPU. Interference on the line, however, might cause the sixth bit to change from 0 to 1 so that the CPU instead receives the message "01000110." Unless the CPU had some way of knowing that a mistake was made, it would wrongly interpret this byte as the letter *F.*

To enable the CPU to detect such transmission errors, ASCII has an additional bit position. This bit, called the **parity bit,** is automatically set to either 0 or 1 to make all the bits in a byte add up to either an even or an odd number. In odd-parity systems, the parity bit makes all the 1-bits in a byte add up to an odd number; in even-parity systems, it makes them add up to an even number (see Figure MC 4-16). The parity bit is automatically generated by the computer system, so its existence is transparent to most users.

Asynchronous versus Synchronous Transmission

Serial transmission can be further classified in terms of whether it is asynchronous or synchronous. In **asynchronous transmission,** one character at a time is transmitted over a line. When the operator strikes a key on the workstation keyboard, the character's byte representation is sent up the line to the receiving device. Striking a second key sends a second character, and so forth. But because even the fastest typist can generate only a very small amount of data relative to what the line can accept, a lot of idle time occurs on the line.

FIGURE MC 4-16 **The parity bit.** If the system used supports even parity, as shown here, the 1-bits in every byte must always add up to an even number. The parity bit is set to either 0 or 1 in each byte to force an even number of 1-bits in the byte.

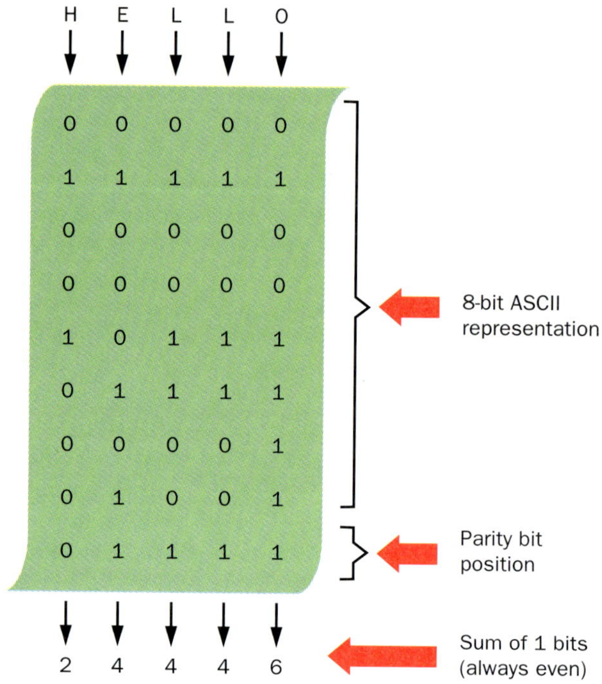

Furthermore, each character sent must be packaged with a *start bit* and *stop bit*, resulting in substantial transmission overhead.

Synchronous transmission corrects for this deficiency by dispatching data in blocks of characters rather than one at a time. Each block can consist of thousands of characters. Because no idle time occurs between transmission of individual characters in the block and less transmission overhead is required, the utilization of the line is much more efficient. Synchronous transmission is made possible by a *buffer* in the sending device—a storage area large enough to hold a block of characters. As soon as the buffer is filled, all the characters in it are sent up the line to the receiving device.

Figure MC 4-17 illustrates the differences between asynchronous and synchronous transmission. Synchronous transmission is commonly used for data speeds above 2,400 bps.

USING MODEM SOFTWARE

Here, we tie together a number of the concepts in this chapter, explaining how terms such as *modems, parity, duplexing,* and several others figure into using the communications software that comes with your computer system.

Modems, like computers, are hardware devices that use software to work. The programs used with modems—which enable you to communicate with remote databases and bulletin boards with your microcomputer system—are commonly referred to in the microcomputing world as *modem software.*

FIGURE MC 4-17 Asynchronous and synchronous transmission. (a) In asynchronous transmission, each byte is sent up the line as soon as it is generated. (b) In synchronous transmission, bytes are collected in a buffer and sent in blocks.

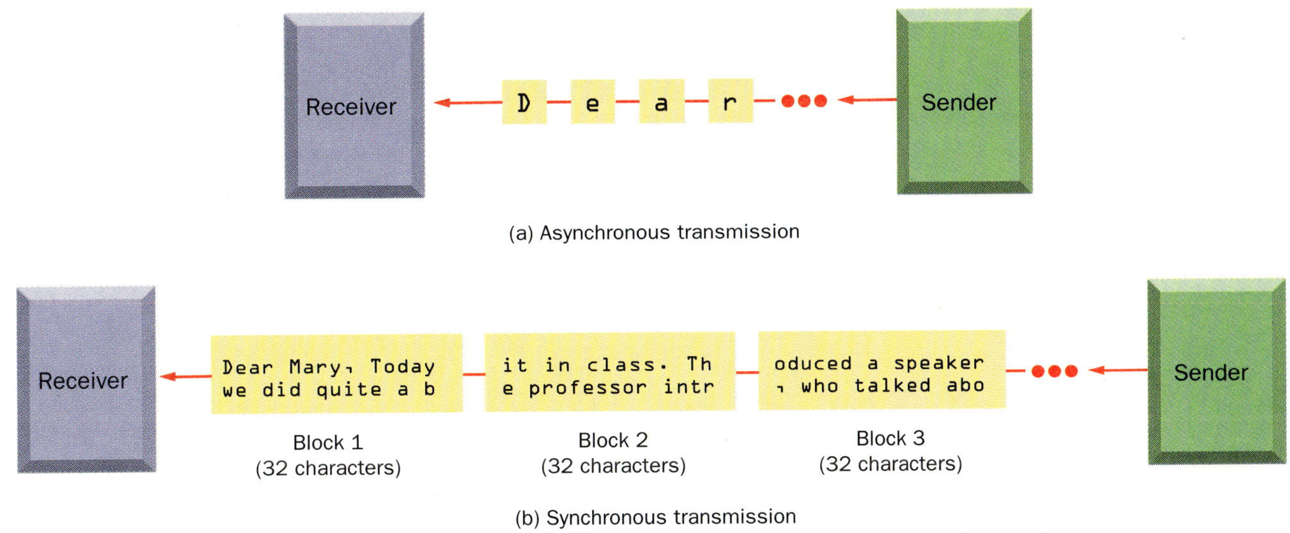

When you buy a modem, you will often get modem software bundled in with it. If not, or if you prefer to buy your own software separately, you can usually acquire it from an independent vendor. There are a variety of well-tested products to choose from, among which are CommWorks, Procomm, Smartcom, and Crosstalk. The prices of such products typically range from about $25 to $200.

Although products in the modem-software marketplace differ in terms of features, most of them let you

- access information services such as America Online, Prodigy, and CompuServe, as well as the Internet.
- receive or send electronic mail.
- exchange disk files with other microcomputers.
- access large computers in other cities, states, or countries.
- turn your modem on and off (to save laptop batteries from drawing down).

In addition, some packages will automatically place and answer calls for you; interface with voice machines; provide security for your files; and simplify a number of routine, phone-related tasks (such as accessing phone directories and keying in passwords to an information service or bulletin board). Figure MC 4-18 shows some of the typical information you may have to supply when setting up a communications application with modem software.

When you summon the software from your operating system, one of the first tasks you will need to do is set up a file of calling parameters for each phone number you want the software to dial. So, for instance, if you regularly called CompuServe, you could create a file with its phone number, your passwords, and other pertinent calling data (see figure). Later, upon supplying the file name associated with CompuServe or clicking its icon with a mouse, and declaring your password, your call would be put through automatically. If you declare *Y* to the auto redial prompt, the modem will keep redialing the phone number at periodic intervals if it is getting a busy signal.

FIGURE MC 4-18 **Modem programs.** Modem programs require setting several calling and transmission parameters to establish outside communication. Generally, the services provider you are connecting to will tell you how to set the parameters or will set them for you automatically.

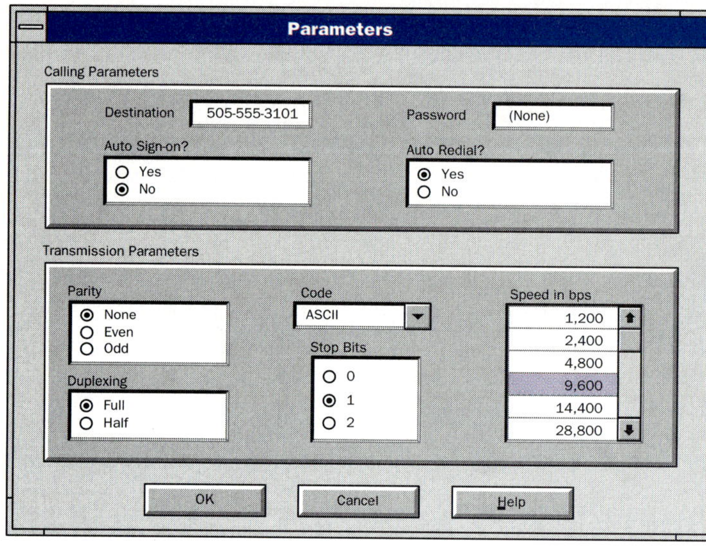

Transmission parameters such as the type of parity and duplexing involved, communications speed, code used, and number of stop bits ensure that your modem sends data in the form the receiver expects. Generally, when you subscribe to a communications service like CompuServe or Prodigy, you will be told what types of settings for these parameters are acceptable. In many cases, the software of the services provider will be able to communicate directly with your modem software—turning the modem on and off, setting the calling parameters automatically for you, and dialing into the service as soon as you click a screen icon. You can edit any parameter files, in the event that settings need to be changed.

Modem software will also turn your microcomputer into a type of answering machine. If you want your computer to receive incoming, electronically encoded messages while you are away, you must leave your computer on, with the modem software set to a "receive calls" mode. As calls come into the system, they are answered by your modem, which establishes a connection with the remote device. The modem sets up a path so that the remote device can send data to it over the phone lines onto your system's hard disk.

WIDE AREA AND LOCAL NETWORKS

An organization generally has two choices for transmitting data between any two points: using a wide area network or using a local network.

Wide Area Networks

Wide area networks (WANs) are communications networks that encompass a relatively wide geographic area. Three common types of WANs are public-access networks, value-added networks, and private WANs.

Public-Access Networks *Public-access networks* most commonly refer to networks that are maintained by the phone companies, or common carriers. **Common carriers** are companies licensed by the government to provide wide area communications services to the general public. Although there are dozens of phone companies in North America alone, virtually all of them are interconnected to give the appearance of a single, seamless network.

Among the most familiar common carriers are the Bell-system phone companies and firms such as US Sprint, MCI, and AT&T Communications. The Bell-system companies provide in-state and nearby-state communications services, and the other firms serve a wider area. Among the less familiar common carriers are the *specialized carrier companies,* such as those that provide satellite transmission facilities.

The Internet is also a public-access network. It is not maintained by the phone companies—thousands of people across the world keep it up and receive no fees for doing so—and it does not cost users anything to use the Internet. All the user pays for is any long-distance charges—the same as if he or she were talking to a person at the other end of the line. The Internet is also an example of a *value-added network* (discussed next) in that it provides over the phone lines a service beyond that provided by the phone company.

Value-Added Networks *Value-added networks (VANs)* generally refer to firms that use the facilities of a common carrier to offer the general subscribing public additional services. These services include information processing, information retrieval, and electronic mail. Individuals and organizations that use the services are billed by both the common carrier (if toll charges are involved) and the VAN company.

One of the most popular types of VAN service is information retrieval, which we discussed earlier. Examples of firms that offer such services are Prodigy, CompuServe, GEnie, and America Online. Once users make phone contact with the VAN company, the firm's software systems generally provide easy-to-use menus of available options.

Private WANs Because many organizations today have such massive communications requirements, a number of them have set up their own exclusive *private WANs.* These networks are created by building certain facilities, leasing capacity on existing satellites, and generally stitching together a variety of cost-effective land- and air-based communications media *dedicated* to delivering a certain level of performance to the organization.

One such network has been built by Sears, the Chicago-based retailer. The Sears network hooks up tens of thousands of hardware devices nationwide and supports the communications needs of both the Sears merchandising group and Sears's member organizations. The network is hosted by an IBM mainframe in Chicago and handles both management information requests and transactions from the millions of users of the Sears Discover card. Sears has also set up a separate organization to sell excess capacity in the network and to sell the communications expertise it has acquired in building the network.

Local Networks

Many firms need communications facilities that connect local resources—say, computers and terminals located on the same college campus or several microcomputer workstations located in the same office. These types of networks are known as **local networks.**

Local networks often are acquired from firms that sell or lease media for private rather than public use. These media may consist of dedicated point-to-point lines, shared lines, switched lines that are unavailable for public use, or networks composed of a combination of these lines. Two common types of local networks are host-independent local area networks and hierarchical local networks.

Local Area Networks For many years, most networks consisted of a large, "central" *host computer*—a mainframe—that controlled many display terminals. With the arrival of inexpensive microcomputers, which could do their own processing, local area networks became possible.

Local area networks (LANs), such as the one shown in Figure MC 4-19, are local networks that do not use a host computer as such. Instead, computers within the network itself manage the devices as they demand the shared facilities. LANs are available in two principal types: client-server LANs and peer-to-peer LANs.

- **CLIENT-SERVER LANS** **Client-server LANs,** such as those that run under Novell's NetWare operating system, are the most prevalent type of LAN. Each workstation getting network service is called a **client,** and the computers (not shown in Figure MC 4-19) managing the network are called **servers.** For example, a *file server* might be used to manage disk-storage activities, enabling workstation users to access any of several available

FIGURE MC 4-19 **A local area network (LAN).** The surge in microcomputer use has made local-area networking a particularly attractive solution for sharing resources.

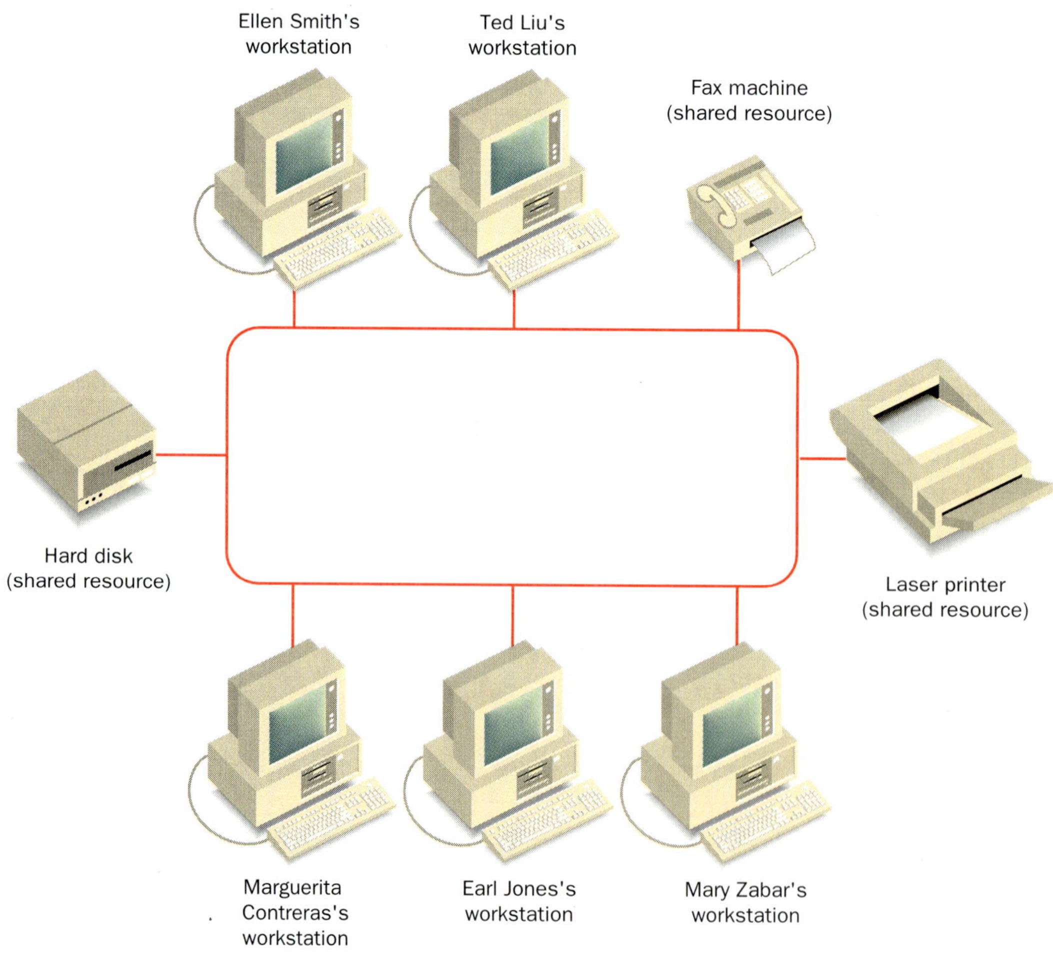

operating systems, applications programs, or data files. Similarly, a *print server* is used to handle printing-related activities, such as managing devices and user outputs. One also sees on LANs such devices as *mail servers* and *fax servers,* which are dedicated to managing electronic mail and facsimile transmissions, respectively. Because servers often need to manage large databases, perform processing chores for clients, and interact with several other computers, powerful microcomputers like those based on advanced Pentium and PowerPC chips are often chosen as servers.

- **PEER-TO-PEER LANS Peer-to-peer LANs,** the most well known of which run under Artisoft's LANtastic, Novell's NetWare Lite, and Microsoft's Windows for Workgroups operating systems, are typically selected for small networks. These LANs do not use clients and servers per se. Instead, all of the devices are on the same level, and any of them can act in a client or server role. Also, users have direct access to each others' workstations. Peer-to-peer LANs were designed as a way to bring networking to small groups without the complexity and expense that normally accompany client-server systems.

LANs are used today for a variety of applications, the simplest of which involve just sharing expensive hard disks and laser printers. Although these were among the first types of LAN applications, LAN technology has evolved to include numerous other uses (see Figure MC 4-20). For instance, some firms that once would have centralized their transaction processing on mainframes are now doing the workload on microcomputer-based LANs. Also, many electronic mailbox systems and computer conferences are run on LANs, and workgroup networks use LANs primarily. Microcomputer-based LANs have a big advantage over systems based on larger computers: Organizations can inexpensively add small increments of extra computing power as their needs grow—say, by adding extra workstations or more servers.

Some LANs are wireless (see Figure MC 4-21). For instance, at sporting events like golf tournaments and the Olympics, where the action is spread out, wireless LANs have made possible faster and better information. Also, at many warehouses today, forklift trucks are equipped with flat-panel display screens and keypads that communicate by radio waves with a local mainframe database, enabling drivers to check product inventory and update it. Wireless LANs are most practical in situations where people are working outdoors or are constantly on the move, or where temporary work groups are formed.

Most LANs, however, use physical wiring, such as coaxial cable or fiber optic cable technology. Cable-based LANs usually employ either a baseband or broadband technology. *Baseband* products consist of a single path over which text, graphics, audio, and video data can pass—but only one type of data at a time. *Broadband* networks, on the other hand, consist of several paths, thereby allowing transmission of many dissimilar types of data simultaneously. Broadband can also cover much longer distances than baseband.

FIGURE MC 4-20 Uses for LANs.

- Sharing expensive devices among several users
- Handling certain types of transaction processing more efficiently than mainframes
- Performing electronic mail operations
- Sharing work among a group of interdependent users

FIGURE MC 4-21 **Wireless LANs.** Wireless LANs are ideal for local applications in which physical lines are impractical. (a) A wireless LAN at a golf tournament enables the results of each swing to be stored in a local database. (b) Radio communication with an onsite inventory database provides realtime information about stock and order levels.

(a)

(b)

Hierarchical Local Networks **Hierarchical local networks** are the oldest type of local network. Traditionally, at the top of the hierarchy has been a big host computer such as a mainframe or minicomputer; at the bottom have been display terminals.

In recent years, however, microcomputers themselves are playing greater roles in hierarchical local networks. In many cases, microcomputer workstations serve as terminals that communicate with a host mainframe or minicomputer through *terminal emulation software.* This type of software tricks the host into thinking it is dealing with an ordinary communications terminal when, in fact, it is communicating with a microcomputer. Thus, a computer like an IBM PS/2 may be made to behave like an IBM 3270 communications terminal when communicating with an IBM mainframe.

Files in hierarchical local networks can be either downloaded from or uploaded to the host. **Downloading** means that copies of existing files can be sent from the host to the microcomputer workstations. **Uploading** means that new data can be created at the microcomputer workstations and sent to the host computer.

Gateways and Bridges Local networks often must communicate with outside resources, such as those available on WANs and on other local networks.

Let's look at an example. An executive working at a microcomputer workstation on a LAN may wish to access a financial database such as Dow Jones News/Retrieval. In this particular case, a facility known as a gateway is necessary for linking the two networks—here, the LAN and the WAN. A **gateway** is a collection of hardware and software resources that enable devices on one network to communicate with devices on another, dissimilar network.

FIGURE MC 4-22 Three network topologies. Networks are often classified by their topology, or shape. The star, bus, and ring are the most widely used network topologies.

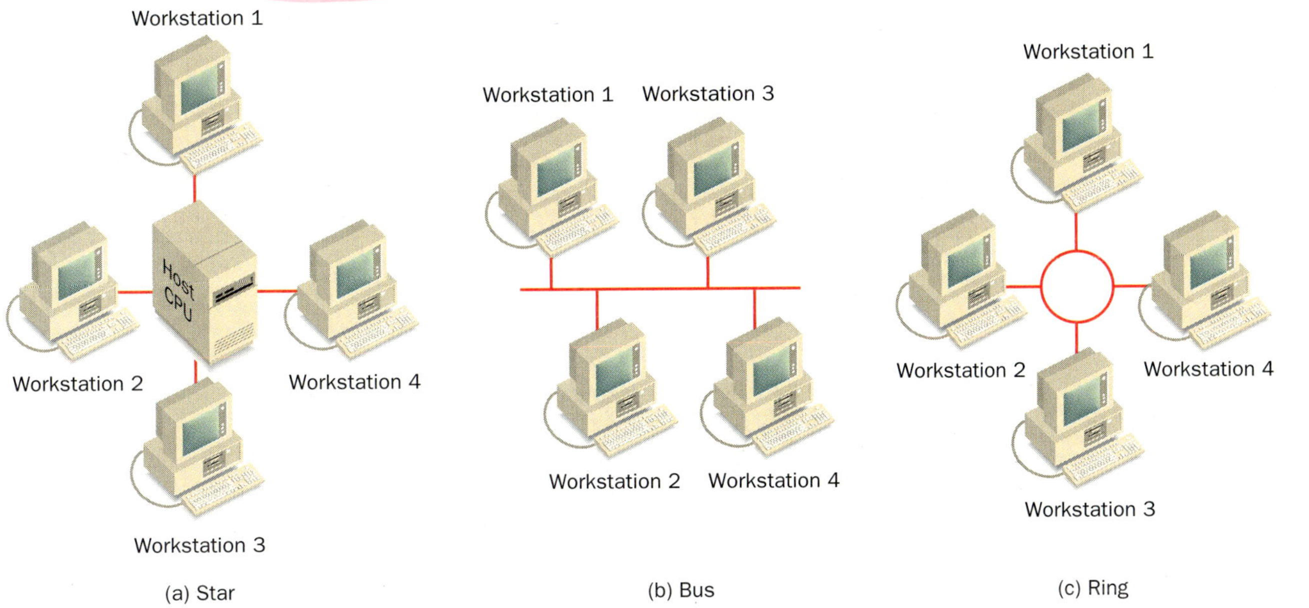

When the two networks being linked—say, a LAN in one campus building and an identical LAN in another nearby campus building—are based on similar technology, a device called a bridge is used to connect them. A **bridge** is a collection of hardware and software resources that enable devices on one network to communicate with devices on another, similar network.

NETWORK TOPOLOGIES

Telecommunications networks can be classified in terms of their *topology,* or shape. Three common topologies are the star, bus, and ring (see Figure MC 4-22).

Star Networks A **star network** consists of a host device that is hierarchically connected to several microcomputer workstations or display terminals in a point-to-point fashion. An example of this configuration is the hierarchical network illustrated in Figure MC 4-22a.

Bus Networks A **bus network** works much like ordinary city buses in ground-based transportation systems. Moreover, the hardware devices are analogous to bus stops and the data are analogous to passengers. For example, the network in Figure MC 4-22b contains four microcomputer workstations (bus stops) at which data (passengers) are "picked up" or "let off." The bus line commonly consists of a high-capacity, high-speed cable, with inexpensive twisted-pair wires dropped off of each terminal station. A bus network contains no host computer.

Ring Networks An alternative to the star and bus networks is the **ring network,** in which a host computer is absent and a number of computers or other devices are connected by a loop. A ring network is shown in Figure MC 4-22c. The LAN in Figure MC 4-19 is also a ring network. One popular implementation of the ring network topology is the *token-ring network* pattern, an IBM LAN that uses the *token-passing* protocol.

PROTOCOLS

Because manufacturers have long produced devices that use a variety of transmission techniques, communications standards for the industry have been a major problem. Everyone recognizes the need for standardizing transmission methods, but the form such standards should take is still widely debated. What is needed is some agreement on matters such as communications protocols.

The term *protocol* originates from the areas of diplomacy and etiquette. For instance, at a dinner party in the elegant home of a social-register family, the protocol in effect may be to wear formal attire, have impeccable table manners, and remain at the table until beckoned to the parlor by the host or hostess. At a backwoods country barbecue, a different protocol will likely exist. In the communications field, protocols have comparable rules.

A communications **protocol** is a collection of procedures used to establish, maintain, and terminate transmission between devices. Protocols specify matters such as how devices will physically connect into a network, how data will be packaged during transmission (for example, asynchronously or synchronously), how receiver devices will acknowledge sender devices (a process called *handshaking*), how competing devices will be given network service, and how errors will be handled. Just as people need an agreed-upon set of rules to communicate effectively, so do machines need a common set of rules to help them get along with one another.

Protocols are found in all types of networks. Many of them are known by their acronyms—TCP/IP, CSMA/CD, SNMP, RIP, NCP, and MAP are all examples of protocols.

Summary

- Telecommunications refers to communications over a distance.
- A wide variety of important applications involve telecommunications. Among these are interorganizational systems (IOSs), electronic data interchange (EDI), electronic mailboxes, voice mail, electronic bulletin boards, computer conferencing, workgroup computing, facsimile (fax) machines, and information retrieval over private and public remote networks.
- All telecommunications networks consist of two or more computers or workstations that are in communication with one another, as well as communications media and devices.
- There are several types of communications media. Wire, such as twisted-pair wires, coaxial cable, and fiber optic cable, constitutes one major class of media. Another class is made up of technologies that send wireless signals—terrestrial microwave stations, communications satellites, and cellular and infrared technology.
- Communications media can be in either the simplex, the half-duplex, or the full-duplex mode. These modes, respectively, refer to whether messages can be sent in a single prespecified direction, two directions but not simultaneously, or two directions simultaneously.
- For two or more digital devices to communicate with each other over the analog phone lines, a device called a modem must be placed between each piece of equipment and the phone lines. Modems perform digital-to-analog and analog-to-digital signal conversion.

- Transmission between machines is done either in parallel, in which each bit of a byte is sent along a different path, or in serial, in which bits of a byte follow each other serially along a single path. Whatever the method used, an extra bit—called a parity bit—is usually appended to the byte representation of each character to check for transmission errors.
- Serially transmitted data are packaged either asynchronously (one byte to a package) or synchronously (several bytes to a package).
- Wide area networks (WANs) are communications networks that encompass a relatively wide geographic area. Three types of WANs are public-access networks, value-added networks, and private WANs.
- Although many organizations take heavy advantage of WANs, a large number of them also build their own local networks to link devices in a single building or at a single site. Two common types of local networks are local area networks (LANs), which typically consist of microcomputers and other devices communicating at the same or different peer level, and hierarchical networks, which consist of powerful host CPUs and workstations subordinate to them.
- Telecommunications networks can be classified in terms of their topology, or shape. Three common topologies are the star, bus, and ring networks.
- A communications protocol is a collection of procedures used to establish and maintain transmission between devices.

Key Terms

Shown in parentheses are the page numbers on which key terms are boldfaced.

Quiz

True/False

___ 1. Electronic data interchange (EDI) enables business documents to be sent directly from one company's computer system to the computer system of another company.

___ 2. Electronic mailboxes allow all mail to be delivered electronically.

___ 3. Only computer-generated documents can be transmitted and received by a fax machine.

___ 4. In half-duplex transmission, messages can be carried in either direction, but only one way at a time.

___ 5. A modem converts analog signals to digital, and vice versa.

___ 6. Serial transmission is much faster than parallel transmission.

___ 7. A file server is another name for the host computer used in a LAN.

___ 8. LANs often employ either a baseband or broadband cable technology.

___ 9. Data are uploaded when they are sent from a microcomputer to a host computer for storage.

___ 10. There are two basic types of communications protocols: uploading and downloading.

Multiple Choice

___ 11. Which of the following applications does NOT require a telecommunications network?
a. Electronic mailbox
b. Voice mail
c. Electronic bulletin board
d. Workgroup computing
e. Image scanning

___ 12. Telecommunications
a. is defined as communications over a distance.
b. refers exclusively to people who work at home using an electronic link to another location.
c. requires the approval of a government agency.
d. refers to a computer network having voice-mail facilities.
e. is another term for distributed transaction processing.

___ 13. The public telephone network is used for telecommunications because
a. government policy requires it.
b. it links virtually any two points in the world.
c. it provides the fastest transmission available.
d. it is the only way to obtain microwave transmission.
e. computer protocols are easier.

___ 14. Microwave transmission works by the
a. transmission of light waves.
b. simplex mode concept.

c. line-of-sight principle.
d. nonamplification principle.
e. bidirectional transmission rule.

___ 15. Fiber optic cable is the telecommunications medium that uses
a. lasers and light waves.
b. satellite transmission.
c. microwaves.
d. the line-of-sight principle.
e. human hair.

___ 16. The phone system carries signals
a. in digital form only.
b. using simplex transmission.
c. in a token ring pattern.
d. in bit notation.
e. predominantly in an analog form.

___ 17. In serial transmission, the bits representing a byte are sent out
a. all at once.
b. only on voice-grade lines.
c. eight bytes at a time.
d. using EBCDIC systems.
e. one at a time.

___ 18. An example that illustrates half-duplex transmission is
a. AM/FM radio transmission.
b. communication using a press-to-talk radio phone in a police car.
c. traffic on a busy two-way street.
d. a conventional telephone conversation.
e. an umpire and manager arguing over a controversial call.

___ 19. A telecommunications network that serially connects computers and other devices, has no host computer, and may implement the token-passing protocol is called a ______________ network.
a. ring
b. bus
c. star
d. token
e. topology

___ 20. A collection of procedures used to establish, maintain, and terminate transmission between devices is called a
a. network.
b. token.
c. traffic manager.
d. protocol.
e. handshaking directive.

Matching

Select the term that best matches each phrase:

a. Electronic mailboxes	g. Modem
b. Twisted-pair wires	h. Voice mail
c. Bulletin board	i. Half-duplex
d. Satellite	j. Full-duplex
e. Fiber optic cable	k. Asynchronous
f. Server	l. Host

___ 21. The central computer in a telecommunications network

___ 22. Hundreds of clear glass strands used as communications media

___ 23. A device that relays communication signals as it orbits the earth

___ 24. A device used to translate analog to digital signals

___ 25. The transmission of data over a line one character at a time

___ 26. A mode that allows data to be transmitted in two directions at the same time

___ 27. A computer file shared by several people who use it to post or broadcast messages

___ 28. Files on hard disk, each file allocated to a different person, for the purpose of receiving and saving electronic messages

___ 29. A form of electronic mail in which spoken phone messages are digitized and stored

___ 30. A network processor that manages a shared device

Answers

True/False: 1. T; 2. F; 3. F; 4. T; 5. T; 6. F; 7. F; 8. T; 9. T; 10. F

Multiple Choice: 11. e; 12. a; 13. b; 14. c; 15. a; 16. e; 17. e; 18. b; 19. a; 20. d

Matching: 21. l; 22. e; 23. d; 24. g; 25. k; 26. j; 27. c; 28. a; 29. h; 30. f

Exercises

1. Pick a services provider such as Prodigy, CompuServe, America Online, or GEnie and determine the following information:
   a. The type of hardware and software you need on your PC to access the service.
   b. The types of information resources available to subscribers. Is there access to the Internet?
   c. The costs involved. Is there a monthly subscription fee? What other types of charges are there?

   Services providers typically maintain 800-area-code phone numbers (call 1-800-555-1212, directory assistance, to get the most current phone numbers) that you can call to be sent product information.
2. If it is possible for you to use a PC with a modem and communications software, command the system to dial up a services provider that you are authorized to access or to dial a free-access bulletin board within your town or on the Internet. Report to the class the type of information you were able to find.
3. Among the most popular features of the Internet are its bulletin boards. While the growing roster of Internet bulletin boards changes almost daily,

many estimates place the number of such boards in the tens of thousands. For your assignment, find ten bulletin boards that interest you, and, for each one, identify the subject matter addressed and how you would access the board on the Internet.

4. Consider the following ASCII representation of a character:

   010100011

   a. What character is represented?
   b. Is odd or even parity in effect?

An Illustrated Glossary for the Internet and the Information Superhighway

Defined below are several terms that users often encounter when working with the Internet. Many of the terms are used in Chapter MC 4 and in other parts of the textbook.

Advanced Research Projects Agency Network (ARPANET) The forerunner to the Internet, named after the group (ARPA) that sponsored its development.

America Online A general-purpose services provider headquartered in Vienna, Virginia; Internet access is one of the many services offered (see Figure 1).

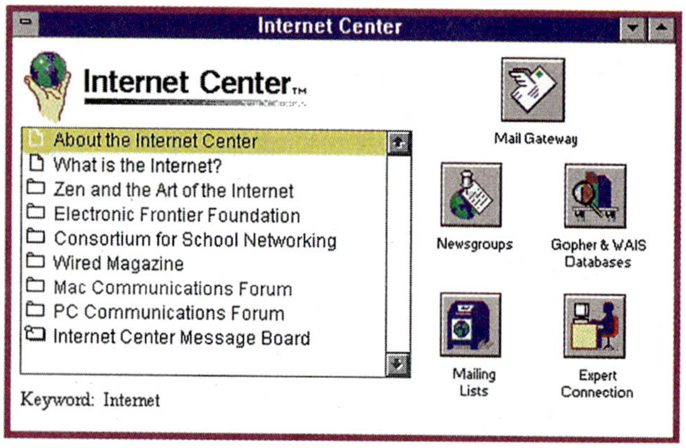

FIGURE 1 America Online (AOL). AOL is one of the leading services providers enabling access to the Internet.

Archie A tool that enables Internet users to search through public servers to find the location of downloadable files on particular subjects (see Figure 2).

ARPANET See Advanced Research Projects Agency Network.

Browser A front-end, menu-oriented software tool that makes it easy for users to navigate through the Internet; two well-known browsers are Mosaic and Cello (see Figure 3).

Bulletin Board An Internet service that provides spaces for users to post messages on thousands of selected topics.

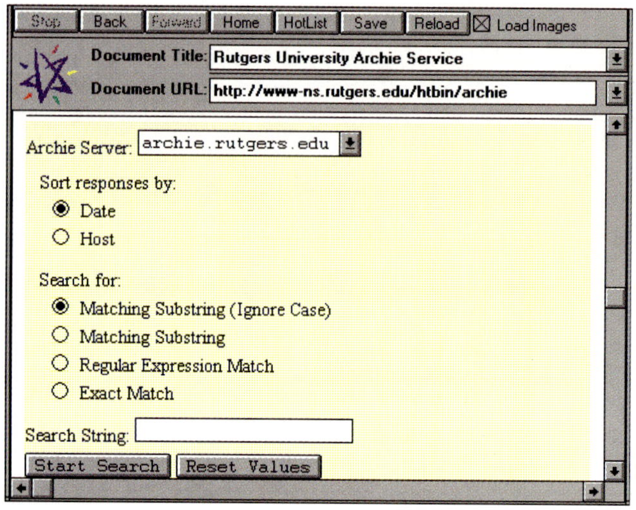

FIGURE 2 Archie Server. Users type in search strings to find the location of files.

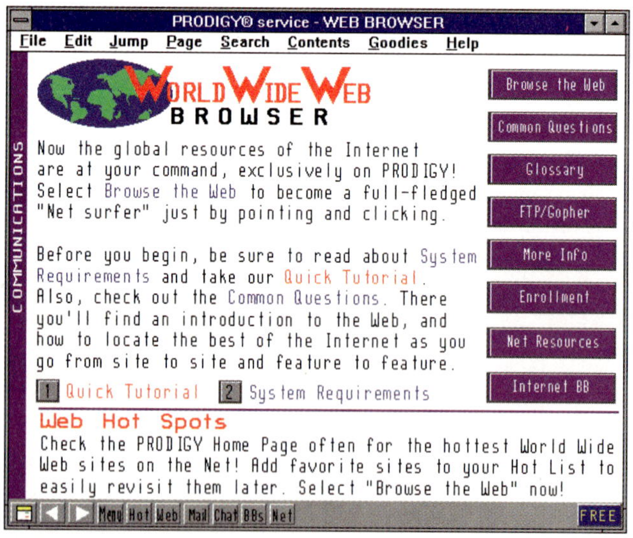

FIGURE 3 Browser. Browsers are graphical screens that make it "supereasy" to navigate the Internet's World Wide Web by repeatedly making menu selections.

Cello A freeware tool that provides an easy-to-use graphical user interface (GUI) for Internet users.

Chat An Internet service that makes possible interactive discussion groups on selected topics (see Figure 4).

FIGURE 4 Chat. A live chat room lets "deadheads"—Grateful Dead fans—meet and exchange ticket information.

CommerceNet An Internet network that specializes in providing such business services to computer users as product ordering and access to product information.

CompuServe A general-purpose services provider headquartered in Columbus, Ohio; Internet access is one of the many services offered (see Figure 5).

Cyberspace A term used loosely to refer to the electronic universe formed by computer hardware, software, and data.

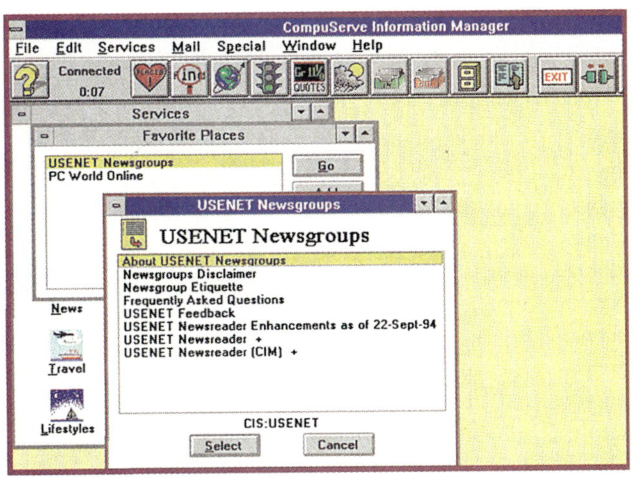

FIGURE 5 CompuServe. CompuServe was one of the earliest online services providers and is still one of the frontrunners.

Delphi Internet A services provider—headquartered in Cambridge, Massachusetts—that specializes in Internet connectivity.

Domains Identifiers, appearing after the @ symbol in an Internet address and separated by periods, that describe the type of user or resource involved. For instance,

jsc.nasa.gov and jsc.nasa.gov.us

respectively show three and four domains. The highest level of domain, which appears last in the address, usually describes the *category* of the account (e.g., com = commercial, edu = educational, gov = government) or the *country* (e.g., us = United States, ca = Canada, uk = United Kingdom). The lowest levels of the domain, which appear first, provide any qualifying information. In the examples, jsc stands for the Johnson Space Center, which is part of the government organization NASA (nasa). See also Internet address.

Electronic Frontier Foundation An organization whose mission is to preserve such rights as free access to information, freedom from censorship, and personal privacy in cyberspace.

Electronic Mail See E-Mail.

E-Mail A facility that enables users to send electronic letters and documents to others with Internet addresses.

eWorld An online service run by Apple that allows both Macintosh and Windows users to connect to the Internet and access other types of information resources.

FAQs See Frequently Asked Questions.

File Transfer Protocol (FTP) The communications protocol that facilitates the transfer of files between a host computer and a user's computer.

Firewall A collection of software and hardware designed to protect internal networks operated by companies from unauthorized use by people on remote computers.

Frequently Asked Questions (FAQs) A collection of common questions asked by newcomers to an Internet bulletin board, newsgroup, or chat room, accompanied by the answers to those questions (see Figure 6).

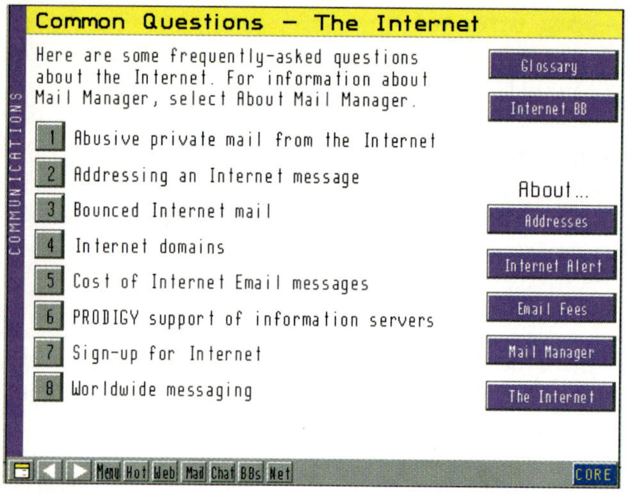

FIGURE 6 FAQS. Answers to any of the eight FAQS listed here can be obtained by clicking the number button to the left of the question.

FTP See File Transfer Protocol.

Gateway A collection of software and hardware that provides access to the Internet. Internet gateways are offered by general-purpose services providers, often as part of a more comprehensive network package.

GEnie An online information service produced by GE Information Services, headquartered in Rockville, Maryland; Internet access is one of the many services offered.

Gopher A browsing tool developed at the University of Minnesota. Gopher generates hierarchical menus that allow users of the Internet to access resources by making selections with an onscreen pointer (see Figure 7).

Home Page An opening screen with a table of contents (see Figure 8).

Host Computer A powerful computer that provides database information or services to Internet users.

HTML See Hypertext Markup Language.

Hyperlink A graphic icon or hypertext within a World Wide Web page that can be selected, thereby summoning to the screen a text file, still image, sound, video clip—virtually any type of data (see Figures 7 and 8). See also Hypertext, World Wide Web.

Hypertext Bolded or underlined text that, when selected, summons to the screen a text file, still image, sound, video clip—virtually any type of data (see Figures 7 and 8).

Hypertext Markup Language (HTML) A language that enables World Wide Web pages to be coded by people developing applications for the Internet.

Information Superhighway A term that loosely refers to the massive collection of computer networks that links online users with electronic information throughout the world.

Intelligent Agent An algorithm that performs a specific type of search task for a network user; for instance, an intelligent agent can be coded to search for all round-trip flights from New York to Bulgaria that cost less than $1,000.

Internaut An Internet user.

The Internet A global, public-access web of tens of thousands of networks connecting, collectively, millions of users, businesses, universities, and government agencies.

Internet Address A unique identifier assigned to a specific location—such as a resource or user mailbox—on Internet. For instance,

mail-server@rtfm.mit.edu

is the address of the server computer at Massachusetts Institute of Technology (MIT) that stores the bank of all Internet mailing lists, while

cspz99a@prodigy.com

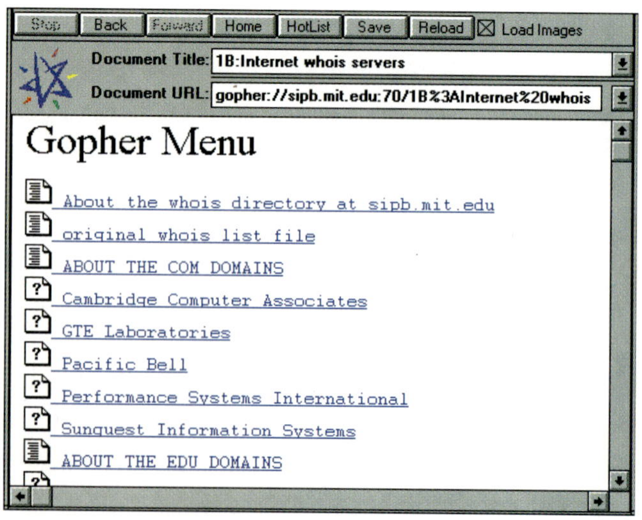

FIGURE 7 Gopher menu. Mouse-selectable hyperlinks are used to access subordinate menus.

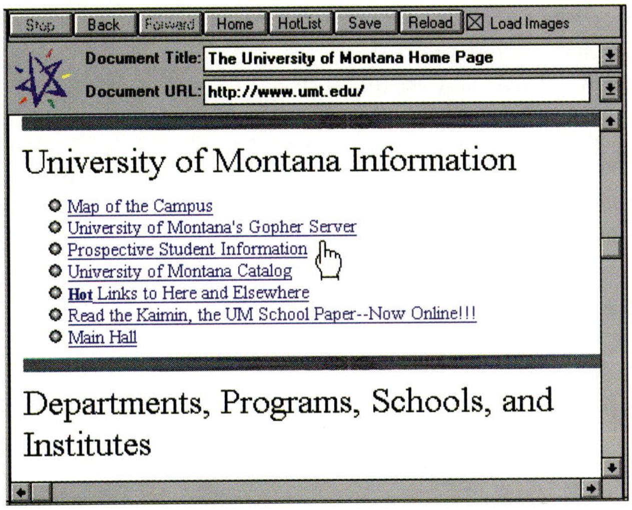

FIGURE 8 Home page. Hypertext on University of Montana's home page can be used to access a wealth of information about the school.

might represent the mailbox of the Prodigy user whose account number is CSPZ99A. As the examples show, an Internet address consists of an identifier, followed by the @ symbol, followed by a list of domains separated by periods. See also Domains.

Lurking Refers to the technique practiced by newcomers to a discussion group whereby newcomers remain observers to the group's activities before becoming active participants.

Mailing Lists An Internet service that provides a list of names of people with interests on a particular topic as well as their electronic addresses. This service enables you to send messages to particular individuals rather than simply post bulletin-board messages, as you would with UseNet.

The Microsoft Network An online service run by Microsoft Corporation that lets users connect to the Internet and access other types of resources.

Mosaic A freeware tool that provides an easy-to-use graphical user interface (GUI) to Internet users. Mosaic is also available in a number of commercial versions.

NetCruiser An Internet browsing program and online service produced by Netcom.

Netiquette Etiquette on the information superhighway. An example: newcomers to discussion groups should read answers to frequently asked questions (FAQs) and lurk around as observers before barging into discussions. See also Frequently Asked Questions.

Netscape An Internet browsing program and online service produced by Netscape Communications Corporation (see Figure 9).

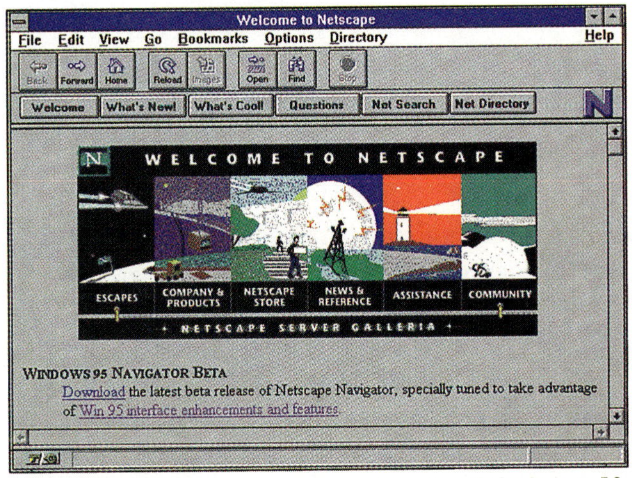

NETSCAPE'S NAVIGATOR 1.2 Internet browser supports Hypertext Markup Language 3.0.

FIGURE 9 Netscape. Netscape's speed and elegance have made it a favorite among Internet browsers.

Net Surfing Refers to browsing the Internet by making repeated menu selections, much as you might "channel surf" cable television stations with a remote pushbutton device.

Newsgroup A bulletin-board-like forum or conference area where messages can be posted on a specific topic (see Figure 10).

The Pipeline Freeware that provides both Internet connectivity and search tools; commercial support is also available from The Pipeline, headquartered in New York City.

Prodigy A general-purpose services provider headquartered in White Plains, New York; Internet access is one of the many services offered (see Figure 3).

Serial Line Internet Protocol (SLIP) A protocol that enables individuals and companies to connect to the Internet over ordinary phone lines, as hosts.

Server A computer that manages the information stored and accessed in Internet databases.

FIGURE 10 UseNet newsgroups. Selecting REC.TRAVEL.CRUISES lets you interact with other travelers, travel agents, and former crew members.

Services Provider An organization or software package that enables access to the Internet. Services providers typically differ with respect to ease of use, the Internet services to which access is allowed, navigational tools, and pricing structures.

SLIP See Serial Line Internet Protocol.

Talk A service that provides the Internet equivalent of a long-distance phone call, with sender and receiver typing interactive messages to each other rather than talking.

TCP/IP See Transmission Control Protocol/Internet Protocol.

Telnet A communications protocol that lets users log onto and log off of Internet networks.

Transmission Control Protocol/Internet Protocol (TCP/IP) A collection of communications protocols that allows PCs accessing the Internet to understand each other and exchange data.

Universal Resource Locator (URL) A unique identifier representing the location of specific files, sites, or features on the Internet.

URL See Universal Resource Locator.

UseNet (User Network) A public network comprised of thousands of bulletin boards organized by topic. UseNet participants can read messages and contribute to the topics (see Figure 10).

Veronica A program that allows users to search Gopher menus for particular keywords. Veronica is an acronym for Very Easy Rodent-Oriented Netwide Index to Computerized Archives.

WAIS See Wide-Area Information Server.

WHOIS A program that lets users search a database for people or network addresses.

Wide-Area Information Server (WAIS) Refers to software that uses keyword searches to navigate across and within large databases.

World Wide Web (WWW) A browsing program that works through hyperlinks to data. The hyperlinks eliminate a user's need to know cryptic programming sequences and Internet addresses. See also Hyperlinks.

Worm A computer virus that infects computers by "eating up" their storage areas.

WWW See World Wide Web.

MC 5 BECOMING A KNOWLEDGEABLE USER

OUTLINE

Overview

The Microcomputer Marketplace
- Microcomputer Products
- Sales and Distribution

Selecting a Computer System
- Analyzing Needs
- Listing Alternatives
- Evaluating Alternatives
- Choosing a System

Operating a Computer System
- Proper Maintenance of Resources
- Security
- Troubleshooting and Repairs

Upgrading
- Functional versus Technological Obsolescence

Learning More about Microcomputers

LEARNING OBJECTIVES

After completing this chapter, you will be able to:

1. Identify several of the leading companies in critical market segments of the microcomputer industry, as well as the key sales and distribution alternatives for microcomputing products.
2. Explain how to go about selecting a microcomputer system for home or office use.
3. Name some practices designed to protect software, hardware, and data resources from damage, as well as some important guidelines to follow in troubleshooting problems and repairing equipment.
4. Describe some of the ways a computer system can be upgraded and explain under what conditions an upgrade should take place.
5. Name several sources for learning more about microcomputer systems.

OVERVIEW

It is increasingly common for a person to own a microcomputer or to use one at work. Consequently, more people than ever are involved with such activities as acquiring their own microcomputer resources, taking care of a system, deciding when to call for outside help, and upgrading a system on their own.

The term *end-user development* is often used to describe activities such as these. End-user development refers to ordinary end users taking on the responsibilities associated with building and maintaining their own computer systems. These responsibilities go far beyond merely using computers; they extend from initially acquiring a microcomputer system to taking charge of the numerous implementation problems that are bound to occur over time. Making you aware of the many ins and outs connected with being a knowledgeable user is the purpose of this chapter.

The chapter opens with a discussion of both the vendors in the microcomputer marketplace and the distribution channels they use to sell their products at the retail level. Then, we look at some of the things you should know when acquiring a microcomputer system for home or for work. From there we turn to several operation and maintenance issues. Next, upgrading a computer system is covered. Finally, we discuss some of the sources that are at your disposal for learning more about microcomputers.

THE MICROCOMPUTER MARKETPLACE

The microcomputer marketplace consists of a wide variety of firms that make hardware and software products and that sell services. Also, because many hardware and software manufacturers do not sell directly to the public, a number of other companies exist solely for sales and distribution purposes.

Microcomputer Products

Only a dozen or so years ago, many of the companies that make today's most familiar microcomputer products were not even in existence. Today, several of them are making more than a billion dollars a year in revenues. Almost overnight, the microcomputer industry has laid claim to being both the fastest-growing and the largest segment of the computer industry.

In the following subsections we look at some of the big players in each of the major market segments of the microcomputer industry. A roster of some of the more familiar company names in the microcomputer marketplace appears in Figure MC 5-1 along with a description of the major product offerings that have made these companies famous.

System Units IBM, Compaq, Packard Bell, and Apple are the big four in the desktop microcomputer marketplace. There are other companies—such as Dell, AST, and Gateway—who, like Compaq, have become highly successful largely by producing IBM-compatible microcomputers. **IBM-compatible microcomputers** are microcomputers that can run the same software as that targeted to most IBM microcomputers. IBM-compatible machines made today will run virtually any major application software product designed to run on IBM microcomputers that use Intel chips and lookalikes.

Laptop and notebook-sized computers are currently the fastest-growing segments within the microcomputer marketplace.

Software Three of the largest independent software producers (and their leading products) are Microsoft Corporation (MS-DOS and Windows operating-system software; Access; Word; Excel; and Works), Lotus Development Corporation (1-2-3, Notes, Ami Pro, and Approach), and Novell Corporation (NetWare, Quattro Pro, and WordPerfect). At one time, many of these companies could be characterized as single-product firms. Today, the leaders in this segment are in a period of aggressive diversification, internally developing new products and acquiring smaller companies with successful, related product lines. Many program packages are increasingly being sold as software suites.

Monitors and Printers With the exception of a few U.S. companies such as IBM and Hewlett-Packard, the monitor and printer markets are dominated by Japanese companies. Some of the major players are Epson, Toshiba, Seiko, Brother, Fujitsu, Canon, NEC, and C. Itoh.

Computer and Memory Chips The chip markets are ruled by Intel, Motorola, and Japanese companies. Intel makes CPU chips for most of the leading IBM and IBM-compatible system units, whereas Motorola makes chips for the Apple Macintosh line of computers. There are also a number of manufacturers such as Cyrix and Advanced Micro Devices (AMD) that produce Intel-compatible chips. Recently, IBM, Motorola, and Apple have teamed up to produce the PowerPC computer chip, which competes head-to-head against Intel chips.

FIGURE MC 5-1 **Who's who in the microcomputer marketplace.** This list shows the products or product lines for which several leading companies are most famous.

Company	Principal Product(s)
Adobe	Assorted desktop publishing software products
Apple	Microcomputer systems
AST	A wide variety of hardware products
Autodesk	AutoCAD design software
Borland	A wide variety of software products
Canon	Printers and related products
Compaq	Microcomputer systems
Computer Associates	A wide variety of software products
Dell	Microcomputer systems
Gateway	Microcomputer systems
Hewlett-Packard	A wide variety of hardware products
IBM	A wide variety of computing products
Index Technology	Excelerator, a CASE product
Intel	Chips for IBM and IBM-compatible computers
Lotus Development	A wide variety of software products
Microsoft	A wide variety of software products
Motorola	Chips for Apple computers; communications products
NEC	A wide variety of hardware products
Novell	A wide variety of software products
Packard Bell	Microcomputer systems
Quadram	A wide variety of hardware products
Qume	Printers
Seagate	Hard disks
Software Publishing	Harvard Graphics presentation software
Symantec	A wide variety of software products
Toshiba	A wide variety of hardware products
Zeos	Microcomputer systems

FIGURE MC 5-2 **Retail computer stores.** Today, computer stores are a common sight along highways and in shopping malls.

Disk Systems Some of the more familiar names in the floppy-disk-drive and hard-disk-drive marketplace are Conner, IBM, Seagate, and Tandon. In the optical-disk-drive marketplace, Canon and Philips are big names. Iomega and SyQuest have done well in the hard-disk-cartridge marketplace.

Sales and Distribution

Hardware and software microcomputing products are most often acquired from computer stores, discount and department stores, mail-order houses, and manufacturers.

Computer Stores Computer stores—such as Computerland, CompUSA, Computer City, and Electronic Boutique (see Figure MC 5-2)—are often used by organizations that need strong local support. Generally, the salespeople at these stores are relatively knowledgeable about computers and many of them will help buyers try out products before making a commitment. Besides hardware, software, and purchasing advice, computer stores also often offer consulting, repair, and other support services to users.

Computer stores come in many varieties. Most are national or multistate chain stores, but there are also outfits that serve only local areas such as a single town or a state. The chains, because they can buy in volume, are likely to have better prices, so many local stores compete by providing superior support. Also, while most computer stores have the floor space of an average mall boutique, massive *computer superstores* have recently become popular. Finally, some computer stores are in actuality *electronics stores,* which sell in addition to computer hardware and software such items as televisions, phones, and electrical supplies.

Other Stores During the last few years, microcomputer hardware and software have become so popular that many other types of retail stores have added such items on their showroom floors (see Figure MC 5-3). Today, you can buy

FIGURE MC 5-3 Computing at a discount. Among the least expensive places to shop for computers are the warehouse clubs, such as Price Club.

hardware and software at discount stores (such as Wal-Mart), warehouse clubs (such as Price Club), department stores (such as Sears), office-supply stores (such as Office Depot), and bookstores (such as Waldenbooks). As a general rule, the discount stores and warehouse clubs have better prices than computer stores, but often less of a selection is available, and many offer little or no technical support to customers.

Mail-Order Firms Another source of computer products is mail-order firms (see Figure MC 5-4). These companies regularly publish price lists in microcomputer journals and many will ship products within 24 hours of a request. Because these companies do not have to pay for a showroom and a large staff of knowledgeable salespeople, their prices generally are much lower than those of computer stores. Also, some of them have access to an enormous stock of goods and can get almost any item to buyers quickly via a private shipper such as United Parcel Service or Federal Express. A disadvantage of mail-order shopping, however, is that buyers need to know exactly what they want.

Manufacturers A fourth alternative for buying hardware and software is going directly to the manufacturer. Some companies—such as Dell, Gateway, and Zeos—are known as *direct manufacturers* in that they sell directly to the public through advertisements in computer journals. Buying directly from manufacturers is not always possible. Many have exclusive selling arrangements with certain wholesalers. Also, although some manufacturers sell directly to the general public, usually they will sell only in large quantities. Buying directly from the manufacturer usually yields lower prices but may not include ongoing support. Such support, if needed, will have to be acquired from another firm.

FIGURE MC 5-4 Mail-order houses. Multiple Zones International is one of several mail-order houses that regularly print catalogs—like the ones featured here—that showcase products for the IBM-compatible and Macintosh-compatible worlds of microcomputing. The catalogs feature hard-to-beat prices on scores of products.

When buying a computer system, consider the possibility of used equipment. Ads for used hardware can usually be found in the ads section of local newspapers. If you take this route, ask to try out the equipment before you buy it. If the equipment functions properly during the trial period, it will probably work fine. Be especially careful to observe how the monitor works over a period of a couple of hours and to check the output quality of the printer.

You should pay significantly less for a used system than you would for a new one. The National Association of Computer Dealers publishes a semi-annual market report called the *Computer Blue Book*—similar to the blue book used-car dealers refer to for used cars—which lists the current worth of computers, monitors, printers, communications equipment, various types of lesser-used peripherals, and software from a variety of manufacturers.

SELECTING A COMPUTER SYSTEM

Chances are, you will need to select a microcomputer system at some point in your life. An important aspect of becoming a knowledgeable user is knowing how to assess your needs and determining the best microcomputer system to meet those needs.

Selecting a microcomputer-based system for home or business use must begin with the all-important question: What do I want the system to do? Once you have decided the uses to which the system will be put, you must then determine the software and hardware alternatives available. Finally, you need a method to evaluate the alternatives and to choose a system.

Analyzing Needs

With regard to computer systems, a *need* refers to a requirement the computer system must be capable of meeting. For instance, at a videotape rental store, a computer system must be able to enter bar codes automatically from tapes being checked in and out, identify customers with overdue tapes, manage tape inventories, and do routine accounting operations. All four of these uses are considered needs. Requiring a computer that you can take with you "on the road" is another example of a need.

Although a person owning a computer system can find dozens of ways to use it, he or she will often justify the acquisition of a microcomputer system on the basis of only one or two needs. For example, many managers do so much financial planning that merely a spreadsheeting capability is enough to justify the entire computer system cost. Many writers, of course, find word processing so indispensable to their livelihoods that it matters little what else the computer system can do. And sales personnel working out of the office can often justify a laptop computer just on the basis of being able to use it as an account-closing tool at client sites.

If you are really not sure what you want a system to do for you, you should think twice about buying one. Computer systems that are specially configured to serve certain applications (say, games) are often poor at others (such as word processing), so you can easily make some very expensive mistakes if you are uncertain.

As part of the needs analysis, you should take a close look at your budgetary restraints. Everyone has many needs, but whether they are affordable is what separates the real needs from the pipe dreams.

Listing Alternatives

Once a set of needs has been established, the next step is to list some alternative systems that might satisfy those needs. You should almost always consider applications software first, then the computer and systems software platform that best meets your applications software requirements.

A **platform** is a set of compatible computer system architecture and systems software choices that limit the user to work in a certain way. For instance, an IBM-compatible Pentium-based system unit running under Microsoft Windows 95 is an example of a platform. With such a base, the user would be able to buy any software that could run under DOS or Windows. Another example of a platform: an Apple PowerMac 7100 running Macintosh System Software version 7.5.

Applications software is selected first because it most closely relates to needs. For instance, if you want a computer system to perform desktop publishing, it would be wise first to look at the various desktop publishing packages available. It makes no sense to choose a system platform first and then find out that it does not support the type of desktop publishing package you most prefer.

Often, in the world of microcomputers, hardware and software decisions are highly interrelated, so that software and hardware must be selected jointly. A software product, for example, may work only on a specific set of hardware. For instance, a certain desktop publishing tool might only be available for an Apple Macintosh computer system, and it might also require a color printer to work most effectively. Or, an illustration software package may work best if a specific type of graphics hardware is in use—say, a digitizing tablet or an image scanner. Also, most illustration packages require a capacious hard disk and run best with a graphics coprocessor, because graphics images require a lot of space and computational power. Because of the interrelatedness of many software and hardware products, it sometimes helps to make a list of system alternatives, where each alternative consists of the principal platform and other hardware and software elements that can be added to it—both now and over time.

You can get a list of software and hardware products from many of the leading microcomputer journals. Often, these journals will also describe the best and worst features of products and will give each product an overall rating (see Figure MC 5-5). These ratings can be used as input for evaluating products—your next step in acquiring a microcomputer system.

Evaluating Alternatives

Alternative products are best examined by trying them out. Keep in mind that when you observe the performance of a software package, you are viewing the performance on a given configuration of hardware. Just because a software package runs smoothly on a Dell Pentium-based computer system does not

FIGURE MC 5-5 **Product evaluation.** One of the most useful features in most microcomputer journals is product evaluation—making relative comparisons among a group of similar products and providing critical reviews of newly released products. A regular feature of *Infoworld* is the "report card," an example of which is shown here summarizing an extensive multipage comparison of four workgroup schedulers.

REPORT CARD — INFO WORLD

Workgroup Scheduler/Mail Packages

	(InfoWorld weighting)	(Your weighting)	The Coordinator II Version 2.1	Office Works Version 2.0	Right Hand Man Version 5.1	Word Perfect Office Version 3.0
List price			$1,800 (10-user)	$495 (six-user)	$1,169 (10-user)	$495 (five-user)
Performance						
Scheduling	(125)	( )	Good	Good	Excellent	Good
Messaging features	(150)	( )	Excellent	Good	Very Good	Very Good
Archiving	(50)	( )	Excellent	Good	Good	Good
Printing/ word processing	(50)	( )	Good	Poor	Good	Very Good
Gateways	(125)	( )	Very Good	Satisfactory	Very Good	Excellent
Documentation	(50)	( )	Very Good	Good	Good	Excellent
Ease of administration	(75)	( )	Very Good	Satisfactory	Very Good	Satisfactory
Ease of learning	(50)	( )	Good	Very Good	Very Good	Satisfactory
Ease of use	(100)	( )	Good	Good	Good	Good
Error handling	(50)	( )	Very Good	Very Good	Good	Very Good
Support						
Support policies	(25)	( )	Satisfactory	Good	Good	Excellent
Technical support	(25)	( )	Satisfactory	Very Good	Very Good	Very Good
Value	(125)	( )	Good	Good	Very Good	Very Good
Final scores			**7.3**	**5.9**	**7.4**	**7.3**
Use your own weightings to calculate your score						

GUIDE TO REPORT CARD SCORES

InfoWorld reviews only finished, production versions of products, never beta test versions.

Products receive ratings ranging from unacceptable to excellent in various categories. Scores are derived by multiplying the weighting (in parentheses) of each criterion by its rating, where:

Excellent = 1.0 — Outstanding in all areas.
Very Good = 0.75 — Meets all essential criteria and offers significant advantages.
Good = 0.625 — Meets essential criteria and includes some special features.
Satisfactory = 0.5 — Meets essential criteria.
Poor = 0.25 — Falls short in essential areas.
Unacceptable or N/A = 0.0 — Fails to meet minimum standards or lacks this feature.

Scores are summed, divided by 100, and rounded down to one decimal place to yield the final score out of a maximum possible score of 10 (plus bonus). Products rated within 0.2 points of one another differ little. Weightings represent average relative importance to *InfoWorld* readers involved in purchasing and using that product category. You can customize the report card to your company's needs by using your own weightings to calculate the final score.

mean the software package will run quite the same on a Compaq 80486SX system, which uses a slightly different architecture and a less powerful chip. Also, the look, feel, and performance of a software package on a computer in the Apple Macintosh line will likely be quite different than it is on an IBM or IBM-compatible machine.

Sometimes it is difficult, when selecting a configuration of hardware and software, to see the entire system running together. Where this is possible, however, it is certainly advisable. What you see is what you get.

Selection Criteria In evaluating software and hardware products, you should base your final selection on a number of criteria.

The most important selection criterion is usually *product functionality*—how well the product performs the work it is supposed to do. For many people, *ease of learning* and *ease of use* follow closely behind. Also, many people strongly prefer products that are widely used rather than unknown ones, because the large user base with the popular products ensures that *vendor support* will be around for a long time. In addition, if you are considering using a microcomputer system in an office environment dominated by, say, Apple Macintoshes, choosing that type of computer would probably be much more convenient from the standpoint of having a lot of *local expertise* available for support. Good written *documentation* showing how to use the package is also important; when a helping hand is not readily available, documentation is often the best alternative for answering a tough question yourself.

A list of important criteria for selecting a microcomputer system is provided in Figure MC 5-6.

Software and Hardware Specifics In looking over software or hardware, you should make a checklist of properties the product should possess—and be sure to examine these during the "test drive." A rehearsed presentation made by a salesperson is likely to point out only the strengths of a product. You will need to discover its weaknesses.

For instance, in looking over a word-processing package, you should note the manner in which standard commands are executed (for example, moving the cursor, centering, moving and copying text, indenting, reformatting, and footnoting), the quality of the spelling-checker and thesaurus features, and the

FIGURE MC 5-6 **Important selection criteria.** Buyers generally select computer systems based on some combination of these criteria.

- Product functionality
- Ease of learning and use
- Cost
- Vendor support
- Local expertise
- Expandability
- Meets industry standards
- Speed
- Favorable reviews
- Delivery
- Documentation

advanced features the word processor possesses (such as desktop publishing features). Again, you need to look at the entire system under consideration. For example, if you are buying an inexpensive, dot-matrix printer that cannot handle proportional spacing, graphics, or subscripts and superscripts, then it may make little difference that a word processor supports these features.

Hardware items that usually will need to be considered when buying a microcomputer system are the system unit and RAM, diskette and hard-disk units, a CD-ROM unit, a monitor, a keyboard and mouse, and a printer.

Some of the questions that should be addressed when buying common types of hardware and software are shown in the appendixes appearing at the end of Chapters 2 and 3.

Choosing a System

After you have looked over the alternatives, it is time to choose a system.

People choose between system alternatives in a number of ways. For instance, some people make a formal list of selection criteria such as those shown in Figure MC 5-6. They quantitatively rate each alternative—say, on a scale of 0 to 10—on each of these criteria. Then they select the alternative that scores the highest overall. Typically, the criteria are also weighted, to reflect relative importance.

Others prefer to make their choices less formally. Often, after thinking about needs and the criteria for evaluating alternatives, they select a computer system as soon as it "feels right." In fact, researchers have found that a large number of microcomputers are purchased individually or in small quantities, and very little formal analysis, if any, is undertaken before the purchase. Although such an acquisition process might be criticized for lack of thoroughness, many managers claim they are too busy to research choices with greater care. There is, of course, a downside to rushed selections. Just as a car buyer can go through years of dissatisfaction driving around in the wrong type of car, so too can a computer buyer wind up with years of headaches from a poor computer system choice. The expense of a computer system mistake, however, may be much greater.

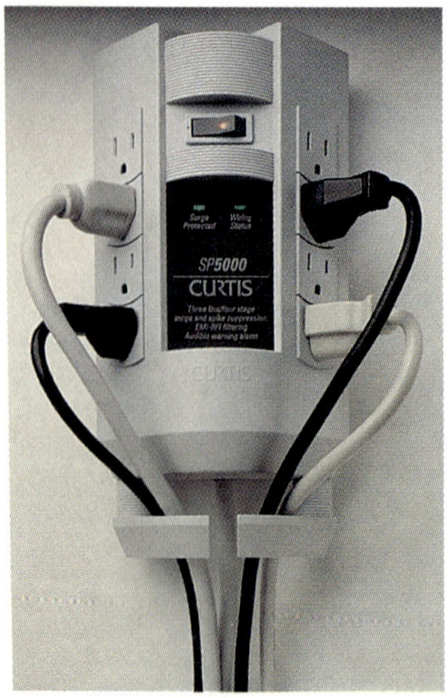

FIGURE MC 5-7
Surge suppressor.
The system unit and its support devices feed into the surge suppressor, which is plugged into a standard wall outlet. This permits you to turn on all of your equipment, as well as a nearby lamp or two, with the flick of a single switch.

OPERATING A COMPUTER SYSTEM

Once you have acquired a computer system, it is important that you develop a set of practices to protect your software, hardware, and data from damage and from costly mistakes. Three precaution areas to consider are proper maintenance of hardware and I/O media, security, and troubleshooting and repairs.

Proper Maintenance of Resources

Microcomputer systems consist of sensitive electronic devices, so they must be treated with appropriate respect. In this section we discuss protecting your computer system with a surge suppressor; caring for disks; protecting your computer system from dust, heat, and static; and protecting printers and monitors.

Surge Suppression One of the best devices to have on your computer system to minimize the chance of unexpected damage is a surge suppressor. A **surge suppressor,** or *power manager,* which is installed between your system unit and the electrical outlet, is a hardware device that prevents random electrical power spikes from damaging your system (see Figure MC 5-7).

The power going into most homes is uneven. Power spikes such as those caused by electrical storms, and power brownouts caused by drops in power, can damage data or your system. Probably the most common problem caused by a spike or brownout is loss of data in RAM. Cases have also been reported, however, of loss of data in secondary storage and destruction of equipment.

A surge suppressor cannot guarantee complete protection. If lightning strikes your house, even a top-of-the-line surge suppressor would probably fail to protect your equipment. The best thing to do if you are working on your computer system when a severe lightning storm approaches is save your work to a disk, turn your system off, and unplug the surge suppressor. Lightning can cause damage to electrical equipment that is plugged in—whether or not it is on or off.

Many people supplement their surge suppressors with an *uninterruptable power supply (UPS)* unit. This device is, in effect, a battery that keeps power going to the computer when the main power goes off, perhaps because of a lightning storm or damage to an outside cable. Most UPSs can run for several hours before they have to be recharged.

Disk Care Precautions taken with diskettes and with hard disks will increase the safety of any data stored on them.

Diskettes are extremely sensitive and must be cared for accordingly. For instance, never touch the exposed diskette surface or bend the diskette in any way. Also, keep the diskette away from magnetic objects, motors, stereo speakers, and extreme temperatures.

With a hard disk, the most important precaution to take is ensuring the disk is in a place where it is likely to be free from being bumped.

Dust, Heat, and Static Each of those tiny processor and memory chips in your hardware units is tightly packed with hundreds of thousands of circuits. Dust particles circulating in the air can easily settle on a chip, causing a short circuit. Many people buy dust covers that fit snugly over each of their hardware devices to prevent foreign particles in the air from causing hardware failure.

System units that support add-in boards require cooling fans. These boards generate heat, and too much heat inside the system unit can cause all sorts of problems. Users inserting boards should place them as far apart as possible to avoid heat buildup. Also, most boards draw power off the system's main power unit (as do many internal hard disks), so you have to be particularly careful about overtaxing the power unit.

Static electricity is especially dangerous because it can damage chips, destroy programs and data in memory, and disable your keyboard. To prevent those nasty little electrical discharges from your fingertips from wreaking havoc, you might consider buying an antistatic mat for under your workstation chair or an antistatic pad to put under your keyboard (see Figure MC 5-8). Static electricity is more likely in dry areas and in the wintertime (when there is less humidity in the air).

Other Causes for Concern CRT-type monitors work by having a phosphorescent surface "lit up" by an electronic gun. If you keep your monitor at a high brightness level and abandon it for an hour or two, the phosphorescent surface may well be "torched" rather than merely lit up. What this means is that ghostly character images will be permanently etched on the screen, making it harder to read. Software packages called **screen savers** are available that will either dim your monitor or create random patterns on the screen when the display remains unchanged for a given number of minutes.

Printers are particularly prone to failure because they are electromechanical devices. If you have an impact dot-matrix printer, the most vulnerable mechanism in the unit is the print head. These print heads, like typewriter keys, will wear down over time. Nonetheless, you can take precautions to pre-

FIGURE MC 5-8 **Antistatic pad.** An antistatic pad dissipates harmful static charges before they have a chance to get at your keyboard. The pad featured here fits unobtrusively below a keyboard or system unit.

vent rapid wear, such as making sure the head is periodically cleaned, not using the printer excessively for graphics (which wears the head more rapidly), and making sure the head is not adjusted for carbon copies (which makes the head strike harder) if you want only single copies.

Naturally, as with other electronic devices, you should not be switching hardware units on and off to an excessive degree.

Security

Security refers to protecting a computer system's hardware, software, and data from unintentional damage, malicious damage, or any type of tampering. There are many ways to secure a computer system, including physical security, password protection, disklock accessories, encryption algorithms, and vaccine programs (for computer viruses).

Physical Security The first line of defense for any microcomputer user is physical security. **Physical security** refers to the use of devices that inhibit physical access to property. For instance, people who have a private office can lock the door while they are gone, thereby making it unlikely that other people can get to their computer systems while they are away. For those whose computer systems are in open offices, various types of physical-locking devices are available. Widely used are lockable security plates that can vacuum-attach computer hardware to a desk, without defacing the furniture, and steel cables that can secure several hardware devices to a desk or any other fixed object (see Figure MC 5-9). Also, many system units today come with built-in locks. By turning a key, you can lock up your computer system so that nobody can use it while you are away. Removable disk cartridges—which require a special hardware device to be read from and written to—are also excellent media for the security conscious. Disk cartridges enable you to remove large volumes of data from the computer system and store them at another site.

FIGURE MC 5-9 **Universal security kit.** The eight-foot padlocked steel cable shown here can secure your system unit and up to three peripherals to a desk or any other fixed object. The cable fits through security brackets that attach to any hardware unit with a removable screw.

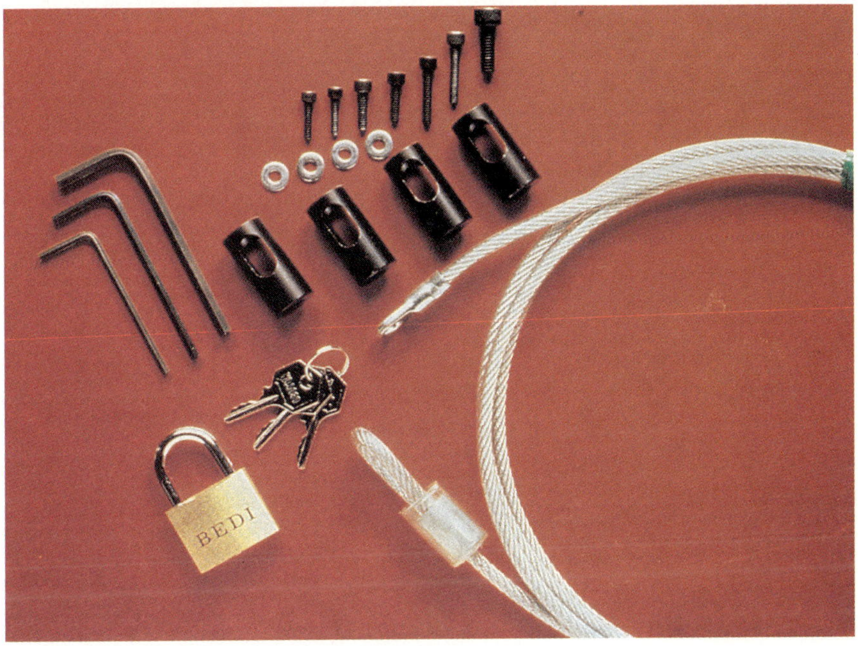

Passwords A number of software solutions also are available that will help you protect data. For instance, access to computer systems is most often restricted by passwords. **Passwords** are "secret" words known only to authorized users and to the professionals charged with safeguarding the system. They are most commonly used on networks, to keep anyone from coming in "off the street" and gaining access to computers. Passwords can also be used at the file and operator level. For instance, a certain password may be necessary to access a specific set of files. Another password may be necessary if the operator wants to update these files in any way.

Disklock Accessories Another popular software-based security solution is the disklock accessory. **Disklock accessories** enable you to lock your hard disk, or selected portions of it, while you are away from your desk. You may make a request to lock a disk at any time, and if you wish, you can also program the accessory to lock the disk if the computer system is unused for a given number of minutes. This way, if you are unexpectedly called away from your desk for a meeting, the screen will go blank on its own and a pop-up box will appear requesting a password to be entered to unlock the system. Because many disklock accessories allow portions of a disk to be protected, security for a computer system is extended to networks and to environments where several people share the same desktop computer system.

Encryption Another popular software solution to security is encryption. **Encryption** allows you to encode files so that they appear as gibberish to anyone trying to read them. Naturally, the encryption package also contains a decoding algorithm. The main disadvantages to encryption are that it takes a long time to encrypt a file and that sometimes files can get destroyed in the encryption process. If you encrypt a file, make sure that you also have an unencrypted version stored in a safe place.

FIGURE MC 5-10 **Vaccine software.** Your system is vulnerable to viruses virtually any time you use it. At high risk are people who work on networks, let others use their computing resources, or use software that comes from unknown origins.

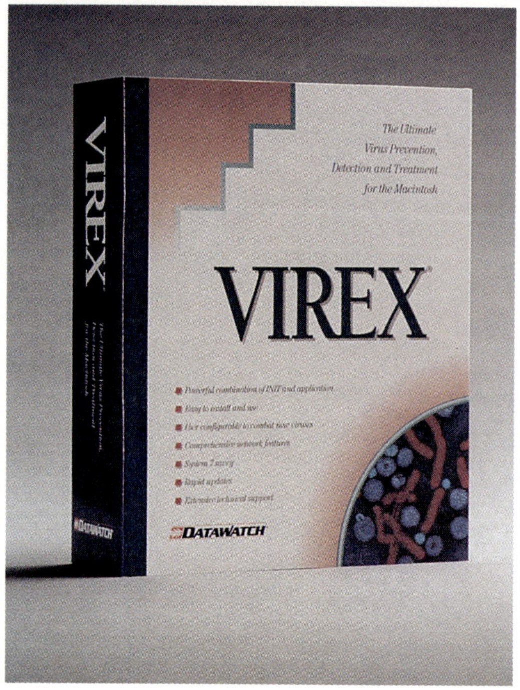

Vaccine Programs for Viruses Virtually everyone concerned about security will want to protect data from computer viruses. A **computer virus** is a small block of code, often hidden inside a larger program, that is designed to create malicious damage or pull a "harmless" prank. Malicious damage includes destroying programs and data, and gumming your computer system up so that it is difficult or impossible to continue work. Pranks include such things as flashing annoying messages on your display screen from time to time.

Viruses often work by writing code of some type onto programs or data on a disk or in memory. Viruses even replicate themselves onto other disks, thereby spreading infection. Some viruses contain a mechanism that will destroy programs or data or pull pranks at a specific time or moment—say, on a specific day or when an infected program performs a certain operation.

To date, a number of vaccine programs have surfaced to combat computer viruses (see Figure MC 5-10). **Vaccine programs** scrutinize code for suspicious patterns. If something looks strange, they often can intercept an activity before it takes place and apprise you of what is going on. Many are also designed to repair damaged files in the event a virus they recognize has infected some programs or data, and they can prevent a program or data with a recognized virus from ever executing. Vaccine programs are generally priced at about $100 or less and are accompanied by a list of the specific types of viruses they can protect your system from picking up.

No matter what you do, it is important to note that no security strategy can give you full protection. Nonetheless, giving a little thought to some of the things that can go wrong and taking a few simple precautions can save you big headaches later on.

Troubleshooting and Repairs

If you work with computers for any length of time, chances are that at some point you will have an experience where your hardware or software does not seem to be working properly. You may turn on your computer system one day and get no response. Or perhaps your monitor screen will begin flickering badly every few seconds or so. Or maybe you will issue a familiar command in a software package you work with regularly and the keyboard will lock up or the command will remain unexecuted. When any such event takes place, you will need to troubleshoot to isolate the underlying problem. If the problem is serious enough, repairs may be necessary.

Troubleshooting *Troubleshooting* refers to any action you take to diagnose or solve a problem situation. Unfortunately, many problems are unique to specific types of hardware and software, so no simple troubleshooting remedy works all of the time. Nonetheless, some simple steps and guidelines will help you out in a surprising number of instances:

- Recall exactly what happened between the time the system was operating properly and the time you began to encounter problems. Maybe there was an electrical storm outside, and your system was plugged in and damaged by lightning. Maybe someone disturbed the room where the computer sits—your hard disk may have been bumped, or the room may have been vacuumed, stirring up dust that entered your keyboard or disk-drive bay. Maybe you installed new system software during your last session, and this change is affecting the way your current application works.
- Try again. Some procedures will work when you try a second or third time. For instance, you may have pressed the wrong keys the first time, or not pressed the keys hard enough. If the problem persists, attempt to save your work, reboot your computer system, and then try again.
- Check to see that all of the equipment is plugged in and turned on and that none of the cables are detached or loose.
- If the problem seems to be caused by software, try going through the same procedure again with a backup version of the software or with another set of data. The problem may be as simple as the original program disk or data disk being defective.
- Be observant. If any strange noises came out of the disk drives when you unsuccessfully tried to boot the system up, those noises might be significant. If the output quality of your printer has deteriorated, check the printhead, observe the printer at work, and save "before" and "after" samples of outputs for further inspection by you or by someone else. Also, you may have been working successfully for several hours before the problem set in—that could be significant, too. Keep in mind that even though solving the problem may be beyond your capabilities, you may be able to supply important facts to the people repairing your system. The faster the repair technicians can diagnose and fix your system, the less money you will spend in repair costs.
- If you cannot solve the problem, temporarily abandon it if possible and work on something else. Sometimes solutions to seemingly insurmountable problems occur to you when you are in the middle of doing another job, or when you approach the problems after a nap or exercise. If you are still stumped, call a repair shop and ask to speak with a repair technician. Maybe, after you describe your problem, the technician can successfully diagnose the problem over the phone so you can fix it yourself—for free.
- Try diagnostic software. *Diagnostic software* enables you to test your system to see if parts of it are malfunctioning or are just giving you poor

FIGURE MC 5-11 **Diagnostic software.** Products such as E-Ware's WinSleuth Gold Plus let you test the speed and reliability of your hard disk.

performance (see Figure MC 5-11). Sometimes, when new equipment is added, compatibility problems arise with existing equipment. Also, hard disks can get fragmented with use over time and may need to be sped up with a disk optimizer. Fragmentation occurs when files become too big to fit in a single, contiguous space on disk and have to be split up among several, noncontiguous empty spaces.

You should weigh the time it takes to solve a problem yourself against the cost of outside repair. It is not a disgrace to give up if the problem is more than you can handle. In fact, it may just be an admission that your time is valuable and that you are wise enough to know when to call a professional for assistance.

Repairs In many cases, a problem is simple enough that no repair is necessary or you can do repairs yourself. However, sometimes the repair is beyond the scope of your capabilities and it may be necessary to seek professional help. Likely sources for professional help are the party that sold you the defective hardware or software, retail computer stores in your area, and computer repair technicians listed in the *Yellow Pages.*

Some of the things that you need to consider when thinking about having someone else diagnose or repair your system are the following:

- Is it better to repair old equipment or to buy new equipment? For instance, if the equipment to be repaired is worth less than $100, it may be cheaper to buy new equipment.
- Will the repair work be under warranty? Most new equipment is sold with a **warranty** stating that the manufacturer will pay for certain repairs if the equipment fails within a given number of days after purchase. If the warranty has not expired, the repair may cost you nothing. Be aware that many

FIGURE MC 5-12 **Repair.** As technicians repair computer systems, many of them also field calls from users about problems.

manufacturers state in their warranty that the warranty becomes void if you attempt to repair the equipment yourself or if a repair is attempted by an unauthorized person or shop. Most equipment manufacturers publish a list of authorized repair shops.

- Can you get an estimate before proceeding with the work? In many cases, repair technicians (see Figure MC 5-12) can give you a free estimate of what the repair will cost. If they cannot, you might want them to diagnose the problem first and call you when they are in a position to give an estimate. You never want to put yourself in a position where you are presented with an unexpected, outrageous bill.
- Is priority service available? People who use their computers as part of their jobs often need repairs done immediately. Many repair shops realize this and will provide same- or next-day turnaround for an extra fee. Regular turnaround time can fluctuate tremendously in any given repair shop—from a matter of hours to a few weeks, depending on how many technicians are currently on staff and how busy they are. Before requesting priority service, find out what the current turnaround time is on regular repair work.

Often, when you buy a computer system you will have the option of buying an extended maintenance contract with it, to cover certain types of repairs beyond those stated in the warranty. Figure MC 5-13 lists a number of the points covered by both warranties and maintenance contracts.

UPGRADING

Hardware and software will generally need to be upgraded over time. **Upgrading** a computer system means buying new hardware or software components that will extend the life and usefulness of your current system. Naturally, you must ask yourself a question when considering a costly upgrade: Should I be doing this, or would it be better to start fresh and buy a completely new microcomputer system?

When you initially acquire a microcomputer system it is extremely important to think about an upgrade strategy. Ideally, you should buy a microcomputer system that adheres to a well-supported standard and is flexible and large enough to be upgraded to meet reasonable future needs over the course of its lifetime. Although it usually is not possible to anticipate all of those needs, not putting any thought at all into system growth can be an invitation to future problems.

Hardware Some common types of hardware upgrades include adding more RAM to a system, installing a second hard disk, adding boards to increase the speed of the CPU or to provide new types of functionality, and adding new input or output equipment such as an image scanner or a film recorder.

Unless your system is powerful enough to handle growth, many upgrades will not be possible. For instance, if you have an Intel 80286-based processor, intensive software upgrades—such as those requiring a Windows-based environment—usually cannot be accommodated. The CPU is not powerful enough. Also, it is important to check the number of expansion slots used for add-in boards. If new peripherals require add-in boards, and all of the expansion slots that allow such boards to communicate with the CPU are used up, upgrading is not possible.

FIGURE MC 5-13 **Contracts.** A good warranty or maintenance contract typically addresses issues such as those listed here.

Coverage. The contract should state that both parts and labor are covered.

Contract period. Many contracts cover a period of one or two years. Some vendors provide a lifetime guarantee on certain types of parts.

Repair procedure. There should be a procedure spelling out clearly what steps will be taken when a problem occurs. Often, the vendor will try first to diagnose the problem over the phone. If this fails, either you will have to take or send the unit to an authorized repair center or a technician will be dispatched to your home or office within so many hours or days. If you cannot afford to be without your computer system for a long period of time, this part of the contract may be the most critical. Some contracts will provide you with a loaner system while yours is being repaired.

Hotline. Many companies provide a hotline for you to call when you have a question or problem. Sometimes you can call toll free and you will not be billed for the vendor's time. A good thing to check is how easy it is to reach the hotline; some of them are so understaffed it takes days for calls to be returned.

Other clauses. Most maintenance contracts will be void if you attempt to repair the equipment yourself or let someone who is not an authorized repairperson do it.

Today, many microcomputer systems sold in the marketplace are being touted as *upgradable PCs.* These devices are designed specifically with replacement in mind, making it easy for users to swap components—like the CPU chip or the internal hard disk—as more powerful ones become available. For instance, as shown in Figure MC 5-14, some PCs come with special sockets in the system board that make it possible to plug in an Intel *overdrive chip* (say, a 150 MHz Pentium processor) that takes over the duties of the resident CPU chip (say, a 66 MHz 486 processor). Although upgradable PCs can make significant upgrades less expensive, they may not be able to take advantage of technology benefits that upgradable-PC designers did not anticipate.

Software Software vendors typically enhance their products in some major way every year or so. Each of these upgrades—generally called **versions**—is assigned a number such as 1.0, 2.0, or 3.0. The higher the number, the later and more powerful the version. Minor versions, called **releases,** are typically numbered in increments of 0.1—say, 1.1, 1.2, and 1.3—and .01—such as 3.1 followed by 3.11.

Each version of a software product is almost guaranteed to be more sophisticated and complex and to require more RAM than its predecessors. For instance, 10 years ago a word processor or spreadsheet may have fit on one or two diskettes and worked within 256 KB RAM. Today, its latest version probably fills a dozen or more diskettes and requires one or more megabytes of RAM. Also, chances are the technical documentation accompanying the software is much thicker in size than it was a few years ago. Fortunately, however, the quality of training has increased dramatically and is geared to people at various levels of expertise.

Generally, software updates will be offered to current users of older versions and releases at a reduced price, to make the upgrade more attractive. The user has to weigh the benefits of using the new package against its costs. The costs include the sticker price of the software, additional training, and, possibly, equipment upgrades. Users are often surprised when they upgrade

FIGURE MC 5-14 **Overdrive chip.** Intel's family of overdrive processors make it easy for users to upgrade their computer systems with a more powerful chip.

USER TIP

Plug and Play

Users frequently have a problem with installing new equipment on their computers. Often, the cover of the system unit has to be taken off and an expansion card put in correctly. Then, device drivers—programs that ensure any hardware you add runs correctly on the hardware and software that you already have—must be installed. From start to finish, the installation process can be time-consuming and stressful. To make matters worse, something can go wrong—and often does.

To make it easier for PC owners to upgrade, many vendors are moving to a plug-and-play approach. Consequently, all users need to do is plug any new equipment into the back of the system unit—as they would plug a lamp or toaster into a wall socket—and they are ready to go. When users start their computers after installing the hardware, the operating environment "talks to" the new equipment and automatically downloads the proper device driver from it.

Equipment installation. What could be easier than letting your computer figure out how to work with new devices?

that the new software crawls at a snail's pace on their current equipment. As more and more software is getting fitted with GUIs and multimedia components, this problem of needing equipment upgrades to run new software is becoming more the rule than the exception.

Most software products tend to be *upward compatible.* This means that applications developed on earlier versions of the software will work on later versions of the software. Downward compatibility, however, is not always possible.

The chapter User Tip covers *plug-and-play* computing, which makes hardware and software upgrades easier than ever.

Functional versus Technological Obsolescence

Many microcomputer products serve needs for several years before they must be replaced. A product is said to be **functionally obsolete** when it no longer meets the needs of an individual or business. However, improvements to hardware and software products are continuous, and often a product is replaced on store shelves with a new version or release before it is functionally obsolete. A product in this latter class is often said to be **technologically obsolete.**

A common problem in upgrading occurs when users believe their product is functionally obsolete when it is merely technologically obsolete. Because of the rapid pace of technology, virtually anyone buying a computer system today will have at least one component technologically obsolete within a matter of months. Consequently it is generally not feasible always to keep current with versions or releases of products as soon as they become available. The most valid reasons for switching from a technologically obsolete product to a newer version are that the older product is also functionally obsolete, the older product results in significantly higher operating costs than the new one would, or support is no longer available for the older product. If you have an older product a lot of other people have, however, there will likely be vendors around for a long time, ready to service applications needs.

FIGURE MC 5-15 Computer shows. One of the largest trade fairs in the world is the Computer Dealer Expo (COMDEX) show in Las Vegas. This event commonly attracts hundreds of vendors and about 200,000 visitors.

LEARNING MORE ABOUT MICROCOMPUTERS

A wealth of resources is available to those who want to learn more about microcomputer systems and their uses. Classes, computer clubs, computer shows, magazines, newspapers, newsletters, books, and electronic media are all sources of information about microcomputers.

Classes A good way to learn about any subject is to take an appropriate class. Many colleges and universities offer microcomputer-oriented courses for undergraduate and continuing-education students. Probably the fastest way to find out about such courses is to phone a local college and ask to speak to the registrar or someone in a computer-related academic department.

Clubs Computer clubs are another effective vehicle for getting an informal education in computers. They are also a good place to get an unbiased and knowledgeable viewpoint about a particular product or vendor. Generally, clubs are organized by region, product line, or common interests. Apple computer enthusiasts join clubs such as Apple-Holics (Alaska), Apple Pie (Illinois), or Apple Core (California). Clubs such as the Boston Computer Society, on the other hand, serve the needs of a more diverse group of microcomputer buffs. Many clubs also function as buying groups, obtaining software or hardware at reduced rates. Computer clubs range in size from two or three members to several thousand.

Shows Computer shows give you a firsthand look at leading-edge hardware and software products. Such shows typically feature a number of vendor exhibits as well as seminars on various aspects of computing. One of the largest trade fairs is November's Computer Dealer Expo (COMDEX) show in Las Vegas (see Figure MC 5-15). This weeklong event commonly attracts hundreds of vendors and around 200,000 visitors, many of them from foreign countries.

COMDEX is a spectacular happening and undoubtedly will remain popular for several years. However, there is a trend today toward smaller, more specialized shows.

Periodicals Periodicals are another good source of information about microcomputers (see Figure MC 5-16). Magazines such as *Byte, Popular Computing, PC Magazine, Infoworld, Lotus, PC Week, MacWeek,* and *MacWorld* focus on microcomputers. Computer magazines vary tremendously in reading level. You can probably find and browse through these publications and more at your local bookstore, computer store, or library.

FIGURE MC 5-16 **Microcomputer periodicals.** Hundreds of periodicals are collectively targeted to general and specialized microcomputer needs. Most periodicals are published on either a weekly or monthly basis.

Books One of the best ways to learn about any aspect of personal computing is to read a book on the subject. A host of softcover and hardcover books are available, ranging from simple to highly sophisticated. Included are "how-to" books on subjects such as operating popular microcomputer systems or productivity software packages, programming in microcomputer-based languages, and the technical fundamentals of microcomputers. You can find such books in your local library, computer stores, and bookstores.

Electronic Media One easy way to learn a subject in our electronic age is to pick up a training disk or view a videotape or television show devoted to the subject. Today many microcomputer-oriented software packages are sold with training diskettes that provide onscreen tutorials, showing you which keys to press and the results. Interactive CD-ROM with full-motion video, as well as other types of professionally prepared "courseware," may also be available. Videotapes are abundantly available for standard videocassette players, so you can see how something works simply by watching your television. Television shows such as PBS's "The Computer Chronicles," which may feature a program on optical disks one week and a program on bus architectures the next, are specifically targeted to microcomputer users.

Summary

- The term *end-user development* describes such activities as users acquiring their own microcomputer resources, using and taking care of their own systems, deciding when to call for outside help, and upgrading systems on their own.
- The microcomputer marketplace consists of a wide variety of firms. Some important market segments are desktop and laptop system units, applications and systems software, monitors, printers, computer and memory chips, and disk systems.
- Users most often buy hardware and software microcomputing products from computer stores, mail-order houses, and manufacturers.
- Selecting a computer system consists of analyzing needs, listing system alternatives, evaluating alternatives, and choosing a system. Although software is normally selected before hardware, with microcomputers, software and hardware choices are often interrelated, so you might consider them jointly.
- There are a number of matters to consider in keeping your microcomputing resources protected from damage. A surge suppressor protects your system from random electrical spikes. Precautions taken with diskettes and hard disks will increase the safety of any data stored on them. In addition, you can take a number of safeguards to protect your system from dust, heat, and static, as well as measures that will extend the life of your monitor and printer.
- Security refers to protecting a computer system's hardware, software, and data from unintentional damage, malicious damage, or any type of tampering. There are many ways to secure a computer system, including physical security, password protection, disklock accessories, encryption algorithms, and vaccine programs.
- Although no two problems with a computer system are ever totally alike, a number of useful guidelines can be followed for troubleshooting problems and repairing equipment. For instance, diagnostic disks sometimes can be used to isolate a problem. When considering a repair, you should check first to see what protections are granted under warranty.
- Upgrading a computer system means buying new hardware or software components that will extend the life of your current system. Software upgrades

are often accomplished by acquiring a new release or version of the program you are currently using. Before upgrading, you need to consider whether it would be better to start fresh and buy a new computer system and whether you are trying to replace a product that is only technologically obsolete instead of functionally obsolete.

- A wealth of resources is available to those who want to learn more about microcomputer systems and their uses. Classes, computer clubs, computer shows, magazines, newspapers, newsletters, books, and electronic media are all sources of information about microcomputers.

Key Terms

Shown in parentheses are the page numbers on which key terms are boldfaced.

Computer virus (MC 154)
Disklock accessory (MC 153)
Encryption (MC 153)
Functionally obsolete (MC 160)
IBM-compatible microcomputer (MC 142)
Password (MC 153)
Physical security (MC 152)
Platform (MC 147)
Release (MC 159)
Screen saver (MC 151)
Security (MC 152)
Surge suppressor (MC 150)
Technologically obsolete (MC 160)
Upgrading (MC 158)
Vaccine program (MC 154)
Version (MC 159)
Warranty (MC 156)

Quiz

True/False

___ 1. The term *end-user development* has been coined to describe the design of computer viruses.

___ 2. The term *IBM-compatible microcomputers* refers only to computers made by IBM.

___ 3. Microsoft and Lotus Development are names of companies in the printer business.

___ 4. Mail-order firms do most of their business through retail computer stores.

___ 5. The *Computer Blue Book* shows the prices you might expect to pay for used computing equipment.

___ 6. Disklock accessories are designed specifically to make duplicate versions of files.

___ 7. A surge suppressor is designed to keep your keyboard free from static that builds up on household carpeting.

___ 8. A screen saver is a transparent cover that fits over your computer screen to cut down on glare.

____ 9. Passwords are commonly used on networks.

____ 10. A major change in a software package is referred to as a version; a minor one, a release.

Multiple Choice

____ 11. Computers that run the same software as that on most IBM microcomputers are called
- a. mainframes.
- b. value-added machines.
- c. IBM-compatible microcomputers.
- d. windowing devices.
- e. Compaq computers.

____ 12. The least expensive computers can generally be found
- a. at computer stores.
- b. from mail-order firms.
- c. in the IBM product line.
- d. listed in the *Computer Blue Book.*
- e. in the Apple product line.

____ 13. A device that protects a monitor from burning out is called a
- a. screen saver.
- b. windowing device.
- c. decelerator.
- d. surge suppressor.
- e. vaccine program.

____ 14. A device that protects a microcomputer from lightning is
- a. a screen saver.
- b. a surge suppressor.
- c. a disklock accessory.
- d. an encryption algorithm.
- e. a CPU chip.

____ 15. Which of the following is NOT a form of computer security?
- a. Disklock accessory
- b. Password
- c. Vaccine program
- d. Encryption algorithm
- e. Modem

____ 16. Disguising data is done by
- a. an encryption algorithm.
- b. a password.
- c. a disklock accessory.
- d. a modem.
- e. a vaccine program.

____ 17. A computer virus
- a. can be transmitted only through a network.
- b. is a block of code that performs unauthorized acts.
- c. can always have its effects reversed through a vaccine program.
- d. is an encrypted password.
- e. can destroy data but not other programs.

____ 18. A major enhancement of a software product is called
- a. a release.
- b. a Class-C upgrade.
- c. a Step-2 revision.
- d. an improvement.
- e. a version.

____ 19. A product that is technologically obsolete
- a. is functionally obsolete.
- b. no longer meets business needs.
- c. is still usable.
- d. is called a revision.
- e. is virtually worthless.

____ 20. Learning more about microcomputers is best accomplished through
- a. attending classes.
- b. going to shows.
- c. reading periodicals.
- d. watching videocassettes.
- e. participating in any of the above alternatives.

Matching

Select the term that best matches each phrase:

a. Compaq
b. Intel
c. Novell
d. Microsoft
e. Canon
f. Hewlett-Packard
g. Motorola
h. Cyrix
i. Lotus Development
j. Apple

____ 21. Makes CPU chips for the Apple Macintosh line of computers

____ 22. The largest U.S.-based maker of IBM-compatible microcomputers

____ 23. Known primarily for making Intel-compatible computer chips

____ 24. Famous for Windows, as well as a wide variety of systems and applications software products

____ 25. Maker of the NetWare operating system

____ 26. Known mostly for 1-2-3 and Notes

____ 27. Most famous for its printers

____ 28. Largest maker of IBM-compatible computer chips

____ 29. Known mostly for its Macintosh computer

____ 30. A Japanese technology company

Answers

True/False: 1. F; 2. F; 3. F; 4. F; 5. T; 6. F; 7. F; 8. F; 9. T; 10. T

Multiple Choice: 11. c; 12. d; 13. a; 14. b; 15. e; 16. a; 17. b; 18. e; 19. c; 20. e

Matching: 21. g; 22. a; 23. h; 24. d; 25. c; 26. i; 27. f; 28. b; 29. j; 30. e

Exercises

1. Select the names of three hardware and three software products. Then check the price of each of these items at a local computer store against prices at a warehouse club or at mail-order houses that advertise in microcomputing journals. Which prices are generally lower? (*Note:* Most products exist in several versions. When making comparisons, make sure you have prices for the same versions of each product.)

2. You are planning to upgrade from an 80486-based computer to a Pentium-based one. You are currently using WordPerfect for DOS and plan to switch to WordPerfect for Windows when you upgrade. What problems might you encounter during the conversion in the following areas:
   a. Compatibility of documents created under the older version of WordPerfect with the newer version
   b. Training yourself to use the new version
   c. Moving from a DOS to a Windows environment

3. There are a large number of microcomputer magazines and books available today, many of them prominently displayed on the shelves of bookstores and computer stores. Supply the name of at least one magazine and book that targets each of the following special-interest areas:
   a. Apple Macintosh computers
   b. Microsoft Windows
   c. The Internet
   d. Multimedia computing applications
   e. Presentation graphics
   f. WordPerfect

MC 6 Advanced Microcomputer Applications

OUTLINE

Overview

Desktop Publishing
- What Is Desktop Publishing?
- Hardware and Software
- Fundamentals of Page Design

Presentation Graphics
- Forms of Presentation Graphics
- Hardware and Software
- Fundamentals of Chart Design

Artificial Intelligence
- Expert Systems
- Natural Languages
- Vision Systems
- Robotics

Multimedia Computing
- Applications Areas
- Hardware and Software

Virtual Reality
- Applications Areas

LEARNING OBJECTIVES

After completing this chapter, you will be able to:

1. Describe what desktop publishing is as well as the hardware and software components that define it.
2. Name several forms of presentation graphics as well as hardware and software that are used to produce them.
3. Explain the role of artificial intelligence in improving the quality of applications software.
4. Identify the components of a multimedia computer system as well as name several multimedia applications.
5. Describe virtual reality and name several uses to which it can be put.

OVERVIEW

In this chapter we cover several important areas of potential interest to advanced users of microcomputer systems. First, we turn to desktop publishing and presentation graphics, both of which are useful to know about if you wish to provide a polished look to your business output. Desktop-published documents are more pleasing to the eye than straight, word-processed text, and thoughtfully prepared presentation graphics can make a difference in how your audiences perceive the information that you present to them. Knowledge in either applications area can make you appear to be more "professional" to others and give you a competitive advantage over someone without presentation skills.

Then we cover artificial intelligence—the ability of computer systems to perform in ways that would be considered intelligent if observed in humans. The main areas of artificial intelligence—all of which are addressed in the chapter—are expert systems, natural languages, vision systems, and robotics.

Next we discuss multimedia computing, in which audio and video data are added to traditional text and graphics in computer-system applications. Using multimedia tools effectively is another way to present information creatively through technology. As we head toward the 21st century, more and more computer systems are becoming equipped with multimedia components.

The final topic in the chapter is virtual reality, the use of computers to create artificial environments that seem almost real. Here we will look at several of the applications areas in which virtual reality techniques hold great promise.

DESKTOP PUBLISHING

The late 1970s introduced desktop computing—an entire computer system capable of fitting on a desktop. Thanks to other major improvements on the software and hardware fronts, we now have desktop publishing—microcomputer-based publishing systems that fit on a desktop.

What Is Desktop Publishing?

Desktop publishing hardware/software systems let you create and combine on a page such elements as text (in a variety of typefaces), art, and photos, thus creating attractive documents that look as if they came off a printer's press. Desktop publishing systems are designed to replace many of the traditionally manual, labor-intensive tasks associated with cutting, arranging, and pasting elements onto a page. Because they make it possible for publishing to be done in-house, they also enable companies to save money, save time, and have more control over the look of finished documents. In the last decade or so, desktop publishing has rapidly evolved into a major applications area within the field of computers. Figure MC 6-1 lists and illustrates several applications for desktop publishing.

As you can see from studying the images in Figure MC 6-1, the basic difference between word processing and desktop publishing is one of document "look." Whereas word processing deals mainly with straight, nontypeset text—and maybe a few simple fonts for emphasis—desktop publishing involves full-fledged typesetting and imagesetting. *Typesetting* implies full control over type styles and sizes as well as spacing between words, letters, and lines. *Imagesetting* involves combining on a page both type and such artwork elements as drawings, photographs, and color.

FIGURE MC 6-1 **Applications for desktop publishing.** Although low-end desktop publishing systems are adequate for simple outputs such as newsletters and price lists, high-end systems are usually required for sophisticated work such as books and brochures.

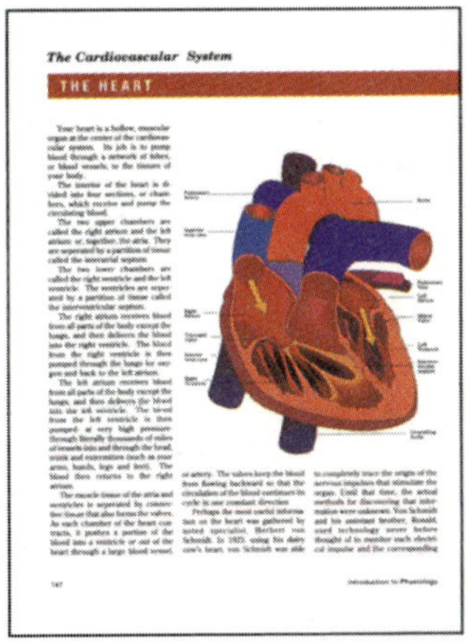

- ☐ Advertisements
- ☐ Annual reports
- ☐ Books
- ☐ Brochures
- ☐ Business reports
- ☐ Catalogs
- ☐ Business cards
- ☐ Resumes
- ☐ Restaurant menus

- ☐ Magazines
- ☐ Newsletters
- ☐ Newspapers
- ☐ Posters
- ☐ Price lists
- ☐ Software/system documentation
- ☐ Stationery and business forms
- ☐ Training manuals
- ☐ Signs

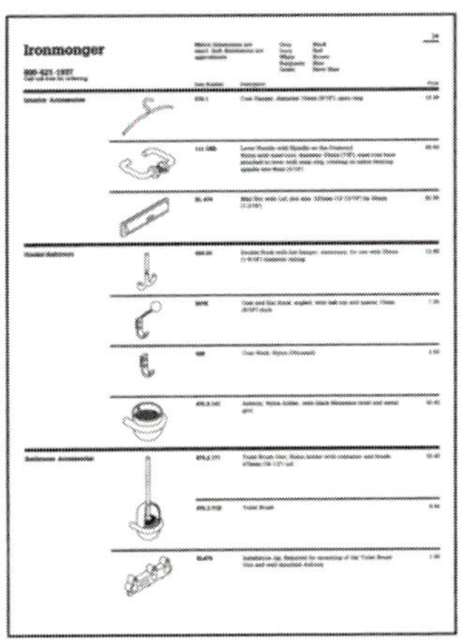

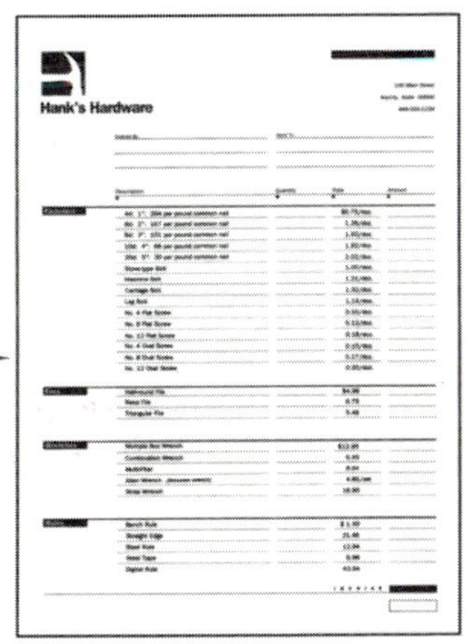

Only a decade or so ago, most users did their desktop publishing by purchasing a standalone page-makeup package. Although you can still buy such packages today, substantial improvements in computer-graphics technology have caused a dramatic change in product offerings. The leading word-processing packages now have so many desktop publishing features that many users are able to use them to produce typeset, image-laden pages. With word-processing packages having improved vastly in their desktop publishing capabilities, the traditional desktop publishing package has, in response, shifted in an upward direction, too. Today's trend is to combine high-end desktop publishing, painting and drawing, and photo manipulation into a single product.

Desktop publishing systems have come a long way in allowing individuals to produce documents that look as if they were professionally prepared, but desktop systems are still a far cry from professional-level publishing systems. Systems falling into this latter category are the preferred choice for producing top-quality printed materials such as corporate annual reports and full-color books.

Hardware and Software

Naturally, not all desktop publishing systems are the same. You can spend less than a hundred dollars for a system that produces simple newsletters, but you will have to pay several times that amount for one that creates stunning and creative color artwork. Desktop publishing systems targeted for commercial applications often consist of several hardware and software components.

Hardware Hardware used for high-end desktop publishing usually includes a high-end microcomputer system, a laser printer, a graphics-oriented monitor, and an image scanner. These devices were covered in depth in Chapter 2 and are therefore addressed only briefly here.

- **HIGH-END MICROCOMPUTER SYSTEM** High-quality desktop publishing requires a microprocessor that packs plenty of power, a respectable amount of RAM, and a hard disk with plenty of storage. Manipulation of graphical fonts, photos, and art can be computationally intensive. A mere two-page newsletter, for instance, can require 200 KB of storage. A set of large characters uses about 150 KB, and a scanned image may need another megabyte. Such work requires a system unit like those based on high-end Intel or PowerPC chips. The systems should have at least 8 to 16 MB of RAM and several hundred megabytes of hard-disk storage.

- **LASER PRINTER** Most laser printers for microcomputer-based desktop publishing applications cost anywhere from about $500 to several thousand dollars. These devices have their own built-in microprocessors, a few megabytes of RAM, and several ROM chips that carry popular fonts. Greater amounts of RAM allow you to output images of greater complexity. Many laser printers output at a resolution of either 300 dpi (dots per vertical and horizontal inch, or 90,000 dots per square inch) or 600 dpi, and some even produce color hard copy. For photographic output, 600 dpi is recommended. If you require higher resolutions, you will need professional typesetting equipment (which works at 1,000 dpi or more).

  The laser printer in your computer system relies on a specific **page description language (PDL)** to carry out its work. The two most common PDLs are Adobe's *PostScript,* which is widely used in the fastest and most expensive laser printers, and Hewlett-Packard's *Printer Command Language (PCL),* which is more popular on slower and less expensive laser printers.

- **GRAPHICS-ORIENTED MONITOR** Most monitors used with microcomputer systems contain a relatively small (15-inch) screen that can comfortably display about half of a standard printed page at a time. On such screens, the resolution usually is adequate for text and some simple graphics. For desktop publishing applications, however, it generally is preferable to have a bigger screen with Super VGA or XGA resolution, both to fine-tune detailed graphics and to see without eyestrain either a full-page or a two-page layout on the screen at one time. Monitors designed for these purposes often have screens up to 50 percent larger than the typical microcomputer display. Like graphics displays with 15-inch screens, they are

FIGURE MC 6-2 **Graphics-oriented monitor.** Shown here is a tiltable monitor that lets you switch between (a) standard portrait mode and, (b) for wide outputs, landscape mode.

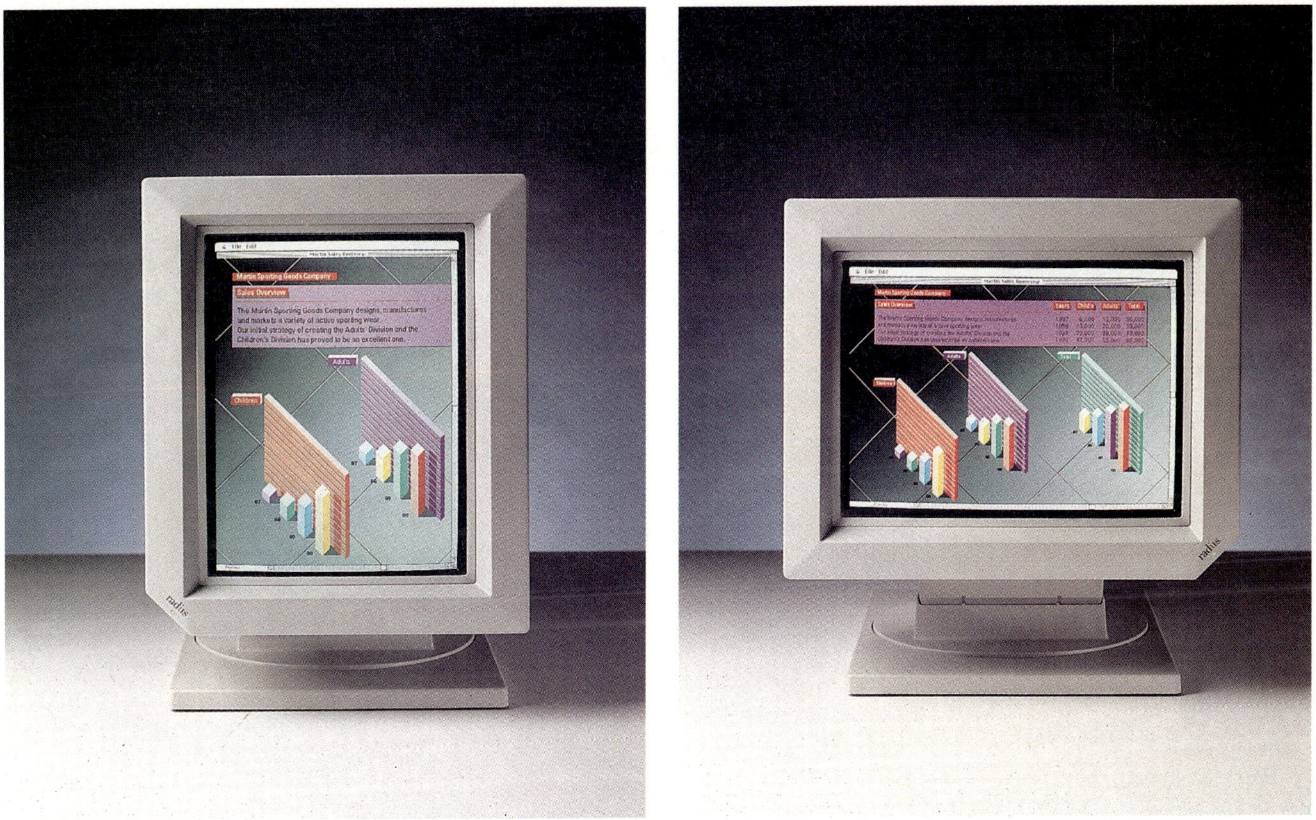

(a) Portrait mode

(b) Landscape mode

capable of **WYSIWYG** (what you see is what you get) output, meaning that users see on the display screen exactly what they will be getting on a printed page.

Figure MC 6-2 shows a monitor targeted to desktop-publishing applications. The product featured in the figure has a tiltable display that can switch between portrait and landscape modes. *Portrait mode* (see Figure MC 6-2a) is used for standard page displays; standard pages are usually 11 inches deep and 8½ inches wide. *Landscape mode* (see Figure MC 6-2b) is for pages that have a reverse orientation—say, 11 inches wide and 8½ inches deep—such as wide tables or worksheets. Most word-processing and desktop publishing packages, and laser printers, will let you output in portrait or landscape modes.

■ **Image Scanner** An image scanner (see Figure MC 2-4) allows you to scan photographs, drawings, or text and digitize them directly into computer memory. Later, you can edit the images with illustration software and hardware. Some image scanners also use optical character recognition (OCR) software, which enables them to recognize certain text characters instead of just digitizing them. Such a feature allows you later to edit any text that you enter with the scanner.

USER TIP

Service Bureaus

You want to create a color brochure on your word processor, but you do not have a color printer. You want to make 35-millimeter color slides for a meeting coming up in two weeks, but you do not have a film recorder to produce them. Someone sent you some important documents on a Macintosh-formatted disk, but you cannot read it—you have an IBM-compatible computer that runs only in a Microsoft Windows environment.

Question: What do you do?

Answer: Consider going to a service bureau.

Service bureaus, which enable to you farm out computer work you cannot do on your own, exist in most towns of reasonable size. A few years ago, many of them were strictly copy centers or print shops, because virtually all they did was duplicate hard-copy documents. Today, many service bureaus have expanded their offerings to include the following types of work: making color copies of disk images in paper, slide, or overhead-transparency form; computer rental; page-layout and typesetting services; creating output for presentations; commercial-art services; and videoconferencing.

Service bureau outsourcing. Farm out the computer work you are unable to do on your own.

Hardware for high-end desktop-publishing and presentation-graphics applications can be expensive. As the chapter User Tip suggests, users who cannot afford all of the equipment they need should consider farming out some of their work to a service bureau.

Software A variety of software and software-based products are used in desktop publishing environments. These include page-makeup software, word-processing software, typefaces and fonts, clip-art libraries, and art and illustration software.

- **Page-Makeup Software** The programs whose principal function is to combine text, photos, and art elements into a finished page are collectively referred to as **page-makeup software.** Some of the leading page-makeup programs are Adobe System's PageMaker, Corel's Corel Ventura, and Quark's Quark Xpress. Corel was one of the first companies to fully integrate page makeup and art preparation into a single package or suite. Its Corel DRAW! 6 package—which now includes the popular Corel Ventura along with the Corel DRAW! illustration program—has virtually all the tools a user needs to produce high-end desktop publishing outputs.

- **Word-Processing Software** In many cases, users can do quite respectable desktop publishing within their word-processing packages. If higher-end page makeup is required, no problem—the vendors of the lead-

FIGURE MC 6-3 Typefaces. A typeface is a collection of visually consistent characters. Shown here are the (a) Courier, (b) Helvetica, and (c) Times typefaces.

(a) Courier (b) Helvetica (c) Times

ing page-makeup programs have designed their products to accept text prepared with several of the leading word processors. When acquiring a page-makeup program, it is always wise to check out which word processors it recognizes. Although most page-makeup programs do contain built-in word-processing features, enabling you to modify any text that you import to them, it is important to recognize that their primary function is page makeup. Consequently, they are not as easy to use for word processing as your average word processor.

■ **Typefaces and Fonts** A **typeface** is a collection of characters—including upper- and lowercase characters, digits, and special symbols—that share a common design (see Figure MC 6-3). Dozens of companies sell typefaces in electronic form. Some companies carry well over a thousand different typefaces. Each typeface is designed to provide a different look.

Typefaces can be either monospaced or proportionally spaced. A **monospaced** typeface is one in which each character takes up the same amount of horizontal space. This textbook, however, like most others, was typeset on a system that proportionally spaces characters. **Proportional spacing** is a feature that allocates more horizontal space on a line to some characters than to others. For example, a capital *M* takes up more space than a lowercase *i*. A microspacing feature may also be available. With **microspacing,** fractions of a full blank space are inserted within each line in places where they are not likely to be noticed so that the left- and right-hand margins are flush. Proportional spacing and microspacing are shown in Figure MC 6-4.

Three widely used typefaces—Courier, Helvetica, and Times—are shown in Figure MC 6-3. *Courier* is a monospaced typeface that is useful when a typewritten look is desired. *Helvetica* is used to achieve a clean, modern feel and also is visually compatible with a wide range of other typefaces, which may need to appear on the same page. *Times* is useful for a wide variety of text applications. Helvetica and Times are proportionally spaced typefaces.

FIGURE MC 6-4 Proportionally spaced characters with microspacing. With proportional spacing, more horizontal space on a line is allotted to some characters than to others. Note, for instance, that a capital *H* takes up more space than the lowercase *t* and *i* combined. Microspacing inserts fractional spaces between characters to make a line appear more attractive to the eye.

How tight is tight?

How tight is tight?

How tight is tight?

How tight is tight?

Some typefaces are related and thus constitute a **typeface family.** Figure MC 6-5 shows four typefaces in Adobe's Times family. Generally speaking, typefaces from the same family produce a compatible look when mixed on a page.

Type is normally measured in points (see Figure MC 6-6). A point is 1/72nd of an inch, and the size of a character in points is called the character's **point size.** Technically speaking, a **font** is defined in the typesetting world as the complete set of characters in a particular typeface and point size. For instance, 12-point Times Roman constitutes a font. In practice, however, many people use the terms *font* and *typeface* interchangeably.

Fonts are of two types: bit-mapped and outline (see Figure MC 6-7). *Bit-mapped fonts* are described by a fixed configuration of dots. Whereas they are the least expensive kind of font, you cannot scale them to different sizes. *Outline fonts* consist of mathematical curves that describe how characters are shaped. They are more expensive than bit-mapped fonts, but you can scale them to virtually any size you want and also create your own fonts. Two widely used outline fonts are *TrueType,* often bundled with Microsoft and Apple software, and *PostScript Type 1,* commonly found in high-end desktop publishing applications.

■ **CLIP-ART LIBRARIES** A **clip-art** library is a collection of prepared art images. You can use these images on their own or as building blocks to create other images. You can even modify them. A sample of clip-art pieces appears in Figure MC 6-8.

Clip-art libraries are bundled into many illustration packages (discussed next) and are also sold separately by third-party vendors. Vendors of illustration packages often use a proprietary format for their clip art, usually one that supports their other products, whereas third-party clip-art vendors typically make their clip art available in a variety of standard formats.

FIGURE MC 6-5 **Typeface family.** Related typefaces form a typeface family. Shown here are four typefaces in Adobe's Times family.

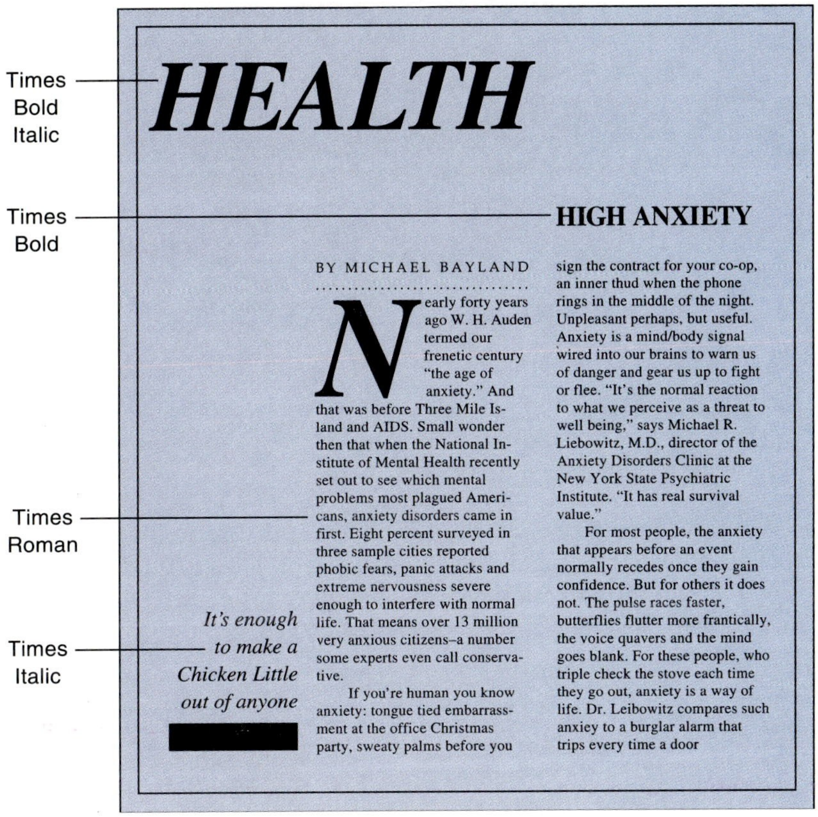

HEALTH

HIGH ANXIETY

BY MICHAEL BAYLAND

Nearly forty years ago W. H. Auden termed our frenetic century "the age of anxiety." And that was before Three Mile Island and AIDS. Small wonder then that when the National Institute of Mental Health recently set out to see which mental problems most plagued Americans, anxiety disorders came in first. Eight percent surveyed in three sample cities reported phobic fears, panic attacks and extreme nervousness severe enough to interfere with normal life. That means over 13 million very anxious citizens–a number some experts even call conservative.

If you're human you know anxiety: tongue tied embarrassment at the office Christmas party, sweaty palms before you sign the contract for your co-op, an inner thud when the phone rings in the middle of the night. Unpleasant perhaps, but useful. Anxiety is a mind/body signal wired into our brains to warn us of danger and gear us up to fight or flee. "It's the normal reaction to what we perceive as a threat to well being," says Michael R. Liebowitz, M.D., director of the Anxiety Disorders Clinic at the New York State Psychiatric Institute. "It has real survival value."

For most people, the anxiety that appears before an event normally recedes once they gain confidence. But for others it does not. The pulse races faster, butterflies flutter more frantically, the voice quavers and the mind goes blank. For these people, who triple check the stove each time they go out, anxiety is a way of life. Dr. Leibowitz compares such anxiey to a burglar alarm that trips every time a door

It's enough to make a Chicken Little out of anyone

■ **Illustration Software** **Illustration software packages** enable artwork to be created from scratch. Also, they accept existing artwork as input and allow it to be modified using the software's image-manipulation facilities.

An image can be input to illustration software in several ways. If you have an image scanner, you can read a hard-copy image directly into RAM. If you have a digitizing tablet, you can trace over a hard-copy image with a stylus, thereby transferring the outline of the image to memory. Or, if the

FIGURE MC 6-6 **Point size.** Point size refers to the size of type. A typeface in a particular point size is commonly called a font.

This is 10-point Helvetica

This is 12-point Helvetica

This is 18-point Helvetica

This is 24-point Helvetica

FIGURE MC 6-7 **Bit-mapped versus outline fonts.** Bit-mapped fonts (left) are made up of a fixed pattern of dots, whereas outline fonts (right) are defined by a series of curves. Outline fonts can be resized to different point sizes; bit-mapped fonts cannot.

image is in a clip-art library, you can transfer the appropriate clip-art directly to the illustration software if both use the same file formats.

High-quality illustration software enables you to size, rotate, flip, recolor, distort, and edit virtually any digitally stored drawing or photograph to your heart's content (see Figure MC 6-9). Because images are manipulated at

FIGURE MC 6-8 **Clip art.** Clip-art libraries are bundled into many illustration software packages and are also sold separately.

FIGURE MC 6-9 **Illustration software.** Illustration packages enable art images to be created and modified. Here, onscreen tools enable the artist to select colors and styling effects.

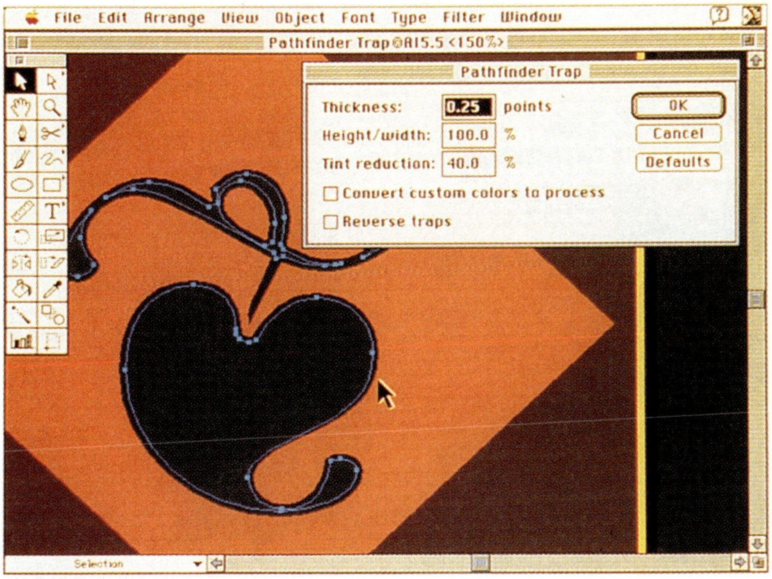

electronically fast speeds, it is possible to try out dozens of possibilities in the time it would normally take to produce only a single image by manual means. Once an image is satisfactory, it can be exported to a dedicated page-makeup program or transferred to the page-makeup routine within the software package that includes the illustration software.

Sometimes illustration software packages are distinguished by whether they are oriented primarily toward painting or drawing. *Painting packages* enable you to create bit-mapped images and to color them pixel by pixel. Usually, the images you create cannot be resized without loss of resolution. For instance, blowing them up may result in jagged edges, whereas reducing them may result in a blurry mess. In contrast, *drawing packages* enable you to create outlines that can be resized. Once properly sized, these outlines can be filled in with colors. Many packages will allow you to both paint and draw.

Several illustration software packages are available today. Among the current best-sellers are Adobe's Illustrator, Corel's Corel DRAW!, and Claris's McDraw and McPaint.

Fundamentals of Page Design

A number of principles have evolved over the years as to what constitutes fundamentally sound page design. Four of these principles—balance, unity, emphasis, and mood—will be covered next. While each of them addresses a separate aspect of page design, keep in mind that the most important thing is for the layout to support the message that the document is intended to deliver.

Balance Page *balance* requires that single pages not be overly weighted by visual elements and that two-page spreads not be visually out of kilter from page to page. Figure MC 6-10 provides examples of balanced and unbalanced

FIGURE MC 6-10 **Balance illustrated.** A layout should be balanced so that it is pleasing to the eye. (a) This piece shows a good balance among the photo, heading, and body-copy text. (b) This piece, which has a "hole" in the middle, is unbalanced. Creating balance is largely a manual, judgmental process left to the talents of the user.

(a) Balanced layout

(b) Unbalanced layout

pages. Often, balance can be enhanced by the use of white space on a page. Of course, balance alone does not make a desktop-published work. Some books can be perfectly balanced and yet be visually boring.

Unity The principle of *unity* requires that all of the elements on a page, page spread, or book be compatible. Unity extends to matters such as consistency in type; consistency in the size and treatment of illustrations, headings, and margins; color compatibility; uniformity in the length of chapters; and a number of other issues. Lack of unity often draws readers to the conclusion that the published output was hastily, whimsically, or amateurishly prepared. Imagine how messy this book would look, for instance, if the typefaces used varied from chapter to chapter, or if half the figures were done in one art style and the other half in another.

Emphasis The whole idea behind *emphasis* is that important elements on a page be drawn to the reader's eye. A technique commonly used in publications to achieve emphasis is the use of *reverses.* See the magazine cover in Figure MC 6-1, where light text is shown against a dark background; this is the reverse of the way copy normally appears—dark text on a light background. Another technique is the use of type proportions, such as making headings large to attract attention. A wise choice of colors and a good use of white space can also effectively increase emphasis.

Mood In the context of publishing, *mood* is a feeling that people get when looking at printed material. Often a mood is established within seconds of looking at something. If the potential reader is put in the wrong mood, the written material may never be fully read. On the other hand, if the potential reader is put in the right mood, the message within the publication may be amplified.

A mood can be imparted by several means, including color and typeface choice.

Bright colors often add excitement to a publication, whereas subdued colors or black and white convey formality. You would not expect a funeral parlor to advertise in bright colors, and you will find few popular magazines on bookstore shelves with black-and-white covers.

Like colors, typefaces have different "personalities." Some are serious, others whimsical. Some have an air of elegance and sophistication, whereas others are intended to be bold and direct.

PRESENTATION GRAPHICS

There is an old saying that a picture is worth a thousand words. If you try to explain to others what you look like, for instance, it may take several minutes. Show them a color photograph, on the other hand, and you can convey the same or better information about yourself within seconds.

Pictures are also extremely useful in business. A person can often spot trends or make comparisons much more quickly by looking at a visual image than by reading text-only or number-only output containing the same information. Furthermore, a point can often be made far more dramatically and effectively by using pictures.

Forms of Presentation Graphics

A **presentation graphic**—sometimes called a *presentation visual* or *chart*—is an image that visually enhances the impact of information communicated to other people. Presentation graphics can take many different forms, a number of which are illustrated in Figure MC 6-11. With the right types of software and hardware, the creation of presentation graphics is limited only by imagination.

There are several compelling reasons to use presentation graphics in business. Trends can be spotted or comparisons made much more quickly when data are in chart form. Presentation graphics can also be used to make a point much more convincingly or dramatically than plain text can. Recent studies have found that presentation graphics also make the presenter look more professional in the eyes of others.

Here, we will discuss in detail four of the most widely used types of presentation graphics—bar, pie, line, and text charts. We will also look at a number of ways in which these charts vary and examine where each is most appropriate. The best graphic in any given situation depends on the point you are trying to make.

Bar Charts **Bar charts** are especially useful for comparing relative magnitudes of items and for showing the frequency with which events occur. They can also be used to illustrate changes in a single item over time.

In a typical bar chart, one axis represents a categorical or *qualitative* phenomenon; the other represents a numeric or *quantitative* one. For instance, in Figure MC 6-12a, the horizontal axis (X-axis) represents months of the year, the qualitative phenomenon, whereas the vertical axis (Y-axis) represents price, the quantitative phenomenon.

A number of different types of bar charts are available, including the simple bar chart, stacked bar chart, grouped (clustered) bar chart, range bar chart, pictograph, and 3-D bar chart (see Figures MC 6-11a through MC 6-11f).

Each type of bar chart has strengths and weaknesses relative to prospective applications. A *range chart,* for instance, would be most useful for show-

FIGURE MC 6-11 **Types of presentation graphics.** Any type of graphical image that enhances the impact of information as it is shown to people is a presentation graphic. Whereas packages vary with respect to the number and types of presentation graphics they produce, most allow you to create simple bar, pie, and line charts.

(a) Simple bar chart
(b) Stacked bar chart
(c) Grouped (clustered) bar chart
(d) Range bar chart
(e) Pictograph
(f) 3-D graphic
(g) Pie chart
(h) Exploded pie chart
(i) 3-D pie chart
(j) Line chart
(k) Multiseries line chart
(l) Area chart
(m) Scatter diagram
(n) Map
(o) Exploded map
(p) Hierarchy chart
(q) Flowchart
(r) Sociogram
(s) Bubble chart
(t) Text chart

ing daily highs and lows of a particular stock in the stock market (see Figure MC 6-12a). A *grouped (clustered) bar chart,* on the other hand, would be more useful for showing something such as overall income comparisons for this year and last year by quarter (see Figure MC 6-12b). Grouped bar charts are especially effective when you want to emphasize a difference between two items over time. When one set of bars is consistently bigger than another set of bars, as is the case here, a *stacked bar chart* can also effectively show the differences between the two sets of bars (see Figure MC 6-12c). A *Gantt chart,* shown in Figure MC 6-12d, is particularly handy for showing when events in schedules begin and end.

FIGURE MC 6-12 **Four bar charts.** Bar charts are especially useful for comparing the relative magnitudes of items and for showing the frequency with which events occur.

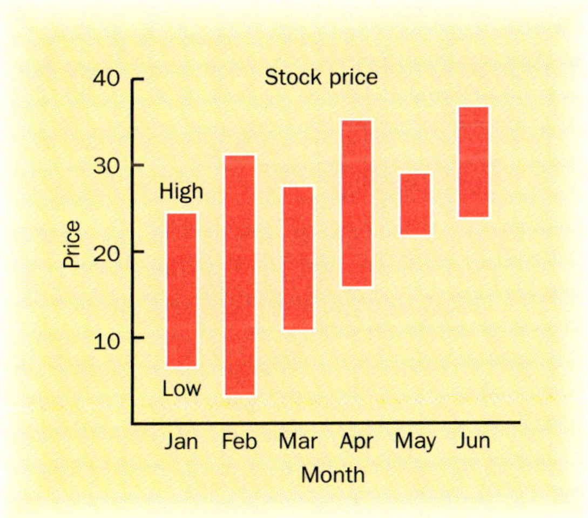

(a) Range chart

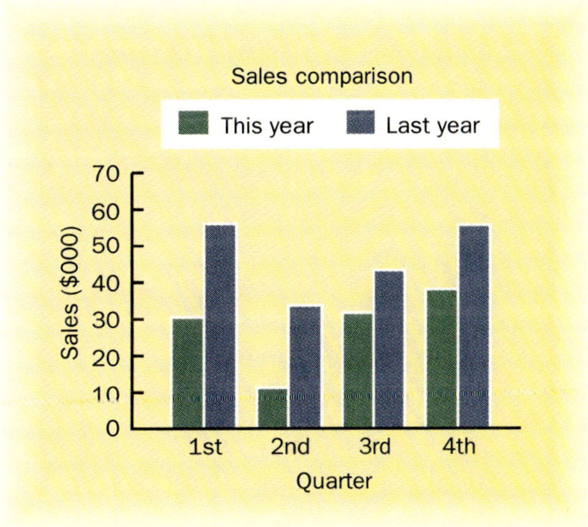

(b) Grouped bar chart

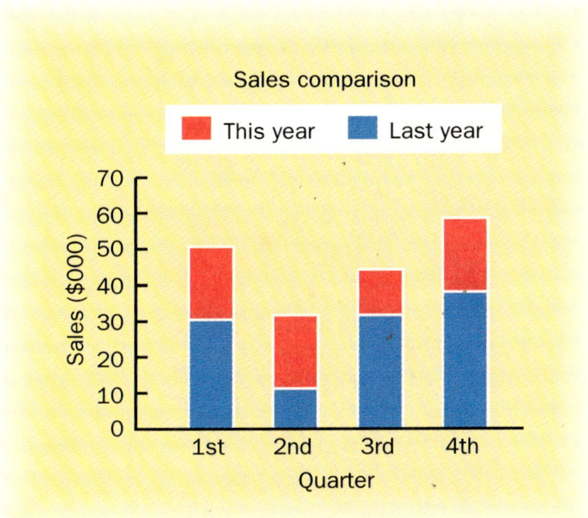

(c) Stacked bar chart

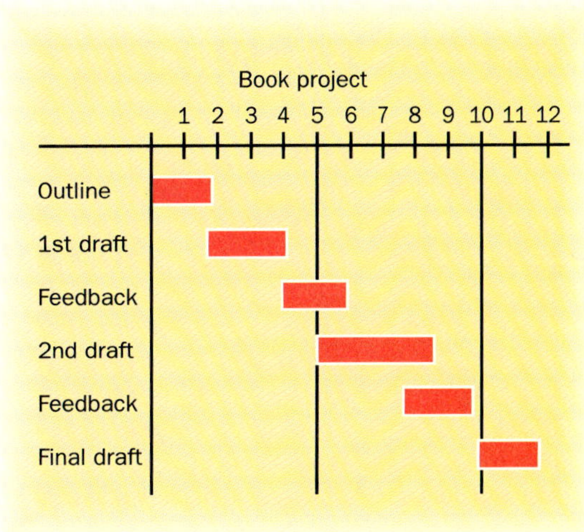

(d) Gantt chart

When designing bar charts, it's a good idea to keep the total number of categories on the X-axis to a half dozen or fewer. Any more than this may be too much information to cram into a single visual.

Pie Charts **Pie charts** are commonly used to show how parts of something relate to a whole (see Figure MC 6-11g to MC 6-11i). Each slice of the "pie," or circle, represents a percentage, or share, of the total. One of the major advantages of the pie chart is that it is extremely easy to understand.

Most presentation graphics packages enable you to "explode" a pie chart to emphasize one or more of the slices, as shown in Figure MC 6-13. The way a pie slice can be exploded varies from one software package to another. Some packages pull the slice out a fixed, predefined distance. Others let you use a mouse to select the slice on the screen and drag it to the place where you want it. Virtually all packages allow you to color or texture each of the pie slices as well, as illustrated in the figure.

Pie charts should not have more than a half dozen or so slices. The more slices there are, the harder it is to recognize relative sizes of the shares they represent. When the number of slices in a pie chart becomes large, the smallest slices should be combined into single slice.

Line Charts **Line charts** (see Figures MC 6-11j to MC 6-11l) are somewhat similar to bar charts. One major difference, however, is that line charts are used in cases where *both* axes represent quantitative phenomena. A second major difference is that, because the line in the chart is unbroken, the effect on the eye can be much more dramatic.

As with bar charts, there is a rich variety of line charts. Two examples are shown in Figure MC 6-14. And as with bar and pie charts, a line chart should not contain too many elements. Lines often cross one another, adding a com-

FIGURE MC 6-13 **Exploded pie chart.** In an exploded pie chart, a single pie slice is moved away slightly from the rest of the pie to call attention to it.

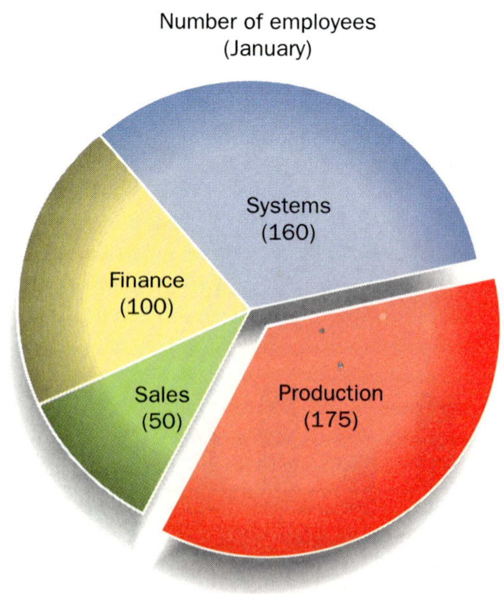

FIGURE MC 6-14 **Line charts.** Because the line in a line chart is unbroken, the effect on the eye can be dramatic.

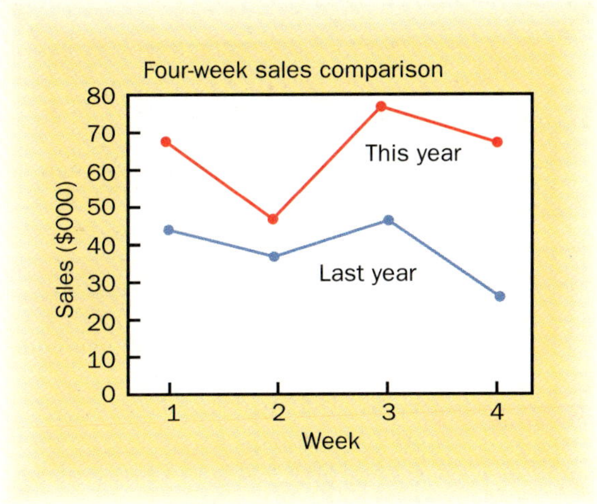

(a) Multiseries line chart

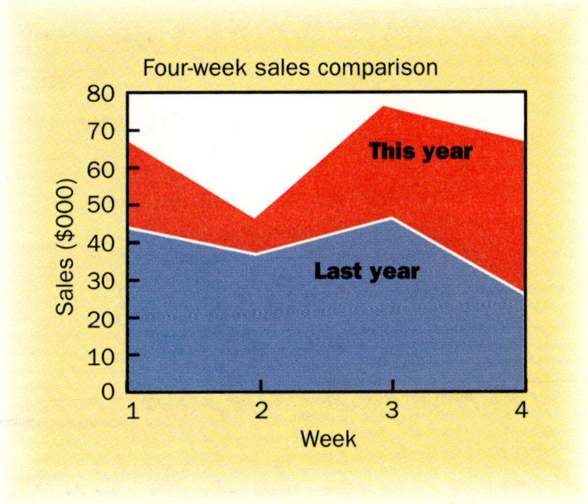

(b) Area chart

plexity not found in a bar or pie chart. Any more than four or five lines will probably make the chart look confusing.

Text Charts Some researchers estimate that approximately 70 or 80 percent of the information presented at meetings is text based. Thus, it is somewhat surprising that, until recently, very little attention has been given in presentation graphics packages to **text charts.** Part of this neglect is due to the "sizzle" that pictures impart to a presentation. Sometimes people come away from a presentation remembering more about how something was presented than about what was actually said in words.

Text charts often use a presentation technique called a *build.* As shown in Figure MC 6-15, text often is presented as a bulleted list that is built bullet by bullet in a series of visuals. This is normally more effective than presenting the entire bulleted list as a single visual, which may be overwhelming. In a build, audience attention is focused on the latest bulleted item in the list.

FIGURE MC 6-15 **Building a list through text charts.** Each text chart shown in the sequence adds a new bulleted item to the list being presented.

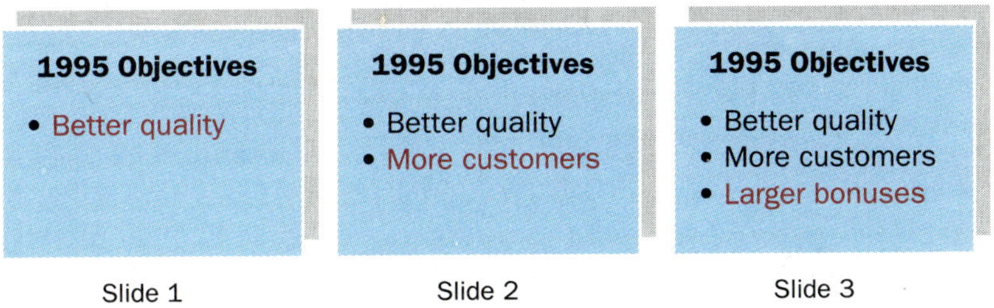

And if some audience members fall asleep, upon awakening they will know exactly which bulleted item is under consideration. As with other types of charts, the creator of a text chart should be careful not to pack too much information into a single visual.

Hardware and Software

A variety of hardware devices and software packages exists for people who prepare and show presentation graphics.

Hardware Hardware used in the preparation of presentation visuals includes many of the same types of devices used in desktop publishing environments. Perhaps the most critical devices are those described in the following subsections.

- **High-End Microcomputer System** Because graphic images generally require lots of computation and storage space, the system should include a state-of-the-art CPU with plenty of RAM and hard-disk storage.
- **Color Plotter and Printer** A color plotter and printer are ideal for preparing hard-copy outputs for meetings. A film recorder is especially useful if the presentation visuals are to be in 35 millimeter film format.
- **Graphics-Oriented Color Monitor** A graphics-oriented monitor enables you to inspect visuals in detail. A monitor that provides color output is usually essential, because color is the standard for most types of presentation graphics.
- **Special Equipment** Presentation visuals are often shown to audiences on special equipment, such as a slide projector, overhead projector, or similar device. Slides and overheads can be either in the traditional hard-copy format or in electronic format. The electronic format makes it possible to run the presentation from the computer, customizing it "on the fly" to the needs of the audience and incorporating dazzling special effects.

Software Presentation graphics software enables you to draw and present bar charts, pie charts, and similar graphics. A variety of presentation graphics packages exist in the marketplace. Most of them fall into one of two classes: dedicated presentation graphics packages and presentation graphics packages that are bundled (integrated) with spreadsheet software.

- **Dedicated Packages** Dedicated packages provide the most powerful types of graphics features—for instance, a wider selection of legend fonts, graph types, and device drivers. Many also come with extensive clip-art libraries and contain painting/drawing software routines to dress up the graphs you create. In short, if your presentation graphics needs are extensive, a dedicated package is more likely to contain the types of features you require. Some examples of widely used dedicated packages are Harvard Graphics, Cricket Presents, Persuasion, Pixie, and Hollywood. There are also dedicated packages that serve specialized needs, such as creating special effects for slide shows or creating animated (moving) images.
- **Spreadsheet Packages** Unfortunately, dedicated packages often lack some of the calculation and data-modeling features available with spreadsheets. Consequently, you either have to type ready-to-go data directly into the dedicated package or import these data from another package. Spreadsheet packages, such as 1-2-3 and Excel, overcome this limitation by integrating data-development and graphing functions into a single product.

They are ideal for users who require a strong data manipulation capability and whose presentation graphics needs are relatively modest. Today, with technology becoming ever more powerful on the average desktop, many of the major spreadsheet packages are incorporating features that just a few years ago could be found only in dedicated packages.

Fundamentals of Chart Design

Earlier in the chapter we looked at several elements of style that are fundamental to desktop publishing. When you think about it, there are many similarities between designing a publication and designing presentation visuals. But whereas publications usually are kept for a time, presentation visuals are fleeting. Each chart is seen for a brief moment, and then it is gone. Consequently, the main objective in creating presentation visuals is to impart short, clear messages that sink into the minds of the audience.

Several general principles govern good chart design, including simplicity, consistency, emphasis, and balance.

Simplicity *Simplicity* suggests that some of the best charts are those that convey a single, strong message. A common error made by beginners is trying to cram too much information into a single image. Although the image may be edifying, its visual impact can easily result in an information overload in the minds of the audience. Generally, the more information added to a graphic, the less attention given by the viewer to the essential information. When a message is complex, it is often best to divide it into a series of simpler messages, each of which can be conveyed in a single chart. The idea, expressed earlier, of limiting the number of bars, pie slices, and lines in a chart is an example of how to apply the principle of simplicity. So, too, is the build concept used with text charts.

Consistency Presentations are usually more effective when given a unified, consistent appearance. *Consistency* can be imparted to a slide presentation by using the same font or typeface throughout or by having a corporate logo or a similar backdrop appear on each slide (see Figure MC 6-16). Many presentation graphics packages have a template feature that enables the user to create and save a **master slide,** containing the logo or backdrop. Every time the user needs to develop a new slide, a fresh copy of the master slide can be summoned to the screen and "pasted up" with text, graphics, or other elements.

Many packages also have a *style sheet* feature that enables storing and recalling specific text formats and fonts. This ensures typographic consistency among all of the images created.

Emphasis *Emphasis* is a matter of making sure that the elements that constitute your graphic support your message fully. Emphasis can be imparted by a number of things. You can use color, for instance, to draw the viewer's eye to an important area of the slide. In pie charts, both the exploding pie slice and the choice of number of pie slices are issues of emphasis. The exploding slice draws the reader's eye to an element, thereby emphasizing it; too many pie slices confuse the eye, thereby diminishing any emphasis.

Balance *Balance* refers to the way the chart is visually weighted with elements. Good balance means that the eyes of the audience are focused on the subject of the visual and not, say, on an element that is out of kilter. It is important that the text be sized in visually appealing proportion to the picture elements. Also, if the chart is to contain a message-rich title, it

FIGURE MC 6-16 **Consistency.** A presentation often looks more professional when its series of images has a consistent background. Putting a corporate logo or a similar backdrop on each visual is possible with a master slide feature.

(a)

(b)

should generally be bold—large enough to attract attention but not so large as to overwhelm the other elements. Subtitles should generally appear under the main title, in smaller type. Such graphic elements as the size of axis labels and the thickness of graph lines should also be in harmony with the rest of the visual.

ARTIFICIAL INTELLIGENCE

The ability of computer systems to perform in ways that would be considered intelligent if observed in humans is commonly referred to as **artificial intelligence (AI).** The field of AI evolved in the 1950s and 1960s from attempts to write programs that would enable computers to rival skilled humans at games such as chess and checkers, to prove difficult mathematical theorems, and so forth.

FIGURE MC 6-17 Benefits of expert systems.

Expert systems

- Capture the knowledge of company experts who someday will retire, resign, or die.
- Place expert knowledge into machine-readable form, where it can be summoned at any time.
- Train newly hired employees to solve problems the way experienced professionals do.
- Are not vulnerable to problems such as fatigue, emotion, and overwork, all of which plague human experts.

Early attempts to use computers to do humanlike thinking primarily exploited the awesome speed of computers. For example, the first chess programs instructed computer systems to make decisions by looking several plays ahead and calculating the effects of all possible moves and countermoves. Unfortunately, planning even 10 moves ahead is a burdensome chore, even for a computer. Also, it is not the way skilled chess players think. Most chess masters rely on intuitive rules of thumb called *heuristics*. For example, one highly successful heuristic for playing chess is to control the center of the board. As programmers began supplying computers with the logic for using heuristics, the quality of chess-playing programs improved dramatically. And as programmers began to incorporate the same "built-in intelligence" into other types of applications, the field of AI started to attract serious notice.

Today the four main areas of AI are expert systems, natural languages, vision systems, and robotics.

Expert Systems

Expert systems are an outgrowth of the heuristics-based chess-playing programs in which the expert knowledge of chess masters was built into programs. An **expert system** is a program or system that provides the type of advice that would be expected of a human expert.

Expert systems have enormous applications potential in business, where they can be used to capture the knowledge of expert business professionals into an active form and can subsequently be employed to improve decision making within the firm or to train individuals (see Figure MC 6-17). Today the application of expert systems to the study of business problems is just beginning to be widespread; Figure MC 6-18 shows a number of present and proposed applications.

Components of an Expert System Most expert systems consist primarily of two parts: data and software.

The data part is commonly called a *knowledge base*. The knowledge base is the part of the expert system containing specific facts about the expert area and any rules, or heuristics, the expert system will use to make decisions based on those facts. For instance, an expert system used to authorize credit for credit-card customers would have in its knowledge base facts about customers, loans, bad debts, and financing, as well as a set of rules such as "Do not automatically authorize credit if the customer has already made five transactions today."

The software part often consists of a variety of different programs. For instance, one program is used to control the entire expert system. Other programs commonly enable users to communicate with the expert system in a natural language such as English or Spanish, provide explanations to users about

FIGURE MC 6-18 Business examples of expert systems. Within the coming decade, say industry analysts, expert system routines will become standard items in many software products.

Business Area	Application
Tax accounting	Assisting tax accountants by providing advice on the best tax treatment for an individual or corporation
Repair	Assisting machine repairpeople by providing expert diagnoses of malfunctions
Insurance sales	Helping an insurance agent tailor an insurance package to a client, given the client's insurance, investment, financial planning, and tax needs
Portfolio planning	Determining the best securities portfolio for a client, given the client's growth and income objectives
Manufacturing	Finding the best way to design, produce, stock, and ship a product
System design	Determining the optimal hardware and software configuration to meet a set of user requirements
Multinational planning	Providing expert advice on whether a given business strategy will work in different countries, each with its own laws and customs
Government tax auditing	Using a complex set of criteria and a knowledge base of past audit cases to decide which individuals and companies to audit to maximize overall return
Credit authorization	Deciding whether to grant credit to individuals and companies based on their past histories and other similar credit cases
Training	Putting newly hired employees into computer-simulated situations in which their performance is aided by or compared with that of experts

how the expert system reached a particular conclusion, and allow computer professionals to set up and maintain the expert system.

Expert systems can be built from scratch or acquired as packages that have all the software components in place but lack a knowledge base. This latter type of package is called an **expert system shell.** Today, shells are a common tool for developing an expert system, especially for companies that do not have personnel available to build an expert system from scratch.

Example of an Expert System To date, one of the best-known, largest, and most successful expert systems is Authorizer's Assistant, which is owned and operated by American Express. The system is designed to help more than 300 human credit authorizers decide whether to allow cardholders whose accounts are at or beyond normal credit limits to make purchases. Authorizer's Assistant was developed to reduce losses—which cost the company hundreds of millions of dollars annually—resulting from bad decisions. The system has also saved the authorizers time, resulted in faster service, and provided consistency in decision making.

From more than a dozen databases, the expert system quickly pulls together relevant data pertaining to a particular transaction decision, evaluates it, and recommends whether credit should be approved. Important data that are usually considered include the cardholder's outstanding balance, payment history, and purchase habits, as well as the amount of risk involved.

Approximately a quarter of the transactions handled by Authorizer's Assistant are straightforward enough that no human intervention is necessary. Every recommendation referred to an operator is accompanied by an explanation and a summary of the key decision-making data that the expert system used in reaching its recommendation. Should the operator question the recommendation, he or she can override it or request further information.

To develop Authorizer's Assistant, the builders interviewed five of American Express's top authorizers and constructed a knowledge base of about 500 rules. These rules deal with things such as customer types and actual cases of good and bad decision making. As the system was refined, the knowledge base gradually increased. Today, it includes several hundred more rules.

American Express reports that when the expert system and operators work together, bad debts have been cut in half and processing time has been reduced by 20 percent.

Neural-Net Computing Most computing today is preprogrammed number crunching. Whether you are reformatting a document, doing spreadsheet computations, searching through a database, compiling a program, or coloring or rotating graphics images, you are simply executing a predetermined procedure at a high speed. Conventional computers are good at this type of thing. But asking them to recognize a handwritten letter is a different matter.

This is where neural nets come in. **Neural-net computing** refers to an AI technology in which a computer system emulates the human brain's pattern-recognition process. Neural-net systems are not preprogrammed to provide predictable responses like conventional algorithms. Instead, they are designed to learn by observation—the way experts largely learn.

Neural nets are usually software programs that work on conventional computers. Some research institutions have gone a step further, however, and have developed hardware-based neural nets—that is, computers with circuitry especially designed to solve pattern-recognition problems.

Neural-net computers translate pattern-recognition processes into small blocks of code that are processed in parallel. These computers simulate a network of hundreds or thousands of interconnected nodes, spanning several layers, that rapidly pass data among the nodes.

Although neural-net computing is largely a technology of tomorrow, several applications involving neural nets have already begun in earnest. These applications—most of which are in the area of expert systems—involve handwriting, speech, and image recognition; credit-risk assessment; crime analysis; and stock analysis.

- **HANDWRITING, SPEECH, AND IMAGE RECOGNITION** Recognition of a person's signature, voice, or face happens so quickly that you scarcely notice how the underlying process works. Neural nets attempt to emulate this process. Consider character recognition, for instance. The lower levels of the neural net may recognize that a character is composed of curves and straight lines. This information is passed to the next layer, which may attempt to determine the number of curves and lines and the way they fit together. Finally, conclusions are passed to a third level, which may recognize the character as a capital *B*. If the character cannot be recognized, the neural net attempts to learn from the problem. One financial-services institution is already using such an algorithm to recognize handwritten numerals on checks. Another company has developed a neural-net program that can recognize human faces with an accuracy of better than 99 percent (see Figure MC 6-19). The program employs levels of recognition, and learning from mistakes, that are similar to the character-recognition process.

- **CREDIT-RISK ASSESSMENT** Subtle patterns also exist in conventional text data, such as those found at financial institutions. If you were very sharp and studied the records of thousands of people who were granted and denied credit, you might eventually be able to discern which types of peo-

FIGURE MC 6-19 **"Faceprinting" through neural networks.** The program featured here, Face-to-Face, works by recognizing subtle patterns in lightness and darkness that define a person's unique features—say, the shape of a nose or mouth—and ignoring variable features such as a day-old beard, glasses, or a new haircut. The program attempts a match by comparing a just-snapped photo of a person with an image on a plastic access card.

ple were good credit risks and which types of people were poor ones. Of course, computers can work much faster than humans and can notice patterns that are hardly discernible. Neural nets are currently being applied to solve credit-risk assessment problems at American Express and other companies. Perhaps in the future, use of neural nets will help to avert catastrophes such as the recent U.S. savings and loan crisis.

- **CRIME ANALYSIS** Neural nets are expected to offer some assistance in solving crimes. Many crimes, of course, display a pattern, and often this pattern is too subtle to be picked up without computer assistance. Police departments and government agencies such as the FBI are not the only organizations using neural-net technology to take a bite out of crime. New York's Chase Manhattan Bank is currently using neural nets to examine hundreds of thousands of transactions daily and to look for fraudulent ones.
- **STOCK ANALYSIS** One exciting neural-net application is a program that examines stock-market data for patterns and helps determine strategies for buying and selling stocks. At Boston-based Fidelity Investments, Brad Lewis—who manages the Disciplined Equity mutual fund—has outperformed the market consistently with a neural-net-based computer model he began developing in business school. The model evaluates 180,000 pieces of data nightly to learn how the market is pricing stocks. It then reviews about a dozen characteristics of 2,000 target stocks to detect subtle patterns that are in line with current market valuations. Stocks are then selected by an attractiveness rating.

Other applications for neural nets in the future abound. In medicine, neural nets may examine detailed records of patients having a specific disease and attempt to uncover an underlying pattern. In quality control, thousands of parts could be studied to uncover subtle structural problems. And, perhaps, the optimal mixture of glue, pulp, and water required to make top-quality paper can be determined with neural nets. Wherever there is a pattern to study, a neural-net application may be useful.

Natural Languages

One of the greatest challenges that scientists in the field of AI currently face is providing computer systems with the ability to communicate in *natural language*—English, Spanish, French, Japanese, and so forth. Unfortunately, this challenge has not been easy to meet. People have personalized ways of communicating, and the meanings of words vary according to the contexts in which they are used. Also, the heuristics that people employ to understand what others are saying are highly complex and still poorly understood by language researchers.

Software that uses a **natural-language interface** enables humans to communicate with the computer system in their native language. The user of a natural-language interface does not have to learn the rules, or syntax, of a particular computer language. Instead, the user types at a keyboard as if writing a memo or instructions to a human assistant.

Natural-language processing is still in its infancy. It is most frequently employed as a "front end" in file or database management packages, handling situations in which users need to retrieve information or generate simple reports. Users type the information request in a natural language. As each request is typed in, the natural-language system builds a command that can be processed by the file or database management package in use. Then the system hands over the request to the package for execution. Theoretically, the same natural-language front end can be used on any software package, so the user can conceivably work with hundreds of different programs without having to know a conventional command set.

A typical natural-language dialogue between the user and computer is shown in Figure MC 6-20. Today, most natural-language systems work with typed requests similar to the one shown in the figure. As voice input and output systems improve, it is likely that the preferred interface for most natural-language applications will not be typed text but voice. Someday you might find a friendly talking head on the screen whose lips are in sync with a computer voice chip and who can personalize the entire interaction for you.

As in human conversation, it is expected that users of natural-language systems will converse using everyday words, whole sentences and sentence fragments, and ambiguous phrases. The user may misspell words, misuse words, or use slang or words with multiple meanings. The natural-language system must contain advanced software that attempts to determine what the user means by looking for key words, making assumptions, and drawing conclusions from earlier dialogue. A good natural-language system interacts heavily with the user to try to clarify each request so that it can take the right action. As you can see from the dialogue in the figure, the natural-language system echoes to the operator any assumptions that it is making as a result of an input.

Vision Systems

Vision systems enable computer-controlled devices to "see." A vision system might work as follows. Parts produced in a manufacturing process are sent

FIGURE MC 6-20 **Natural language.** A good natural language provides users considerable latitude in composing queries, and it echoes—for verification purposes—how the computer system is interpreting them.

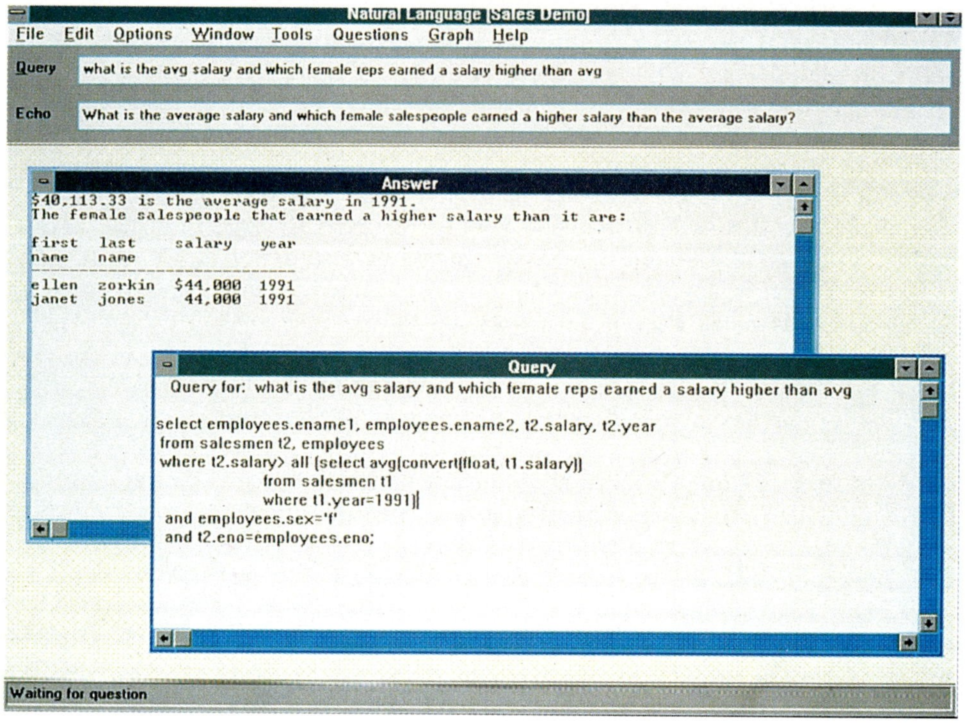

along an assembly line for inspection. A vision system located at a station along the line takes a digital photograph of each part as it passes by the station. The photo is decomposed into vital data that are compared with other data—showing how the part would look if produced correctly—in the vision system's electronic memory. An expert system within the vision system uses heuristics to judge whether the part has been correctly made or is flawed. If the part is flawed, the system determines the nature of the flaw and the necessary corrective action.

Robotics

Robotics plays an integral role in computer-aided manufacturing (CAM) systems. Although robots may seem "dumb," they are often aided by a number of other AI techniques to enable them to identify objects and states in their environments and act accordingly. Robots designed for warehouses, for instance, are equipped with vision systems. These "eyes" allow them to gauge distances and speeds while they navigate among stationary aisles of goods and moving forklift trucks. And scientists are busily producing ant-sized robots that will fit inside the human body and perform delicate tasks, such as unclogging arteries. The ultimate AI product, of course, will be a robot that is virtually indistinguishable from a human being. Such a robot could be scaled to virtually any dimension and be given superhuman powers. Researchers working in AI are still far from realizing this goal.

MULTIMEDIA COMPUTING

Applications in which several types of data intermingle are known as **multimedia** computing applications. Currently, this is still a new application area for computers.

The marriage by computer of text, graphics, sound, and video data in a single application is among the most exciting new technological frontiers we will explore in the 1990s and the upcoming 21st century. As many of the major hardware and software vendors jockey to position their products in a potential multibillion-dollar market, one question remains unanswered: In which applications areas will multimedia take off?

Applications Areas

A variety of multimedia applications are now being reported in the press. Four of these are discussed in the following subsections.

Education and Training Multimedia is increasingly being used as an educational and training tool in educational institutions and in industry. Figure MC 6-21 features a multimedia application at Alabama Power Company, in which maintenance personnel are taught about boiler feed pumps. Users of the system can pull up video and audio clips of demonstrations, check reference materials about operations, and run "what-if" simulations. Education is seen today as a prime area for multimedia product development. Some people have gone so far as to say that multimedia will completely change the way most people learn. Several companies are now aggressively using multimedia to train their employees, and colleges and universities have also embraced multimedia with open arms.

Entertainment Entertainment is an area where multimedia is already a success. As computer technology enables more and more types of information to be presented in new ways, a new breed of consumer product has evolved—the multimedia book, which combines some of the best features of a video and a book. Say, for instance, you wanted to learn about a subject like the planets. You would buy a CD-ROM-based multimedia product such as the one shown in Figure MC 6-22. With the CD-ROM loaded up on your computer system, you could listen to audio and video clips that would give you a guided tour of the celestial heavens. You could also read or browse through the contents of several books on the subject, using electronic keyword searches to find specific topics that interested you.

Live television is also likely to be packaged with a multimedia component in the future. Imagine watching a football game and being able to access football trivia or even another game in a window that you could blow up to any size. Multimedia may soon bring us to an age of "intelligent television."

Presentations Organizations and individuals are increasingly turning to multimedia to make presentations to important clients, to colleagues, and to hot business prospects. For instance, Figure MC 6-23 shows two stills from a multimedia presentation created by a dentist for meetings at which he speaks. Knowing that business leaders are used to slick presentations, the city of Aurora, Colorado, also recently turned to a multimedia approach to woo new businesses to its area.

Another popular use of multimedia as a presentation tool is in the design of self-guided tours. Texas A&M opted for this approach when it set up a new visitor center. The center features a multimedia presentation that lets visitors use a mouse at kiosk stations to get information about the school.

FIGURE MC 6-21 Multimedia as a training tool. With multimedia technology, trainees have access to text, audio and video clips, and diagrams to help them see how something works. Featured here are two stills from a multimedia training program on the maintenance of a boiler pump.

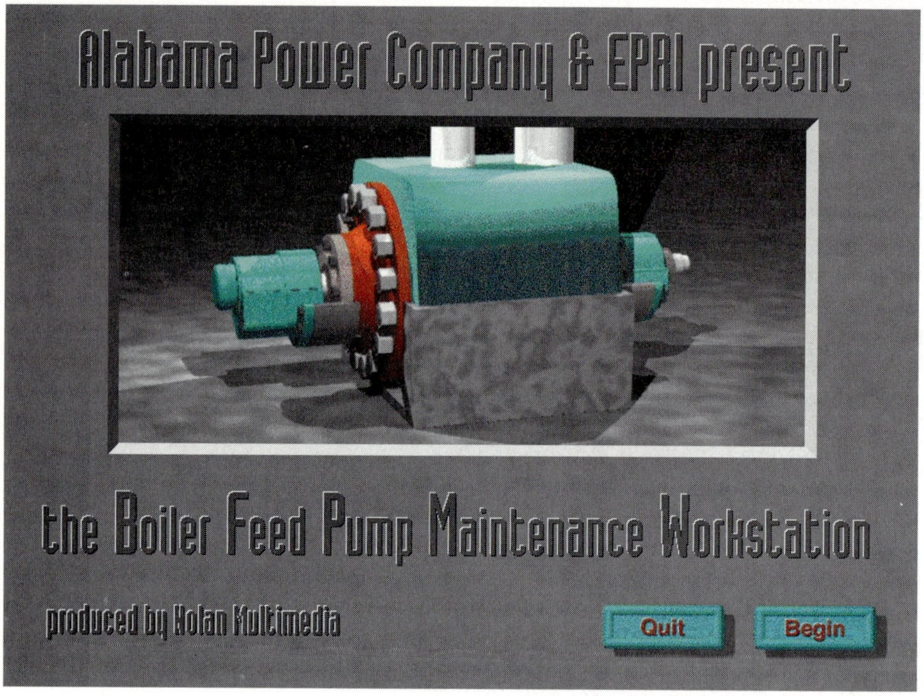

(a)

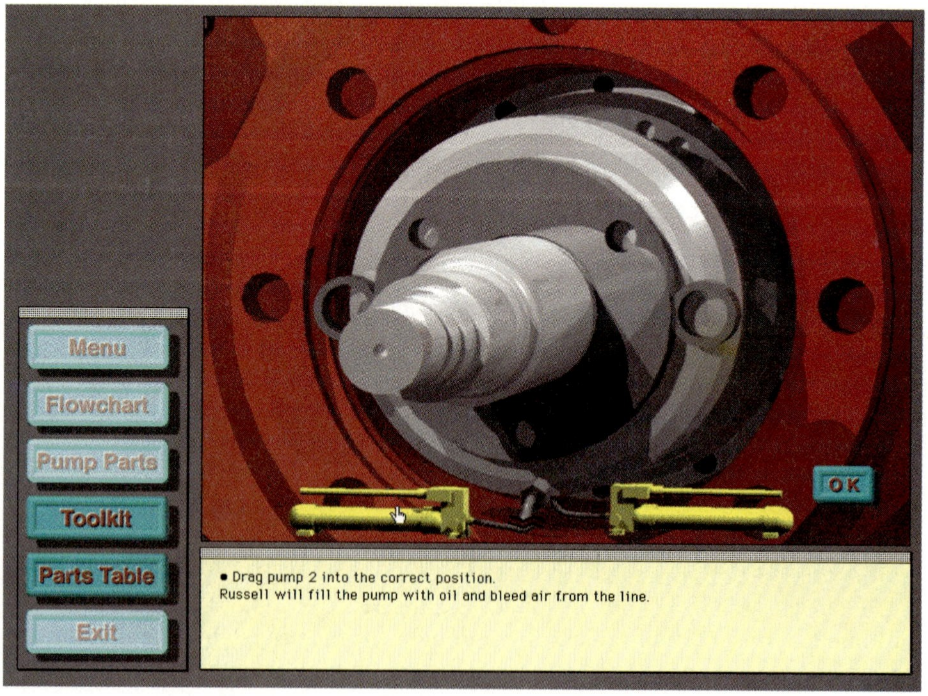

(b)

FIGURE MC 6-22 **Multimedia as entertainment.** Multimedia is often used in the creation of products that are both fun and educational. Shown here are two images from *The View from Earth*, an optical disk product that contains the contents of three books from the *Voyage through the Universe* hardbound-book series. You can go on a guided tour of planets or access specific information through menus, a glossary, and an index.

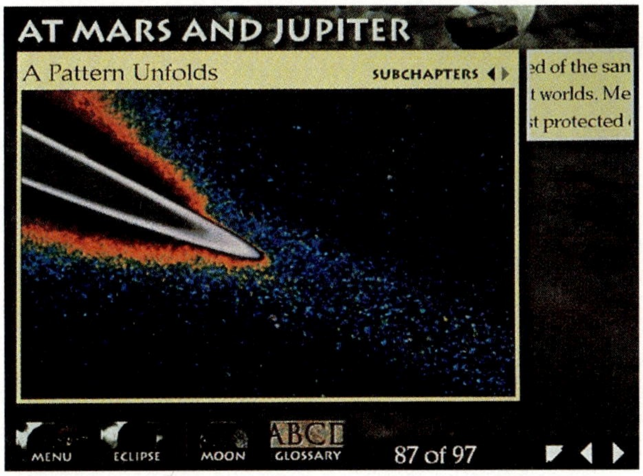

(a)

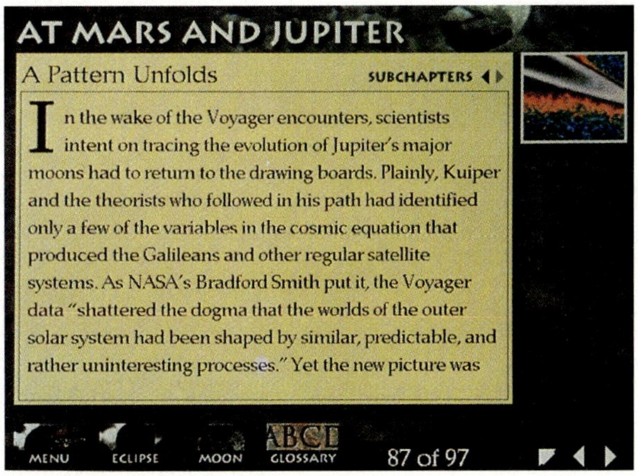

(b)

FIGURE MC 6-23 **Multimedia as a presentation tool.** Multimedia is being increasingly employed as a presentation tool, by both corporations and individuals. Shown here are two stills from a presentation made by a dentist who is a frequent speaker at various dental conventions and symposiums.

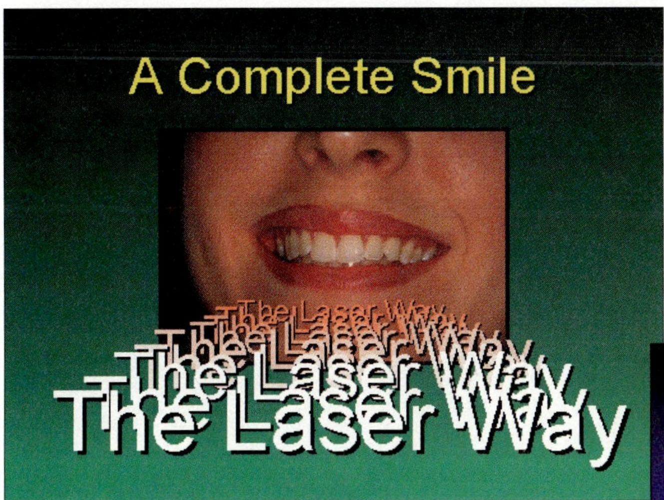

(a)

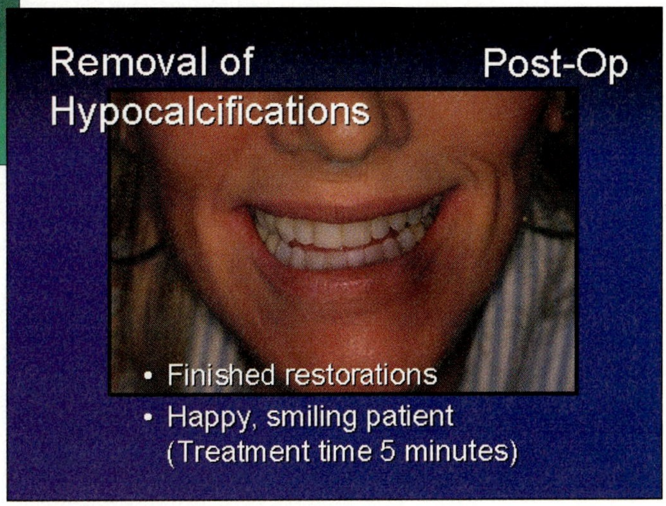

(b)

Reference This area is a natural for multimedia and optical disks since reference materials—such as encyclopedias and atlases—usually must contain a wealth of text and picture information. Because sound and video clips can also be put on the disk and because electronic searches are possible through the computer, a multimedia reference product can be much more powerful than its hard-copy counterpart. Some of the leading multimedia reference products today are encyclopedias, atlases, almanacs, and resource books (see Figure MC 6-24).

Hardware and Software

Special hardware and software are required to run multimedia applications. A description of these follows:

Hardware Microcomputer systems that let users run multimedia applications—called **multimedia PCs**—have become extremely popular during the last couple of years. These computer systems are equipped with a system unit that sports a powerful CPU with plenty of RAM and hard-disk storage, a CD-ROM optical disk unit, a graphics-oriented color monitor, sound and video boards, and speakers. Such hardware was covered in an earlier chapter (see Figure MC 2-29). Many computer-industry insiders predict that in just a few years it will be common for multimedia PCs to receive television broadcasts and also channels that specialize in bringing added excitement to these PC-and-TV-set hybrids (see Figure MC 6-25).

FIGURE MC 6-24 **Multimedia as a reference tool.** Microsoft's *Cinemania* is a multimedia reference product for movie buffs. It covers some 20,000 films, and, for many of them, features short audio and video clips, publicity stills, celebrity biographies, and reviews.

FIGURE MC 6-25 Sunday afternoon at the PC. If you are tired of Windows, consider turning on John Elway or the Raiders.

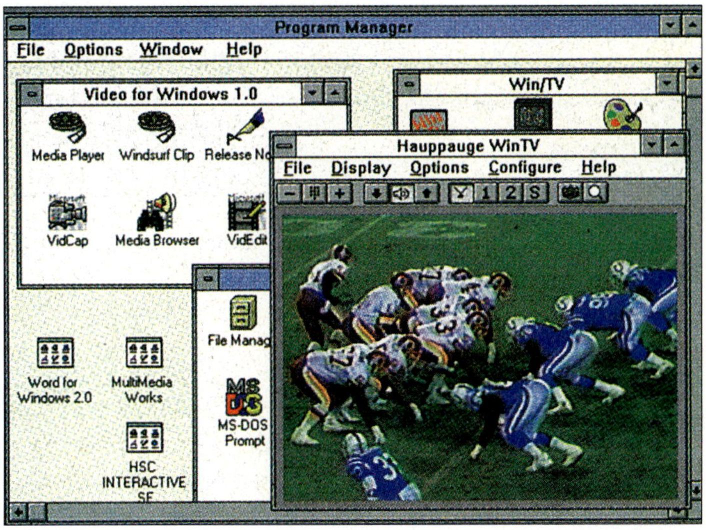

While a basic multimedia PC system may cost only two or three thousand dollars, a hardware system capable of developing commercial multimedia applications can cost up to ten times as much. These latter systems will typically include specialized equipment for capturing and editing audio and video data as well as an MO optical-disk system for output. Furthermore, such systems need to be equipped with *authoring software* (discussed next).

Software Multimedia software is of two types: applications software and authoring software. Earlier in the book and in Figures MC 6-21 through MC 6-24, we covered several types of applications-software products. Professional developers create such products with multimedia **authoring software,** packages that come with special programming tools for manipulating and synchronizing text, graphics, audio, and video data.

Multimedia authoring software has a wide number of uses. One, of course, is to develop the types of applications already covered, such as entertainment and reference products. It can also be used to improve existing applications. For instance, you can spice up Microsoft Windows and outgoing electronic-mail messages with voice greetings or you can program a computer to show a small video clip if certain commands are executed by the computer operator. Additionally, multimedia authoring software is widely used to develop touch-screen "kioskware" for museums, exhibits, and trade shows (see Figure MC 6-26). Applications-software development is more fully covered in Chapter 7.

VIRTUAL REALITY

You are lazing away on a warm beach in Mexico when the sun begins to nudge toward the horizon. The hills to your left take on an orange glow, gulls are diving for fish, and each harmless cloud in the sky looks wildly three-dimensional

FIGURE MC 6-26 Authoring software. Multimedia authoring software enables multimedia applications—those involving text, still pictures, sound, and video—to be rapidly developed. Here, an authoring package is used to develop a kiosk presentation for those who take a tour at Ben & Jerry's—the Vermont ice cream company. (a) A storyboard being prepared. (b) A still from the finished presentation.

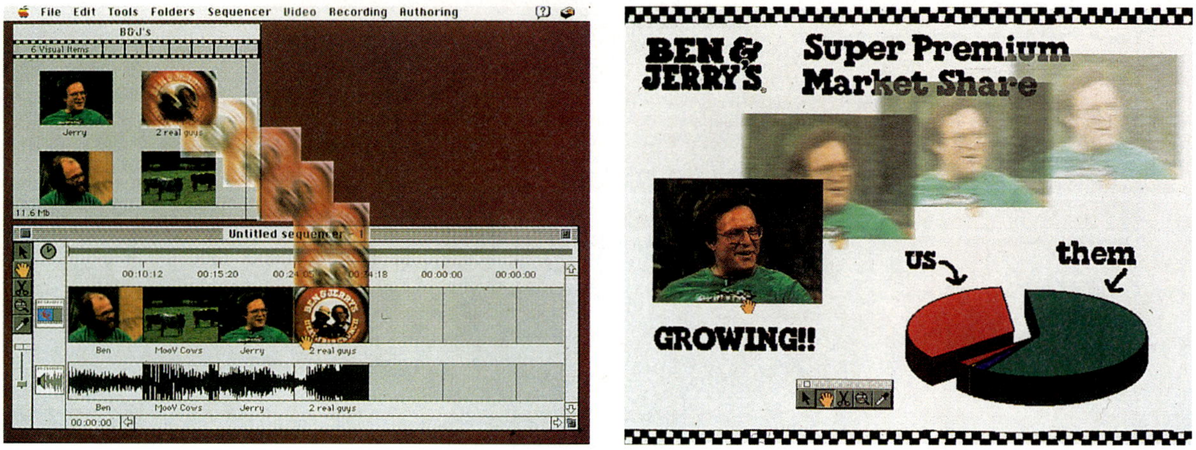

(a) (b)

and is painted with its own special color. "If only this could go on for another hour," you think. It does . . . and not because it is actually happening. You have used a computer system to create a virtual reality.

Virtual reality refers to the use of computers to create artificial environments that seem, to the computer operator, as if they were real. Although we are still far from the virtual reality that science fiction writers tell us about, there are many who believe that computer technology will someday make it possible to create such illusions.

Applications Areas

Several pioneering virtual reality applications are visible in the marketplace today, including those discussed in the following subsections.

Architecture It is now possible to take "tours" of offices and buildings whose foundations are yet to be poured. How? A computer model of the office or building is made in three dimensions (see Figure MC 6-27). Once the building is mathematically specified, what a person can see if standing at any specific point in the building, looking in any specified direction, can be mathematically determined.

Assume the client taking the tour wants to look at the top floor first and see the lounge before the offices. The tour can be taken in "real time," which enables the client to move as he or she chooses, deciding which facilities to view before others, how much time to spend at each facility, and what to see there. Lighting routines are available that can show how natural light falls in the building on a sunny or rainy day and how artificial light changes a room. Does the client hate the look and size of the lounge? No problem. With a remodeling software package, it can be reshaped, repainted, relighted, refurnished, and ready for reinspection—in just a few minutes.

FIGURE MC 6-27 **Office tours.** Virtual reality can be used as a tool for touring offices before they are ever built. Such a feature minimizes the risk that the building will not be suited to its potential tenants.

Entertainment Virtual reality applications have begun to arrive in full force in the entertainment industry, where illusion is the principal product. In many cities, shops have sprouted up that feature virtual reality games in which players can battle demons on a realistic, computer-generated landscape (see Figure MC 6-28). In many cases, the virtual reality participant must don special goggles, which project computer-generated images directly toward the eye, and wear gloves with built-in sensors, which change the images when the hands are moved (see Figure MC 6-29). Coming next to your town: virtual reality theaters.

Investments In the field of investment analysis, virtual reality techniques are now being applied to the study of securities. One of the problems inherent in conventional analysis is that it is often difficult to tell when a group of securities is moving relative to the market as a whole. With virtual reality, stocks belonging to a certain group—say, technology stocks—can each be given a characteristic color. When general stock movements are viewed in three dimensions over time, which is simulated by animation techniques, the analyst can more clearly visualize how the technology group, or any other group, is behaving.

Other Applications In addition to applications in architecture, entertainment, and investments, a variety of other virtual reality applications have been reported by the press:

FIGURE MC 6-28 Virtual reality in entertainment. Virtual reality games enable players wearing special equipment to enter their own computer-generated environments, where they can assume active roles and do battle with such villains as dragons and evil people.

(a) (b)

- In the field of law, virtual reality techniques were recently used to recreate a murder scene—and perhaps sway a jury. The prosecution prepared a videotape of the crime "starring" electronic models of the characters involved. Basing the videotape on collected evidence, the prosecution then persuaded the judge to show it to the jury. The defendant was convicted and is appealing—in part because of the damaging videotape. The use of such tapes in trials is highly controversial because their expense favors wealthy defendants and because juries may confuse what they see on tape with reality.
- Virtual reality techniques have helped in the creation of the *Talking Glove*. People who have difficulty speaking use sign language with the gloved hand. The glove sends signals to a pendant around the user's neck—the pendant

FIGURE MC 6-29 **Virtual reality hardware.** Virtual reality hardware is among the most specialized and diverse in the computer industry. Many applications feature special goggles and gloves, as shown here, and some even require full body suits.

is normally hidden under clothing—that converts the finger spellings into words and then outputs them as synthesized speech (see Figure MC 6-30).

- Boeing and the University of Seattle are jointly working on a project that would enable engineers to "walk through" a computer-designed plane, to test it for safety and comfort, before the plane is ever built.
- Medical researchers are working on techniques that would enable a computer-simulated medical operation to "take place" on a patient before a scalpel ever touches the patient's body.
- In sports, researchers are using virtual reality techniques to discover subtle body movements that make certain athletes fantastically successful.

Virtual reality may also someday enable the exploration of planets without actually going there, make possible educational and therapeutic experiences in which human confrontation is realistically simulated, and allow people to take virtual vacations.

FIGURE MC 6-30 Virtual reality and the speaking impaired. Virtual reality techniques have led to the development of the Talking Glove, which sends signals to a neck-worn transmitter that outputs words in a synthesized voice.

Summary

- Desktop publishing systems let you combine on a page such elements as text (in a variety of fonts), art, and photos, thus creating attractive documents that look like they came off a printer's press.
- Whereas word processing deals mainly with straight, nontypeset text—perhaps using a few simple fonts for emphasis—desktop publishing involves full-fledged typesetting and imagesetting.
- Hardware used in quality desktop publishing usually includes a high-end microcomputer system, a laser printer, a graphics-oriented monitor, and an image scanner. Software and software-based products include page-makeup software, word-processing software, typefaces and fonts, clip-art libraries, and art and illustration software.
- Page layout often conforms to a set of design principles. Good layouts are frequently perceived as such because they convey a proper balance, unity, emphasis, and mood.
- A presentation graphic is an image that visually enhances the impact of information communicated to other people. Four widely used types of presentation graphics are bar charts, pie charts, line charts, and text charts.
- Hardware used in the preparation of presentation visuals includes a high-end microcomputer system; a color plotter, laser printer, or film recorder (or all three); a graphics-oriented color monitor; and various types of presentation equipment. The software used may include spreadsheet packages and dedicated graphics packages.

- Several principles govern good chart design. Among these are simplicity, consistency, emphasis, and balance.
- The ability of computer systems to perform in ways that would be considered intelligent if observed in humans is commonly referred to as artificial intelligence (AI).
- The four main areas of AI are expert systems, natural languages, vision systems, and robotics.
- Many expert systems consist of an expert system shell and a knowledge base. Recently, neural-net technology has been used successfully in the development of expert systems.
- Applications in which several types of data—text, graphics, sound, and video—intermingle are known as multimedia computing applications. Four promising areas for multimedia are education and training, entertainment, making presentations, and storing reference materials.
- Virtual reality refers to the use of computers to create special, customized environments that seem, to the user, as if they were real. Three promising areas for virtual reality are architecture, entertainment, and investments.

Key Terms

Shown in parentheses are the page numbers on which key terms are boldfaced.

Artificial intelligence (AI) (MC 188)
Authoring software (MC 199)
Bar chart (MC 181)
Clip art (MC 176)
Desktop publishing (MC 170)
Expert system (MC 189)
Expert system shell (MC 190)
Font (MC 176)
Illustration software package (MC 177)
Line chart (MC 184)
Master slide (MC 187)
Microspacing (MC 175)
Monospacing (MC 175)
Multimedia (MC 195)
Multimedia PC (MC 198)
Natural-language interface (MC 193)
Neural-net computing (MC 191)
Page description language (PDL) (MC 172)
Page-makeup software (MC 174)
Pie chart (MC 184)
Point size (MC 176)
Presentation graphic (MC 181)
Proportional spacing (MC 175)
Robotics (MC 194)
Text chart (MC 185)
Typeface (MC 175)
Typeface family (MC 176)
Virtual reality (MC 200)
WYSIWYG (MC 173)

Quiz

True/False

___ 1. Landscape mode means the output image is more deep than wide.

___ 2. Page-makeup programs are often loosely referred to as illustration programs.

___ 3. Courier is a monospaced typeface.

___ 4. An image scanner is one of the most important types of hardware to consider when buying a multimedia PC system.

___ 5. A font is a typeface in a particular point size.

___ 6. In a typical bar chart, both axes represent qualitative phenomena.

___ 7. The field of artificial intelligence began in the 1990s, from attempts to rival skilled humans at chess.

___ 8. An expert system is software that provides the type of advice that would be expected of a human expert.

___ 9. Virtual reality refers to the area of artificial intelligence known as robotics.

___ 10. A Gantt chart is a type of pie chart.

Multiple Choice

___ 11. You combine text, photos, and art elements into finished pages using
a. page-makeup software.
b. word processing.
c. halftoning.
d. a page description language.
e. virtual reality.

___ 12. You can enhance someone else's art images, or do your own, using
a. a PCL.
b. illustration software packages.
c. WYSIWYG.
d. sans serif.
e. page-makeup software.

___ 13. Adobe's PostScript and Hewlett-Packard's Printer Command Language (PCL) are examples of
a. fonts.
b. page description languages (PDLs).
c. WYSIWYG.
d. dingbats.
e. illustration software packages.

___ 14. WYSIWYG applies to
a. the image displayed on all monitors.
b. seeing on the screen exactly what a printed document will look like.

c. digitizers.
d. word processors but not desktop publishing systems.
e. graphics but not text.

___ 15. Type size is normally measured in
a. fonts.
b. inches.
c. centimeters.
d. serifs.
e. points.

___ 16. Which of the following is generally not an essential piece of hardware in a multimedia PC system?
a. A CD-ROM unit
b. A plotter
c. A keyboard
d. A sound card
e. Speakers

___ 17. Side-by-side columns are the principal charting element with
a. bar charts.
b. pie charts.
c. text charts.
d. all presentation graphics.
e. line charts.

___ 18. Special gloves and full body suits are common pieces of equipment in which of the following technology areas?
a. Vision systems
b. Neural-net computing
c. Multimedia computing
d. Virtual reality
e. Natural-language computing

___ 19. A bar chart variant that is useful for setting up schedules is the
a. column chart.
b. Gantt chart.
c. slice chart.
d. range chart.
e. stacked bar chart.

___ 20. Both axes represent quantitative phenomena in a
a. line chart.
b. pie chart.
c. clustered bar chart.
d. text chart.
e. stacked bar chart.

Matching

Select the term that best matches each phrase:

a. Virtual reality
b. Font
c. Point size
d. Authoring software
e. Expert systems
f. Bar chart
g. Line chart
h. Typeface
i. Text chart
j. Pie chart
k. Helvetica
l. Template

___ 21. A type of presentation graphic that uses a build technique

___ 22. A proportionally spaced typeface

___ 23. A type of presentation graphic in which both axes represent quantitative phenomena

___ 24. A range chart is an example

___ 25. A branch of AI

___ 26. Used to create multimedia products

___ 27. A type of presentation graphic that is often exploded

___ 28. A typeface in a particular point size

___ 29. The use of computers to create artificial environments

___ 30. A collection of characters that share a common design

Answers

True/False: 1. F; 2. F; 3. T; 4. F; 5. T; 6. F; 7. F; 8. T; 9. F; 10. F

Multiple Choice: 11. a; 12. b; 13. b; 14. b; 15. e; 16. b; 17. a; 18. d; 19. b; 20. a

Matching: 21. i; 22. k; 23. g; 24. f; 25. e; 26. d; 27. j; 28. b; 29. a; 30. h

Exercises

1. Clip-art libraries are sold by a number of different vendors. Choose a particular clip-art library and report to the class the number of different categories of images that can be found in this library (sports, business, and so on), the total number of images in the library, and its approximate cost. Also, if possible, collect some clip-art samples to show to the class. (*Note:* Many microcomputer journals regularly have articles on clip art; these articles are a good source of information for this exercise. Another good source is softcover trade books on computer products, such as Harvard Graphics, that contain clip-art features. Computer books are available in many bookstores and microcomputer stores.)

2. Peruse periodicals or journals for at least one example of an advertisement that is well designed and at least one example of an advertisement that is poorly designed. List your reasons why each ad is well or poorly designed. (*Note:* You should have no trouble finding examples. Ads appearing in print are designed both by sophisticated professionals and by rank novices.)

3. Using the data in Figures MC 6-12b and MC 6-12c and the presentation graphics package available to your class, produce the bar charts shown in the figures.

4. Using the data in Figure MC 6-13 and the presentation graphics package available to your class, produce the pie chart shown in the figure. If the

package you are using allows colors or cross-hatched patterns, try one or the other with the pie slices. Also, if your package allows exploding pie slices, try exploding the Production slice.

5. Using the data in Figure MC 6-14a and the presentation graphics package available to your class, produce the line chart shown in the figure.
6. Look through the computer journals in your school or local library and identify at least three cases where a company is using expert-system technology. In each case, identify the benefit provided.
7. Search through the computer journals for an advertisement for a multimedia PC. What extra hardware and software features does this computer have that make it a multimedia PC, and what is the cost of these features?
8. Virtual reality amusement centers have become popular in recent years, offering a variety of entertaining adventure games. Find an example of such a game and prepare a short report on it for your class. Be prepared to answer questions such as the following: What do people do in the game? How long does it take to play? How much does it cost to play? What makes the game a virtual reality product?

MC 7 APPLICATIONS DEVELOPMENT ON MICROCOMPUTERS

OUTLINE

LEARNING OBJECTIVES

After completing this chapter, you will be able to:

1. Identify and describe the activities involved with applications development on microcomputers.
2. Describe a number of program design tools.
3. Identify several of the language options available to code programs.
4. Explain the importance of debugging, maintaining, and documenting programs.
5. Explain the role played by computer-aided software engineering tools.
6. Appreciate the scope of applications development in database environments.

OVERVIEW

If you wanted to build a house, you would probably begin with some research and planning. You might speak to various people about home design, draw up some floor plans, estimate the cost of materials, and so on. In other words, you would not start digging a hole and pouring concrete on the very first day. Creating successful applications also requires considerable planning.

Microcomputer users may need to develop their own applications from time to time. Applications development may involve using a programming language to code new applications programs from scratch or, possibly, using a variety of database management tools to fashion a custom database application. Whatever is involved, the goal is to produce an applications program.

In this chapter we will study useful practices for developing applications programs. As you read this chapter, keep in mind that it is never enough just to write a program that works. Good programs must also be easy to understand and to maintain. A well-planned program may take longer to write initially, but the subsequent savings in maintaining it usually will make the effort worthwhile.

The chapter opens by covering the sorts of activities that need to be considered when a new application is required. From there, we turn to the make-or-buy decision, which deals with choosing either to develop applications software from scratch or to buy it prepackaged. Next we address three of the chapter's most important topics: program design, programming languages, and program coding. Then we turn to a discussion of program debugging and testing and, subsequently, maintenance and documentation. Following that is a brief introduction to one of the most promising new software-development technologies—computer-aided software engineering. The chapter closes with a discussion of applications development in a database environment.

APPLICATIONS DEVELOPMENT ACTIVITIES

You can acquire programs to meet your applications needs in two principal ways: developing them from scratch or buying them in prepackaged form from an outside source. The alternative chosen generally depends on factors such as the quality of software available in the marketplace, the nature and importance of the application, the level of difficulty involved, and cost. The developer of the software—whether it be you, a colleague, or an outside vendor—should follow certain steps to ensure that the software does its job.

The steps associated with creating successful applications programs are called **applications software development.** Applications software development consists of the four following activities or steps:

- *Program Design.* Planning the specific software solution to meet the program specifications
- *Program Coding.* Writing the program
- *Program Debugging and Testing.* Finding and eliminating errors in the program
- *Program Maintenance.* Making changes to the program over time

While each of these critical development activities is taking place, there should be ongoing *documentation*—such as "writing up" the details about what the program does and how it works. Later in the chapter, we will address both this type of documentation and also the type that you receive from vendors of commercial software packages.

For most microcomputer users, applications development is done either through a public-domain programming language such as BASIC, C, or COBOL or through a proprietary language tool that is available, say, through a database management system. This chapter focuses on these two types of applications development.

THE MAKE-OR-BUY DECISION

Once you know that a software solution to a problem is required, you must decide whether to create the programs from scratch or to acquire them "off the shelf," from a software vendor. This consideration is frequently called the *make-or-buy decision.*

During the last several years, prewritten applications programs for such tasks as payroll, accounting, financial planning, and project scheduling have become more widely available from specialized vendors. These programs, called **applications packages,** consist normally of an integrated set of programs, documentation (usually of fairly high quality), and, possibly, training. Because they often provide immediate results at a reasonable cost, applications packages are becoming increasingly popular.

But although applications packages offer many compelling advantages, they are not always appropriate, nor do they always completely spare the user from doing any type of programming. For instance, if a package was originally developed for a business that works differently from yours and the vendor has made only superficial attempts to adapt it for general use, it may prove to be more trouble than it is worth. Also, for some applications, little or no appropriate packaged software exists—in such cases, developing software yourself, from the ground up, may be your only alternative. Finally, you may acquire a package and realize that it comes with state-of-the-art programming tools for developing advanced applications that you can use. This is when you may be thankful that you learned how to develop applications.

PROGRAM DESIGN

The program design, or plan, must address all the tasks that a program must do as well as the way to organize or sequence these tasks when coding the program. Only when the design is complete does the next stage—the actual program coding—begin.

Program Design Tools

Program design tools are, essentially, planning tools. They consist of various kinds of diagrams, charts, and tables that outline either the organization of program tasks or the steps the program will follow. Once a program has been coded and implemented, program design tools serve as excellent documentation.

Structure Charts

Structure charts depict the overall organization of a program. They show how the individual program segments, or modules, are defined and how they relate to one another.

FIGURE MC 7-1 Structure chart for a payroll application. Structure charts subdivide a program into individual modules, each of which represents a well-defined processing task. The modules are then arranged hierarchically in a top-down fashion, as illustrated here for a payroll application.

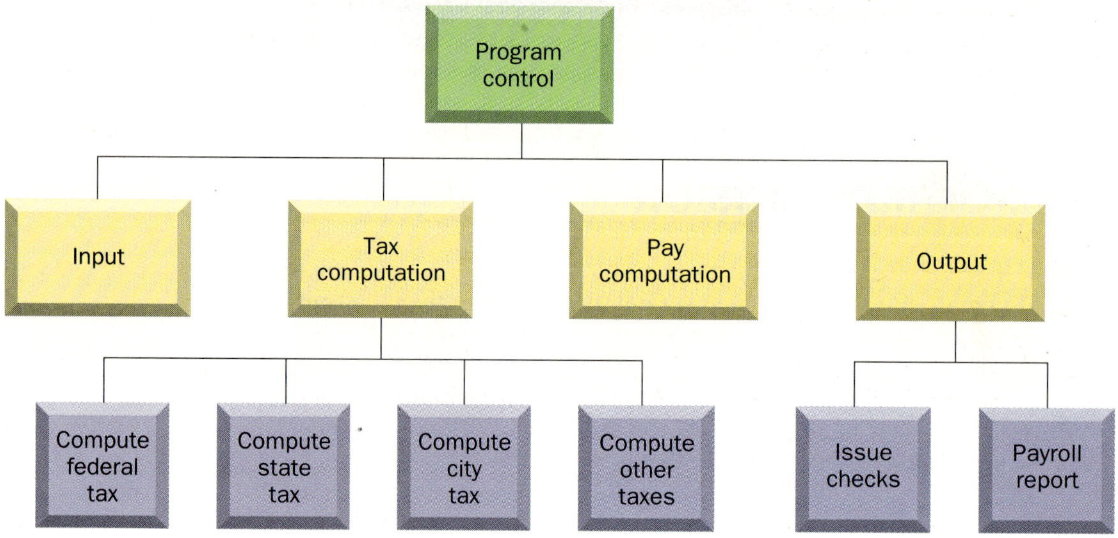

A typical structure chart, with its several rows of boxes connected by lines, looks like a corporate organization chart. Each box represents a program *module*—that is, a set of logically related operations that perform a well-defined task. The modules in the upper rows serve control functions, directing the program to process modules under them as appropriate. The modules in the lower boxes serve specific processing functions. These modules do all the program "work." The lines connecting the boxes indicate the relationship between higher-level and lower-level modules. Figure MC 7-1 is a structure chart for a payroll application.

Structure charts commonly embody a **top-down design**—modules are conceptualized first at the highest levels of the hierarchy and then at progressively lower levels.

Logically speaking, establishing how a program is organized should be the first step in program design. Once all of the functions of the program are carefully laid out in a structure chart or some equivalent tool, the next step—showing the step-by-step logic that is to take place in each module—can be started.

Program Flowcharts

Program flowcharts use *geometric symbols,* such as those in Figure MC 7-2, and familiar *relational symbols,* such as those in Figure MC 7-3, to portray graphically the sequence of steps involved in a program. The steps in a flowchart occur in the same logical sequence that their corresponding program statements follow in the program. To help you understand what these symbols mean and see how to use them, consider an example.

Scanning a File for Names of Employees with Certain Characteristics A common activity in information processing is scanning an employee file for names of people with certain characteristics. Suppose, for

FIGURE MC 7-2 Program flowchart symbols.

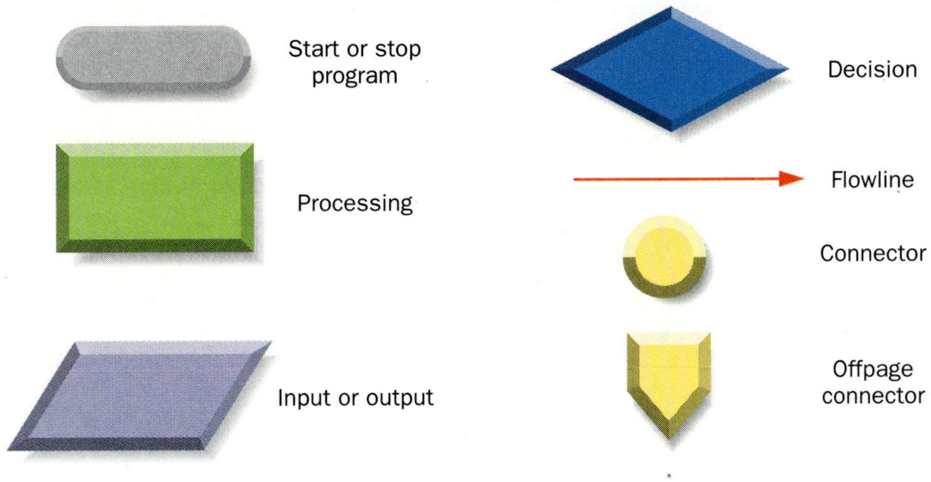

example, a company's personnel department wants a printed list of the names of all employees with computer experience and at least five years of company service. A flowchart that shows how to accomplish this task and also totals the number of employees who meet these criteria is shown in Figure MC 7-4.

This particular flowchart uses five symbols: start/stop, processing, decision, connector, and input/output. The lines with arrows that link the symbols are called *flowlines;* they indicate the flow of logic in the flowchart.

Every flowchart begins and ends with an oval-shaped *start/stop symbol.* The first of these symbols in the program contains the word *Start,* and the last contains the word *Stop.* The diamond-shaped *decision symbol* always indicates a question, which generally will have only two possible answers—yes or no (true or false). Decision symbols should always have one flowline entering and two flowlines (representing the two possible outcomes) exiting.

The rectangular *processing symbol* contains an action that needs to be taken—for example, "Set counter to 0" or "Add 1 to counter." The *connector symbol* provides a logical meeting point for several flowlines. The *input/output symbol* enables the logical process depicted in the flowchart to accept data or output them.

FIGURE MC 7-3 Relational symbols used in flowcharts.

Symbol(s)	Meaning
<	Less than
<= or ≤	Less than or equal to
>	Greater than
>= or ≥	Greater than or equal to
=	Equal to
≠ or < > or ><	Not equal to

FIGURE MC 7-4 **Scanning an employee file.** The operation that the flowchart represents is as follows: Print the names of all people in an employee file who have computer experience and at least five years of company service. Also, count the number of such people and print out this count.

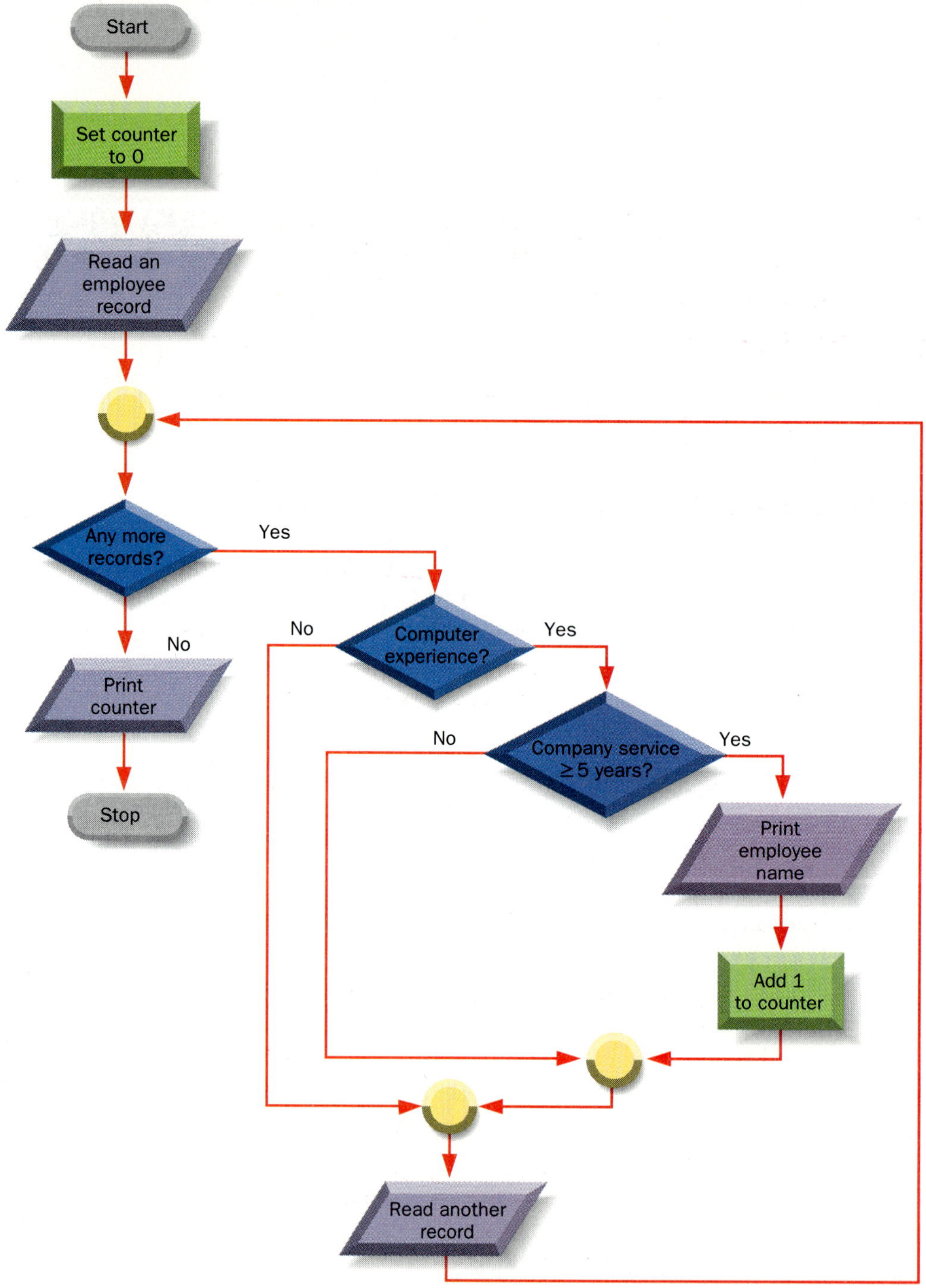

The flowchart in Figure MC 7-4 involves a looping operation. We "read" a record, inspect it, and take an action; then we read another record, inspect it, and take another action; and so on until the file is exhausted. When the computer reads a record, as indicated by the input/output symbol, it brings the record into memory and stores its contents (or field values). If a record meets both search criteria, we increment a counter by 1. After the last record is read and processed, we print, before ending the program, the value of the counter.

The Three Basic Control Structures Beginning in the 1960s, a number of researchers began to stress program design (planning) and the merits of separating the design process from the actual program coding. Many of their proposed ideas caught on, and over the last few decades a group of methods has evolved that has made program design more systematic and programs themselves easier to understand and maintain. These methods usually are grouped together under the term **structured programming.**

Advocates of structured programming have shown that any program can be constructed out of three fundamental **control structures:** sequence, selection, and looping. Figure MC 7-5 illustrates these structures using flowchart symbols.

A **sequence control structure** is simply a series of procedures that follow one another. A **selection** (or **if-then-else**) **control structure** involves a choice: *If* a certain condition is true, *then* follow one procedure; or *else*, if false, follow another. A *loop* is an operation that repeats until a certain condition is met. As Figure MC 7-5 shows, a **looping** (or **iteration**) **control structure** can take one of two forms: DOWHILE or DOUNTIL.

With **DOWHILE**, a loop is executed as long as a certain condition is true ("do *while* true"). With **DOUNTIL,** a loop continues as long as a certain condition is false ("do *until* true"). You should also note another major difference between these two forms of looping. With DOUNTIL, the loop procedure will always be executed at least once, because the procedure appears before any test is made about whether to exit the loop. With DOWHILE, the procedure may not be executed at all, because the loop-exit test appears before the procedure.

The three basic control structures are the major building blocks for structured program flowcharts and pseudocode. We discuss pseudocode later in the chapter.

The Case Structure By nesting two or more if-then-else control structures, you can build a fourth structure known as the **case control structure.** For example, in Figure MC 7-4, the two individual choices—"Computer experience?" and "Company service ≥ 5 years?" —result in the following four possibilities, or cases:

Case I: No computer experience, company service < 5 years

Case II: No computer experience, company service ≥ 5 years

Case III: Computer experience, company service < 5 years

Case IV: Computer experience, company service ≥ 5 years

One Entry Point, One Exit Point An extremely important characteristic of the control structures discussed so far is that each permits only one entry point into and one exit point out of any structure. This property is sometimes called the **one-entry-point/one-exit-point rule.** Observe the marked entry and exit points in Figure MC 7-5. The one-entry-point/one-exit-point convention encourages a modular, building-block programming approach that makes programs more readable and easier to maintain.

Pseudocode

An alternative to the flowchart that has become extremely popular in recent years is **pseudocode.** This structured technique uses Englishlike statements

FIGURE MC 7-5 The three fundamental control structures of structured programming. Note that each structure has one entry point and one exit point.

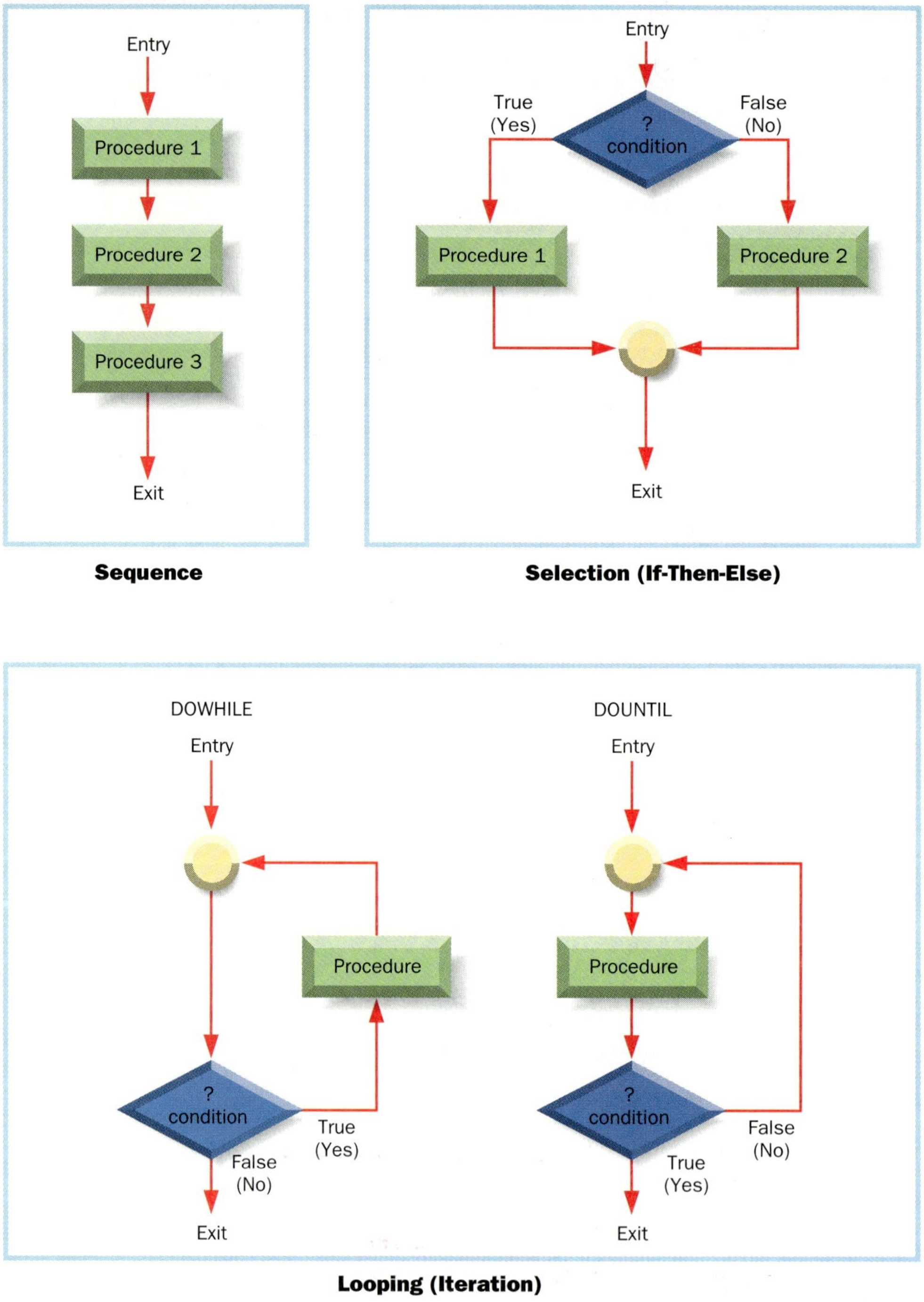

in place of the flowchart's graphic symbols. An example of pseudocode is shown in Figure MC 7-6.

Pseudocode looks more like a program than a flowchart. In fact, it is often easier to code a program from pseudocode than from a flowchart, because the

FIGURE MC 7-6 Pseudocode for solving the employee file problem of Figure MC 7-4 The problem requires printing the names of all people in an employee file with computer experience and at least five years of company service. A count of the number of such people is also required as output.

```
Start
Counter = 0
Read a record
DOWHILE there are more records to process
 IF computer experience
    IF company service ≥5 years
       Print employee name
       Increment Counter
    ELSE
       Next statement
    END IF
 ELSE
    Next statement
 END IF
 Read another record
END DO
Print Counter
Stop
```

former provides a codelike outline of the processing to take place. As a result, the program designer has more control over the end product—the program itself. Also unlike a flowchart, pseudocode is relatively easy to modify and can be embedded into the program as comments. However, flowcharts, being visual, are sometimes much better than pseudocode for designing logically complex problems.

There are no standard rules for writing pseudocode, but Figure MC 7-7 describes one set of rules that has a wide following. Note that all words relating to the three control structures of structural programming are capitalized and form a "sandwich" around other processing steps, which are indented. As Figure MC 7-6 shows, indentation is also used for readability. The keywords *Start* and *Stop* are often used to begin and end pseudocode.

Action Diagrams Pseudocode is now being widely employed in the creation of **action diagrams,** tools used to develop applications programs rapidly while online to the CPU. Action diagrams are composed of brackets into which pseudocodelike statements are written (see Figure MC 7-8). These statements, from which the computer is automatically able to develop executable code, are usually created with an *action-diagram editor.* Each control structure used in the diagram—sequence, selection, looping, or case—is accompanied by its own set of brackets.

When the programmer signals that a particular control structure is to be used, the action-diagram editor creates both the appropriate pseudocode keywords and brackets. As programmers provide various conditions or field names at certain places within the brackets, the editor checks to see that the code is both valid and consistent with the existing code for the application. If there is

FIGURE MC 7-7 Some rules for pseudocode. In addition to the rules shown here governing program control structures, pseudocode often begins with the keyword *Start* and ends with the keyword *Stop*.

Sequence Control Structure

```
BEGIN processing task
    Processing steps
END processing task
```

The steps in the sequence structure are normally written in lowercase letters. If the steps make up a well-defined block of code, they should be sandwiched between the keywords BEGIN and END.

Selection Control Structure

```
IF condition
    Processing steps
ELSE
    Processing steps
END IF
```

The keywords IF, ELSE, and END IF are always capitalized and tiered. The condition and processing steps normally are written in lowercase letters. The processing steps are indented from the keywords in the manner illustrated.

Looping (DOWHILE and DOUNTIL) Control Structures

```
DOWHILE condition            DOUNTIL condition
    Processing steps             Processing steps
END DO                       END DO
```

The keywords DOWHILE (or DOUNTIL) and END DO are always capitalized and tiered. The condition and processing steps follow the same lowercase convention and indentation rules as the selection control structure.

a problem, the editor will issue a warning or error message. Once an action diagram has been completed, it is automatically translated into executable code with a *code generator.* Action diagrams are an example of CASE tools, which are covered later in the chapter.

PROGRAMMING LANGUAGES

A **programming language** is a set of rules that describe how computer instructions are to be created. Programming languages used in microcomputing environments are commonly divided into three classes: low-level languages; high-level languages; and fourth-generation, or very-high-level, languages.

Low-Level Languages

The earliest programming languages—machine and assembly languages—are called *low-level languages* because programmers who code in them must write instructions at the finest level of detail: the base level of the machine. In both machine language and assembly language, each line of code corresponds to a single action of the computer system.

Virtually no one writes machine-language programs anymore. *Assembly languages* were developed in the 1950s to replace the 0s and 1s of machine language with symbols that are easier to understand and remember. The big advantage of assembly-language programs is executional efficiency; they are fast and consume little storage compared with their higher-level counterparts.

FIGURE MC 7-8 An action diagram. Action diagrams, which are created and modified with a special editor, are used to design and code pseudocodelike programs that are capable of being executed.

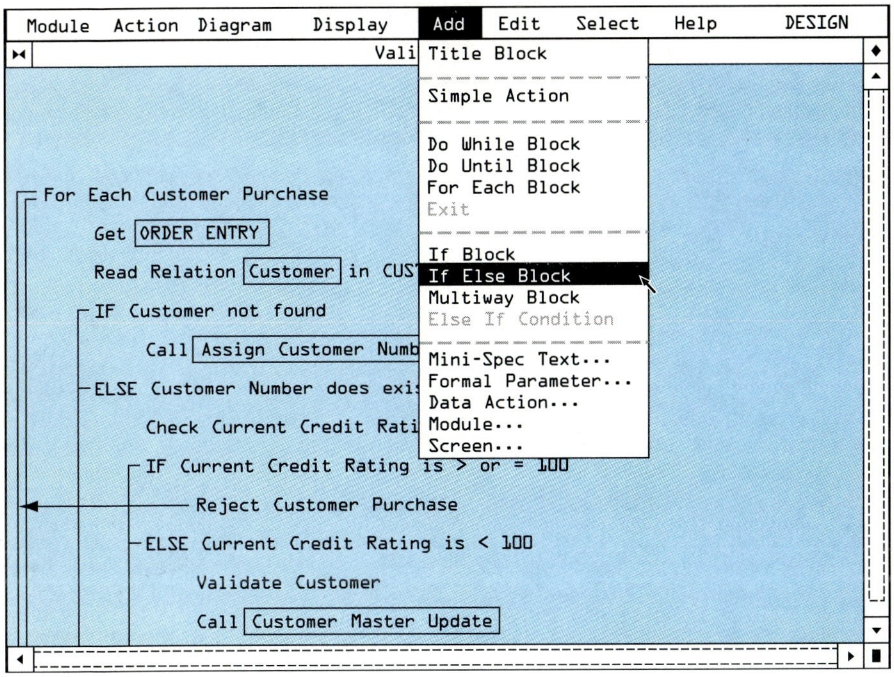

Unfortunately, assembly-language programs take longer to write and maintain than programs written in higher-level languages.

High-Level Languages

High-level languages differ from their low-level predecessors in that they require less coding detail and make programs easier to write. Included in this class are what have come to be known as third-generation programming languages—BASIC, COBOL, FORTRAN, Pascal, PL/1, APL, and many others. A number of high-level languages that one commonly finds on microcomputer systems are briefly discussed in the following list:

- **BASIC** (Beginner's All-purpose Symbolic Instruction Code) was designed as an easy-to-learn beginner's language that would work in a "friendly," nonfrustrating programming environment. Over the years, BASIC has evolved into one of the most popular and widely available programming languages. Because it is easy to learn and use, and because the storage requirements for its language translator are small, BASIC works well on almost all microcomputers. A conventional BASIC program is illustrated in Figure MC 7-9. A Visual BASIC program is shown in Figure MC 7-10. *Visual BASIC* is a version of the BASIC programming language that is used to develop applications in the Microsoft Windows environment.
- **C** combines the best features of a structured, high-level language and assembly languages—that is, it is relatively easy to code and uses computer resources efficiently. Currently it is one of the hottest languages for programmers to learn, largely because of its role in commercial software development. Recently, a new version of C called C++ has been developed to

FIGURE MC 7-9 **A sample BASIC program and its output.** This program is designed to accept as input the name of a product, its unit selling price, and the number of units sold and to output this information along with the total dollar value of sales.

(a) BASIC program

```
REM Program to compute sales
REM Author - C.S. PARKER
PRINT "     DESCRIPTION           PRICE       UNITS      TOTAL VALUE"
A$="\                    \    $###.##      #,###      $###,###"
READ Item$, Price, Units
WHILE Item$ < > "Last record"
   Value = Price * Units
   PRINT USING A$; Item$, Price, Units, Value
   READ Item$, Price, Units
WEND
DATA "SMALL WIDGETS",150,100
DATA "LARGE SKY HOOKS",200,50
DATA "BLIVETS",100,3000
DATA "Last record",0,0
END
```

(b) Output from the program

```
    DESCRIPTION           PRICE       UNITS      TOTAL VALUE
SMALL WIDGETS            $150.00        100       $ 15,000
LARGE SKY HOOKS          $200.00         50       $ 10,000
BLIVETS                  $100.00      3,000       $300,000
```

FIGURE MC 7-10 **Visual BASIC.** Microsoft's Visual BASIC is a version of the BASIC programming language that is used to develop applications in Microsoft Windows environments. The product includes tools for adding messaging, pen-computing, and audio and video components to applications.

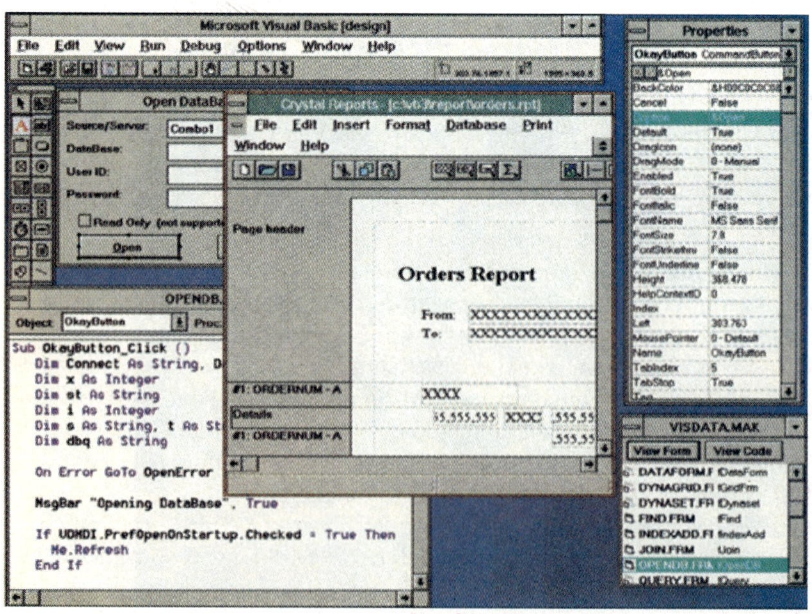

FIGURE MC 7-11 **C++.** C++, a graphically oriented version of C, has been developed to encourage better design and coding practices with the C language.

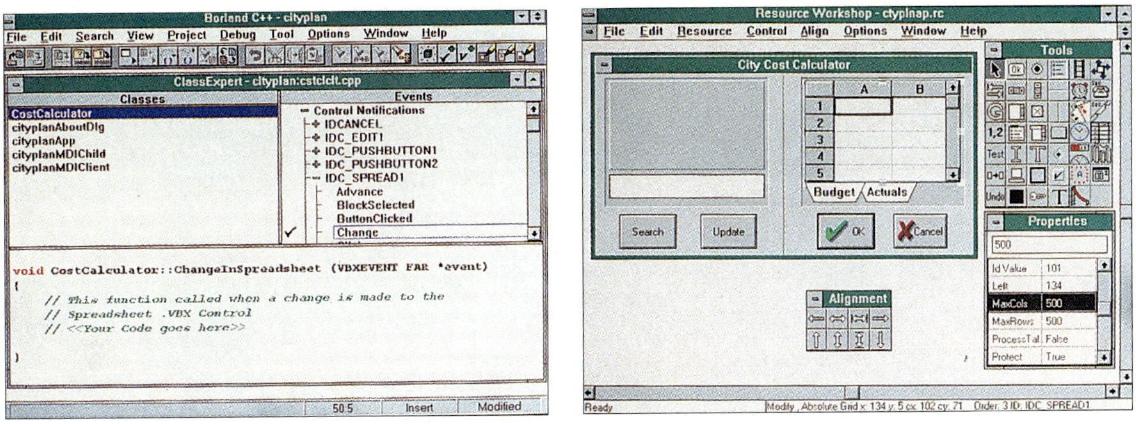

encourage better design and programming practices (see Figure MC 7-11). C++ is a superset of C, making all C programs understandable to C++ compilers. It is also an *object-oriented programming language* (discussed shortly). During the last few years, interest in C++ has taken off and C++ has become even more popular than C itself.

- **COBOL** (COmmon Business-Oriented Language) is the primary transaction processing language in use today. Transaction processing involves such activities as managing orders and recording purchases and payments. Currently most transaction processing applications in large organizations are coded in COBOL. Not too long ago, COBOL was too large a language to be used on microcomputer systems; today, however, many top-of-the-line microcomputers have computational power and storage capacity exceeding that of large computers that existed only a decade or so ago. Consequently, microcomputer-based COBOL is a fast-growing trend in business (see Figure MC 7-12).
- *Pascal,* named after the mathematician Blaise Pascal, was created primarily to fill the need for a teaching vehicle that would encourage structured programming. *Structured programming* refers to a philosophy of programming intended to make programming more systematic. Pascal uses a modular, building-block approach to programming; that is, each program is created from smaller subprograms. Today, Pascal is widely used in academia as a model for how a programming language should be designed.
- *FORTRAN* (FORmula TRANslator), which dates back to 1954, is the oldest surviving commercial high-level language. It was designed by scientists and is oriented toward scientific, mathematical, and engineering problem solving. The key strengths of FORTRAN are fast program execution and a large bank of preprogrammed subroutines.
- *PL/1* (Programming Language 1) was introduced in the mid-1960s by IBM as a general-purpose language; that is, it was designed for both scientific and transaction processing applications. It is a powerful language and has strong capabilities for structured programming.
- *APL* (A Programming Language) was developed in the early 1960s to enable programmers to code rapidly. It is an extremely compact language, with con-

FIGURE MC 7-12 Microcomputer-based COBOL. Because communications workstations connected to mainframes often lack color and graphical user interfaces, many programmers prefer developing mainframe-based COBOL applications on microcomputers.

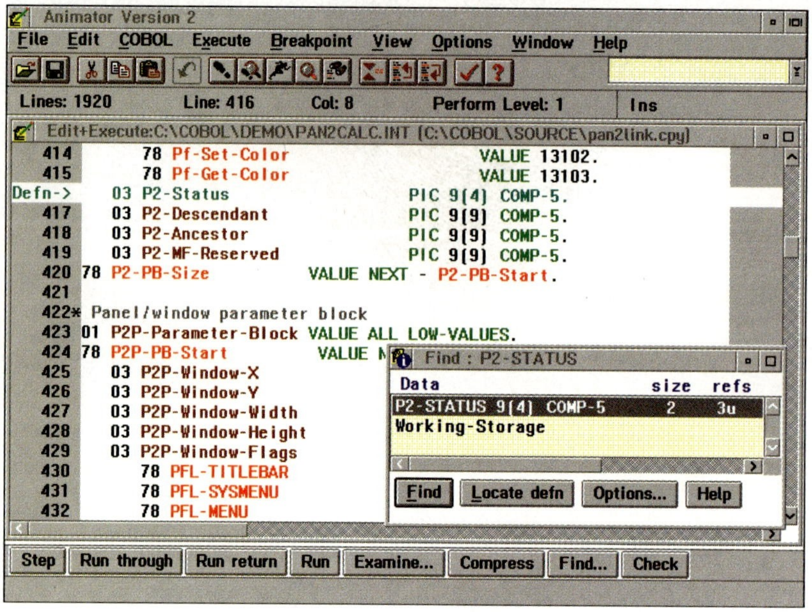

ventions that are quite different from those in other programming languages. APL requires a special keyboard.

- *Ada,* a superset of Pascal, is a relatively new structured language initiated by the U.S. Department of Defense. As a superset of Pascal, it shares many of Pascal's properties. It is still too early to predict how successful it will be in the business and academic worlds.
- *LISP* (for LISt Processor) and *Prolog* are used to develop applications in the field of artificial intelligence. LISP, a programming language that is nearly as old as FORTRAN, is often implemented on a special, dedicated computer system. Prolog, created around 1970, is designed to run on an ordinary computer.
- *Smalltalk,* pioneered at the University of Utah in the late 1960s, was the first successful object-oriented language commercially available. Whereas the trend today in language development is to pick up on the breakthroughs established by Smalltalk, Smalltalk itself has fallen into virtual obscurity.

Fourth-Generation Languages (4GLs)

Machine language and assembly language characterized the first and second generations of computing. During the third generation, languages such as FORTRAN, BASIC, and COBOL became dominant. Today, in the so-called fourth generation of the computer age, a new breed of languages has arrived. These *very-high-level languages* are appropriately called **fourth-generation languages (4GLs).** In contrast to lower-level languages, they are much easier to use and, consequently, they result in increased on-the-job productivity.

The 4GLs found in the market are diverse and serve a wide range of application areas. Some are targeted to users, some to programmers, and some to

FIGURE MC 7-13 Types of fourth-generation languages (4GLs). 4GLs have evolved to make end users and programmers more productive.

Language	Application
Report generators	Used to generate reports quickly
Retrieval and update languages	Used to retrieve information from files or databases and to add, delete, or modify data
Decision support system tools	Used to create financial schedules, budgets, models of decision environments, and the like
Graphics generators	Used to prepare presentation graphics quickly
Applications packages	Prewritten programs for applications such as word processing, payroll, and various accounting tasks
Applications generators	Used to prepare applications programs quickly

both. Six types of 4GLs commonly found in commercial software products are described in Figure MC 7-13. Many of these language functions overlap in a single product. For instance, Lotus Development Corporation's 1-2-3 spreadsheet is a decision support system tool with facilities for report generation, retrieval and update, and graphics generation. And dBASE and Paradox, popular database management systems, have language features that support report generation, retrieval and update, decision support, and applications generation. Most types of productivity software packages have a 4GL that has at least one of the functions covered in Figure MC 7-13.

Object-Oriented Programming

Probably few would argue today that the latest rage on the programming language scene is *object-oriented programming (OOP)*. The basic idea behind OOP is to make program preparation more intuitive. That, OOP advocates hope, will widen the scope of applications development to include the ordinary user and make professionally prepared programs easier to develop and maintain (see Figure MC 7-14).

An **object-oriented programming language** works with **objects**—program modules that encapsulate both instructions and data—rather than with a set of instructions and a separate set of data, as in traditional languages. Some experts think that at some point in the future, object-oriented languages will dominate the programming language landscape. Three key features that distinguish OOP languages are encapsulation, inheritance, and polymorphism.

Encapsulation Perhaps the key feature of OOP languages is *encapsulation*—bundling data and programs into objects. Here is an example of how it works at the user level. An icon on a display screen might be called *Sales*. When a user selects the Sales icon—which is an object—a menu might appear on the screen offering several choices. The choices might be (1) display sales for last week, (2) display year-to-date sales, and (3) display a sales chart. These, too, are objects, and the user would again select one of them. Each time an object appears on the screen it contains some type of *data*, and each time the user selects an object, the object knows what to do—that is, it exe-

FIGURE MC 7-14 OOP at work. The trend in commercial software today is toward context-sensitive icons and menus that are encapsulated objects.

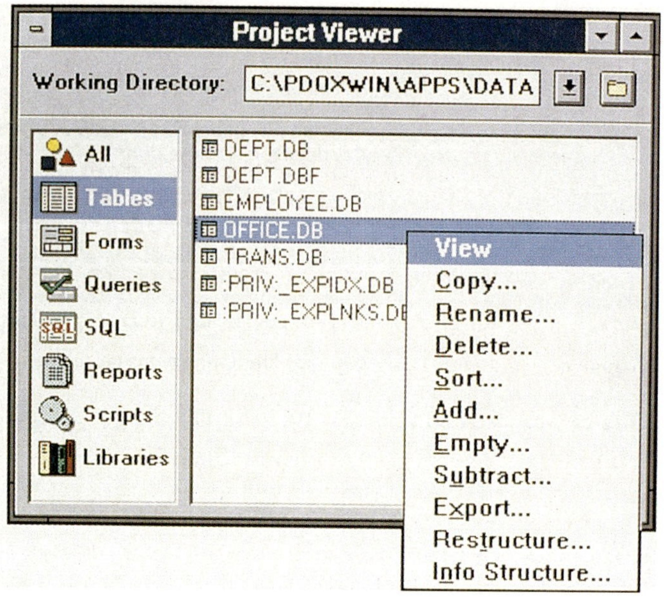

cutes encapsulated *instructions.* These instructions are passed on as "messages" to other objects.

Many industry observers feel that the encapsulation feature of OOP is the natural tool for making the transition to complex applications in which speech and moving images are integrated with text and graphics. With moving images and voice built into the objects themselves, program developers avoid the sticky problem of deciding how each separate type of data is to be integrated and synchronized into a working whole.

Inheritance *Inheritance* allows OOP developers to define one set of objects, say, "Employees at the Dearborn plant," and a specific instance of this object, say, "Welders." Thus, if employees at the Dearborn plant are eligible for a specific benefits package, welders automatically qualify for the package. If welder John Smith is later relocated from Dearborn to Birmingham, Alabama, where a different benefits package is available, there will be no problem. An icon representing John Smith—such as John Smith's face—can be selected on the screen and dragged with a mouse to the icon representing the Birmingham plant. John Smith then automatically will "inherit" the Birmingham benefits package.

Polymorphism *Polymorphism* means that different objects can receive the same message but deal with them in different ways. For instance, consider again the Sales icon mentioned earlier and the subsequent menu that appears when this icon is selected. If the user asks to display sales for last week (that is, a "display message" is sent to the sales-for-last-week object), the sales-for-last-week object may look for a routine that tells it how to display monochrome text in a window and add a scroll bar to it. On the other hand, if the user asks to display a sales chart (that is, the same display message is sent to the display-sales-chart object), the sales object may instead consult a routine that tells it how to paint colors onto the screen.

The combination of encapsulation, inheritance, and polymorphism leads to two major benefits: code reusability and the ability to make changes rapidly. **Reusable code** refers to "generic" code segments that can be used over and over again by several programs. Related programs often use the same blocks of code. Thus, reusable code enables programs to be cut and pasted quickly from pretested, error-free code segments. With respect to OOP, all the user has to do is access a library of reusable objects and stitch them into a working whole. Code reusability is critical in programming because it eliminates the need to write code from scratch and then debug it. Thus, reusability makes both program development and program maintenance faster. Such productivity gains can be influential to the corporate bottom line; recent studies have shown that about 80 percent of commercial programmer time is spent keeping existing programs up-to-date.

Although OOP has gotten rave reviews so far, it is still too early to tell what its full impact will be. To date, many languages still lack object-oriented interfaces. Also, many traditional programmers find object-oriented programming counterintuitive to the way they have been trained for years to think about development. In addition, object-oriented tools for users are still too new to predict reliably what their eventual effect might be. Although the corporate world is impressed so far, it is wary of jumping in feet first where new technology is concerned.

PROGRAM CODING

Once the program design is complete and the development language has been chosen, the next step is to code the program. **Coding** is the actual process of writing the program in a programming language.

During coding, knowledgeable programmers often take advantage of a number of special tools and methods to improve productivity. The purpose of these techniques is to produce code rapidly while creating programs that are both easy to maintain and as error-free as possible. Two techniques that are useful in microcomputing environments are coding standards and data dictionaries.

Coding Standards

Good programmers often follow a set of *coding standards*—essentially a list of rules designed to standardize programming style. The rules may cover items such as acceptable program structures, field-naming conventions, and comment conventions. Rules such as these help make programs easy to modify if the need ever arises.

Data Dictionaries

A **data dictionary** is similar to an ordinary dictionary in that it contains rules of usage for an alphabetical list of words. The words are those encountered in an application environment, for example, names of fields, records, files, and programs in a particular database.

Data dictionaries can be active or passive. An *active* data dictionary is online to an application as a programmer is developing it. If, say, you attempt to use a field name improperly or inconsistently, the active data dictionary will immediately warn you, and it may prohibit the alleged infraction from being part of the finished software product. A data dictionary that is not online during application development is *passive.* Later, in the section on database management systems, we will look more closely at the potential value of data dictionaries.

DEBUGGING AND TESTING

Debugging is the process of ensuring that a program is free of errors, or *bugs.* Debugging is usually a lengthy process, sometimes amounting to more than 50 percent of a program's development time.

Preliminary Debugging

The debugging process often begins after the program is initially entered into the computer system. Rarely is any program error-free the first time the programmer attempts to execute it. A very long program may have well more than a hundred errors of one sort or another—and maybe even thousands—at the outset. The computer's systems software usually provides the programmer with a list of informative error messages indicating the source of many of the bugs. At this point, the programmer again checks the code to see what is wrong, makes the necessary corrections, and reexecutes the program. This "execute, check, and correct" process will probably be repeated several more times before the program is free of bugs.

Testing

At some point in the debugging process, the program will appear to be correct. At this point, the original programmer—or, preferably, someone else—runs the program with extensive *test data.* Good test data will subject the program to all the conditions it might conceivably encounter when it is finally implemented. For example, will the program issue a check or a bill in the amount of $0.00? Also, many programs are beta tested. In a *beta test,* preliminary versions of the software are scrutinized by users for bugs and for ease of use (see the chapter User Tip). Although rigorous testing significantly decreases the chance of surprise when a program is implemented, there is no foolproof guarantee that the completed program will be problem-free.

Proper debugging and testing are vital, because an error that may cost a few dollars to fix at this stage in the development process may cost many thousands of dollars to correct after the program is released. Incidentally, rarely are commercial programs completely free of errors upon release. If an error is serious enough, a new release of the software product, with the bug fixed, will have to be considered.

PROGRAM MAINTENANCE

Virtually every program, if it is to last a long time, requires ongoing maintenance. Program **maintenance** is the process of updating software so that it continues to be useful. For instance, if new types of data are added to a database and existing programs must be modified to use these data, program maintenance is necessary. Program maintenance is also commonly triggered by new software releases, new equipment announcements, and changes in the way business is conducted.

USER TIP

Beta Testing

If you want to try commercial software before it becomes available for sale, then consider becoming part of a beta test. Today, with the number of hardware and software combinations on the desks of ordinary users being far too large to catalog, software vendors have turned to the users themselves to be guinea pigs. To ensure that the programs will hold up under a wide variety of conditions when released, the more testers the better. To put Windows 95 through its paces, for instance, Microsoft sent out more than 50,000 beta copies of the product while it was under development. Beta testers, for their efforts, often receive a free copy of the software when it comes out and perhaps some promotional items, such as a T-shirt and mug. The vendor, in return, expects some type of reporting on a regular basis.

User testing. User testing helps root out bugs that might otherwise show up after release.

Program maintenance is costly and time-consuming. It has been estimated that many organizations spend well over half of their programming time just maintaining existing applications programs. One of the major reasons that such tools as coding standards and data dictionaries are so popular today is that they can result in lower program-creation and maintenance costs. The goal is to do it right the first time or you will wind up doing it again. And perhaps again and again.

DOCUMENTATION

Documentation refers to a written description of a system, procedure, or program. If you have ever been frustrated by trying to get something to work from poorly written instructions, you can appreciate how valuable good documentation can be. Microcomputer users developing their own applications may encounter documentation in several different ways.

One way is through the professionally prepared support materials that come with the programming language or the productivity software package that is being used to build applications. This type of documentation is sometimes called *vendor documentation,* and it normally consists of such tools as a reference manual, a learning workbook, and tutorial disks. Good vendor documentation and support are becoming increasingly important to users who do their own applications development.

Another way developers encounter documentation is through the *user documentation* they prepare themselves. If you build an application for others, you need to provide support telling them what they need to know to be able to work with the software you create. User documentation should include instructions for running programs, a description of command sequences to follow when doing work procedures, examples of situations users are likely to encounter, and a troubleshooting guide to help with difficulties.

Finally, developers often must prepare *programmer documentation,* which usually consists of any tools that will simplify later maintenance of programs—by either the original developer or someone else. Tools might include program narratives, flowcharts and structure charts, program listings, and descriptions of inputs and outputs. There might also be a set of procedures to test programs when modifications are made.

COMPUTER-AIDED SOFTWARE ENGINEERING (CASE)

Software development has never been an easy process. In fact, a partner at Arthur Andersen & Co. recently estimated that the average business applications program takes some 32,000 hours to develop from start to finish—an effort worthy of a team of three dozen programmers working for almost three years. And that represents only the programs that get finished! No wonder people are looking for a better way to get programs developed.

In the last dozen years, a number of solutions have surfaced. Among the most promising are **computer-aided software engineering (CASE)** tools. The objective of CASE tools is automating one or more stages of applications software development. Although CASE is in its infancy and has numerous wrinkles to be worked out, many people believe that most commercial software will be developed through a CASE-type approach in the not-too-distant future.

Many of the CASE products now offered in the marketplace are called *software engineering workbenches.* Like a carpenter's workbench, which comprises a number of the tools of the carpentry trade—hammers, saws, chisels, drill bits, and the like—software engineering workbenches contain a number of design, programming, and maintenance tools that get software products developed faster. For instance, such a workbench might consist of an action-diagram editor, a 4GL, a code generator, an active data dictionary, and tools that help turn unstructured programs into structured ones. The specific tools included in the workbench vary from one vendor to another. Figure MC 7-15 features Systems Architect, a CASE product from Popkin Software and Systems that supports a wide number of development methodologies and diagram types.

No company has yet developed an everything-but-the-kitchen-sink CASE package, the panacea that will cure every company's applications software development headaches. Consequently, an organization may have to shop around for several CASE products that collectively will meet its needs. This is easier said than done; many CASE tools are incompatible with one another and may not interface well with other proprietary software products that the organization is using. Fortunately, CASE vendors realize this and currently are attempting to forge alliances with other vendors to establish standards that will increase CASE applicability.

DATABASE MANAGEMENT ON MICROCOMPUTERS

Applications are often developed for use in a database environment. Database management systems on microcomputers often come with their own 4GL tools that enable a user/developer to write conventional computer programs and that

FIGURE MC 7-15 **A CASE package.** Systems Architect is a CASE product that enables information systems professionals to work with a wide assortment of design methodologies and diagram types.

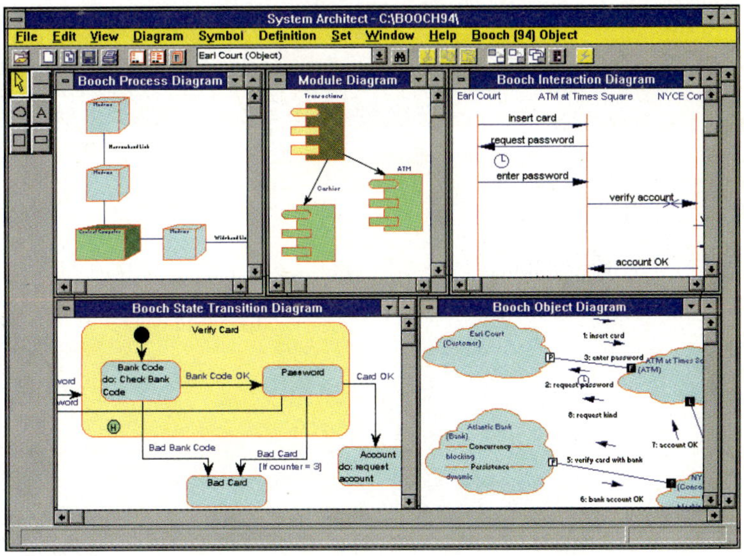

make it easy to retrieve and update data, generate reports, and the like. Here, we look at what both users and developers should know about microcomputer-based database management systems.

A **database management system (DBMS)** is a software system that integrates data in storage and provides easy access to them. The data themselves are placed on disk in a **database,** which can be thought of as an integrated collection of related files. The three files shown in Figure MC 7-16, which we will discuss shortly, collectively form a database. In a nondatabase environment, these data would normally exist as independent files.

The best way to understand what a microcomputer-based DBMS does and how one works is to turn immediately to an example. Many different DBMSs are commercially available. Not all of them work the same way, nor are they all equally easy to comprehend. In the example that follows we will look at a **relational database management system**—the type of DBMS found on most microcomputers and probably the easiest type to understand.

A Simple Example

Imagine that you are a sales manager at a ski-equipment warehouse, and an order comes in for 160 pairs of ski boots. You first need to find out if the order can be filled from stock in inventory. If it cannot, you next need to know how long it will be before enough stock is available. You have an impatient client on the phone who requires an immediate response.

Because rapid access to more than one file's worth of data is required, this type of task is especially suited to a relational DBMS. An *inventory file* is used to store current stock levels, an *order file* is used to keep track of future shipments, and a *product description file* is used to store the product descriptions. The very notion of files is often not apparent to the database end user, who

FIGURE MC 7-16 Using a database management system (DBMS). Data in various files can be quickly pulled together by their common fields (shaded here).

Product name	Product number	Supplier	Price
Skis	A-202	Ellis Ski Co.	90.00
Boots	A-211	Ajax Bros.	60.00
Poles	A-220	Bent Corp.	25.00
Bindings	A-240	Acme Co.	15.00
Wax	A-351	Candle Industries	3.00

(a) Product description file

Product number	Uncommitted stock	On order?
A-202	15	Yes
A-211	90	Yes
A-220	30	Yes
A-240	25	Yes
A-351	80	No

(b) Inventory file

Shipment date	Product number	Amount
1/8	A-202	30
1/8	A-240	15
1/9	A-211	50
1/9	A-202	40
1/10	A-220	35
1/12	A-211	60

(c) Order file

Product number	Product name	Date	Total stock
A-211	Boots	Today	90
		1/9	140
		1/12	200

(d) Information screen

sees only a screenful of information and usually has no idea from where the database system is extracting it.

The following scenario would be ideal. At the microcomputer workstation on your desk, you key in the product description, "Boots." The computer system responds with a screen that shows the status of this product, including the current level of uncommitted stock, future delivery dates, and future delivery amounts (see Figure MC 7-16d). Within seconds, you are able to pull together the information necessary to satisfy the client's request and place the order.

Data from several files are combined quickly by a relational DBMS through the fields (columns) that the files have in common. Relational DBMSs are so named because they *relate* data in different files by common fields in those files. In the example we just covered, data from the three files were pulled together through a common product-number field (the highlighted column in Figure MC 7-16).

Interacting with the DBMS

Users interact with the DBMS through either an easy-to-use retrieval/update facility that accompanies the database package or an applications program written in a programming language.

FIGURE MC 7-17 Database environment. The DBMS serves as an interface between users at one end and data and programs at the other.

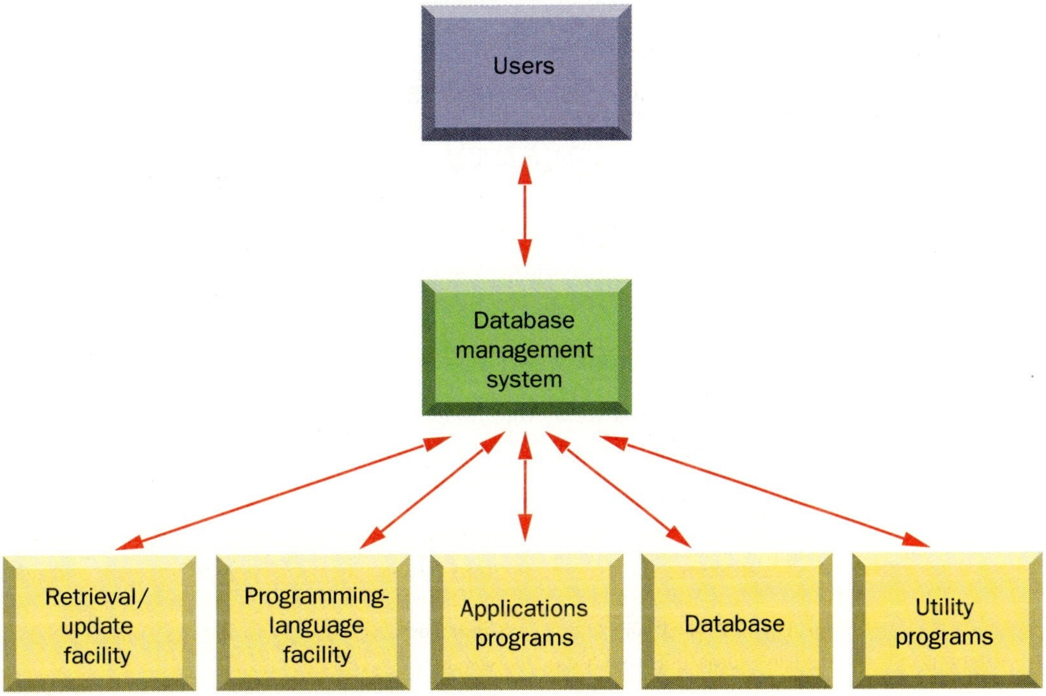

Usually the *retrieval/update facility* contains a graphical, menu-driven interface that lets users select choices onscreen and an easy-to-use language interface that allows commands to be typed in. Such a facility is designed primarily to satisfy the database needs of ordinary users. Among the most critical of these needs are creating the database, updating database data, and retrieving information from the database (making queries).

The *programming-language facility* allows users to create complete computer programs. It often is targeted to more sophisticated users who want to design custom menus or screens or to create applications that go well beyond the standard ones offered with the database package. Most microcomputer-oriented DBMSs come equipped with their own proprietary programming language. Some also support applications developed in such public-domain programming languages as C, BASIC, and COBOL.

A database processing environment for a typical microcomputer system is illustrated in Figure MC 7-17. The DBMS serves as an interface between the user at one end and the data and programs at the other. As users develop programs and database data at their workstations, DBMS *utility programs* such as the data dictionary ensure that the data are properly prepared before storing them on disk. Other utility programs, such as a help facility, can be summoned quickly when the user needs assistance with executing a command or troubleshooting an error condition.

Users of microcomputer-based DBMSs must be able to do at least two principal tasks: (1) set up databases (an activity called *data definition*) and (2) create and use databases (an activity called *data manipulation*). Usually, database packages come with a single, proprietary language that can handle both these activities. Typically, this language can also be used to develop applications programs.

Data Definition

Setting up the database, or **data definition,** mainly involves creating a *template* for each file in the database. Templates for the database shown in Figure MC 7-16 are given in Figure MC 7-18. Usually, each template will ask for the following types of information about the file:

- The name of each field
- The maximum length of each field
- The type of data (say, character or numeric) that is to go into each field

This information is commonly referred to as a **file structure.** Each file will have its own structure. For example, suppose you have informed your microcomputer's relational database package that you want to create a file called "INVENTORY" (see Figure MC 7-18b). The package will ask you to describe each data field of the records that will go into the file. You might respond as follows:

Field Name	Field Type	Width	Decimals
PRODUCT-NUMBER	Character	5	N/A
UNCOMMITTED-STOCK	Numeric	5	0
ON-ORDER?	Logical	1	N/A

Roughly translated, this structure declares that there will be three fields in the "INVENTORY" file: PRODUCT-NUMBER, UNCOMMITTED-STOCK, and ON-ORDER?. The PRODUCT-NUMBER field is composed of text, or *character,* data. The width of 5 means that product numbers will be five or fewer characters in length. UNCOMMITTED-STOCK will consist of *numeric* data that will have a maximum width of five characters. Because stock is counted in units of product, there will be no decimal places. ON-ORDER? will be a *logical* field. A logical field contains either the value *T* (for true, or yes) or *F* (for false, or no). For instance, a product that was on order would typically be given the value *T;* a product not on order would receive the value *F.*

Generally, arithmetic computations can be performed on data that have been declared as numeric but not on data declared as character or logical. The "character," "numeric," and "logical" designations are commonly called **field descriptors.**

In many database environments, templates can be customized to meet a variety of data-entry needs. In Paradox, for instance, there is a feature called Form Expert that lets users choose exactly which type of data are to appear in a screen template and how these data will be displayed onscreen (see Figure MC 7-19).

The DBMS uses file structures and other characteristics of the file to construct the data dictionary for the application. On most microcomputers, the data dictionary is kept *active* to the application. This means that when data are placed into the template and later used, the data dictionary monitors the applications environment and ensures that no data are entered or used in any conflicting way. So, for instance, you could not enter a seven-character product number if the dictionary expected all product numbers to be five characters long. Nor would the dictionary allow you to add a character field and a numeric field.

FIGURE MC 7-18 **Data definition.** Data definition requires developing a file structure, or template, for each database file. The template (shown to the right of each file) contains such data as field names, field widths, and field types.

(a) Product description file

Product name	Product number	Supplier	Price
Skis	A-202	Ellis Ski Co.	90.00
Boots	A-211	Ajax Bros.	60.00
Poles	A-220	Bent Corp.	25.00
Bindings	A-240	Acme Co.	15.00
Wax	A-351	Candle Industries	3.00

PRODUCT
PRODUCT-NAME
PRODUCT-NUMBER -
SUPPLIER
PRICE

(b) Inventory file

Product number	Uncommitted stock	On order?
A-202	15	T
A-211	90	T
A-220	30	T
A-240	25	T
A-351	80	F

INVENTORY
PRODUCT-NUMBER -
UNCOMMITTED-STOCK
ON-ORDER?

Shipment date	Product number	Amount
1/8	A-202	30
1/8	A-240	15
1/9	A-211	50
1/9	A-202	40
1/10	A-220	35
1/12	A-211	60

ORDER
SHIPMENT-DATE / /
PRODUCT-NUMBER -
AMOUNT .

(c) Order file

In many database systems, the data dictionary is also used to protect certain data from unauthorized use or alteration. Sensitive data such as salaries can be hidden so that only certain users of the database, furnished with the proper password, are authorized to retrieve them. Also, only users with access to another password would be allowed to update these data.

Data Manipulation

The process of using the database in some hands-on fashion is called **data manipulation.** There are generally two ways to manipulate data in a microcomputer-oriented DBMS—through the retrieval/update facility that is provided with the DBMS and through an applications program developed with the programming-language facility.

Data manipulation encompasses a variety of activities. The following subsections briefly cover some of the most important of them.

FIGURE MC 7-19 **Preparing customized templates.** In many database environments, templates can be tailored to meet specific data-entry needs. In Borland's Paradox DBMS, users can summon a Form Expert feature that takes them through a series of easy-to-follow steps to design templates.

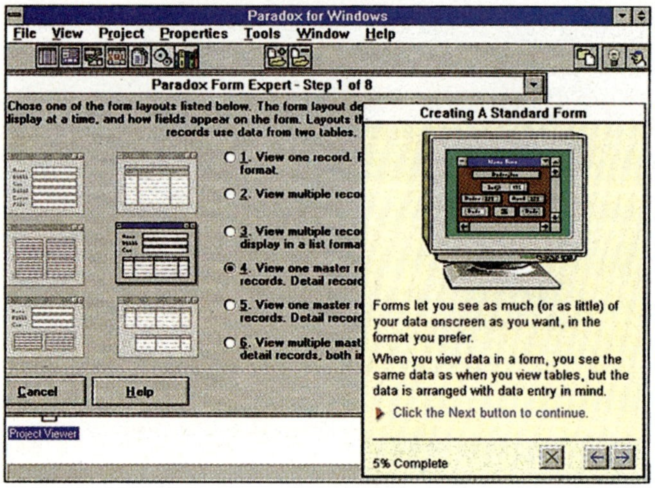

(a)

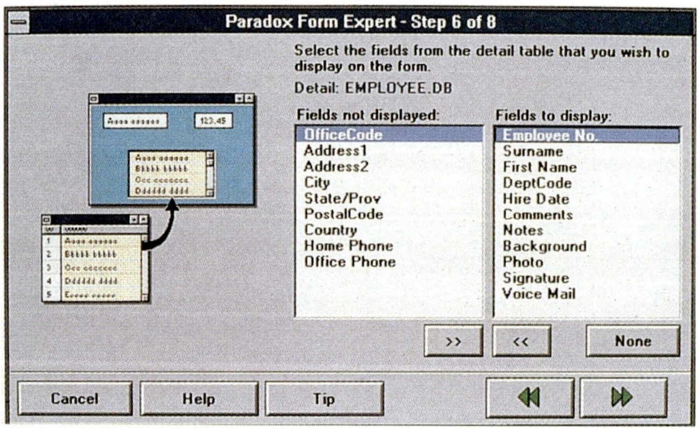

(b)

Creation of Database Data Creating database data consists of developing records for the database. Each template in the database is successively brought to the screen and filled with the records that pertain to it. In Figure MC 7-18, for example, you might first summon the template for the product description file. Then you would type in the first record in that file and enter it. After you did this, a fresh template would appear on the screen. You would type in the second record, and so forth. When you had finished entering all the records for the product description file, you would do the same thing for the next file—say, the inventory file.

File Maintenance File maintenance consists primarily of updating records. This involves adding new records from time to time, deleting records

FIGURE MC 7-20 Examples of database queries. The queries given here can be directed to the database data described in Figures MC 7-16 and MC 7-18. Each of the queries conforms to SQL, the de facto standard for information retrieval from relational databases.

Query

```
SELECT   PRODUCT-NUMBER, PRODUCT-NAME
FROM     PRODUCT
WHERE    PRICE < 20.00
```

Selects all records in the product file that have a price of less than $20; outputs only the product number and product name on each selected record. That is,

Response

```
A-240   Bindings
A-351   Wax
```

Query

```
SELECT   PRODUCT-NUMBER, UNCOMMITTED-STOCK, ON ORDER?
FROM     INVENTORY
WHERE    UNCOMMITTED-STOCK > 20    AND    ON-ORDER? = T
```

Selects all records in the inventory file that have an uncommitted stock level of more than 20 and that are on order (that is, the value of ON-ORDER is *T*, for true); outputs all fields of each selected record. That is,

Response

```
A-211   90   T
A-220   30   T
A-240   25   T
```

Query

```
SELECT   SHIPMENT-DATE, PRODUCT-NUMBER
FROM     ORDER
WHERE    SHIPMENT-DATE  >= 1/9 OR AMOUNT >= 30
```

Selects all records in the order file where the shipment date is 1/9 or later, the amount is 30 or more units, or both. Outputs only dates and product numbers. That is,

Response

```
1/8    A-202
1/9    A-211
1/9    A-202
1/10   A-220
1/12   A-211
```

Query

```
SELECT   PRODUCT-NAME, ON-ORDER?
FROM     PRODUCT, INVENTORY
WHERE    PRODUCT.PRODUCT-NUMBER = INVENTORY.PRODUCT-NUMBER
```

Creates new records by linking the product and inventory files through their common field, PRODUCT-NUMBER. The new records show the name of each product and whether it is on order. That is,

Response

```
Skis       T
Boots      T
Poles      T
Bindings   T
Wax        F
```

that are no longer needed, and making modifications to records. Modifications are necessary because data such as prices and delivery schedules can change and also because errors are sometimes made in entering data.

Information Retrieval (Query) The information on the screen in Figure MC 7-16d, where we needed to find out amounts and delivery dates of uncommitted stock, is an example of information retrieval, or query. Database queries can be simple or very complex. Figure MC 7-20 illustrates several queries from the database data described in Figures MC 7-16 and MC 7-18. Also provided are the DBMS's responses to those queries. One important fact you should keep in mind is that if you can *manually* pull together the data

FIGURE MC 7-21 **Simplifying SQL with GUIs.** The trend in database software today is toward graphical user interfaces (GUIs) that make it easier for ordinary users to construct SQL commands. Shown here are two different GUI approaches to the language interface illustrated in Figure MC 7-20. (a) Easy SQR lets users compose queries by placing search fields, search operators, and search criteria in separate windows. (b) Data Partner enables users to construct queries by connecting icons that symbolize access routines.

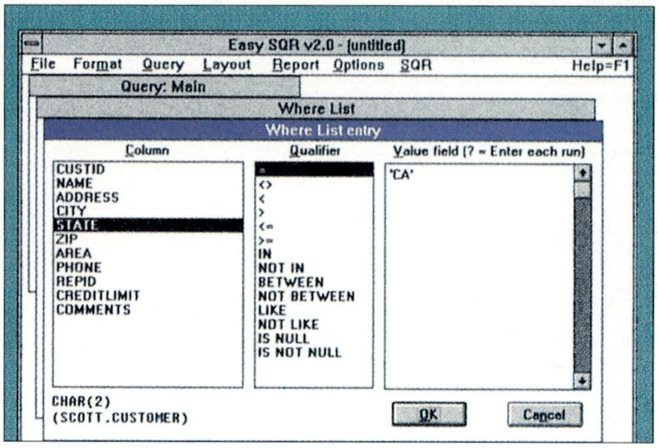

(a)

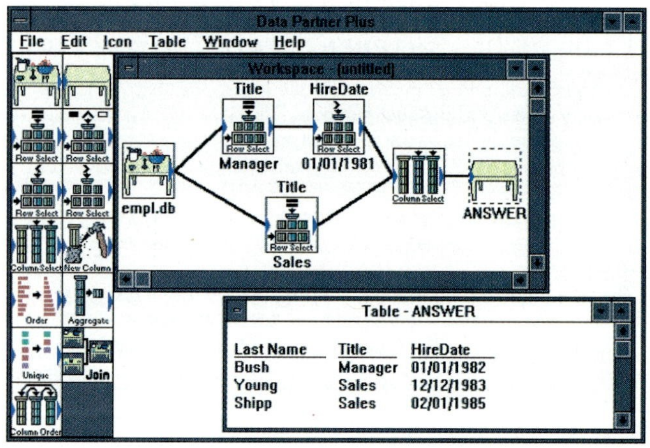

(b)

you need, you should be able to get your DBMS to pull these same data together *automatically*—and a lot faster, too.

Every DBMS has its own way of letting users query the database for information. The style shown in Figure MC 7-20 is based largely on **Structured Query Language (SQL),** which is recognized as today's de facto standard for information retrieval in relational databases. Recently, a number of GUI tools have become available from both database vendors and vendors of add-on packages to make it easy for users to construct database queries without having to remember language syntax (see Figure MC 7-21).

Increasingly, databases are enabling the storage and retrieval of graphical information as well as traditional text (see Figure MC 7-22).

Reporting Reporting is the process of arranging the information you need in a formal report. Most DBMSs require that you produce a *report form* for each type of report you need. The report form specifies what the report will

FIGURE MC 7-22 **Graphics data.** Database management packages are increasingly being used for storage and retrieval of graphics-oriented data. (a) Photographic data are included along with regular text data in an electronic insurance record. (b) Lotus Development's Notes contains a feature that enables a database of newspaper articles to be scanned by keywords and selected articles retrieved.

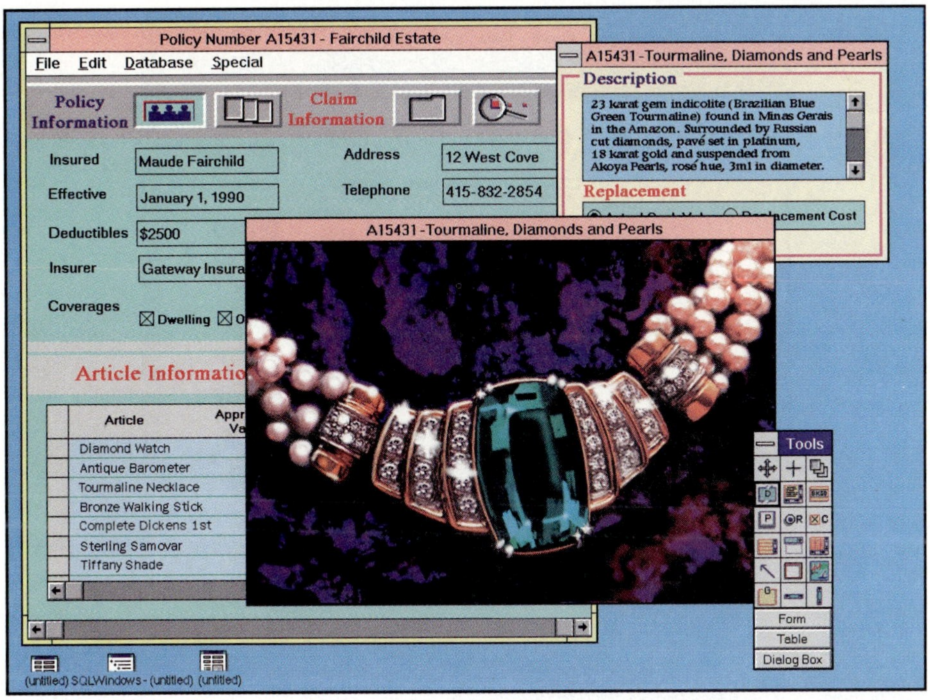

(a)

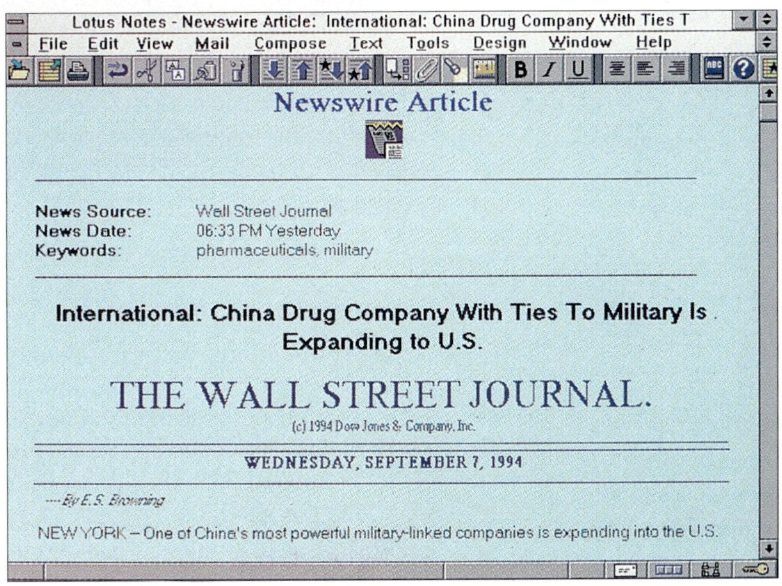

(b)

look like when it is output—how the report title and column headings will look, which fields will be placed into which columns, the criteria used to select records for the report, how records are to be arranged in the report, and the like. Typically, a series of easy-to-use menus will guide users through report preparation (see Figure MC 7-23).

FIGURE MC 7-23 **Developing a report form.** DBMS packages, such as Lotus Development's Approach, are increasingly employing mouse-driven, point-and-click tools that enable users to design reports onscreen.

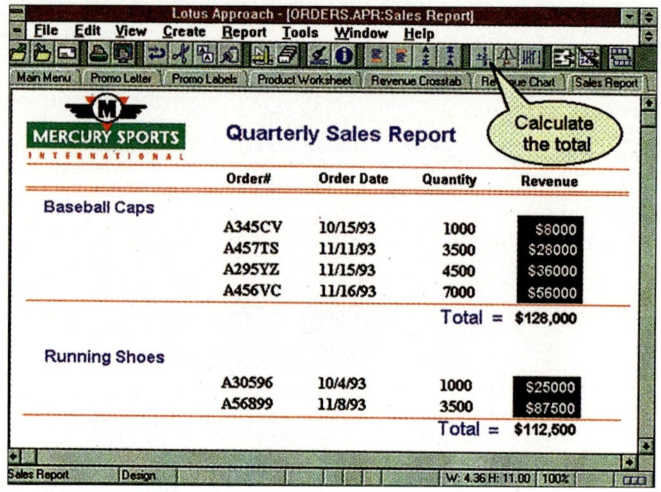

Sorting Sorting is the process of arranging records in some order. Most DBMSs are equipped with the necessary tools to help you arrange records in virtually any sequence you desire. As with spreadsheets, you can choose several sort keys if you wish to do sorts within sorts.

Calculations Often it is necessary to compute sums for columns, take averages, count records, and so forth. Although spreadsheet software is especially suited to these particular applications, DBMSs also include several such math features.

Summary

- Applications software development consists of program design, coding, debugging and testing, and maintenance. Documentation is also generally carried out during each stage of the development process.
- Before any software development takes place, a critical decision that must be made is whether the software should be created from scratch or acquired off the shelf.
- The program design stage often consists of using design tools such as structure charts, program flowcharts, and pseudocode. It is usually desirable that programs follow standard design practices.
- Programming languages used to code applications include low-level languages, high-level languages, and very-high-level (or fourth-generation) languages. When coding, programmers often follow strict coding practices and use a data dictionary to maintain the integrity of the application.
- Once programs are coded, they must be debugged and tested. Proper debugging and testing is vital, because an error that may cost a few dollars to fix at this stage in the development process may cost many thousands of dollars to repair after the program is implemented.

____ 15. Which is executed as long as a certain condition is true?
   a. The case control structure
   b. Pseudocode
   c. A DOWHILE loop
   d. The sequence control structure
   e. A DOUNTIL loop

____ 16. When does debugging occur in program development?
   a. During documentation
   b. Before coding
   c. After the program is released
   d. After coding
   e. Before design

____ 17. An information-retrieval standard most relational databases follow is
   a. the report generator.
   b. limitation to use of data from one file.
   c. SQL.
   d. the use of secondary keys only.
   e. the report form.

____ 18. Files in a relational database are interrelated using
   a. the database administrator.
   b. updating.
   c. common fields.
   d. sorting.
   e. the math feature.

____ 19. A collection of information about the fields of a file (names, lengths, types) is referred to as
   a. a field descriptor.
   b. a file structure.
   c. an SQL.
   d. an applications generator.
   e. a Create command.

____ 20. A code used to describe whether a data field is numeric, character, logical, or some other type is the
   a. file structure.
   b. view.
   c. field descriptor.
   d. key field.
   e. SQL.

Matching

Select the term that best matches each phrase:

a. Looping control structure
b. 4GL
c. Structure chart
d. Sequence control structure
e. Case control structure
f. Documentation
g. Programming language
h. COBOL
i. Field descriptors
j. Selection control structure
k. C
l. Debugging

____ 21. LISP and Smalltalk are examples

____ 22. A special case of an if-then-else control structure

____ 23. A written description of a program

____ 24. A programming language that combines the best features of a high-level language and an assembly language

____ 25. A control structure that comes in two types: DOWHILE and DOUNTIL

____ 26. A diagram that looks like a hierarchical organization chart

____ 27. A very-high-level language

____ 28. The act of removing errors from a program

____ 29. A transaction-processing-oriented programming language

____ 30. Character, numeric, and logical are types

Answers

True/False: 1. F; 2. T; 3. T; 4. F; 5. F; 6. F; 7. F; 8. T; 9. T; 10. F

Multiple choice: 11. d; 12. d; 13. b; 14. b; 15. c; 16. d; 17. c; 18. c; 19. b; 20. c

Matching: 21. g; 22. e; 23. f; 24. k; 25. a; 26. c; 27. b; 28. l; 29. h; 30. i

Exercises

1. Create a flowchart that reads a list of positive values and outputs the number of those values that are greater than 25.
2. Each employee record in a large employee file contains the name and ID number of an employee, the hours worked this week by that employee, and the employee's hourly wage rate. Create a flowchart that reads these records and, for each employee processed, outputs the employee ID number, the amount of overtime earnings to be received by that employee, and total earnings. Employees earn "time and a half" for overtime (that is, for each hour worked beyond 40 hours, employees earn an extra 50 percent above what they would normally earn).
3. Prepare pseudocode to solve Exercise 2. Label all fundamental control structures (sequence, selection, looping) in the pseudocode.
4. For each of these languages—COBOL, C, and BASIC—answer the following questions. Assume in each case that the language is to be implemented on the microcomputer system you are using in class.
   a. Is a version available that will fit on your system? If so, name the version. If not, determine how your system would need to be upgraded to accommodate the version best suited to it.
   b. What is the suggested list price of the version you identified in item a?
5. Choose a CASE package targeted to microcomputers and a system platform on which the package is used. Then answer the following questions:
   a. What are the hardware and storage requirements for the particular package and platform chosen?

   b. What types of program design tools does this package contain?
   c. What is the suggested list price of this package?

6. Compare the latest versions of any two of the following five DBMSs with respect to suggested list price, available platforms (for example, DOS, Windows, Macintosh), RAM and hard-disk requirements, number of files that can be related in a single application, maximum number of records allowed per file, maximum number of fields allowed per record, and maximum number of characters allowed per field.
   a. dBASE
   b. Access
   c. Foxbase
   d. Oracle
   e. Paradox
   f. Approach

MC 8 DEVELOPING BUSINESS SYSTEMS

OUTLINE

LEARNING OBJECTIVES

After completing this chapter, you will be able to:

1. Explain what a system is.
2. Describe several types of computer systems commonly found in business.
3. Define the roles of various people and information systems areas involved in the systems development process.
4. Identify and describe the components of the systems development life cycle (SDLC).
5. Describe several approaches used to develop systems.

OVERVIEW

In previous chapters, we considered primarily the hardware, software, data, or applications development procedures that go into building a microcomputer system. Here, we turn to the larger context of putting together microcomputers with other technology elements, with people, and with procedures to form complete computer systems in business organizations.

All organizations have various sorts of systems—systems that attend to accounting activities such as sending out bills and processing payrolls, systems that provide information to help managers make decisions, systems for word processing and electronic mail tasks, systems that help run factories efficiently, and so on. Such systems require considerable effort to design, build, and maintain. The process that includes planning and implementing systems is called *systems development.*

Unfortunately, since no two situations are exactly alike, there is no surefire formula for successful systems development. A procedure that works well in one situation may fail in another. These facts notwithstanding, there is a set of general principles that, if understood, will enhance the likelihood of a system's success. Those principles are the subject of this chapter.

The chapter opens with a general discussion of systems and systems development. Then we cover the types of systems commonly found in business. From there we turn to the computer professionals who are hired to develop systems in organizations and consider some of their primary responsibilities. Then we look at the systems development life cycle—the set of activities that are at the heart of every serious systems-building effort. The chapter concludes with a discussion of the major approaches to systems development.

ON SYSTEMS

A **system** is a collection of elements and procedures that interact to accomplish a goal. A football game, for example, is played according to a system. It consists of a collection of elements (two teams, a playing field, referees) and procedures (the rules of the game) that interact to determine which team is the winner. A transit system is a collection of people, machines, work rules, fares, and schedules that get people from one place to another. Similarly, a computer system is a collection of people, hardware, software, data, and procedures that interact to perform information processing tasks.

The function of many systems, whether manual or computerized, is to keep an organization well managed and running smoothly. Systems are created and altered in response to changing needs within an organization and shifting conditions in its surrounding environment. When problems arise in an existing system or a new system is needed, systems development comes into play. **Systems development** is a process that consists of analyzing an applications environment, designing a new system or making modifications to an old one, acquiring needed hardware and software, and getting the new or modified system to work.

Systems development may be required for any of a number of reasons. New laws may call for the collection of data never before assembled; for example, the government may require new data on personnel. The introduction of new technology, especially new computer technology, may prompt wholesale revision of a system. Or, as is the trend today, a company may decide to convert certain applications into a global, networked environment. These and other kinds of pressure often can bring about major changes in any system in an organization.

BUSINESS SYSTEMS

Undoubtedly, you have already encountered many types of business systems. When you go into the supermarket, you generally see electronic cash registers and various handheld or laser scanning devices that are obviously a part of some supermarket system. Or, when you registered for classes, perhaps you have observed someone at a display device checking to see whether a certain class you want to take is still open or whether you have paid all your bills—apparently as part of a registration system.

Though there are hundreds of types of computer systems in existence today, many of those in business and most other organizations fall into one or more of four categories: transaction processing systems, information systems, office systems, and design and manufacturing systems. Here we will look more closely at each of these.

Transaction Processing Systems

Virtually every business must support a number of routine operations, most of which involve some form of tedious recordkeeping. These operations, such as payroll and accounts receivable, were some of the earliest commercial applications of computers in organizations and are still among the most important. Because these systems involve processing of business transactions—such as paying employees, recording customer purchases and payments, or recording vendor receipts and payments—they are called **transaction processing systems.**

At one time, almost all transaction processing systems relied heavily on mainframe computers. Today, however, microcomputer systems have made automated transaction processing affordable to almost all businesses (see Figure MC 8-1). Even large organizations have acquired microcomputer systems at record rates for their transaction processing. These organizations are finding that microcomputer-based networks are often cheaper than mainframes and, also, that data automatically captured into machine-readable form at the point of purchase are more accurate and are available for immediate analysis.

Some of the functions commonly found as part of a transaction processing system are discussed in the following subsections.

Payroll *Payroll programs* compute deductions, subtract them from gross earnings, and write paychecks to employees for the remainder (see Figure MC 8-1a). These programs also contain routines that prepare reports for management and for taxing agencies of the federal, state, and local governments.

Accounts Receivable *Accounts receivable* refers to the amounts owed by customers who have made purchases on credit. Accounts receivable programs are charged with keeping track of customers' purchases, payments, and account balances. They also calculate and print invoices (see Figure MC 8-1b), and monthly statements, and provide information to management. Other output includes sales analyses, which describe changing patterns of products and sales, as well as detailed or summary reports on current and past-due accounts.

FIGURE MC 8-1 **Transaction processing.** Transaction processing systems are the backbone of most businesses. Here, Peachtree Accounting for Windows, a PC-based accounting and general-ledger system, is featured performing a variety of accounting tasks.

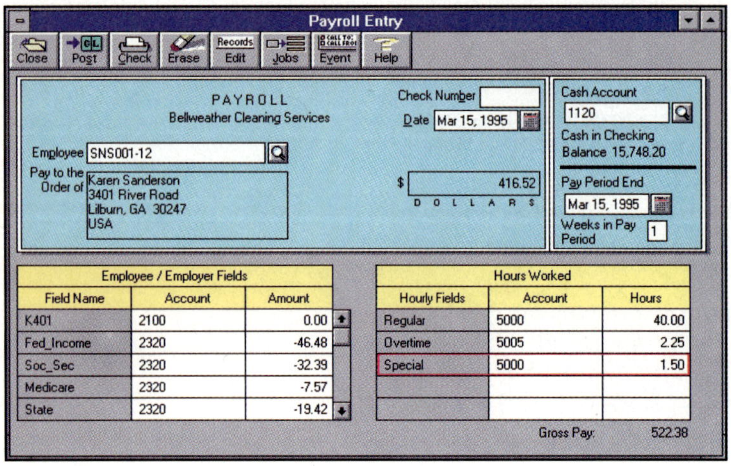

(a) Preparing a payroll check.

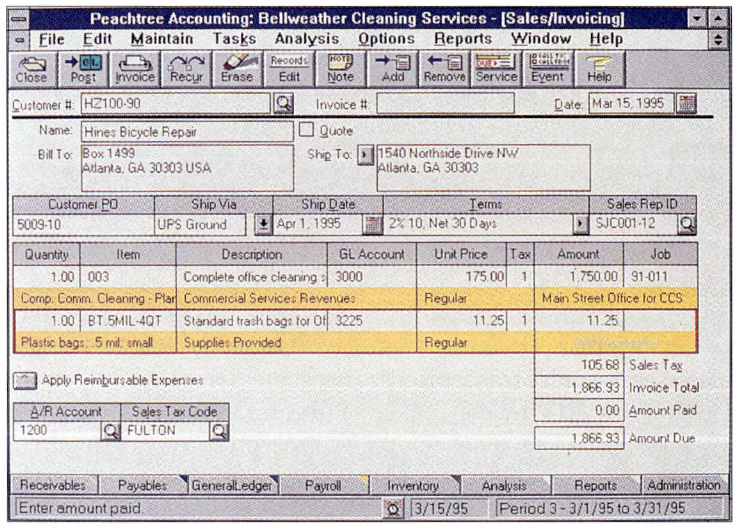

(b) Producing a sales invoice.

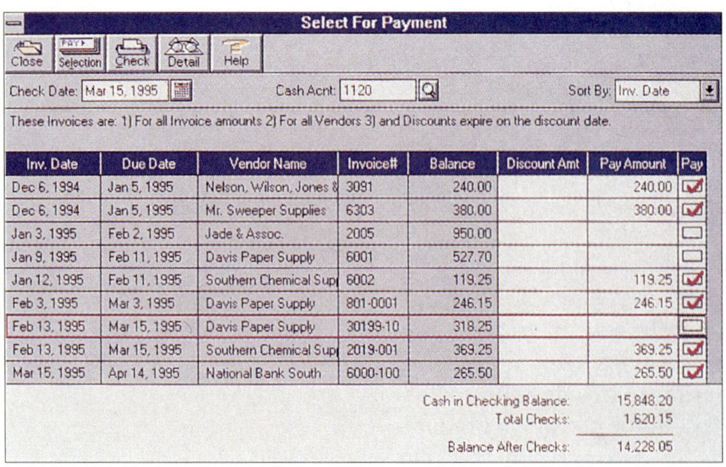

(c) Preparing a list of vendors to pay.

Accounts Payable *Accounts payable* refers to the money a company owes other companies for the goods and services it has received. Accounts payable programs keep track of bills and often generate checks to pay them. They record who gets paid and when (see Figure MC 8-1c), handle cash disbursements, and advise managers whether the company should accept discounts offered by vendors in return or early payment.

Order Entry Many businesses handle some type of order processing on a daily basis. Customers either call in orders by phone, send in written orders by ordinary mail or by computer, or place orders in person. The programs that record and help manage such transactions are called *order-entry software.*

Inventory Control The units of products that a company has in stock to sell at a given moment are called its inventory. *Inventory control programs* closely monitor the number of units of each product in inventory and ensure that reasonable quantities of products are maintained. In the automotive industry, state-of-the-art computer technology has made it possible for dealers to know what is available on lots other than their own and to know what is scheduled for production—a phenomenon known as *virtual inventory.* If your local car dealer does not have precisely the vehicle you want in stock, the dealer can simply enter your requirements into the computer to find out where the closest unallocated vehicle of that description is and how soon it can be made available.

General Ledger *General ledger (G/L) programs* keep track of all financial summaries, including those originating from payroll, accounts receivable, and accounts payable (see Figure MC 8-2). They also ensure that the company's books balance properly. In addition, G/L programs produce accounting reports such as income statements, balance sheets, and general ledger balances.

Information Systems

During the early days of commercial computing, businesses purchased computers almost exclusively to perform routine transaction processing tasks. Used in this way, the computer could cut clerical expenses considerably. However, as time passed, it became apparent that the computer could do much more than replace clerks. It could also provide information to assist management in its decision-making role.

A system that generates information for use by decision makers is often called an **information system.** With an information system, management can incorporate much more information into decisions and spend less time gathering it. As a result, managers have more time to do the things that they do best—thinking creatively and interacting with people.

Two major types of information systems are information reporting systems and decision support systems.

Information Reporting Systems **Information reporting systems** were the first type of information system. They provide management with preselected types of information, generally in the form of computer-generated reports. The types of information that some managers receive are preplanned, just like the information you see on your monthly checking account statements. The individual *values* on your statements, such as check numbers and amounts, may change from month to month, but the *types* of information you receive remain the same. Also, you and every other person mailed checking account statements by your bank receive exactly the same type of information.

Many information reporting systems provide managers with information that is a by-product of the data generated through transaction processing.

FIGURE MC 8-2 The relationships among transaction processing systems. All systems eventually tie into the general ledger system, which keeps track of all financial transactions.

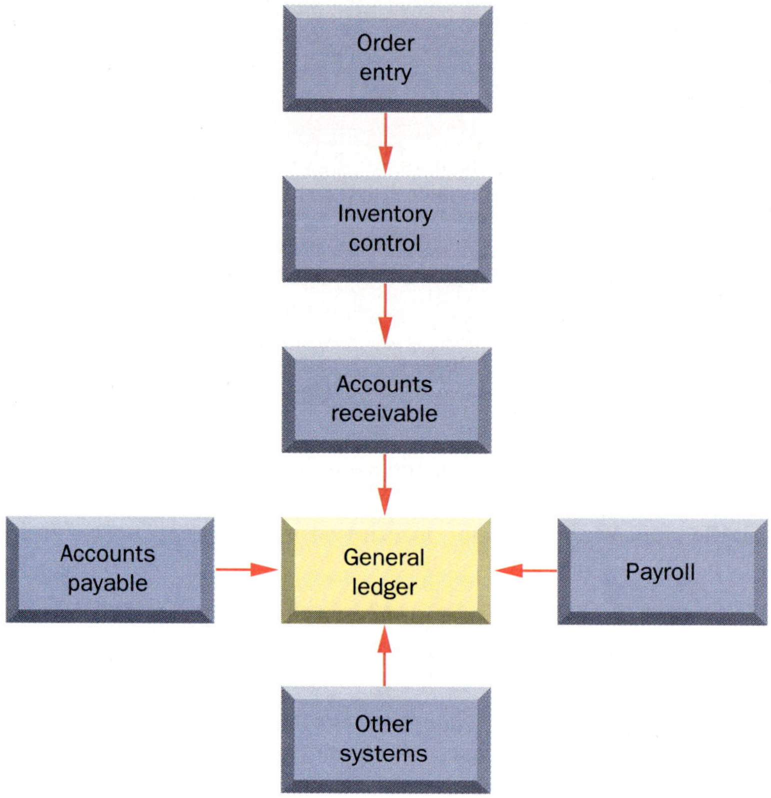

Decision Support Systems During the 1970s, many companies began to call for systems that could field extemporaneous questions from managers. Such systems were expected to be particularly useful to top-level managers, whose requirements for information are somewhat unpredictable and unstructured. In response to this situation, the computer industry developed the decision support system.

A **decision support system (DSS)** helps people organize and analyze their own decision-making information. Thus, a "sales support system" is the name typically given to a DSS aimed at the special decision-making needs of salespeople or marketing personnel. A "fire-suppression support system" might be a DSS targeted to helping the director of a forest area develop specific strategies for fighting forest fires.

In order to appreciate the usefulness of flexibility in a DSS, consider this example. To assist with making product pricing decisions, a sales manager uses a DSS that has been set up on a microcomputer system. At the keyboard, the manager first requests the price of an item. Then he or she decides to ask for the average price of several other items, and then for the inventory turnover of yet a different item. A model may be used to predict the sales volume of items five years into the future. The manager can pose questions as the need evolves and receive answers at once. At the end of the interactive session, the

FIGURE MC 8-3 Decision support systems (DSSs). Management often uses mapping software to help make decisions.

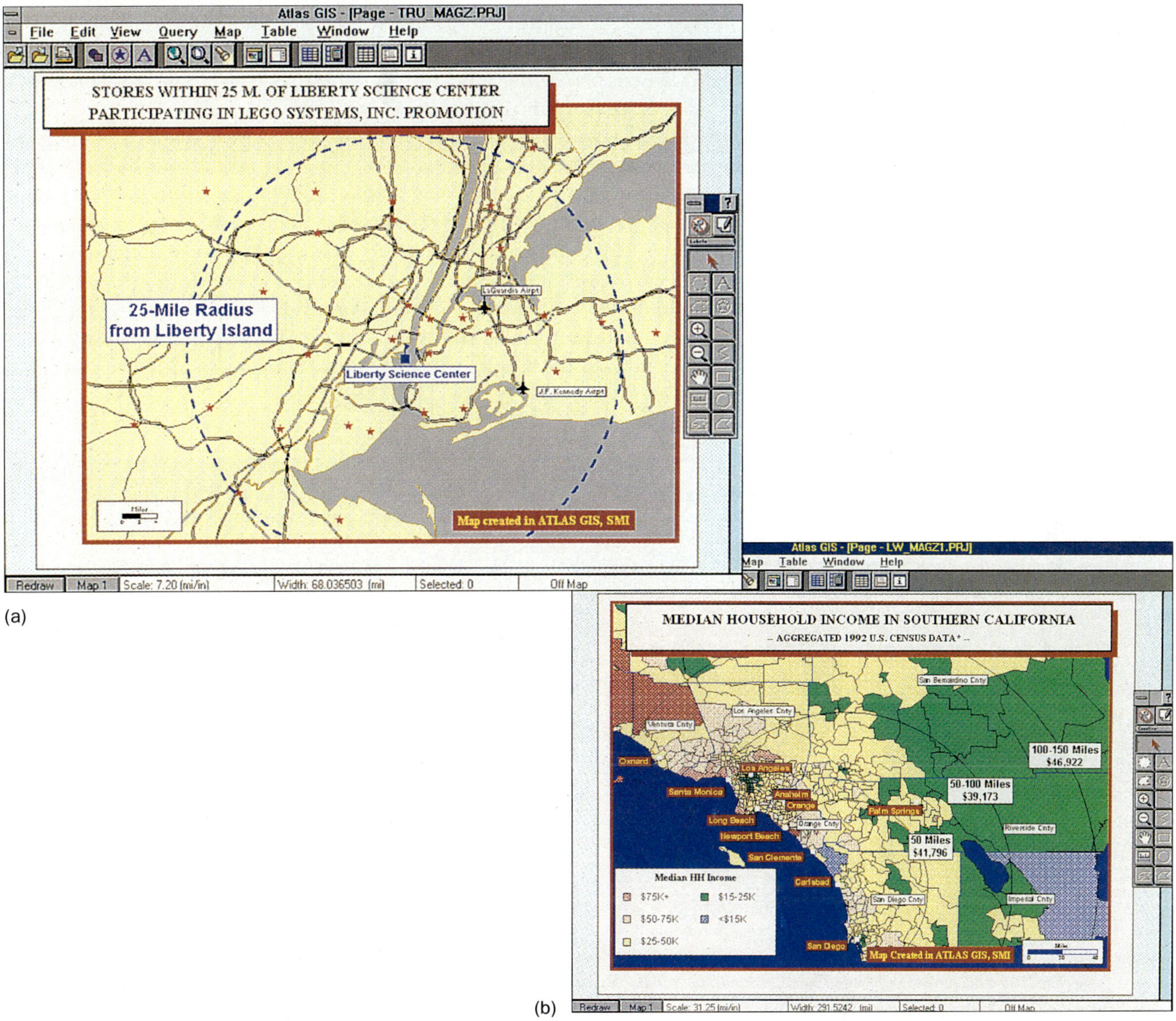

(a)

(b)

manager uses the DSS to prepare a summary of important findings and some bar charts for a meeting. The next time the manager uses the DSS, other types of information may be collected and analyzed.

Generally, the DSS is built from a number of other productivity software tools that we have covered in this textbook. For instance, the sales manager might acquire a spreadsheet package or a DBMS to build the sales support system just described. Figure MC 8-3 illustrates a DSS at work.

A relatively recent development in the DSS area has been emergence of the **group decision support system (GDSS).** A GDSS is a system in which several people routinely interact through a computer network to solve common problems. In fields such as newspaper publishing, architectural design, insurance, and banking, a GDSS allows workers to share ideas and collaborate on decisions through computer and communications technology. Workers can electronically route their outputs to other workers in the chain and even meet electronically when a bottleneck of some sort occurs. An example of this computer-age phenomenon is illustrated in Figure MC 8-4. GDSSs are sometimes referred to as **workgroup computing.**

Executive information systems (EISs) are DSSs customized to meet the special needs of individual executives—those people at the highest organizational level. As some executives see it, the business world today is so competitive and fast paced that they need instant access to fresh information. Among executives' favorite applications are using database management systems to access corporate and financial data, using electronic mail systems to streamline contact with subordinates, and using customized spreadsheet programs to display important ratios and trends in a graphical format. Many executives, because they do not know how to type, require easy-to-learn graphical

FIGURE MC 8-4 **Using a GDSS to process an insurance claim.** (a) Accident photos, estimates, and reports are scanned into electronic files. (b) A customer representative can pull up any document on the screen when the customer has a question about a claim. (c) An appraiser electronically writes her comments on a form with a digitizing tablet and stylus and adds a digitized voice message.(d) The adjuster reviews all of the paperwork and approves the payment.

(a) (b) (c) (d)

interfaces (see Figure MC 8-5). With the right type of system, it simply takes some pointing and, perhaps, a few keystrokes or mouse clicks to get what these executives want in exactly the form they require.

Office Systems

In recent years, computer technology has been applied to the task of increasing productivity in the office. The term **office automation (OA)** has been coined to describe this trend. Automating the office can be done through a wide variety of technologies and processing techniques, several of which are discussed in the following subsections.

Document Processing *Document processing* refers to the use of computer technology in the preparation of text-intensive documents such as letters, manuscripts, legal documents, articles, books, restaurant menus, or reports. Two principal document-processing tools—word processing and desktop publishing—were covered in earlier chapters.

Electronic Mail **Electronic mail** (or **E-mail**) makes it possible to send informative messages and documents from one terminal or computer system to another. Two familiar examples of electronic mail are the *fax (facsimile) machine,* which is used to transmit images of hard-copy documents over the phone wires, and *electronic mailboxes,* computer files that are set up to store any transmitted message that can be created in or converted to electronic form. Fax machines and electronic mailboxes were covered in Chapter 4.

Desk Accessories *Desk accessories,* sometimes called *personal information managers (PIMs)* or *desktop organizers,* are packages that provide the electronic equivalent of features commonly found on an office desktop. Desk accessory software varies from vendor to vendor, but many packages offer such features as a calendar (see Figure MC 3-28), clock, calculator, and Rolodex-type file. Often, the feature is implemented in a window, which appears when a specific sequence of keys is activated.

FIGURE MC 8-5 **Executive information systems (EISs).** EISs are DSSs customized to meet the needs of executives, many of whom are not technology experts. Consequently, EISs are usually characterized by easy-to-use graphical interfaces and simplified procedures for making information requests.

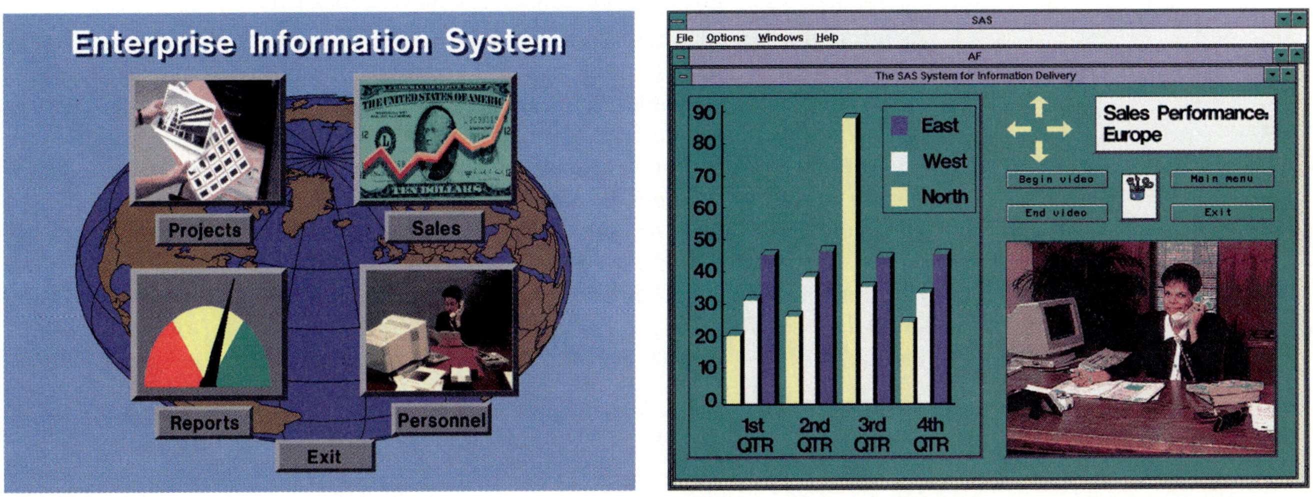

(a) (b)

USER TIP

Forms Software

Most business systems rely heavily on form documents—tax forms, invoices, purchasing orders, and the like. For many years, the need for such documents was filled entirely by the paper-forms industry. Today, with graphically oriented computers and laser printers widely available, the situation is rapidly changing. Using *forms software,* individuals and businesses now have simple tools to design their own forms—often, for a fraction of the cost. Further, the wait that is entailed in sending the work outside can almost be eliminated; if the forms are needed immediately, they can be designed and printed within hours.

Depending on the system to be implemented, the forms can be generated as paper copies or left in the computer system as electronic documents. Electronic documents have the advantages of being hard to misplace, less prone to errors, easy to tally, and less costly overall.

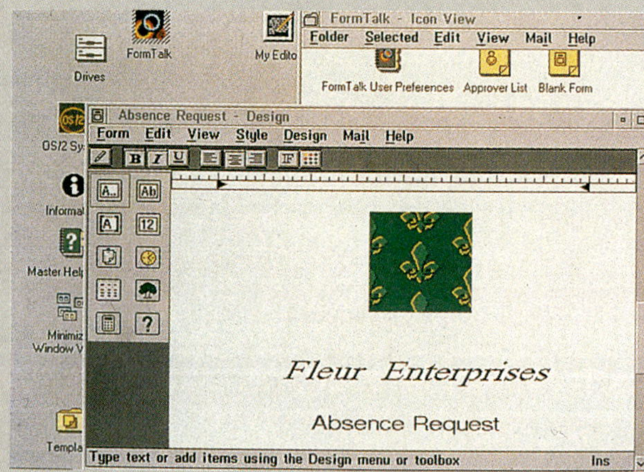

Designing forms. The computer has made form creation easy, fast, and inexpensive.

Also, another type of program—called *workflow software*—makes it possible to monitor electronic records. Workflow software can determine how long forms have been in the hands of individuals who must route them elsewhere within the organization and, consequently, help eliminate processing bottlenecks.

Decision Support Tools Since many decisions are made by white-collar workers in offices, it is understandable that many decision support systems are found in offices. Among the tools that are useful in such a setting are spreadsheets, presentation graphics, plotters and laser printers, color monitors, and relational database systems. All of these software and hardware tools have been discussed earlier in the book and have contributed to streamlining life at the office.

Electronic Document Handling *Electronic document handling,* sometimes called *image processing,* refers to the use of optical-disk-based computer systems to store and manipulate electronic copies of form documents and the like. The GDSS system featured in Figure MC 8-4 is an example. Relative to paper copies of documents, electronic documents are cheaper to handle, capable of being instantaneously transmitted, and far less likely to get misplaced or be mismanaged. Also, several people in different locations can access the same documents simultaneously. Increasingly, as the Chapter 8 User Tip explains, *forms software* is used to design and print the forms that—after being filled in by hand out in the field—become the scanned-in electronic documents.

Teleconferencing **Teleconferencing** makes it possible for two or more people to meet electronically, thereby avoiding the time and expense they would incur if they were to physically get together in one spot (see Figure MC 8-6). *Audio teleconferencing*—also known as the conference phone call—allows a meeting to take place between several people on a phone system.

FIGURE MC 8-6 **Teleconferencing.** Teleconferencing is available for large groups in specially equipped conference rooms and, as shown here, for individuals and smaller groups at the desktop level. The biggest benefit to teleconferencing is its ability to bring problem-solving expertise together quickly.

Video teleconferencing systems, on the other hand, permit participants to see each other on video screens as well as to hear each other. *Computer teleconferencing,* which takes place at computer workstations, allows a conference to develop through messages sent to electronic mailboxes.

Today, many teleconferencing sessions involve a combination of audio, video, and computer components. Desktop tools called *whiteboards* have also recently become available that enable teleconferencing participants to create images and annotate them while interacting with colleagues (see Figure

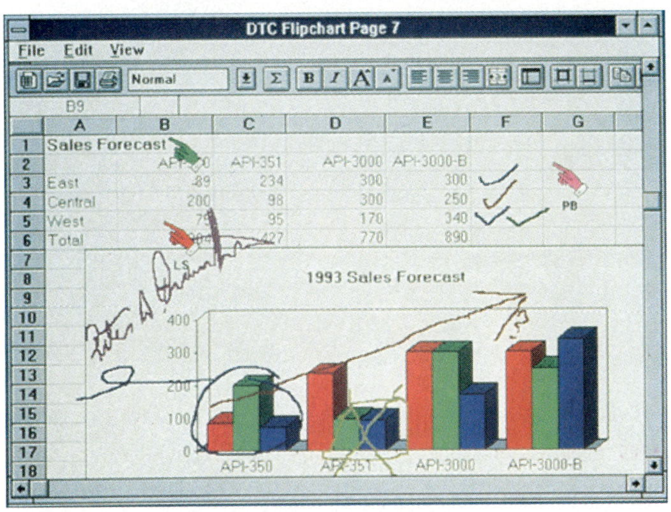

FIGURE MC 8-7 **Desktop teleconferencing tools.** Electronic packages called whiteboards let conference users create and edit computer images, using pointing and annotating tools. Whiteboards are the electronic equivalents of conventional blackboards and flip charts.

MC 8-7). Travel savings notwithstanding, the biggest benefit to teleconferencing is something most technology experts never anticipated—the ability to bring together company expertise quickly to solve problems.

Telecommuting **Telecommuting** refers to people working at home and linking up to their employers through a microcomputer workstation, fax machine, or virtually any other type of computer-age tool that can communicate (see Figure MC 8-8). Many typists and computer programmers, for example, telecommute to their jobs, perhaps because they prefer to do so or because they do not need supervision and are more productive at home. Telecommuting can save workers both the time and expense involved in traveling to work. It can also save business the expense of maintaining office and parking space. On the negative side, telecommuting limits the interpersonal contact that often makes working in an office lively and productive.

Design and Manufacturing Systems

Computers are widely used in business to improve productivity both at the design stage—through computer-aided design—and at the manufacturing stage—through computer-aided manufacturing. With technology becoming ever more sophisticated, serious attempts have been made recently to integrate design, manufacturing, and other business functions more closely—a concept known as computer-integrated manufacturing.

Computer-Aided Design Using **computer-aided design (CAD),** product designers can dramatically reduce the time they spend at the drawing board. For example, using light pens and specialized graphics workstations, engineers can sketch ideas directly into the computer system, which can then be instructed to analyze the proposed design in terms of how well it meets a number of design criteria (see Figure MC 8-9). Taking into account the sub-

FIGURE MC 8-8 **Telecommuting.** Computer and communications technologies have made it possible for individuals to conduct business out of the office and to build careers around the lifestyles they prefer.

sequent output of the computer, the designer can modify the drawings until a desirable design is achieved. Before the arrival of CAD, the designer had to produce by hand preliminary sketches and then advanced designs, representing refinements on the sketches. After physical models were built and tested, the designer had to prepare production drawings, which were used to build the equipment needed to manufacture the new product, whether it was a truck or a new toaster. Today, computer-aided assistance with all of these tasks is fairly common. CAD is especially helpful in the design of products such as automobiles, aircraft, ships, buildings, electrical circuits (including computer chips), and even running shoes.

Computer-Aided Manufacturing Computer applications are not limited to the design phases of product development. In fact, computers were used on the factory floor well before engineers used them interactively for design. With each passing day, more and more of the actual process of production on the factory floor is becoming computerized.

Computer-aided manufacturing (CAM) includes the use of computers to help manage manufacturing operations and to control machinery used in manufacturing processes. One example is a system that observes production in an oil refinery, performs calculations, and opens and shuts appropriate valves when necessary. Another system, commonly used in the steel industry, works from preprogrammed specifications to perform the shaping and assembly of steel parts automatically. Increasingly, robots are being used to carry out processes once solely in the human domain (see Figure MC 8-10). CAM is also widely employed to build cars and ships, monitor power plants, manufacture food and chemicals, and perform a number of other functions.

Computer-Integrated Manufacturing Over the last few years, serious efforts have been afoot to implement **computer-integrated manufac-**

FIGURE MC 8-9 **Computer-aided design (CAD).** Perhaps no field has been altered more by CAD than architecture. (a) Computer modeling of Nashville Metropolitan Airport. (b) Computer modeling of a Nordstrom's department store.

(a)

(b)

FIGURE MC 8-10 **An industrial robot.** Robots take on jobs that are too physically demanding, monotonous, dangerous, or expensive for humans to perform. The robot shown here is helping to assemble a laptop computer at an IBM plant.

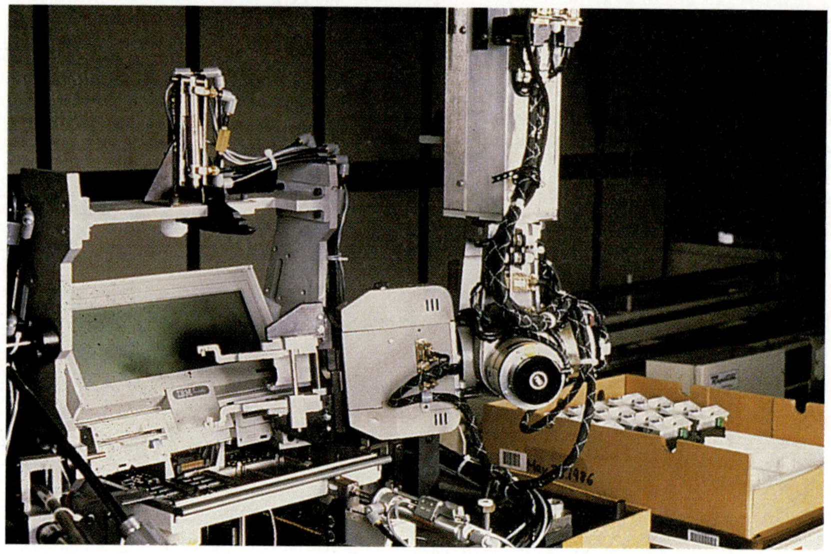

turing (CIM) systems. The idea behind CIM is to tie together CAD, CAM, and other business activities (see Figure MC 8-11).

Here is how CIM might work: A large auto distributorship uses a microcomputer workstation to call an auto manufacturer, to check out the feasibility of changing a styling detail on 500 cars that are to be produced next month. The CAD part of the integrated system checks out the design change to see whether it can be done and, also, what types of assembly-line changes are necessary. The CAD subsystem then automatically routes this information to computers on the factory floor—which determine if the assembly line can make the shift and if new parts can be made available on time. To find out about the availability of the new parts, the factory computers may have to call up the computers of parts suppliers, which are also integrated into the system. Finally, all of the information is forwarded to accounting department computers, which calculate the cost impact of the change.

In the CIM system just described, the distributor has the required information within a short period. Without CIM, such a request may take days or weeks for a human to answer. Human labor is expensive and carries with it a greater chance of error. Today, with many organizations having thousands of computers and with so many ways available to tie together information from these computers usefully, some level of integration is a necessity.

RESPONSIBILITY FOR SYSTEMS DEVELOPMENT

In large organizations—with thousands of employees and thousands of operational details to keep track of—there are usually thousands of systems, ranging from personal systems to systems that operate at an enterprisewide level. Deciding which systems best support the direction of the enterprise, and how

FIGURE MC 8-11 Computer-integrated manufacturing (CIM). CIM enables CAD, CAM, and other business activities to be tied together by computers. In the auto industry, CIM makes it possible to check quickly the effect of a design change on parts inventories, production schedules, and costs.

much attention to give each one, is essentially where systems responsibility begins. In the typical business organization, a number of computer professionals share responsibility for the development of all but the very smallest of systems.

The *chief information officer (CIO)* holds primary responsibility for systems development. Often this position is at the level of vice-president. One of the CIO's duties is to develop a corporate strategy that defines the role of information processing within the organization. Another is to oversee the formulation of a five-year plan that maps out which systems are to be studied and possibly revamped during that period.

Because information processing affects not only the accounting functions in most firms but also most other departments, including marketing, manufacturing, and personnel, a *steering committee* composed of top-level executives normally approves the plan. This committee also sets broad guidelines for performing computer-related activities. However, it does not become highly involved with technical details or the administration of particular projects, which are the responsibility of the information systems department.

The Information Systems Department

The **information systems department** varies widely in structure from one company to another. In one form the department is divided into three parts, as shown in Figure MC 8-12. The *data processing area* has primary responsibility for the development of large transaction processing systems—that is, those systems costing more than $100,000 and that keep track of the money coming in and going out of the entire organization. The *information center* normally is involved with smaller projects, say, those that help individual

FIGURE MC 8-12 A possible organizational structure for an information systems department. Many information systems departments consist of three principal areas: data processing, an information center, and office automation.

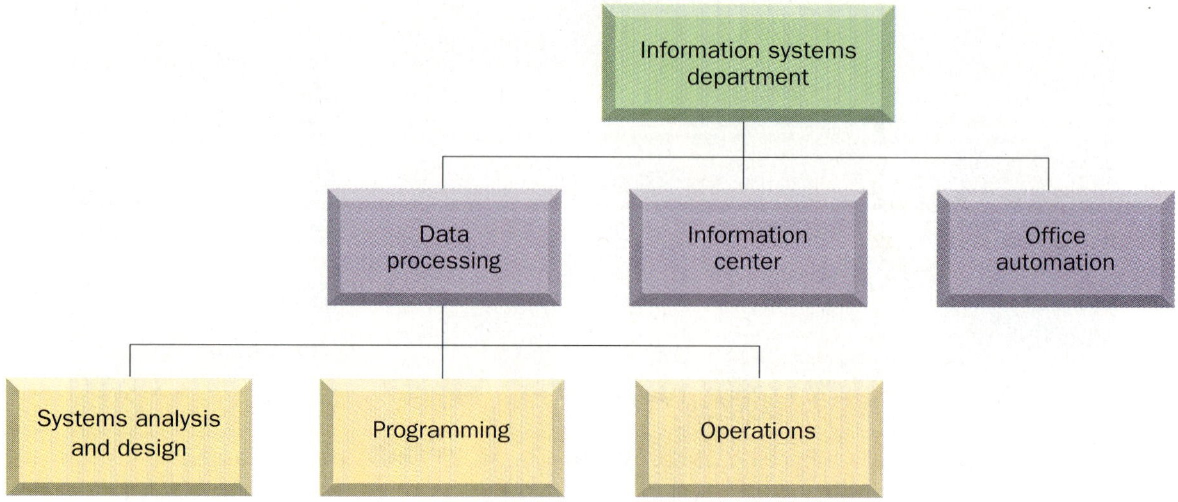

end users or end-user departments select microcomputer resources for their own, local use. The *office automation area* is in charge of ensuring that the organization takes full advantage of technologies such as desktop publishing and electronic mail.

Data Processing Area The **data processing area** predates all other areas within the information systems department and is still considered by many to be the most important. After all, if their computers stopped processing high-volume business transactions, most large organizations would have to shut down.

Within the data processing area, the *systems analysis and design group* analyzes, designs, and implements new software and hardware systems. The *programming group* codes computer programs from program design specifications. The *operations group* manages day-to-day processing once a system has become operational.

The person most involved with systems development is the **systems analyst.** Generally speaking, the systems analyst's job in the data processing area is to plan and implement large systems that will use the computers the organization has or will acquire. When such a system is needed, the systems analyst interacts with current and potential end users to produce a solution. The analyst generally is involved in all stages of the development process.

In most large projects, a team of people will be involved. A systems analyst will probably be appointed as *project manager* to head the team. Other people on the team might include users, programmers, an outside consultant, a cost accountant, and an auditor.

Information Center The **information center (IC)** was originally conceived to help the individual end users in the organization make intelligent choices about the microcomputer hardware and software they need to perform their jobs better, as well as to promote an orderly acquisition of microcomputing resources within the organization as a whole. Many ICs are staffed primarily with *information center consultants* (systems analysts having special skills in the microcomputing area) and with *trainers.*

ICs often are set up similarly to a typical microcomputer store. A user walks in and talks to a consultant about specific microcomputing needs. Perhaps the user is a sales manager who needs a small DSS to keep track of a field sales force. The manager and consultant sit down at one or two machines and experiment with some appropriate, off-the-shelf software. Eventually, through trial and error, they put together a small system.

Office Automation Area In many organizations, the **office automation (OA) area** is one of the newest, smallest groups within the information systems department. The OA area is responsible for developing a cost-efficient, integrated approach to using office technologies such as electronic document processing and electronic mail. Typical duties, which resemble those of the IC, are arranging product demonstrations and helping end users and end-user departments select systems.

Outsourcing

When an organization does not have the staff on hand to build or operate a system it needs, an outsourcing option is often chosen. **Outsourcing** involves turning over certain information systems functions to an outside vendor (see Figure MC 8-13). For instance, a manufacturer might have only a PC-based LAN at its headquarters to accept orders. The remote mainframes doing the processing workload might be owned and operated by a third-party company skilled at high-volume transaction processing.

Why do companies outsource? A small firm might find it too expensive to keep in-house information systems personnel on hand, given its current work volume. Or a large company might not have the capacity or capital to expand its operations in-house, so it may outsource some of them temporarily. And many firms have found it easier to outsource operations in areas in which it is too hard to find or too expensive to hire new personnel. Many firms also turn to an outsourcer when they think that the outsourcer could do the job better or cheaper than they could.

Outsourcing exists in a variety of different forms. In some cases, the outsourcer has its own computer center and supplies terminals and a network to the client. In other cases, the client firm has its own equipment and, needing someone to operate it, turns to the outsourcer to supply personnel. Virtually any conceivable support arrangement is available through outsourcing.

THE SYSTEMS DEVELOPMENT LIFE CYCLE

Systems development often is subdivided into five steps, or phases:

- *Phase 1:* Preliminary investigation
- *Phase 2:* Systems analysis
- *Phase 3:* System design
- *Phase 4:* System acquisition
- *Phase 5:* System implementation

Collectively, these phases often are referred to as the **systems development life cycle (SDLC)** because they describe a system from the time it is first studied until the time it is put into use. When a new business pressure necessitates a change in a system, the steps of the cycle begin anew. The five steps

FIGURE MC 8-13 **Outsourcing.** At Electronic Data Systems (EDS), a leading outsourcer, building information systems is Job One. Shown here is EDS's Information Technology Center in Plano, Texas.

of the SDLC apply in principle both to the large, multimillion-dollar information systems that run large corporations and to the $3,000 microcomputer systems that sit on many desk tops in homes. The activities carried out during each phase of systems development are described in Figure MC 8-14.

The five steps of the SDLC do not always follow in a predetermined sequence. Frequently, analysis and design are interleaved. For instance, to look at an example from everyday life, when people develop a seven-day vacation plan, they often do not completely design the plan as the first step and execute it, without modification, as the second step. They might design a plan for day 1, and when the day is over, analyze what has happened and use their experiences to design a plan for day 2. After day 2, further analysis is done to design day 3. And so on. Many systems are designed this way as well.

APPROACHES TO SYSTEMS DEVELOPMENT

Depending on the system being built, organizations will follow one or more of three approaches to systems development: the traditional approach, prototyping, and end-user development.

FIGURE MC 8-14 Activities carried out during each of the five phases of systems development.

Preliminary investigation During this phase the problem is studied briefly and a few possible solutions are suggested so that management can decide whether the project should be pursued further.

Systems analysis If management decides after the preliminary investigation that further systems development is warranted, the existing applications area is studied in depth and specific recommendations for change are made.

System design During this phase a model of the new system is developed, software and hardware needs are specified, and a detailed list of benefits and costs is prepared.

System acquisition Upon management approval of the design model, it must be decided from which vendors to acquire software and hardware.

System implementation After the components of the system have been acquired, the lengthy process begins of adapting existing files to the new system, preparing specifications for programmers, training, and so forth.

The Traditional Approach

In the **traditional approach,** the phases of systems development are carried out in a predetermined order: (1) preliminary investigation, (2) systems analysis, (3) system design, (4) system acquisition, and (5) implementation. Each phase is begun only when the one before it is completed. Often, the traditional approach is reserved for the development of large transaction processing systems. Because the traditional approach is usually expensive and extensive, it is normally carried out by knowledgeable professionals—that is, by systems analysts.

Traditional systems development requires system users to consider proposed system plans by looking at detailed diagrams, descriptive reports, and specifications of the proposed new system. The entire system is specified and built before anyone gets to use it. As each phase of development is completed, users sign off on the recommendations that the analyst presents to them, indicating their acceptance.

In many organizations, the traditional approach to systems development has recently fallen into disfavor. First, systems often take too long to analyze, design, and implement under the traditional approach—especially with technology changing so rapidly. By the time a system is finally put into operation, important new needs that were not part of the original plan may surface. Second, the system being developed is often the wrong one. Managers almost always have difficulty expressing their information needs, and it is not until they begin to use a system that they discover what they really need.

Prototyping

To avoid the potentially expensive disaster that could result from completing every phase of systems development before users ever lay their hands on a system, many analysts have advocated prototyping as a means of systems development. In **prototyping,** the focus is on developing a small model, or a *prototype,* of the overall system. Users work with the prototype and suggest modifications. The prototype is then modified, resulting in an improved prototype. As soon as the prototype is refined to the point at which higher man-

FIGURE MC 8-15 **Prototyping.** Prototyping is an iterative process; after each prototype is built, the user and analyst try it out together and attempt to improve on it. Eventually, the prototype evolves into a finished system.

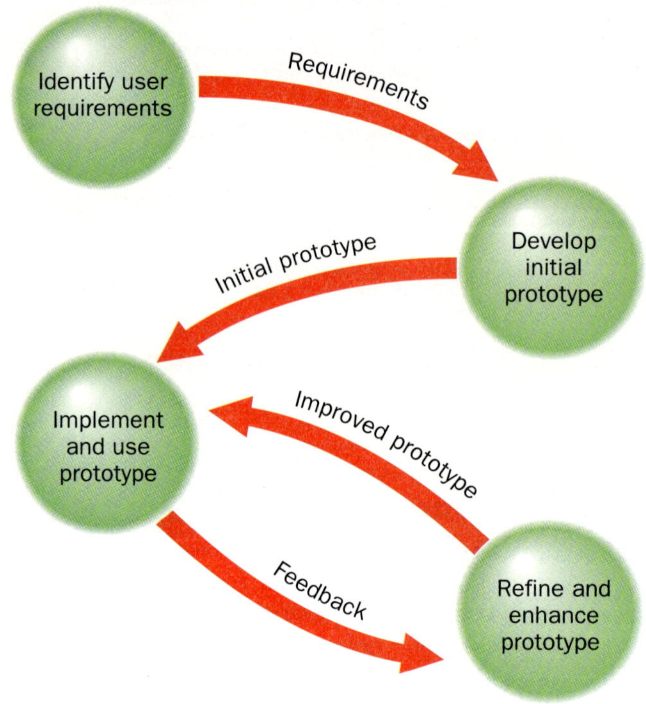

agement feels confident that a larger version of the system will succeed, either the prototype can be gradually expanded or the organization can proceed with the remaining steps of systems development.

In prototyping, analysis and design generally proceed together, in small steps that finally result in a completed system. The idea behind the prototyping process is virtually identical to the one described earlier for developing vacation plans. Prototyping is illustrated in Figure MC 8-15.

End-User Development

End-user development is a relatively new form of systems development—one that has evolved from the microcomputing revolution. It is defined as a systems development effort in which the end user is primarily responsible for the development of the system. This is in contrast to other types of development, in which a qualified computer professional, such as a systems analyst, takes charge of the systems development process.

As you might guess, end-user development is feasible only in cases where the system being acquired is within the purview of the end user and is relatively inexpensive. A good example is the situation in which an end user purchases a microcomputer system and develops applications on his or her own. In developing the system, the end user might follow a prototyping approach or a method similar to traditional development.

End-user development was covered in considerable detail in Chapter 5.

___ 15. Robots are humanlike machines that are directed by
a. decision support systems.
b. computers.
c. fax boards.
d. natural languages.
e. information reporting systems.

___ 16. A collection of elements and procedures that interact to accomplish a goal is known as a(n)
a. preliminary investigation.
b. system.
c. OA.
d. systems development life cycle.
e. systems analyst.

___ 17. The group of professionals within the information systems department charged with building large transaction processing systems is the
a. data-entry staff.
b. data processing area.
c. steering committee.
d. office automation area.
e. CIO.

___ 18. The individual generally charged with building systems in an organization is the
a. CIO.
b. end user.
c. systems analyst.
d. trainer.
e. information center consultant.

___ 19. With end-user development, the main burden of developing a system falls on the
a. crisis staff.
b. systems analyst.
c. control clerk in the data processing area.
d. end user.
e. steering committee.

___ 20. An alternative to the traditional systems development process is to develop a small
a. prototype.
b. SDLC.
c. systems analyst.
d. systems analysis crisis command center.
e. checklist.

Matching

Select the term that best matches each phrase:

a. DSS
b. CAD
c. SDLC
d. GDSS
e. CAM
f. End-user development
g. CIM
h. Prototyping
i. Outsourcing
j. OA
k. Telecommuting
l. Teleconferencing

___ 21. Refers to the use of computers in manufacturing

___ 22. An approach to systems development that involves building a small model of a system and gradually expanding it

___ 23. Refers to going outside the company to obtain assistance with system building

___ 24. Refers to the use of computers in design

___ 25. Refers to the five stages of systems development

___ 26. A technology that ties together CAD, CAM, and other business functions

___ 27. Refers to the use of computers to streamline office work

___ 28. An acronym that represents another name for workgroup computing

___ 29. Systems development carried out by people who are not computer professionals

___ 30. Refers to situations in which computers enable people to work at home rather than at a centralized office site

Answers

True/False: 1. F; 2. F; 3. T; 4. T; 5. F; 6. T; 7. F; 8. T; 9. F; 10. F

Multiple Choice: 11. a; 12. b; 13. d; 14. b; 15. b; 16. b; 17. b; 18. c; 19. d; 20. a

Matching: 21. e; 22. h; 23. i; 24. b; 25. c; 26. g; 27. j; 28. d; 29. f; 30. k

Exercises

1. Until recently, executives have been willing to sign checks for computers to be used by the office staff but have been unwilling to use computers directly in their own work. One reason was because computers were too hard to learn about and use. Name several other reasons. *Hint:* This phenomenon has been researched and reported in information systems journals, many of which are probably available in your school library. Feel free also to use your intuition to guess reasons.
2. Look through the computer journals in your school or local library and identify at least one case in which a company is using a GDSS to link its workers. Report your findings to the class.
3. Several studies have claimed that despite the billions of dollars spent on office automation during the past several years, there has not been until recently any appreciable gain in white-collar-worker productivity. How do you account for this?

4. Many observers of the computing scene have pointed out that some of the biggest problems in getting a system to work properly are people-related and have little to do with the technology itself. Provide at least three examples that show how people problems could make a system fail.

5. Can the prototyping approach to development be useful in situations in which computer systems are not involved? If you think so, provide an example from everyday life.

6. What types of problems are likely to surface when end users within an organization rather than trained computer professionals develop desktop computer systems for themselves or their departments? *Hint:* This problem area has been widely researched and reported in information systems journals, many of which are probably available in your school library. Feel free to use your intuition to answer this question.

MC 9 Social Issues Involving Computers

OUTLINE

LEARNING OBJECTIVES

After completing this chapter, you will be able to:

1. Describe some health-related concerns that people have regarding computers.
2. Explain what computer crime is, give several examples of it, and describe how it can be prevented.
3. Appreciate how computer technology can encroach on people's privacy and describe some of the legislation enacted to prevent such abuses.
4. Explain what is meant by *ethics,* and provide several examples of ethical misbehavior as regards computer-related matters.

OVERVIEW

Since the early 1950s, when the era of commercial computing began, computers have rapidly woven their way into the fabric of modern society. In the process, they have created both opportunities and problems. Consequently, they have been both cursed and applauded—and for good reason.

So far in this book, we have focused on the opportunities. However, although the computer "revolution" has brought undeniable benefits to society, it has also produced some troubling side effects. Like any fast-paced revolution, it has been disruptive in many ways. Some jobs have been created, others lost, and still others threatened. In addition, an increasing variety of health-related concerns affecting people who work with computer-related technologies have surfaced. Computers have also immensely increased access to information, creating new possibilities for crime—even at the international level—and threatening personal privacy. Clearly some controls to limit the dangers that these awesome devices pose will always be needed. In this chapter, we highlight four important problem areas: computers and health in the workplace, computer crime, computers and privacy, and ethical uses of technology.

Microcomputers have only been around since the 1970s, so many of the problems covered in this chapter have been inherited rather than initiated by their use. However, microcomputers have added an important dimension to the social concerns posed by technology: Because more than 100 million of them are in use and they are so easy to operate, microcomputers have made many problems far more pervasive.

COMPUTERS, WORK, AND HEALTH

Computers have been said to pose a threat to our mental and physical well-being. Although the body of scientific evidence supporting this claim is far from conclusive, and is likely to be that way for many more years, we should all be aware of the major concerns raised about the possible effects of computers on our health and the environment.

Stress-Related Concerns

Emotional problems such as financial worries, feelings of incompetence, and disorientation often produce emotional *stress*. This stress may be triggered by layoff or reassignment, fear of falling behind, or job burnout.

Layoff or Reassignment One of the first criticisms leveled at computers was that their very presence in the workplace resulted in job-related stress. When computers came in, many people were laid off and had to find new jobs. Clerical workers especially worried about job security. Many employees feared the full potential of computers in the office, never knowing when machines might replace them. These fears are still widespread today.

Even people who were not laid off found that their jobs had changed significantly and that they had no choice but to retrain. Airline agents, for example, had to learn how to manipulate a database language and to work with display terminals. Secretaries were pressured into learning word processing (and perhaps electronic spreadsheets, electronic data management, and electronic mail) to keep in tune with state-of-the-art office work. Many workers never made the transition successfully.

Because of computers, fewer people are needed to do many types of work today. Computers are also regularly changing the way work is done—often in ways that are difficult to predict. Even modern computer networks are posing a new threat to workers in that companies no longer have to staff each location as heavily with local expertise. Networks also mean that work can be transferred overseas more easily.

Fear of Falling Behind The microcomputing boom has placed computing power of awesome dimensions at almost everyone's fingertips. Some researchers perceive a widespread fear that failure to learn how to use these machines will make people fall behind. One example is the numerous non-computer-oriented executives, managers, and educators who see themselves being upstaged by their computer-knowledgeable colleagues. The surge of interest in microcomputers has even made many programmers who work in mainframe environments feel that they are somehow falling behind.

Burnout Burnout is caused not by fear of computers (*cyberphobia*) but by overuse of them (*cyberphelia*). The infusion of microcomputers into home and office has raised new concerns about what will happen to children who withdraw into their computer systems, to computer-bound managers who have inadvertently been swept into the tide of the computer revolution, or to couples or families whose intimacy may be threatened by computer overuse in their homes.

To date, little research has been done on computer burnout. What makes this area so controversial is the compelling flip-side argument that most victims of computer burnout would burn out on something else if computers did not exist.

Ergonomics-Related Concerns

Ergonomics addresses such issues as making products and work areas comfortable and safe to use. With respect to technology, ergonomics covers the effects on workers from such things as display devices, keyboards, and workspaces.

Dangers Posed by Display Devices For nearly a decade, large numbers of data-entry operators have reported a variety of physical and mental problems stemming from their interaction with display devices. The complaints have centered on visual, muscular, and emotional disorders resulting from long hours of continuous display device use. These include blurred eyesight, eyestrain, acute fatigue, headaches, and backaches. In response to these problems, several states and cities (such as San Francisco) have passed laws that curb display device abuse. In addition, vendors of these devices have redesigned their products with features such as tiltable screens and detachable keyboards to make them more comfortable to use.

Dangers Posed by Keyboards Years ago, computer keyboards frequently were built into display units, making it difficult for operators to move them about as freely as they could if the keyboards had been detached. Most claims that a computer keyboard could result in injury seemed to be put to rest after keyboard manufacturers started making detachable keyboards—that is, until recently. Today, some people are experiencing a condition known as *carpal tunnel syndrome*, a painful and crippling complex of symptoms affecting the hand and wrist that has been traced to the repetitive finger movements routinely made when using a keyboard. The condition, which may not strike everyone who puts in long hours on a keyboard, and which can disappear in some cases, makes it difficult to use a keyboard, drive long distances, or even

FIGURE MC 9-1 Stress-reducing keyboard. Standard keyboards are often criticized for straining the tendons that run through the wrist and connect the fingers to the forearm muscles. To reduce such stress, the Select-Ease™ Keyboard can be split so that users can make the back higher than the front, make the middle higher than the sides, or configure the unit in a variety of other ways.

hold up a book to read. Physicians recommend that to minimize the chance of such an injury, workers take breaks every hour or so and relax their arms and hands so that blood flows freely throughout the body. Recently, a number of innovative keyboards have been designed that attempt to reduce stress in the hands and wrists (see Figure MC 9-1).

Workspace Design Display devices and keyboards are not the only things that can torture people at workstations. For example, the furniture may be nonadjustable, forcing the user into awkward positions that are guaranteed to produce body kinks. Or the lighting may be so bright that it causes a headache-producing glare on the display screen. There may even be disconcerting noise levels present due to poorly designed office equipment or acoustics. Ergonomics researchers are constantly studying such problems, and the results of their efforts are becoming apparent in the consumer products now being offered to the ergonomics-conscious buyer. Figure MC 9-2 illustrates some principles of good workspace design.

Environment-Related Concerns

The surge in microcomputer use during the last several years has caused a variety of environmental concerns. One example is the question of power use. The U.S. Environmental Protection Agency (EPA) has estimated that home and office microcomputer systems now annually consume about $2 billion worth of electricity. This has indirectly resulted in the discharge of tons of pollutants into the atmosphere. The microcomputer industry has responded by adding a variety of energy-saving devices into computer hardware, including power-management software that puts the CPU, hard-disk unit and display into a "sleep mode" when they are not being used; low-power-consumptive chips and boards; and flat-panel displays. Of course, users can help, too. EPA statistics suggest that most of the time a microcomputer system is turned on, it is not in use.

FIGURE MC 9-2 **Workspace design.** Features such as detachable keyboards, tilt capabilities on keyboards and display devices, and adjustable furniture have contributed to making life more pleasant for display device users.

The pollution problem, however, goes much deeper than just electrical use. Other major concerns include the following:

- Many laptop-computer batteries are of the nickel cadmium (nicad) type. Cadmium is a highly toxic material that requires special disposal procedures. The trend today is toward batteries with less toxicity.
- Toner cartridges for laser printers and personal copiers are getting to be a common sight at landfills. Although such cartridges can be refilled or recycled, relatively few are.
- The so-called paperless office that many visionaries predicted for the computer age has become a myth. Because computer outputs are so easy to produce, more paper than ever is now being consumed. It is estimated that U.S. businesses generate almost 800 billion pages a year—an amount that would stack 50,000 miles high. Recycling and cutting down on paper use are two solutions.

Other Areas of Concern

Besides the aforementioned concerns, there are many other social-related worries regarding computers. One is whether we rely on them too much. Dr. Joseph Weizenbaum of MIT, a luminary in the field of artificial intelligence, has voiced one such concern: Will future generations rely on computers so much that they lose sight of the fundamental thought processes that computers are intended to model? Many teachers complain that some children who own pocket calculators cannot do arithmetic by hand.

There is no question, of course, that computers have altered the structure of work and play just as mechanized farm machinery changed the nature of agriculture and airplanes and automobiles changed the nature of travel. Many people have accepted these disruptions as the price of progress.

COMPUTER CRIME

Computer crime is loosely defined as the use of computers to commit unauthorized acts. The law is spotty on computer crime. The federal government, through the Computer Fraud and Abuse Act of 1984 and its amendments, has made it a felony to access confidential programs or data knowingly and fraudulently in federal-level computers. Most states also have laws that address some aspect of computer crime. Such laws notwithstanding, computer crime is hard to pin down.

One reason is that it is often difficult to decide when an unauthorized act is really a crime. No one would doubt that a bank employee who uses a computer system to embezzle funds from customers' accounts is committing a crime. But what about an employee who "steals time" on a company computer to balance a personal checkbook for a home or business? Or someone who uses the same computer to write a personal letter? These acts are also unauthorized. Where does one draw the line?

Another problem in pinning down computer crime is that judges and juries often are bewildered by the technical issues involved in such cases. Also, companies that discover computer criminals among their employees frequently are reluctant to press charges because they fear adverse publicity.

Types of Computer Crime

Computer crime has many forms. Some cases involve the use of a computer for theft of financial assets, such as money or equipment. Others concern the copying of information processing resources such as programs or data to the owner's detriment. Still other cases involve manipulation of data, such as grades, for personal advantage. By far, the majority of computer crimes are committed by insiders.

The cost of computer crime to individuals and organizations is estimated at billions of dollars annually. No one knows the exact figure, because so many incidents are either undetected or unreported. Today, with so much talk about building an information superhighway to connect government, businesses, hospitals, schools, and individuals, there are new fears about the potential for computer crime.

As in many fields, a specialized jargon has evolved in the area of computer-related crime. Following is a sampling of some of the specific forms computer crime can take.

Data Diddling *Data diddling*, one of the most common ways to perform a computer crime, involves altering key production data on the computer system in some unauthorized way. Data diddlers often are found changing grades in university files, falsifying input records on bank transactions, and the like.

The Trojan Horse The *Trojan horse* is a procedure for adding concealed instructions to a computer program so that it will still work but will also perform unauthorized duties. For example, a bank worker can subtly alter a program that contains thousands of lines of code by adding a small "patch" that instructs the program not to record withdrawals from his or her account.

Salami Shaving *Salami shaving* involves manipulating programs or data so that many small monetary amounts—say, a few cents of interest payments—are shaved from a large number of transactions or accounts and accumulated elsewhere. The victims of a salami-shaving scheme generally are unaware that their funds have been tapped, because the amount taken from each individual is trivial. The recipient, however, can benefit substantially from the aggregation of these small amounts. Some of the earliest of these schemes were perpetrated by unscrupulous programmers working on their own behalf in banks. Recently, several supermarkets have been accused of salami shaving at the checkout counter by not conscientiously updating computer-stored prices to reflect lower shelf prices (see Figure MC 9-3).

Superzapping *Superzapping* is made possible by a special program, available on most computer systems, that bypasses all system controls when the computer crashes and cannot be restarted with normal recovery procedures. This program, in effect, is a "master key" that can provide access to any part of the system. The superzap program is a highly privileged "disaster aid" that few computer professionals are authorized to use. In the wrong hands, it can be used to perform almost any unauthorized task.

Trapdoors *Trapdoors* are diagnostic tools, used in the development of systems programs, that enable programmers to gain access to various parts of the computer system. Before the programs are marketed, these tools are supposed to be removed. Occasionally, however, some blocks of diagnostic code are overlooked. Thus, a person using the associated systems program may be given unauthorized views of other parts of the computer system.

Logic Bombs *Logic bombs* are programs or short code segments designed to be executed at random or at specific times to perform unauthorized acts. In one documented case, a programmer inserted into a system a logic bomb that would destroy the company's entire personnel file if his name was removed from it.

FIGURE MC 9-3 **Is that price correct?** Despite the fact that supermarket scanners are both accurate and fast, they are only as good as the people who update the price data. During the last several years, several supermarkets have been accused of salami shaving at the checkout counter by not conscientiously updating computer-stored prices to reflect lower shelf prices.

Computer Viruses A **computer virus** is a piece of program code—often transmitted to a computer system from a floppy disk or from code downloaded off a network—that is designed to damage files or perform pranks. There are now over 3,000 viruses of one sort or another in existence. Some are like logic bombs; they may lay dormant for months and then activate on a specific date or when a specific operator action is taken. Viruses can replicate themselves, infecting other programs and files as well.

Scavenging As its name implies, *scavenging* involves searching through trash cans, offices, and the like for information that will permit unauthorized access to a computer system. Students, for example, will sometimes look through discarded listings at the mainframe computer site for an identification number that will open to them the resources of others' accounts. Many organizations use document shredders to deter scavengers.

Data Leakage Some pieces of data generated by organizations are highly confidential and not intended for outsiders' eyes. Generally these organizations carefully control any computer output that leaves their premises. In *data leakage,* however, confidential data are coded in sophisticated ways so that they can be removed undetected. For example, sensitive data can be transformed through a coding process called *encryption* (discussed shortly) into useless nonsense. Then, after these data leave the premises unnoticed, they are decoded into their original form and used for unauthorized purposes.

Eavesdropping Examples abound involving the use of technology to eavesdrop on information intended for others. One of the earliest types of such acts, and still one of the most common, was *wiretapping*. Modern computer systems have made it possible to eavesdrop in new ways. For instance, by simply having access to an identification number, it is possible to view files and even steal from them. In recent years, people have used technology in other such ways to engage in criminal activity; two examples are acquiring descrambling systems to intercept satellite transmissions and using scanners to listen to calls made over wireless phones.

Cellular Phone Fraud The goal of cellular phone fraud, which takes eavesdropping a step further—is to make calls without paying for them—thereby sticking either the cellular-phone owner or phone company with the charges. Cellular phones use unique internal electronic serial numbers to verify phone numbers and billing. These numbers are broadcast when the phone is in use or even just turned on. Eavesdroppers pluck them out of the air and then use the numbers illegitimately.

Software Piracy **Software piracy,** the unauthorized copying or use of a computer program, is often a crime. It is definitely a crime to copy a program and then attempt to sell it for profit. The law is generally more lenient if someone just uses an unauthorized copy that was made by someone else, but this use may constitute a crime as well. The person who makes the unauthorized copy of a program can be guilty of breaking copyright laws.

Hacking **Hacking** is a computer term referring to the activities of people who use computers or computer workstations to crack the security of remote computer systems. Many people engage in hacking purely for the challenge of cracking codes; others do it to steal computer time or to view confidential information. Intentions aside, hacking often is considered a breaking-and-entering crime similar to forced entry into someone's car or home.

Counterfeiting Hard as it is to believe, microcomputer-based color copier technology is so sophisticated today that it has opened the door to a new type of computer crime—counterfeiting (see Figure MC 9-4). The U.S. Secret Service recently arrested a person who made more than $1 million worth of photocopied money and traveler's checks. In another case that involved counterfeit rail tickets on a commuter line, an official of the railroad conceded that the fake, copier-produced tickets looked more authentic than the real ones. But would-be counterfeiters, beware. Many of the new color copiers print "invisible" codes on outputs, making counterfeit money easier to spot. Also, laws are being introduced that will make it easier to identify the owner of a machine from its output.

Bulletin Board Crimes The rise of microcomputers and electronic bulletin boards have contributed to new varieties of criminal activity that most people scarcely could have imagined years ago. For instance, a man was recently arrested who systematically stalked young boys through a computer bulletin board. In another case, a student at a prestigious eastern university was indicted for running an Internet bulletin board over which copyrighted software was allegedly distributed. Bulletin boards have also given rise to *cyberporn,* the distribution of pornographic material over networks.

Preventing Computer Crime

Organizations can combat computer crime in many ways. The following subsections offer several tips for crime prevention.

FIGURE MC 9-4 **Counterfeiting.** Checks, tickets, certificates, and even money have been easier to counterfeit in recent years because of the widespread availability of personal computers, laser printers, and color copiers. Although no one is certain how much counterfeiting costs the public annually, some experts estimate the loss to be $10 billion or more.

Hire Trustworthy People Employers should carefully investigate the background of anyone being considered for sensitive computer work. Some people falsify résumés to get jobs. Others may have criminal records. Despite the publicity given to hackers, studies have consistently shown that most computer crimes are committed by insiders.

Beware of Malcontents The type of employee who is most likely to commit a computer crime is one who has recently been terminated or passed over for a promotion, or one who has some reason to get even with the organization. In cases in which an employee has been terminated and potential for computer crime exists, security records should be updated immediately to indicate that the person involved is no longer an employee.

Separate Employee Functions An employee with many related responsibilities can commit a crime more easily than one with a single responsibility. For example, the person who authorizes adding new vendors to a file should not be the same one who authorizes payments to those vendors.

Restrict System Use People who use a computer system should have access only to the things they need to do their jobs. A computer operator, for example, should be told only how to execute a program and not what the program does. People who need only to retrieve information should not also be given updating privileges. Additionally, to ward off the threat of hackers, many companies have built firewalls. A *firewall* is a collection of hardware or software intended to protect computer networks from remote attack by unauthorized users.

Limit Access to Programs and Data On many systems, users can restrict access to programs and data with **passwords.** For example, a user might specify that anyone wanting access to a program named AR-148 must first enter the password FRED. Users can change passwords frequently and also can protect particularly sensitive files with several passwords. Today many organizations use measures such as *access cards* and sophisticated *biometric security devices* in place of or in combination with passwords. **Access cards,** such as those used in automatic teller machines at banks, activate a transaction when they are used in combination with a password or number. **Biometric security devices** activate a transaction by recognizing some unique physiological characteristic of a person—such as a fingerprint or handprint—or some unique learned characteristic—such as a voice or signature (see Figure MC 9-5).

Use Site Licensing Software vendors often protect their products from unauthorized copying with site licenses. A **site license** allows organizations buying a software product to make copies of it and to distribute the copies among employees for internal use.

Disguise Programs or Data through Encryption Some users and vendors encrypt data or programs to protect them. **Encryption** is the process of disguising data and programs by using some coding method. The encrypting procedure must provide for both coding and decoding. As with passwords, the encryption method should be changed regularly if it is to protect particularly sensitive materials. Some software packages, such as Microsoft's Excel, have built-in encryption routines.

Use Crime-Prevention Software Recently, a variety of software products have become available to help fight computer crime. For instance, *vaccine software*—such as Datawatch's Virex and Symantec's SAM—is available

FIGURE MC 9-5 **Biometric security.** Biometric security devices work by recognizing some unique physiological characteristic of a person—such as a fingerprint or handprint—or some unique learned characteristic—such as a voice or signature.

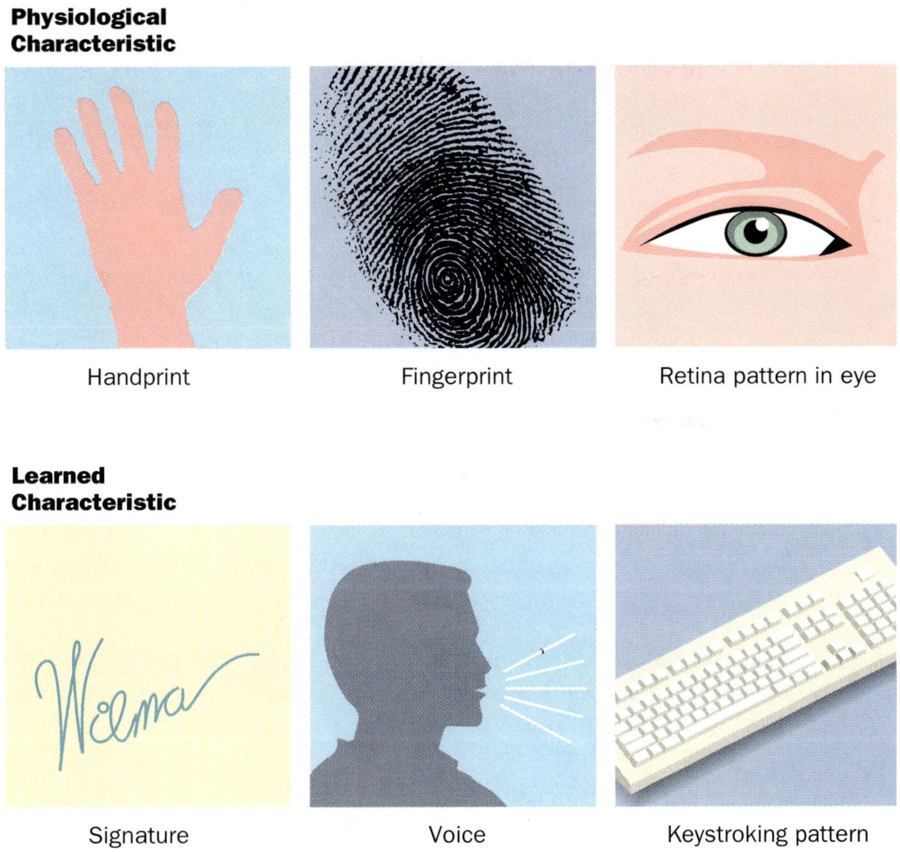

to help detect and eliminate computer viruses. Also, just as computers are often used to file false claims for insurance, government benefits, and so on, businesses and government agencies can also use computers to analyze such claims for suspicious patterns.

Devise Staff Controls Overtime work should be carefully scrutinized, because computer crimes often occur at times when the criminal is unlikely to be interrupted. Sensitive documents that are no longer needed should be shredded. Access to the computer room or program/data library should be strictly limited to authorized personnel. **Callback devices,** which hang up on and call back people phoning in from remote locations, should be used in communications systems to deter hacking and virus implantation.

Monitor Important System Transactions The systems software should include a program for maintaining a log of every person gaining or attempting to gain access to the system. The log should contain information on the terminal used, the data files and programs used, and the time at which the work began and ended. Such a log allows management to isolate unauthorized system use.

Conduct Regular Audits Unfortunately, many crimes are discovered by accident. Key elements of the system should be subjected to regular **audits**—inspections that certify that the system is working as expected—to ensure that no foul play has occurred.

Educate Employees One of the best ways to prevent computer crime is to educate employees about security matters. People should be told about various types of computer crime and the conditions that foster them, informed of the seriousness of computer crime, and instructed on what to do when they suspect a computer crime is taking place or is about to occur.

Crime Legislation

Federal law has also sought to deter computer crime. Congress has regularly amended the law regarding criminal use of computers to broaden its scope and to clarify its intent. For example, the *Computer Fraud and Abuse Act of 1984* specifically outlawed unauthorized access to data stored in federal government computers. The *Computer Fraud and Abuse Act of 1986* expanded the 1984 law to include federally regulated financial institutions and crimes that span two or more states. More recently, the *Computer Abuse Amendments Act of 1994* broadened the law still further to include the transmission of damaging code such as computer viruses.

Under the most recent amendments, actions taken with intent to harm are classified as felonies, whereas actions performed merely with "reckless disregard" are classified as misdemeanors. Although these provisions were added to make it easier to drag hackers into court, critics complain that under current law a hacker who is merely "curious" may not be guilty of a crime at all.

The rapid growth of online computer bulletin boards—such as the thousands that exist on the Internet—has recently pushed the possibility of censorship legislation into the forefront. There have long been laws addressing such offenses as sending indecent material through the mail, libel, harassment, inciting hatred, and the like, but how should those laws apply to computer networks? One problem is jurisdictional; because networks can be global, it may be hard to determine where a crime is being committed and whose laws apply. A second problem is that many existing laws do not transfer well to networks. Should, say, inflammatory comments over a network be treated like chat in a telephone conversation or like words sent through the mail? A third problem deals with responsibility and enforcement issues. Whose job is it to read the massive number of messages sent over computer networks daily? Will the right to personal privacy be abused? Will the public be willing to pay for the potentially exorbitant cost of having networks policed?

COMPUTERS AND PRIVACY

Almost all of us have some aspects of our lives that we prefer to keep private. These may include a sorry incident from the past, sensitive medical or financial facts, or certain tastes or opinions. Yet we can appreciate that sometimes selected people or organizations have a legitimate need for some of this information (see Figure MC 9-6). A doctor needs accurate medical histories of patients. Financial information must be disclosed to credit card companies and college scholarship committees. A company or the government may need to probe into the lives of people applying for unusually sensitive jobs.

No matter how legitimate the need, however, once personal information has been made available to others, there is always the danger that it will be mis-

FIGURE MC 9-6 **Computers and privacy.** Organizations often have a legitimate need to run background checks on people. At TRW, one of the largest holders of credit information in the world, some 2.7 trillion pieces of credit data are stored on consumers and businesses.

used. Some of the stored facts may be wrong. Facts may get to the wrong people or may be taken out of context and used to draw distorted conclusions. Facts about an individual may be collected and disseminated without that person's knowledge or consent. People who are victimized may be denied access to incorrect or sensitive data. The term **privacy,** in the context of information processing, refers to how information about individuals is used and by whom.

The problem of how to protect privacy and ensure that personal information is not misused existed long before electronic computers were developed. But modern computer systems, with their ability to store and manipulate unprecedented quantities of data and to make those data available to many locations, have added a new dimension to the privacy issue. The greater the ability to collect, store, use, and disseminate information, the greater the potential for abuse of that information.

Privacy and Electronic Mail

The infamous case involving Lieutenant Colonel Oliver North and the hearings on arms sales to Iran, in which electronic mail messages between White House staffers were sought as evidence, raised a new issue concerning technology and right to privacy. Some people believe that the objective of electronic mail is to promote a free-flowing dialogue between workers—that is, to increase the effectiveness of organizational communication. They claim that electronic mail should be viewed as the modern-day version of informal chatting around the water cooler, and that electronic mail messages should

USER TIP

Watch Your E-Mail

Electronic mail, or E-mail, is midway between speaking to someone and sending them a formal letter. As such, users frequently do not know quite what to make of it. The sender is often in a rush to get a job done and does not think about polishing words, and there is a certain intimacy to electronic mailboxes that makes the messaging seem almost like spoken communication. The bottom line is that people sending E-mail are often sloppy about expressing themselves and it sometimes comes back to haunt them.

Want an example? One E-mail exchange went as follows. The sender instructed, "Destroy the evidence." The receiver responded, "Acknowledging your request. Evidence destroyed." The time-stamped dialogue was retrieved by lawyers representing an outside party, and the company was subsequently sued and had to settle for considerable out-of-court damages. In general, courts treat E-mail like paper evidence.

Loose lips sink ships. What you create on your computer can be used against you.

not in any way be confused with official company records. Others claim that the law applies to hard-copy and soft-copy data in the same way, and that any business document created on the premises of an organization is not the property of the individual but of the organization. Currently under consideration are several pieces of legislation that address such issues, as well as the key matter of when it is appropriate to destroy government electronic mail backups. Recently, a law professor at a leading university recommended that companies in the private sector should not keep backups on file longer than ten days.

The matter of whether or not companies should be allowed to eavesdrop on their employees' electronic-mail messages is now a matter of heated debate. Many companies are quick to point out that they have to protect themselves from unauthorized use of their electronic mail systems (see the chapter User Tip). Privacy rights advocates often counter that companies do not casually go rifling through people's desks or file cabinets for security reasons, so why should they peek at computer files? Also, the advocates point out, monitoring of electronic mail can be used for political purposes. Presently, eavesdropping by companies on their electronic mail systems is totally legal and there is no law requiring that employees be informed that messages could be monitored. A recent survey in *Macworld* magazine reported that 60 percent of companies that eavesdrop on their employees' electronic mail messages conceal doing so.

Privacy and Marketing Databases

Marketing databases contain information about the consuming public. These databases record where people live, what they are inclined to do, and what they buy. Using this information, companies attempt to determine the best way to promote specific products to specific people. Virtually any time you leave

FIGURE MC 9-7 **Shotguns and pickups.** Through such data as your occupation, past purchasing habits, age, and place of residence, the micromarketer makes an educated guess as to what category to slot you in.

traceable information about yourself anywhere, there is a good chance that it will eventually find its way into somebody's marketing database.

When you buy a house, for example, your name, address, and the sales price are recorded in a county courthouse. These records are available to the public, including *micromarketers*—companies that specialize in creating marketing databases and selling them to companies that produce consumer goods and services. The micromarketer typically breaks down the neighborhoods in a region into several dozen categories. Consumers are placed into one of these categories according to their address. For instance, a "Blueblood Estates" category might be a neighborhood in which the very wealthy live. A "Shotguns and Pickups" category, by contrast, might refer to a rural area where trailers are the likely abode (see Figure MC 9-7). There are also categories for urban professionals, the elderly, and so on.

Each category is correlated in the micromarketer's computer system with certain buying preferences, a technique known as *geodemographics*. "Blueblood Estates" types are likely to buy expensive cars and take trips to places such as Aspen, St. Thomas, and Patagonia. Those of the "Shotguns and Pickups" sort are more likely to be interested in fishing equipment, chainsaws, western wear, and Elvis collectibles. This information helps companies customize a direct mail (unaffectionately called "junk mail") campaign to consumers' specific tastes.

In addition to geodemographic data, micromarketers also collect data showing consumers' past purchasing behavior. Every time you make a computerized purchase, valuable data can be gathered about your purchasing tastes and entered into a computer system. Records kept by stores, credit-card companies, banks, the companies whose magazines you subscribe to, and other organizations are sold to the micromarketer. Even the government sells information!

Caller Identification

Caller identification refers to a technology in which a telephone contains a microprocessor and a tiny display that will output the phone number and—more recently—the name of an incoming caller. Thus, the party receiving the call can identify the person at the other end of the line before picking up the phone, regardless of whether the caller is aware of this or wants his or her identity known. Many people have praised caller identification systems as a good way of screening or cutting down on unwanted calls. Also, businesses such as pizza parlors and take-out restaurants are guaranteed a measure of protection against callers who order food and then do not show up. Some people, however, have been less enthusiastic, seeing these systems as a potential invasion of privacy. For instance, a person living in an apartment or house in a dangerous neighborhood might be afraid to report a crime taking place outside, fearing that his or her identity could be leaked and cause the criminal to take revenge at some point in the future.

Some companies have designed phone systems that connect caller identification systems to customer and vendor databases. Thus, for each incoming call, the computer system can pull up and display certain types of information related to the transaction about to take place (see Figure MC 9-8).

Caller identification is not available everywhere. Whereas most states permit its use, some do not.

Privacy Legislation

Since the early 1970s, the federal government has sought to protect citizens' rights by passing legislation to limit the abuse of computer data banks. Some important laws enacted for this purpose are the Fair Credit Reporting Act, the Freedom of Information Act, the Education Privacy Act, and the Privacy Act.

- The *Fair Credit Reporting Act (1970)* is designed to prevent private organizations from unfairly denying credit to individuals. It stipulates that people must have the right to inspect their credit records. If a reasonable objection about the integrity of the data is raised, the credit reporting agency is required by law to investigate the matter.
- The *Freedom of Information Act (1970)* gives individuals the right to inspect data concerning them that are stored by the federal government. The law also makes certain data about the operation of federal agencies available for public scrutiny.
- The *Education Privacy Act (1974)* protects an individual's right to privacy in both private and public schools that receive any federal funding. It stipulates that an individual has the right to keep matters such as course grades and evaluations of behavior private. Also, individuals must have the opportunity to inspect and challenge their own records.
- The *Privacy Act (1974)* primarily protects the public against abuses by the federal government. It stipulates that collection of data by federal agencies must have a legitimate purpose. It also states that individuals must be allowed to learn what information is being stored about them and how it is being used and that individuals must have the opportunity to correct or remove erroneous or trivial data.

FIGURE MC 9-8 **Caller identification.** Caller identification systems can help provide better service to customers. At one large appliance company, when a call comes in on a customer-assistance line, the phone number and the area code are given to a computer that checks a customer database to determine the customer's identity and the agent in charge. If a match is found, both the call and customer file are automatically routed to the correct agent.

Many people inside and outside the computer industry feel that privacy legislation is woefully out of date and due for an overhaul. As you can see, most of the major laws were enacted more than two decades ago and are restricted to the conduct of the federal government and the organizations to which it supplies aid. A lot of things have changed since then. Twenty years ago, most information was centralized on large, mainframe computers and was available only in hard-copy form, whereas today it is common for data to travel over networks and never make it beyond electronic form. Also, few privacy guidelines apply to the private sector, and the public is getting increasingly concerned about privacy being invaded by such things as junk mail. In a recent poll, 78 percent of Americans said they were very concerned about threats to personal privacy, as compared to 64 percent in 1978.

ETHICAL ISSUES REGARDING COMPUTERS

Ethics refers to standards of moral conduct. For example, telling the truth is a matter of ethics. An unethical act is not always illegal, but sometimes it is. For example, purposely lying to a friend is unethical but normally is lawful, but perjuring oneself as a courtroom witness is a crime. Whether or not criminal behavior is involved, ethics plays an important role in shaping the law and in determining how well we get along with other people. Some questions to ask when considering an action that might be ethically questionable are provided in Figure MC 9-9.

FIGURE MC 9-9 **Ethical guidelines.** When considering an action that bothers you from an ethical viewpoint, ask yourself these questions. Answering yes to certain key questions might be a tipoff that something you are considering doing is wrong. The propriety of an act must ultimately be a matter resolved in your own conscience.

- Will you benefit in any way from the questionable action you are considering taking?
- Are you not disclosing certain facts to others because you are afraid they will disapprove of the action?
- Are you purposely coloring facts to portray a situation as being better or worse than it actually is, to bias someone in a certain way?
- If the same action that you are considering was instead done to you, would you feel taken advantage of, used, lied to, disrespected, or abused in any way?
- Could anyone possibly object to the action as being unfair?
- Will anyone be harmed by the action?
- Do you feel yourself rationalizing your behavior in some way?
- Could the action ultimately result in the evolution of a destructive practice or socially undesirable trend?

Some Examples

Today, there are a number of ethical concerns in the computer area. Following are several examples of these:

- People tend to use computer resources casually in ways that, although not criminal, are ethically questionable. For instance, some people regularly use a software package that they do not own for personal purposes, claiming they are doing so just to "get the feel of it." Although most vendors encourage limited experimentation with their products, they frown on someone who has not bought the package using it regularly.
- A student casually eavesdrops on a university mainframe system on data not intended for his or her use. This may entail neither a prosecutable crime nor a major security threat, but that makes the act no less ethically reprehensible.
- A computer professional working for one software company leaves and takes a job for a competing company. During the first few days with the new employer, the professional divulges product-development secrets that were entrusted in confidence by the former employer, putting the latter at a distinct competitive disadvantage.
- A medical programmer is assigned to code a software routine quickly that is to be part of a system that monitors the heart rate of hospital patients. Before the program can be fully tested, the programmer is ordered to hand it over, so that the system can meet its promised deadline. The programmer tells the project supervisor that the code may contain serious bugs. The supervisor responds, "It's not our fault if the program fails and someone dies because the deadline is too tight."
- A large software company, hearing that a small competitor is coming out with a new product, spreads a rumor that it is working on a similar product. Although the large company never provides a formal release date for its product, it leaves potential users with the fear that they will be taking

a major risk by adopting the small competitor's product. (Software that exists more in people's imaginations than in actuality is sometimes referred to as **vaporware.**)

Why Study Ethics?

Why has ethics become such a hot topic? Undoubtedly, ethics has taken on more significance in recent years because the workplace has become increasingly multicultural and diverse. Different cultures have different values—what might seem ethically problematic to a person in the United States might be a normal way of doing business in, say, Mexico or China, and vice versa. Consider, for example, the question of bribery. In the United States, both bribing and accepting bribes are generally considered morally reprehensible. They are also illegal. In other countries, not only may bribery be culturally tolerated, but also the salaries of workers may be adjusted downward to reflect that bribes are a normal and reasonable part of the compensation package. Such phenomena as increasing divorce rates and changing family structures have tended to broaden ethical norms within cultures over time.

Many scholars think that educating people about ethical matters is being pushed aside today in the rush to achieve measurable results. A movement is afoot to change this, however. Several professional computer organizations—such as the Data Processing Management Association (DPMA) and the Association for Computing Machinery (ACM)—have established codes of ethics for computer professionals. Also, ethics is frequently a topic in computer journals and at professional conferences today.

Whose job it is to teach ethics? The consensus seems to be that primary responsibility lies with parents. Many people believe that ethics should be part of school curricula, but a debate rages over where it should be taught: Should special classes be devoted to ethical behavior, or should an ethics component be added in each course? In the workplace, some 90 percent of the largest U.S. corporations have written codes of ethics, and some even conduct training in the area.

Summary

- Computers have triggered several health-related concerns, including fears about the future, stress due to burnout, and a host of ergonomics- and environment-related concerns.
- A variety of computer crimes have been reported in the press, including data diddling, the Trojan horse technique, salami-shaving methods, unauthorized use of superzap and trapdoor programs, logic bombs, computer viruses, scavenging, data leakage, eavesdropping, cellular-phone fraud, software piracy, hacking, counterfeiting, and bulletin-board crimes.
- Organizations can combat computer crime in many ways, including hiring the right people and educating them about computer crime, acquiring software and hardware that can detect unauthorized acts, and developing control procedures that are aimed at thwarting and detecting crime.
- Although concerns about privacy existed before computers were developed, computers—with their ability to store, manipulate, and distribute data more effectively—have arguably heightened the threat to personal privacy.
- Ethics refers to standards of moral conduct. Today, many people use computers in ways that—although not criminal—are certainly ethically questionable.

Key Terms

Shown in parentheses are the page numbers on which key terms are boldfaced.

Access card (MC 282)
Audit (MC 284)
Biometric security device (MC 282)
Callback device (MC 283)
Caller identification (MC 288)
Computer crime (MC 278)
Computer virus (MC 280)
Encryption (MC 282)
Ergonomics (MC 275)
Ethics (MC 289)
Hacking (MC 280)
Marketing database (MC 286)
Password (MC 282)
Privacy (MC 285)
Site license (MC 282)
Software piracy (MC 280)
Vaporware (MC 291)

Quiz

True/False

___ 1. Carpal tunnel syndrome is a type of computer virus.

___ 2. Cyberphobia refers to people who tend to overuse computers.

___ 3. Salami shaving often involves manipulating programs or data so that many barely noticeable monetary amounts are removed from a large number of accounts and accumulated elsewhere.

___ 4. Ergonomics is a computer crime that involves changing an organization's computer data in an unauthorized way.

___ 5. A computer virus refers to renegade computer code that is transmitted during a copy operation.

___ 6. A biometric security device might be used to recognize a fingerprint.

___ 7. The Computer Fraud and Abuse Act was designed to head off unethical uses of computers.

___ 8. Caller identification is a technology that involves the use of callback devices.

___ 9. Micromarketers are companies that specialize in creating marketing databases.

___ 10. Vaporware refers to software that does not exist.

Multiple Choice

___ 11. The danger posed by radiation levels in display devices is a matter of
a. ethics.
b. computer crime.
c. ergonomics.
d. privacy.
e. biometric security.

____ 12. Much computer crime is discovered
a. before the crime itself actually is committed.
b. by trapdoors.
c. while superzapping.
d. accidentally.
e. by data banks.

____ 13. The process of legitimately disguising data and programs is referred to as
a. wiretapping.
b. salami shaving.
c encryption.
d. hacking.
e. scavenging.

____ 14. Computer crime is hard to pin down because
a. it is not clear whether some unauthorized acts are crimes.
b. judges and juries tend to be ignorant of technical issues involving computers.
c. much computer crime is undiscovered.
d. much computer crime is unreported.
e. all of the above.

____ 15. Vaporware refers to
a. the Trojan horse technique.
b. a type of computer virus.
c. software that exists more in people's imagination than in reality.
d. the use of computer technology in the noxious-chemical area.
e. a method used to fight computer crime.

____ 16. All of the following are generally accepted methods for combatting computer crime except
a. access cards.
b. passwords.
c. separating employee functions.
d. geodemographics.
e. conducting regular audits.

____ 17. Which legislation stipulates that any data federal agencies collect must have a legitimate purpose?
a. Freedom of Information Act
b. Privacy Act
c. Fair Credit Reporting Act
d. Education Privacy Act
e. Communications Privacy Act

____ 18. Which of the following does not refer to a computer crime technique?
a. Trojan horse
b. Scavenging
c. Computer virus
d. Auditing
e. Data diddling

____ 19. One way to help prevent computer crime is to
a. use the Trojan horse technique.
b. replace the computer printer with a document shredder.
c. hire trustworthy people.

d. provide easy access to the computer system for all currently employed personnel.
e. eliminate computer personnel altogether.

___ 20. Taking off small monetary amounts in numerous, randomly selected accounts and posting them to another account is a type of computer crime known as
a. data diddling.
b. postcreation perturbation.
c. superzapping.
d. salami shaving.
e. shifting.

Matching

Select the term that best matches each phrase:

a. Geodemographics
b. Caller identification
c. Ethics
d. Biometric security device
e. Computer virus
f. Trapdoor
g. Encryption
h. Trojan horse
i. Vaporware
j. Software piracy
k. Carpal tunnel syndrome
l. Fair Credit Reporting Act

___ 21. An event that was motivated to protect the privacy of individuals

___ 22. Refers to standards of moral conduct

___ 23. Provides access to a computer system

___ 24. A means used to disguise data

___ 25. A technology that, although useful, threatens to invade the privacy of some individuals

___ 26. Used to develop marketing databases

___ 27. A program product that does not yet exist

___ 28. Caused by poor keyboard use

___ 29. Program code that can replicate itself from one disk to another

___ 30. The adding of concealed instructions to a program

Answers

True/False: 1. F; 2. F; 3. T; 4. F; 5. T; 6. T; 7. F; 8. F; 9. T; 10. T

Multiple Choice: 11. c; 12. d; 13. c; 14. e; 15. c; 16. d; 17. b; 18. d; 19. c; 20. d

Matching: 21. l; 22. c; 23. d; 24. g; 25. b; 26. a; 27. i; 28. k; 29. e; 30. h

Exercises

1. In a recent editorial in *Computerworld,* a software consultant touched off a flood of protest by remarking that software piracy is overblown as an issue. He argued the following:
   a. Most people who pirate software would not have bought the software in the first place, so pirated software does not necessarily represent lost revenue to a company.
   b. Pirates who like a product often buy future releases of it to access new features, so pirating often has a positive effect on future sales.
   c. The estimate of the loss due to stolen software—which ranges from $170 million to $4 billion a year—overstates the real drain on profits because it multiplies the number of illegal copies times sales price.

   Please comment.

2. A software developer creates a program to protect against computer viruses. To finance the advertising campaign for this product, the developer decides to call several computer executives at large firms to ask them to put up $5,000 each. This, the developer believes, will produce the funds needed and make the executives more likely to buy the product for their companies. Does this strategy seem sound to you from both a business and an ethical standpoint?

3. As discussed in the chapter, there is considerable fear that marketing databases can be used to invade a person's privacy. What issues do you think the government should address to ensure that the privacy of individuals is not invaded by micromarketers? For instance, one critical area concerns *access;* that is, who will have access to the marketing data, and under what circumstances access will be granted.

GLOSSARY

This glossary covers terms discussed in both the long version (Chapters 1–9) and the short version (Chapters 1–5) of *Microcomputer Concepts.*

Access card. A plastic card that, when inserted into a machine and combined with a password, permits access to a system. (MC 282)

Accounting package. A software package that processes an organization's business transactions, such as those coming from payroll, order entry, accounts receivable, accounts payable, and inventory operations. (MC 91)

Action diagram. A tool that helps programmers code structured programs. (MC 219)

Add-in board. A card with electronic circuitry that may be inserted into the computer's system unit to perform one or more functions. (MC 32)

Analog transmission. The transmission of data as continuous wave patterns. (MC 118)

Applications package. A fourth-generation-language product that, when the user sets a few parameters, becomes a finished applications program ready to meet specific needs. (MC 213)

Applications software. Programs that do useful work—such as payroll, inventory control, and accounting tasks—for end users of a computer system. Contrast with systems software. (MC 11)

Applications software development. The process of designing, coding, debugging and testing, maintaining, and documenting applications software. (MC 212)

Artificial intelligence (AI). The ability of a machine to perform actions that are characteristic of human intelligence, such as reasoning and learning. (MC 188)

ASCII. (American Standard Code for Information Interchange.) A fixed-length, binary-based code widely used to represent data for processing and communications. (MC 8)

Asynchronous transmission. The transmission of data over a line one character at a time. Each character is preceded by a *start bit* and followed by a *stop bit.* Contrast with synchronous transmission. (MC 121)

Audit. An inspection used to determine if a system or procedure is working as it should or if claimed amounts are correct. (MC 284)

Authoring software. Software used to develop applications in such areas as multimedia computing, virtual reality, and the like. (MC 199)

Backup. Making duplicate copies of programs or data. (MC 40)

Bar chart. A presentation graphic that uses side-by-side columns as the principal charting element. (MC 181)

BASIC. An easy-to-learn, high-level programming language developed at Dartmouth College in the 1960s. (MC 221)

Binary. A number system with two possible states. The binary system is fundamental to computers because electronic devices function in two states—for example, *on* or *off, current present* or *current not present, clockwise* or *counterclockwise.* (MC 7)

Biometric security device. A device that, upon recognition of some physiological or learned characteristic that is unique to a person, allows that person to have access to a system. (MC 282)

Bit. A binary digit, such as 0 or 1. Computer systems use the 0 and 1 states to take advantage of the binary nature of electronics. Bits are often assembled into bytes when manipulated or stored. (MC 7)

Bits per second (bps). A measure of the speed of a communications device. (MC 119)

Bridge. An interface that enables two similar networks to communicate. Contrast with gateway. (MC 129)

Bus. A set of wires that acts as a data highway between the central processing unit (CPU) and other devices. (MC 33)

Bus network. A telecommunications network that consists of a line that taps into several devices, allowing them to communicate with one another. The network is so named because data are passed around from device to device similar to the way in which passengers are picked up and dropped off at city bus stations. (MC 129)

Byte. A configuration of 7 or 8 bits used to represent a single character of data. (MC 9)

C. A programming language that has the portability of a high-level language and the executional efficiency of an assembly language. (MC 221)

Callback device. A device on the receiving end of a communications network that verifies the authenticity of the sender by calling the sender back. (MC 283)

Caller identification. Refers to the use of a telephone or answering device that displays the phone numbers of incoming calls. (MC 288)

Cartridge disk. A magnetic disk in which a single disk platter is contained in a sealed plastic case. (MC 41)

Cartridge tape. Magnetic tape in which the supply and take-up reels are contained in a small plastic case that is mounted onto a tape unit when data are to be read from or written to the tape inside. (MC 42)

Case control structure. A control structure that can be formed by nesting two or more selection control structures. (MC 217)

Cellular phone. A wireless phone that uses special ground stations called *cells* to communicate with the regular phone system. (MC 116)

Central processing unit (CPU). The piece of hardware, also known as the *computer,* that interprets and executes program instructions and communicates with input, output, and storage devices. (MC 3)

Client. A device designed to receive service in a client-server network. (MC 126)

Client-server LAN. A local area network (LAN) that is composed of *client* devices, which receive networking service, and *server* devices, which provide that service. (MC 126)

Clip art. Prepackaged artwork that can be imported into text documents by desktop publishing software. (MC 176)

Coaxial cable. A transmission line developed for sending data and video images at high speeds. (MC 115)

COBOL. A high-level programming language developed for transaction processing applications. (MC 223)

Coding. The writing of programming-language instructions. (MC 227)

Common carrier. A government-regulated, private organization that provides communications services to the public. (MC 125)

Communications medium. The intervening substance, such as a telephone wire or cable, that connects two physically distant hardware devices. (MC 114)

Communications satellite. An earth-orbiting device that relays communications signals over long distances. (MC 116)

Compiler. A computer program that translates a source program written by a user or programmer in a high-level programming language into machine language. The translation takes place before the translated program is executed. Contrast with interpreter. (MC 82)

Computer. See Central processing unit.

Computer-aided design (CAD). A general term applied to the use of computer technology to automate product design functions. (MC 258)

Computer-aided design (CAD) software. A graphically oriented program package that is used to automate product design functions. (MC 92)

Computer-aided manufacturing (CAM). A general term applied to the use of computer technology to automate manufacturing functions in industry. (MC 259)

Computer-aided software engineering (CASE). Program products that automate systems and program development activities. (MC 230)

Computer crime. The use of computers to commit unauthorized acts. (MC 278)

Computer-integrated manufacturing (CIM). The use of technology to tie together computer-aided design (CAD), computer-aided manufacturing (CAM), and other business systems. (MC 259)

Computer system. A collection of elements that includes the computer as well as components that contribute to making the computer a useful tool. (MC 2)

Computer virus. A small block of unauthorized code, transmitted from program to program by a copy operation, that performs destructive acts when executed. (MC 154, 278)

Context sensitive. Refers to an online feature that provides assistance relating to the type of operation the user is currently trying to perform. (MC 69)

Control structure. A pattern for controlling the flow of logic in a computer program. (MC 217)

CRT (cathode-ray tube). A long-necked display-tube mechanism similar to those in television sets. (MC 48)

Cursor. A highlighting symbol that appears on a video screen to indicate where the next character to be typed will appear. (MC 44)

Data. A collection of raw, unorganized facts. (MC 5)

Database. An integrated collection of data stored on a medium such as a disk. (MC 10, 231)

Database management system (DBMS). A software package designed to integrate data and provide easy access to them. (MC 87, 231)

Data definition. The process of describing the characteristics of data that are to be handled by a database management system. (MC 234)

Data dictionary. A facility that manages important information about characteristics of data or programs in a database or a computer system. (MC 227)

Data manipulation. The process of using language commands to add, delete, modify, or retrieve data in a file or database. (MC 235)

Data processing area. The group of computer professionals charged with building transaction processing systems. (MC 262)

Debugging. The process of detecting and correcting errors in computer programs or in the computer system itself. (MC 228)

Decision support system (DSS). A system that provides tools and capabilities to managers to help them satisfy their own information needs. (MC 252)

Desk accessory. A software package that provides the electronic counterpart of tools commonly found on a desktop. (MC 91)

Desktop computer. A microcomputer system that fits on a desktop. (MC 28)

Desktop publishing. A microcomputer-based publishing system that can fit on a desktop. (MC 89, 170)

Dialog box. A box that requires the user to supply information to the computer system about the task being performed. (MC 72)

Digital transmission. The transmission of data as discrete impulses. (MC 118)

Direct access. Reading or writing data in storage so that the access time involved is relatively independent of the location of the data. Also known as *random access.* (MC 35)

Diskette. A small, removable disk made of a tough, flexible plastic and coated with a magnetizable substance. (MC 36)

Disklock accessory. A software package that is used to restrict access to a hard disk. (MC 153)

Documentation. A detailed written description of a program, procedure, or system. (MC 229)

DOUNTIL. A looping control structure in which the looping continues as long as a certain condition is false (that is, "do until true"). (MC 217)

DOWHILE. A looping control structure in which the looping continues as long as a certain condition is true (that is, "do while true"). (MC 217)

Downloading. The process of transferring data or information from a large computer system to a smaller one. Contrast with uploading. (MC 128)

Electronic bulletin board. A computer file that is shared by various people, enabling them to post messages. (MC 105)

Electronic mail (E-mail). A facility that enables users to send letters, memos, documents, and the like from one hardware device to another. (MC 255)

Electronic mailbox. A disk storage area used to hold a person's electronic mail. (MC 105)

Encryption. A method of disguising data or programs so that they are unrecognizable to unauthorized users of a computer system. (MC 153, 282)

End-user development. Systems development carried out by the end user. (MC 266)

Ergonomics. The field that studies the effects of things such as computer hardware, software, and workspaces on employees' comfort and health. (MC 275)

Ethics. A term that refers to standards of moral conduct. (MC 289)

Executive information system (EIS). A decision support system that is tailored to the needs of a specific, top-level individual in an organization. (MC 254)

Expert system. A program providing the type of advice that would be expected of a human expert. (MC 94, 189)

Expert-system shell. A prepackaged expert system that lacks only a knowledge base. (MC 190)

Facsimile (fax) machine. A device that can transmit or receive hard-copy images of text, pictures, maps, diagrams, and the like over the phone lines. (MC 106)

Fiber optic cable. A cable composed of hundreds of hair-thin, transparent fibers along which data are passed as light waves from lasers. (MC 115)

Field. A collection of related characters. (MC 10)

Field descriptor. A code used to describe the type of data—say, numeric, character, or logical—that occupies a given field in a data record. (MC 234)

File. A collection of related records. (MC 10)

File directory. A directory on a disk that provides for each stored file such information as the file's name, length, and starting address. (MC 37)

File structure. A collection of information about the records of a file, including the names, lengths, and types of the fields. (MC 234)

Flat-panel display. A slim-profile display device. (MC 48)

Floppy disk. See Diskette.

Font. A typeface in a particular point size (for instance, 12-point Helvetica). (MC 176)

Formatting. The process of preparing a disk for use on a computer system by dividing it into addressable locations. (MC 37)

Fourth-generation language (4GL). An easy-to-learn, easy-to-use language that enables users or programmers to code applications much more quickly than they could with traditional languages. (MC 224)

Full-duplex transmission. A type of transmission in which messages may be sent simultaneously in two directions along a communications path. (MC 118)

Functionally obsolete. Refers to a product that no longer meets the needs of an individual or business. (MC 160)

Function key. A special keyboard key that executes a preprogrammed routine when pressed. (MC 24)

Gateway. An interface that enables two dissimilar networks to communicate. Contrast with bridge. (MC 128)

Gigabyte (GB). Approximately one billion bytes. (MC 9)

Graphical user interface (GUI). Refers to the computer graphics screens that make it easier for users to interact with software. (MC 64)

Group decision support system (GDSS). A decision support system in which several people routinely interact through a computer network to solve common problems. Also called *workgroup computing.* (MC 252)

Hacking. Using a microcomputer system or terminal to penetrate the security of a remote computer system. (MC 280)

Half-duplex transmission. Any type of transmission in which messages may be sent in two directions—but only one way at a time—along a communications path. (MC 117)

Hard copy. A permanent form of usable output—for example, output on paper or film. Contrast with soft copy. (MC 43)

Hard disk. A rigid platter that has been coated with a magnetized substance. (MC 39)

Hardware. Physical equipment in a computing environment, such as the computer and its support devices. Contrast with software. (MC 11)

Hierarchical local network. A local network in which a relatively powerful central processing unit (CPU) is the host computer and less powerful CPUs and workstations serve users who depend on the host. (MC 128)

IBM-compatible microcomputer. A microcomputer that can run the same software as that run by IBM microcomputers. (MC 142)

Icon. A graphic image on a display screen that, when selected by the operator, invokes a particular program action. (MC 25, 67)

Illustration software package. A program package that enables users to paint or draw. (MC 177)

Impact dot-matrix printer. A printer whose print head is an impact dot-matrix mechanism. (MC 48)

Information center (IC). A facility in an organization charged with developing small systems. (MC 262)

Information reporting system. An information system whose principal outputs are preformatted reports. (MC 251)

Information system. A system designed to provide information to managers to enable them to make decisions. (MC 251)

Information systems department. The area in an organization that consists of computer professionals. (MC 261)

Ink-jet printer. A printer that works by spraying small dots of charged ink onto a page. (MC 48)

Internet. A public-access, worldwide web of over 50,000 networks connecting more than 15 million private users and thousands of universities, businesses, and government agencies. (MC 108)

Interpreter. A computer program that translates a source program written by a user or programmer in a high-level language into machine language. The translation takes place on a line-by-line basis as each statement is executed. Contrast with compiler. (MC 83)

Keyboard. An input device that is composed of keys arranged in a configuration similar to that of a typewriter. Computer keyboards also have a number of special keys that can initiate preprogrammed routines. (MC 24)

Kilobyte (KB). Approximately 1,000 (1,024, to be exact) bytes. Memory on smaller computer systems is often measured in kilobytes. (MC 9)

Language translator. A systems program that converts an applications program into machine language. (MC 72)

Laptop computer. A portable computer that is light enough to be operated while resting on a user's lap. (MC 28)

Laser printer. A printer, yielding excellent output quality, that works on a similar principle to that of a photocopier. (MC 50)

Line chart. A presentation graphic in which the principal charting element is an unbroken line. (MC 184)

Local area network (LAN). A hostless local network that usually consists of microcomputer workstations and shared peripherals. (MC 126)

Local network. A privately run communications network of several machines located within a mile or so of each other. Contrast with wide area network. (MC 125)

Looping (iteration) control structure. The control structure used to represent a looping operation. (MC 217)

Machine language. A binary-based programming language that can be executed directly by the computer. (MC 9)

Macintosh system software. The operating system that is used primarily on Apple's Macintosh line of computer systems. (MC 79)

Maintenance. The process of making upgrades to systems or software over time. (MC 228)

Marketing database. A database containing information useful for marketing products to consumers. (MC 286)

Master slide. An electronic slide image that contains chart elements common to several slides and that is used as the starting point to prepare these other slides. (MC 187)

Megabyte (meg or MB). Approximately one million bytes. (MC 9)

Memory. Also known as random access memory (RAM), a type of computer storage that temporarily holds data and program instructions awaiting processing, intermediate results, and processed output. (MC 7)

Menu. A set of options from which the user chooses to take a desired action. (MC 65)

Menu bar. A horizontal list of choices that appears on a highlighted line, usually below the window title. Often called the *main menu.* (MC 65)

Microcomputer system. The smallest and least expensive type of computer system. Also called a *personal computer system.* (MC 2)

Microspacing. A technique used by some printers and software packages to insert fractional spaces between characters to give text a typeset look. (MC 175)

Microwave. An electromagnetic wave in the high-frequency range. (MC 116)

Modem. (A contraction of the words *modulation* and *demodulation.*) A communications device that enables computers and their support devices to communicate over ordinary telephone lines. (MC 118)

Monitor. A video display device. (MC 44)

Monospacing. A printing feature that allocates the same amount of space on a line to each character. (MC 175)

Mouse. A device used to move a cursor rapidly around a display screen. (MC 25)

MS-DOS. An operating system widely used by microcomputer systems similar to those made by IBM. (MC 77)

Multimedia. A type of computing in which text, graphics, sound, and video are intermixed in applications. (MC 195)

Multimedia PC. A microcomputer system equipped with a powerful microprocessor and plentiful storage as well as an optical disk (CD-ROM) unit, a graphics-oriented color monitor, sound and video boards, and speakers. (MC 198)

Multitasking. Refers to the ability of an operating system to execute two or more programs or program tasks from a single user concurrently. (MC 77)

Natural-language interface. Software that allows users to communicate with the computer in a conversational language, such as English, Spanish, or Japanese. (MC 193)

NetWare. The most widely used operating system on microcomputer-based networks. (MC 82)

Neural-net computing. An expert-system technology in which a computer system emulates the human brain's pattern-recognition process. (MC 191)

Object. An element in an object-oriented programming environment that consists of instructions and data—possibly even several types of data. (MC 225)

Object-oriented programming language. A language that works with objects and messages rather than with separate instructions and data. (MC 225)

Office automation (OA). The use of computer-based, office-oriented technologies such as word processing, desktop publishing, electronic mail, and video teleconferencing. (MC 255)

Office automation (OA) area. The group of computer professionals charged with managing office-related computer activities within the organization. (MC 263)

One-entry-point/one-exit-point rule. A rule stating that each program control structure will have only one entry point into it and one exit point out of it. (MC 217)

Operating system. The main collection of systems software that enables the computer system to manage the resources under its control. (MC 74)

Optical disk. A disk that is read by laser beams rather than by magnetic means. (MC 41)

OS/2. The operating system designed for the high end of the IBM line of microcomputers. (MC 81)

Outsourcing. The practice by which one company hires another company to do some or all of its information processing. (MC 263)

Page description language (PDL). A language used to communicate instructions to a laser printer. (MC 172)

Page-makeup software. Programs used to compose page layouts on a desktop publishing system. (MC 174)

Parallel transmission. Data transmission in which each bit in a byte has its own path and is transmitted simultaneously. Contrast with serial transmission. (MC 120)

Parity bit. An extra bit added to the byte representation of a character to ensure that either an odd or an even number of 1-bits is transmitted with every character. (MC 121)

Password. A word or number used to provide selected individuals access to a system. (MC 153, 282)

PC-DOS. The operating system most widely used on IBM microcomputers. (MC 77)

Peer-to-peer LAN. A local area network (LAN) in which all of the user workstations and shared peripheral devices operate on the same level. (MC 127)

Physical security. Refers to devices that inhibit physical access to a system. (MC 152)

Pie chart. A presentation graphic in which the principal charting element is a pie-shaped image that is divided into slices, each of which represents a share of the whole. (MC 184)

Pixel. A single dot on a display screen that is used to compose dot-matrix characters and other images. (MC 44)

Platform. A set of compatible computer-system architecture and systems software choices that limits the user to work in a certain way. (MC 147)

Plotter. An output device used for drawing graphs and diagrams. (MC 52)

Point size. A measurement used in the scaling of typefaces. (MC 186)

Port. An outlet on the computer's system unit through which a peripheral device may communicate. (MC 33)

Presentation graphic. A visual image, such as a bar chart or pie chart, that is used to present data in a highly meaningful form. (MC 181)

Presentation graphics package. A productivity software package used to prepare line charts, bar charts, pie charts, and other information-intensive images. (MC 89)

Printer. A device that places computer output onto paper. (MC 48)

Privacy. In a computer processing context, refers to how information about individuals is used and by whom. (MC 285)

Productivity software. Easy-to-learn, easy-to-use program packages—such as word processors, spreadsheets, and database management systems (DBMSs)—that are designed to make ordinary workers more productive at their jobs. (MC 11, 83)

Program. A set of instructions that causes the computer system to perform specific actions. (MC 5)

Program flowchart. A visual design tool showing step by step how a computer program will process data. (MC 214)

Programming language. A set of rules used to write computer programs. (MC 220)

Project manager. A software package that is used to coordinate and schedule activities in large projects. (MC 92)

Prompt. Displayed text or symbols indicating that the computer system is awaiting input. (MC 62)

Proportional spacing. A printing feature that allocates more horizontal space on a line to some characters than to others. (MC 175)

Protocol. A set of conventions used by machines to establish, maintain, and terminate communication with each other. (MC 130)

Prototyping. A systems development alternative whereby a small model, or *prototype*, of the system is built before a full-scale systems development effort is undertaken. (MC 265)

Pseudocode. A technique for structured program design that uses English-like statements to outline the logic of a program. (MC 217)

Pull-down menu. A menu of subcommands that drops down vertically from a horizontal menu bar or to the right of another pull-down menu. (MC 66)

Random access memory (RAM). See Memory. (MC 7, 31)

Read-only memory (ROM). A software-in-hardware module that can be read but not written on. (MC 32)

Record. A collection of related fields. (MC 10)

Relational database management system. A database management system that links data in related files through common fields. (MC 231)

Release. A minor upgrade of a software product. (MC 159)

Reusable code. Program segments that can be reused several times in constructing applications programs. (MC 227)

Ring network. A telecommunications network in which machines are connected serially, in a closed loop. (MC 129)

Robotics. The field devoted to the study of robot technology. (MC 194)

Screen saver. A software product designed to protect the phosphor coating on the inside of a display screen from damage when the display is turned on but is not used for an extended period. (MC 151)

Scroll bar. A horizontal or vertical bar along an edge of a window indicating that the window is too small to display all the information involved. (MC 70)

Secondary storage. Storage on disk and tape that supplements memory. (MC 7)

Sector. A pie-shaped area on a disk. Many disks are addressed through sectors. (MC 37)

Security. Refers to protecting a computer system's hardware, software, and data from damage or any type of tampering. (MC 152)

Selection (if-then-else) control structure. The control structure used to represent a decision operation. (MC 217)

Sequence control structure. The control structure used to represent operations that take place sequentially. (MC 217)

Sequential access. Fetching records in storage in the same order in which they are physically arranged. (MC 35)

Serial transmission. Data transmission in which all bits in a byte must travel down the same path, one after the other. Contrast with parallel transmission. (MC 120)

Server. A computer that manages a shared device—such as a laser printer or high-capacity hard disk—on a local area network (LAN). (MC 126)

Shortcut keystrokes. Keystrokes that make it possible for commands to be entered with minimal keystroking. (MC 63)

Simplex transmission. Any type of transmission in which a message can be sent in only a single, prespecified direction along a communications path. (MC 117)

Site license. A right purchased by an organization that enables employees to use or copy software freely for specific, authorized purposes. (MC 282)

Soft copy. A nonpermanent form of usable output—for example, display output. Contrast with hard copy. (MC 43)

Software. Computer programs. Contrast with hardware. (MC 11)

Software piracy. The unauthorized copying or use of computer programs. (MC 280)

Spreadsheet package. A productivity software package that enables operators to create tables and financial schedules quickly by making entries into cells on a display-screen grid. (MC 84)

Star network. A telecommunications network that consists of a host device directly connected to several other devices. (MC 129)

Statistical package. A software product designed to assist in the interpretation of data. (MC 94)

Structure chart. A program design tool that shows the hierarchical relationship between program modules. (MC 213)

Structured programming. An approach to program design that makes program code more systematic and maintainable. (MC 217)

Structured Query Language (SQL). A popular language standard for information retrieval in relational databases. (MC 238)

Surge suppressor. A hardware device that is installed between the system unit and the electrical outlet to prevent random electrical power spikes from damaging the system. (MC 150)

Synchronous transmission. The transmission of data over a line one block of characters at a time. Contrast with asynchronous transmission. (MC 122)

Syntax. The grammatical rules that govern a language. (MC 62)

System. A collection of elements and procedures that interact to accomplish a goal. (MC 248)

System board. The board that contains the computer; sometimes called a *motherboard.* (MC 30)

Systems analyst. A person who studies systems in an organization to determine what actions need to be taken and how these actions may best be achieved with computer resources. (MC 262)

Systems development. The ongoing process of improving ways of doing work. (MC 248)

Systems development life cycle (SDLC). The process consisting of the five phases of system development: preliminary investigation, systems analysis, system design, system acquisition, and system implementation. (MC 263)

Systems software. Computer programs—such as the operating system—that do background tasks for users and programmers. Contrast with applications software. (MC 11, 74)

System unit. The hardware unit that houses the computer and its memory, as well as a number of other devices such as add-in boards and related circuitry. (MC 28)

Technologically obsolete. Refers to a product that, although superseded by a newer version or release, still meets the needs of an individual or business. (MC 160)

Telecommunications. The transmission of data over a distance—via the phone lines, privately owned cable, or satellite, for instance. (MC 104)

Telecommuting. Working at home and being connected by means of electronic devices to other workers at remote locations. (MC 258)

Teleconferencing. Using computer and communications technology to carry out a meeting in which not all the participants need be present at the same place or time. (MC 256)

Terrestrial microwave station. A ground station that receives microwave signals, amplifies them, and passes them on. (MC 116)

Text chart. A presentation graphic in which the primary element is text. (MC 185)

Top-down design. A structured design philosophy whereby a program or system is subdivided into well-defined modules and organized into a hierarchy. (MC 214)

Track. A path on an input/output medium on which data are recorded. (MC 36)

Traditional approach. An approach to systems development whereby the five phases of the systems development life cycle are carried out in a predetermined sequence. (MC 265)

Transaction processing system. A system that handles an organization's business transactions. (MC 249)

Twisted-pair wires. A communications medium that consists of pairs of wires that have been twisted together and bound into a cable. The telephone system consists mainly of twisted-wire cabling. (MC 115)

Typeface. A collection of characters that share a common design. (MC 175)

Typeface family. A collection of related typefaces. (MC 176)

UNIX. A multiuser, multitasking operating system. (MC 80)

Upgrading. The process of buying new hardware or software that will extend the life of a computer system. (MC 158)

Uploading. The process of sending data from a small computer system to a larger computer system, for storage or processing purposes. (MC 128)

User interface. Generally refers to the *software* user interface, or the manner in which a program package makes its resources available to users. (MC 62)

Utility program. A program used to perform some frequently encountered operation in a computer system. (MC 83)

Vaccine program. A program that scrutinizes code for suspicious patterns that might indicate the presence of a computer virus. (MC 154)

Vaporware. Software that exists more in people's imaginations than in actuality. (MC 291)

Version. A major upgrade of a software product. (MC 159)

Vertical-market software. Productivity software products designed to meet the needs of niche markets, such as doctors, lawyers, real-estate appraisers, or farmers and ranchers. (MC 94)

Virtual reality. Refers to the use of computers to create special, customized environments that seem, to the user, as if they were real. (MC 200)

Voice mail. An electronic mail system in which spoken phone messages are digitally recorded and stored in an electronic mailbox. (MC 105)

Warranty. A formal statement saying that a manufacturer will pay for certain repairs if equipment or software fails to meet certain expectations within a given number of days after purchase. (MC 156)

Wide area network (WAN). A communications network that covers a wide geographic area. Contrast with local network. (MC 124)

Window. A box of related information that is overlaid on a display screen. (MC 69)

Windows 3.x. A graphically oriented operating environment, for MS-DOS, created by Microsoft Corporation. (MC 77)

Windows 95. The operating system that is the heir apparent to DOS-with-Windows 3.x. (MC 78)

Windows NT. A high-end operating system designed by Microsoft Corporation for 32-bit microcomputers in corporate networking applications. (MC 79)

Word processing. The development of text materials such as letters, legal contracts, and manuscripts on a computer system. (MC 83)

Workgroup computing. A computer application in which a group of workers interdependently use the same software and data on a network. Also known as a *group decision support system (GDSS).* (MC 106, 254)

WYSIWYG (*w*hat *y*ou *s*ee *i*s *w*hat *y*ou *g*et). Refers to the capability of showing on the display screen an output image identical or very close to the final, printed image. (MC 173)

INDEX

This index covers terms discussed in both the long version (Chapters 1–9) and the short version (Chapters 1–5) of *Microcomputer Concepts.*

CREDITS

These credits cover terms discussed in both the long version (Chapters 1–9) and short version (Chapters 1–5) of *Microcomputer Concepts.*

Chapter MC 1

Figure MC 1-1a & b
Courtesy of International Business Machines Corporation.

Figure MC 1-1c
Apple Computer, Inc.

Figure MC 1-1d
Reprinted with permission of Compaq Computer Corporation. All rights reserved.

Figure MC 1-2
Courtesy of International Business Machines Corporation.

Figure MC 1-4
Courtesy of International Business Machines Corporation.

User Tip
© The Miami Herald.

Figure MC 1-11
Reprinted by permission from THISCO and Prodigy Services Company.

Chapter MC 2

Figure MC 2-3a
Image courtesy of AST Research, Inc.

Figure MC 2-3b
Image supplied by Logitech, Inc.

Figure MC 2-3c
Image supplied by Logitech, Inc.

Figure MC 2-3d
Source: Wacom.

Figure MC 2-4a
Reprinted with permission by Plustek USA, Inc.

Figure MC 2-4b
Image courtesy of Primax Electronics.

Figure MC 2-5a
Courtesy of International Business Machines Corporation.

Figure MC 2-5b
Courtesy of Apple Computer, Inc.

Figure MC 2-5c
Courtesy of International Business Machines Corporation.

Figure MC 2-5d
Courtesy of Sharp Electronics.

Figure MC 2-7a
Intel Corporation.

Figure MC 2-7b
Courtesy of International Business Machines Corporation.

Figure MC 2-8a
Courtesy of Micro Solutions.

Figure 2-8b
Courtesy of International Business Machines Corporation.

Figure MC 2-17a
Courtesy 3M.

Figure MC 2-17b
Courtesy of International Business Machines Corporation.

Figure MC 2-17c
Courtesy of 3M.

Figure MC 2-17d
Pioneer Communications of America.

Figure MC 2-18a & c
Photo courtesy of Macromedia.

Figure MC 2-18b
Screen shot reprinted with permission from Microsoft Corporation.

Figure MC 2-19
Iomega Corporation.

Figure MC 2-20
Photo courtesy of Everex Systems, Inc.

Figure MC 2-21a
Reprinted with permission of Compaq Computer Corporation. All rights reserved.

Figure MC 2-21b
Image courtesy of AST Research, Inc.

Figure MC 2-23a & b
Reprinted from PC COMPUTING, October 1991. Copyright © 1991, Ziff-Davis Publishing Company.

Figure MC 2-24a
Eric Hanson/Gensler & Associates.

Figure MC 2-24b
Courtesy of Zenographics, Inc.

Figure MC 2-24c
Courtesy of Toshiba American Information Systems.

Figure MC 2-26
Canon and BJ are registered trademarks of Canon Inc. and Bubble Jet is a trademark of Canon Inc. Reprinted with the express written consent of Canon Computer Systems, Inc. All rights reserved.

User Tip
Image courtesy of Tektronix, Inc.

Figure MC 2-27a
Photo courtesy of Hewlett-Packard Company.

Figure MC 2-28
Image courtesy of Tektronix, Inc.

Figure MC 2-29a
Courtesy of International Business Machines Corporation.

Figure MC 2-29b
Courtesy of Toshiba American Information Systems.

Figure MC 2-30a & b
Photo courtesy of CalComp.

Chapter MC 3

Figure MC 3-2
WordPerfect is a registered trademark of Novell, Inc. WordPerfect for Windows screen shot, © 1991 Novell, Inc. All rights reserved. Used with permission.

Figure MC 3-3
Image reprinted with permission from Microsoft Corporation.

Figure MC 3-4
Image reprinted with permission from Microsoft Corporation.

Figure MC 3-5a
Screen shot courtesy of Lotus Development Corporation. Used with permission of Lotus Development Corporation. Lotus Notes is a trademark of Lotus Development Corporation.

Figure MC 3-5b
Screen shot reprinted with permission from Microsoft Corporation.

Figure MC 3-5c
Courtesy of Apple Computer, Inc.

Figure MC 3-6a & b
Image reprinted with permission from Microsoft Corporation.

Figure MC 3-8
Image reprinted with permission from Microsoft Corporation.

Figure MC 3-9
Image reprinted with permission from Microsoft Corporation.

Figure MC 3-10
Image reprinted with permission from Microsoft Corporation.

Figure MC 3-11
Image reprinted with permission from Microsoft Corporation.

Figure MC 3-12
Image reprinted with permission from Microsoft Corporation.

Figure MC 3-13
Image reprinted with permission from Microsoft Corporation.

Figure MC 3-14
Image reprinted with permission from Microsoft Corporation.

Figure MC 3-17
Image reprinted with permission from Microsoft Corporation.

Figure MC 3-18
Screen shot reprinted with permission from Microsoft Corporation.

Figure MC 3-19
Screen shot reprinted with permission from Microsoft Corporation.

Figure MC 3-20
Courtesy of Apple Computer, Inc.

User Tip
Mapland by Software Illustrated. Mapland is a trademark of Software Illustrated.

Figure MC 3-25
Image courtesy of Adobe Systems, Inc. All rights reserved.

Figure MC 3-26
Screen shot courtesy of Lotus Development Corporation. Used with permission of Lotus Development Corporation.

Figure MC 3-27a
Photo courtesy of Lotus Development Corporation. Used with permission of Lotus Development Corporation.

Figure MC 3-27b
Image reprinted with permission from Microsoft Corporation.

Figure MC 3-28
Image courtesy of Day-Timer Technologies.

Figure MC 3-29
Courtesy of SAS Institute, Inc., Cary, NC. SAS, SAS/BIS, SAS/AF, and SAS/OR are registered trademarks of SAS Institute, Inc., Cary, NC, USA.

Figure MC 3-30
Eric Hanson/Gensler & Associates

Chapter MC 4

Figure MC 4-1
Image from CompuServe Information Service.

Figure MC 4-2
Screen shot courtesy of Lotus Development Corporation. Used with permission of Lotus Development Corporation. Lotus Notes is a trademark of Lotus Development Corporation.

Figure MC 4-3b
Source: Delrina.

Figure MC 4-4a–d
© 1994 America Online, Inc. This screen shot is reprinted with the permission of America Online, Inc. The America Online® service is a registered service mark of America Online, Inc. All rights reserved.

Figure MC 4-5
Prodigy Services Company.

Figure MC 4-6
Prodigy Services Company.

Figure MC 4-8
Image courtesy of Spyglass.

User Tip
Courtesy of International Business Machines Corporation.

Figure MC 4-10
Courtesy of Motorola.

Figure MC 4-14
Source: Sierra Wireless.

Figure MC 4-21a
Photograph courtesy of Norand Corporation; Cedar Rapids, Iowa.

Figure MC 4-21b
Photo courtesy of Intermec Corporation.

An Illustrated Glossary for the Internet and the Information Superhighway

Figure 1
© 1994 America Online, Inc. This screen shot is reprinted with the permission of America Online, Inc. The America Online® service is a registered service mark of America Online, Inc. All rights reserved.

Figure 2
Sources: Rutgers University and Prodigy Services Company.

Figure 3
Prodigy Services Company.

Figure 4
Source: Arista Records.

Figure 5
Image from CompuServe Information Service.

Figure 6
Prodigy Services Company.

Figure 7
Sources: MIT and Prodigy Services Company.

Figure 8
Sources: University of Montana and Prodigy Services Company.

Figure 9
Source: Netscape.

Figure 10
Source: Carnival Cruise Lines.

Chapter MC 5

Figure MC 5-2
Courtesy of Computerland, San Diego.

Figure MC 5-3
Courtesy of Price Costco.

Figure MC 5-4
Image courtesy of Robert LaPrelle Photography.

Figure MC 5-7
Image courtesy of Curtis Manufacturing Company, Inc.

Figure MC 5-8
Image courtesy of Curtis Manufacturing Company, Inc.

Figure MC 5-9
Image courtesy of Curtis Manufacturing Company, Inc.

Figure MC 5-10
Datawatch Corporation.

Figure MC 5-11
Image courtesy of E Ware.

Figure MC 5-12
Courtesy of International Business Machines Corporation.

Figure MC 5-14
Intel Corporation.

User Tip
Charles S. Parker.

Figure MC 5-15
The Interface Group.

Figure MC 5-16
Image courtesy of Robert LaPrelle Photography.

Chapter MC 6

Figure MC 6-1a, c, & d
What Can Adobe 88 Illustrator Do For You? © 1988 Adobe Systems Incorporated. All rights reserved.

Figure MC 6-1b
Architrave Magazine. © 1990 Adobe Systems Incorporated.

Figure MC 6-2a & b
PrecisionColor Pivot distributed by both Radius Inc. and Portrait Display Labs.

User Tip
Courtesy of AlphaGraphics, Inc.

Figure 6-4
© 1990–1993 Adobe Systems Incorporated. All rights reserved.

Figure 6-5
© 1990–1993 Adobe Systems Incorporated. All rights reserved.

Figure 6-8
Gold Disk Inc.

Figure MC 6-9
Image courtesy of Adobe Systems, Inc. All rights reserved.

Figure 6-10a & b
Guide to Basic Design © Adobe Systems, Inc. All rights reserved.

Figure MC 6-16
Source: Computer Associates International, Inc.

Figure MC 6-19
Miros, Inc., Wellesley, MA.

Figure MC 6-20
Natural Language Inc., Berkeley, California.

Figure 6-21a & b
Nolan Multimedia (producers), Alabama Power Company. Electric Power Research Institutes.

Figure MC 6-22a & b
Image courtesy of Warner New Media.

Figure MC 6-23a & b
Presentek, Inc.

Figure MC 6-24
Screen shot reprinted with permission from Microsoft Corporation.

Figure MC 6-25
Source: Huppauge Computer Works, Inc.

Figure MC 6-26a & b
Images are copyright of Ben & Jerry's Homemade Ice Cream, Inc. 1992.

Figure MC 6-27
Kohn, Pedersen, Fox.

Figure MC 6-28a & b
Courtesy Evans & Sutherland Computer Corporation.

Figure MC 6-29
Source: VPL Research, Inc.

Figure MC 6-30
Virtual Technologies *Talking*Glove ™. Photo by Charles Painter, courtesy of Virtual Technologies.

Chapter MC 7

Figure MC 7-10
Screen shot reprinted with permission from Microsoft Corporation.

Figure MC 7-11a & b
Product is a trademark or registered trademark of Borland International.

Figure MC 7-12
Image courtesy of Micro Focus.

Figure MC 7-14
Product is a trademark or registered trademark of Borland International.

User Tip
Photo courtesy of Hewlitt-Packard Company.

Figure MC 7-15
Screen shots created using System Architect Version 3, provided by Popkin Software & Systems, Inc.; New York, NY.

Figure MC 7-19a & b
Product is a trademark or registered trademark of Borland International.

Figure MC 7-21a
Sybase, Inc.

Figure MC 7-21b
Courtesy of Icons International.

Figure MC 7-22a
Reprinted by permission of Gupta Technologies, Inc.

Figure MC 7-22b
Screen shot courtesy of Lotus Development Corporation. Used with permission of Lotus Development Corporation. Lotus Notes is a trademark of Lotus Development Corporation.

Figure MC 7-23
Screen shot courtesy of Lotus Development Corporation. Used with permission of Lotus Development Corporation. Lotus Approach is a trademark of Lotus Development Corporation.

Chapter MC 8

Figure MC 8-1a–c
© Peachtree Software, 1994.

Figure 8-3a & b
Courtesy of Strategic Mapping, Inc.

Figure 8-4a–d
Source: Wang Laboratories.

Figure MC 8-5a & b
Courtesy of SAS Institute, Inc., Cary, NC. SAS, SAS/EIS, SAS/AF, and SAS/OR are registered trademarks of SAS Institute, Inc., Cary, NC, USA.

User Tip
Courtesy of International Business Machines Corporation.

Figure MC 8-6a
Photograph courtesy of Viewpoint Systems, Inc.

Figure MC 8-6b
VTEL Corporation.

Figure MC 8-7
Desktop conferencing screen image provided by Fujitsu Networks Industry, Inc. USA.

Figure MC 8-8
Photo courtesy of Hewlett-Packard Company.

Figure MC 8-9a
Gobbell Hayes Partners/Pat McMillan.

Figure MC 8-9b
Image courtesy of the Callison Partnership, Seattle Washington.

Figure MC 8-10
Courtesy of International Business Machines Corporation.

Figure MC 8-11
Courtesy of International Business Machines Corporation.

Figure MC 8-13
Image courtesy of EDS.

Chapter MC 9

Figure MC 9-1
Image courtesy of Lexmark International, Inc.

Figure MC 9-3
Courtesy of International Business Machines Corporation.

Figure MC 9-4
Courtesy of International Business Machines Corporation.

Figure MC 9-6
TRW, Inc.

Figure MC 9-7
VF Corporation.

Figure 9-8
Courtesy of Whirlpool Corporation.